Theorising Tenure:
Land Division and Identity in Later Prehistoric Dartmoor, South-West Britain

Helen Wickstead

BAR British Series 465
2008

This title published by

Archaeopress
Publishers of British Archaeological Reports
Gordon House
276 Banbury Road
Oxford OX2 7ED
England
bar@archaeopress.com
www.archaeopress.com

BAR 465

Theorising Tenure: Land Division and Identity in Later Prehistoric Dartmoor, South-West Britain

ISBN 978 1 4073 0311 6

Printed in England by CMP (UK) Ltd

All BAR titles are available from:

Hadrian Books Ltd
122 Banbury Road
Oxford
OX2 7BP
England
bar@hadrianbooks.co.uk

The current BAR catalogue with details of all titles in print, prices and means of payment is available free from Hadrian Books or may be downloaded from www.archaeopress.com

Theorising Tenure:

Land Division and Identity in Later Prehistoric Dartmoor, South-West Britain

Tenure describes certain relations between people and material things. It has long been an important theme in archaeology, especially in the interpretation of ancient land division. How do archaeologists approach this subject, and which approaches have the most potential? This monograph explores tenure through analysis of Bronze Age land division on Dartmoor. The research has two aims:

1. To develop existing approaches to tenure
2. To interpret land division and tenure on Dartmoor during the second millennium BC

The research applies a series of different theories of, and approaches to tenure to data from Dartmoor. Methods used include spatial analysis of land division and settlement patterns, metrological analysis, experimental reconstruction and synthesis of palaeoenvironmental, excavation and artefactual data. The results are used to advance an interpretation of land division and tenure on Dartmoor and to reflect critically on approaches to tenure.

The findings suggest that tenure on Dartmoor was not an exclusive individual right, but involved inclusive claims and obligations held in persons and groups. Spatial analysis suggests relationships were valued more than accumulation of individualised land-holdings. Intensification cannot be proved, but land division allowed greater flexibility in land rotation and commoning. The lay out of landscapes materialised the value of exchanges of labour and resources involved in building structures. Through tenure, aspects of identity were exchanged and personhood was 'translocated' around exchange networks. Tenurial transactions gave groups and persons claims over long distance interactions.

I conclude that tenure is best approached as part of the constitution of identity. In archaeological terms, this approach describes tenure as part of how persons 'matter'. I attempt to move tenure studies away from approaches that concentrate narrowly on land use or boundaries. As an aspect of identity, tenure should be approached by looking across many different sources of evidence.

Acknowledgements

This monograph would not have been possible without information amassed in published and unpublished sources. Jeremy Butler kindly allowed me to digitise his original aerial photograph transcriptions - part of an ongoing survey of Dartmoor archaeology. Simon Probert of English Heritage offered invaluable advice on unpublished survey data. Staff of Devon Sites and Monuments Record were unfailingly helpful, especially Bill Horner and Faye Glover who assisted with records of lithics and metalwork finds. Frances Griffith advised on the question of measuring field lengths on the ground, and sent the analysis off in a new direction (see appendix E). Peter Weddell of Exeter Archaeology lent 'grey literature' on excavations. Thanks also to Devon Library and Information Services, Dartmoor National Park Authority, and Ordnance Survey's EDINA Digimap Service for allowing me to access vital information and for permission to reproduce some of the illustrations.Several authors generously sent copies of theses and dissertations including Mats Widgren, Bob Johnston, Andy Jones, Alan Lambourne, and Jo Brück. Others granted previews of unpublished or forthcoming work, for which I thank Mark Lake, James Connolly, Ralph Fyfe , Chris Carey, Adrian Chadwick, Howard Williams, Matthew Johnson, Jo Brück, Bob Johnston, and Helen Lewis.

Mark Lake supervised the research and Sue Hamilton acted as second supervisor. Supplementary guidance was offered by Mats Widgren, Andrew Fleming, Seamus Caulfield, Jeremy Butler, Bob Johnston, Mark Edmonds, Josh Pollard, Fay Stevens, Helen Lewis, Chris Cumberpatch and Jo Brück. Mark Lake's genius for analysis was indispensable. Karl Petruso offered advice on metrology; Bill Wickstead on statistics and programming; Andy Jones and John Chapman suggested references.

Many people helped with fieldwork. Thanks are due to Seamus Caulfield, Eoin O'Sullivan and Neil Price for their hospitality. Phil Emery, Trevor Ashwin, Bob Johnston and Paul Quinlan as well as students from Bangor University and from UCL helped research the laying-out of field systems. Experimental reconstructions were made possible by Jim, Darren and Richard James. I also thank everyone who has helped and/or continues to help with the Shovel Down excavation project.

Friends and family were both a help and a hindrance. Publication was hampered by the arrival of my baby son four months ago and it is largely thanks to Paul Quinlan that I have been able to make it to my desk every now and then. Nicola Smith and Emily Davey also lent a hand in these busy weeks. Thanks to the Wickstead family and Ian Battersby for discussions on land and Englishness. Conversations with Adrian Chadwick, Chris Deter, Sarah McCarthy and Caroline Sandes kept me thinking, while Lesley McFayden and the Cambridge Theory Group set the seeds for new ideas. Gary Robinson was an oasis of calm and good humour. Gerry, David and the staff of Archaeopress were pleasant and helpful throughout. Finally I dedicate this monograph to three people who read some terrible drafts, criticised them, but somehow remained enthusiastic about my ideas:

to Helen Lewis, Chris Cumberpatch and Jo Brück

Contents

Preface   **7**

1. 'The first who bethought himself of saying 'this is *mine*'...'   **11**
A Thematic Review of Theories of Tenure
1.1 Land and Territorialisation   11
1.2 Classical Theories of Property   14
1.3 The Labour Theory of Property   17
1.4 Approaching Tenure through Personhood   19
1.5 Tenure and Relational Identity   22
Conclusions   24

2. Dartmoor and Archaeologies of Tenure: Significance and Potential   **26**
2.1 Archaeologies of Land Division in North West Europe   27
2.2 Previous Archaeologies of Tenure on Prehistoric Dartmoor   30
2.3 The Archaeology of Dartmoor   34
2.4 Databases and Frameworks for Analysis   39
Conclusions   44

3. 'A Post-hoc Explanation': Classical Theories of Property   **45**
3.1 Maximisation, Efficiency and Scarcity in Classical Theories   45
3.2 Maximisation and Land Division   48
3.3 Coaxial Land Division and Land Scarcity   51
3.4 Settlement Pattern, Scarcity and Maximisation   61
3.5 Property and Hierarchy   66
Conclusions   71

4. Labour isn't working: The Labour Theory of Property and Intensification   **72**
4.1 The Labour Theory of Property and Intensification Theory   72
4.2 Assessing Intensification on Dartmoor   75
4.3 Flexibility, Agriculture and Land Division   81
4.4 Production, Value, and the Labour Theory   87
Conclusions   89

5. 'Self-Evident Domains': Territories, Houses and Tenure   **91**
5.1 Territorialisation, Translocation and Identity   91
5.2 Excavations of Buildings   94
5.3 Building Biographies   99
5.4 Territorialisation and Coaxial Landscapes   102
Conclusions   109

6. 'Keeping-for-Giving': Tenure and the Constitution of Identity   **111**
6.1 Tenure and Bronze Age Exchange   111
6.2 Cairns, Territory and Tenure   114
6.3 Mortuary Practices Assessed   117
6.4 Metalwork and 'Gifts to the Gods'   120
6.5 Tenure and the Constitution of Identity   126
Conclusions   128

7. Arithmetic of Tenure and Identity: Measurement and Value in Coaxial Landscapes   **129**
7.1 Mathematics, Personhood and Value   129
7.2 Previous Metrological Studies   132
7.3 Metrological Analysis of Coaxial Landscapes   135
7.4 Measuring Practices in Coaxial Landscapes   140
7.5 Mathematics, Value and Tenure   146

Conclusions 148

8. From one 'becoming' to another: Contribution and Future Projects **150**
8.1 Findings of the Study 150
8.2 Contribution of the Interpretation and Methodology 152
8.3 Critique of 'Personhood' Approaches and Further Work 155
8.4 Future Projects Emerging from the Study 157
Conclusions 159

9. Tenure and How Persons Matter: Contribution to Tenure Studies **161**
9.1 Findings of the Study and their Implications 161
9.2 Contribution of Archaeology to Tenure Studies 164
9.3 Classical Theories make Individuals matter 166
9.4 Territorializing Tenure makes the 'Indigenous' matter 168
9.5 The Future of Tenure Studies 170
Conclusion 172

Bibliography **221**

Appendices

Appendix A:	Excavations of Dartmoor Settlements	173
Appendix B:	Relocating Early Excavations of Prehistoric Buildings	175
Appendix C:	Methodology and Quality of Archaeological Excavations before 1950	177
Appendix D:	Key for Map of Pollen Sampling Sites in and around Dartmoor	178
Appendix E:	Dealing with the lie of the land	180
Appendix F:	Recalibration of Dates for Enclosures and Buildings	182
Appendix G:	Recalibration of Dates from Reaves on Dartmoor	185
Appendix H:	Recalibration of Dates from Cairns and Barrows at Shaugh Moor, Upton Pyne and Dainton	187
Appendix I:	Condensed Version of Needham's Chronological Framework	189
Appendix J:	Frequencies of Enclosure areas within size classes	190
Appendix K:	Measurements of Strip Widths	193
Appendix L:	Lithic Scatters from Dartmoor	198
Appendix M:	Areas of Blocks of Pastureland	200
Appendix N:	Possible Common Pastures within Coaxial Landscapes	201
Appendix O:	Characteristics of Hearth Architecture from Excavations after 1930	202
Appendix P:	Early Excavations of Charcoal-filled 'Troughs' or 'Cooking Chambers'	203
Appendix Q:	Numbers and Percentages of Excavated Buildings Associated with Hearths, Cooking Pits, Pot-Boilers and Paving Compared Between Settlement Types	204
Appendix R:	Frequencies of Excavated Buildings with Different Features at various Elevations	206
Appendix S:	Cumulative Frequency Graphs Comparing the Numbers of Buildings at a range of Distances from Boundaries with Nine Random Simulations	207
Appendix T:	Database of Metalwork for Dartmoor and its Surrounding Area	208
Appendix U:	Metalwork Findspots in North East Dartmoor	212
Appendix V:	Pacing Experiments	213
Appendix W:	Metrological Analysis Using Kendall's Formulation. Cosine Quantograms for Eight Sample Coaxial Landscapes	214
Appendix X:	Coaxial Pattern at Kestor South	217
Appendix Y:	Coaxial Pattern at Halsanger and Horridge Commons	218
Appendix Z:	Potential for Further Work on Partially Excavated Buildings	219

List of Figures

Chapter 2

2.1: Location of the Study Area (© Crown Copyright/database right 2002. An Ordnance Survey/EDINA supplied service)
2.2: Reave on Rippon Tor with tor cairn on skyline
2.3: Reaves used in Fleming's 'diagrammatic representations' of land division
2.4: Previous Archaeological interventions on Dartmoor (Data from: Butler 1997 and Unpub., Ordnance Survey)
2.5: Dates of Archaeological Interventions
2.6: Locations of Excavations after 1950
2.7: Palynological Samples (published and unpublished reports)
2.8: Fleming's Model implemented using latest survey data
2.9: Chronology of Prehistoric and Roman Sites (From Dartmoor National Park 2004)
2.10: Date Ranges of Recalibrated Non-Anomalous Dates; Reaves and Cairns compared
2.11: Date Ranges of Recalibrated Non-Anomalous Dates; Enclosures, Houses and Cairns compared

Chapter 3

3.1: Rainfall Intensity compared with Elevation
3.2: Growing Season Length compared with Elevation
3.3: Edge of Enclosed Land and Distribution of survey data
3.4: Interquartile Range for Elevation
3.5: Interquartile Range for Elevation
3.6: Frequency within aspect classes
3.7: 50mm Contours of Long-term Rainfall Intensity compared with distribution of Settlement and Coaxial Features
3.8: Frequency of Coaxial Sites within Rainfall Intensity Contours
3.9: Map Calculations and Reclassifications used to Model Results of Location Analysis
3.10: Land with characteristics preferred by builders of coaxial land division compared with locations of known coaxial sites
3.11: Land with characteristics preferred by builders of coaxial land division compared with locations of all known sites
3.12: Areas of Coaxial Land Division used in analysis
3.13: Reaves per hectare
3.14: Reaves per hectare compared with buildings per hectare
3.15: Numbers of buildings within 100m (all buildings)
3.16: Numbers of buildings within 100m (buildings in coaxial areas)
3.17: Log log plot of numbers of buildings within 100m (all buildings)
3.18: Log log plot of numbers of buildings within 100m (buildings in coaxial areas)
3.19: Frequencies of enclosures of different sizes
3.20: Inter-Quartile Ranges of Enclosures within each area
3.21: Strips of similar widths (from Butler, 1997a)
3.22: Five Coaxial Landscapes from Dartmoor Showing Varying Plot Sizes.

Chapter 4

4.1: Possible Realms of Flexibility in Agricultural systems (from Adams & Mortimore, 1997)
4.2: Distribution and Circumstances of Recovery of Neolithic and Early Bronze Age Lithics
4.3: Dates of Lithics Found at each Findspot
4.4: Circumstances of Recovery of Lithics
4.5: Elevations of Lithic Findspots with and without association with Mesolithic material
4.6: Degrees Slope of Lithic Findspots with and without association with Mesolithic material
4.7: Reconstruction of a reave on Shovel Down. Following excavations at Shovel Down a reave was reconstructed as originally built by two professional Dartmoor wallers (Brück et al., 2005).
4.8: Estimates of Labour Hours involved in Reave Construction
4.9: Enclosures used in orientation and slope analysis
4.10: Random Quadrangles used in orientation and slope analysis
4.11: Elevation Ranges of enclosures in each sample compared
4.12: Cumulative Frequencies of Coaxial and Random samples
4.13: Possible Commons within Coaxial Landscapes
4.14: Maximum Elevation of Coaxial Enclosures against area

List of Figures

Chapter 5

5.1: Buildings with evidence for features associated with burning at Watern Oke
5.2: Proportions of Excavated buildings of different settlement types
5.3. Difference between Percentages of Buildings with Hearths, Cooking Pits, Pot-Boilers and Paving compared with Percentage of Buildings within each Settlement Type
5.4: Percentages of different site types associated with reaves
5.5: Buildings linked to Reaves in Three non-coaxial landscapes.
5.6: Axial Reaves within three coaxial landscapes and percentages associated with boundaries
5.7: Cumulative Frequency of Buildings Against Distance from Axial Boundaries at Holne Moor, Shaugh Moor and Shovel Down
5.8: Buildings Linked to Axial Reaves in Three Coaxial landscapes

Chapter 6

6.1: Excavations of Cairns, Barrow and Cemeteries
6.2: Proportions of excavated cairns with different materials
6.3: Distribution of Bronze Age Metalwork
6.4: Metalwork Chronology (Adapted from Pearce 1999)
6.5: Frequencies of metal finds over time
6.6: Contexts of Finds in Each Period
6.7: Numbers of Finds per Findspot by Period
6.8: The Pinhoe Hoard (Copyright Exeter City Council)

Chapter 7

7.1: Kendall's Formula
7.2: Results from Application of Kendal's Formula to widths of coaxial enclosures
7.3: Cosine Quantogram of widths of coaxial enclosures
7.4: Quantogram of widths of enclosures in eight coaxial areas
7.5: Results from Application of Kendal's Formula to eight coaxial areas
7.6: Spatial distribution of deviation from quantum
7.7: Re-analysis of Part of Kestor Area
7.8: Deviation from quantum at Holne Moor
7.9: Absolute error against multiplication of quantum (Shovel Down)
7.10: Absolute error against multiplication of quantum (Shaugh Moor)
7.11: Subdivision on Shaugh Moor
7.12: Subdivision on Shovel Down
7.13: Chi Square Test of subdivision in coaxial landscapes
7.14 Widths of smallest enclosures
7.15: Errors on lengths subdivided by eye
7.16: Errors in actual examples of subdivision
7.17: Viewshed analysis showing none intervisibility of ends of subdivided enclosures (Kestor)
7.18: Viewshed analysis showing none intervisibility of ends of subdivided enclosures (Shovel Down)

Preface

Tenure is an important aspect of relations involving people and material things. Archaeologists often evoke tenure but less often subject this concept to sustained examination. In this monograph I explore the subject of tenure. The root of the word tenure is the French verb '*tenir*' (to hold). It is thus concerned with possession, and is related to the concept of property. Dictionary definitions of tenure outline three main senses in which the word tenure is used: Firstly, tenure refers to the holding or possession of something, especially of property and land; Secondly, it also means the duration, term or conditions on possession, and thus encompasses a greater range of relations than can be described by 'property'; Thirdly, it is also possible to speak of 'getting tenure' – by which is meant the attainment of a permanent office, linked to achieving a certain personal status within a profession. At first sight this third sense seems very different to the first two. However it points to the history of a concept that is closely bound up with personhood. For example, the word 'property' derives from the Latin '*proprius*' and French '*propiete*'. The words property and propriety thus overlap indicating the historical connections between property and ideas of moral personhood ('self-possession'). 'Ownership', related to the German '*eigen*', also refers to identity through its historical link with 'belonging' - the word was once used to describe blood ties between kin as well as possession of objects (Verdery & Humphrey, 2004a: 5). The concept of tenure is more complicated than it may at first appear, referring to many different sense and forms of possession simultaneously.

How should archaeologists approach tenure? Finding an answer to this question drives my research here. In the pages that follow I carry existing approaches to tenure in archaeology in new directions. My method involves the analysis of a case study that has been important in previous archaeologies of tenure – Dartmoor during the second millennium BC. My research thus has two related aims:

- To develop existing approaches to tenure
- To interpret tenure on Dartmoor during the second millennium BC.

I begin this short preface outlining the thrust of my argument. I set out the methods and objectives of the research. I then discuss ethical issues that arise from the application of GIS in the study. Lastly, I outline the structure of the work that follows.

Translocating Tenure

My thesis is that tenure can be seen as part of how persons come to matter. It can be envisaged as an aspect of how identities are constituted. To understand this process, I consider how it involves the valuing of persons and things. 'Translocating tenure' thus develops theories of tenure in new directions. Traditional approaches to 'land tenure' tend to assume tenure is a variety of territorialisation. Other approaches subsume tenure within property seeing it as the right of individuals to exclude others. I offer an alternative perspective linking tenure and identity.

I adopt the term 'translocation' from Nancy Munn (Munn 1987, 1990) using it to help understand the ways in which personhood can be said to extend through tenure. 'Translocation' describes 'how … the subject's present forms a 'network branching out in listening posts to somewhere else' (Munn, 1990: 2, citing Hobson). Events in the here and now, Munn suggests, are constituted by 'protensions' of the future and 'retentions' of the past, forming 'horizons of the present'. Similar dynamics constitute the event's spatiality. Munn illustrates this concept through detailed studies of Gawa, Papua New Guinea (Munn, 1987, 1990). On Gawa, tenure involves actions whose value is translocated within ever widening levels of spatiotemporal extension. The value of actions is ultimately realised at the highest level of spatiotemporal extension, in transactions involving kula valuables. The translocal is therefore not the same as the 'regional'. The regional denotes a pre-given territorial construct. 'Translocation', however, describes a process, an 'experiential synthesis', through which time and space configure events.

I understand the extendibility of persons in tenure as involving processes of valuing. I employ an 'anthropological theory of value' developed by David Graeber (Graeber, 2001). Following Munn, Graeber argues that value is the importance of actions congealed in objects. Pursuing meaningful projects of value, people create society. This is a process of which they can be only partially conscious. Actions undertaken as part of projects of value coordinate to produce social 'totalities'. These totalities later become the contexts within which value is later realised. Graeber's theory unites economic value with moral and social values. Processes of valuing reproduce values which are simultaneously moral, social and economic. I use this theory of value to understand how tenure makes persons matter. The materiality of tenure, I suggest, involves valuing persons and things. Projects of value shape identities and create totalities within which the value of identities is realised.

In this monograph I 'translocate' tenure by moving the theory of tenure away from traditional accounts which link it to land division and agricultural production. By considering tenure as part of the constitution of identities I move it away from a narrowly conceived category of productive labour and the 'subsistence economy'. I argue that archaeologies of tenure must engage with many different sources of evidence, seeing tenure within wider interpretations of personhood and materiality.

Aims, Methods and Objectives

My research develops existing approaches to tenure in archaeology reflexively through analysis of Dartmoor during the second millennium BC. As was stated above the first aim of the research is to develop approaches to tenure. To meet this aim I begin with a review of previous theories of tenure. I group existing approaches within four themes. My methodology applies approaches from each theme to the Dartmoor datasets. This method allows me to reflect critically on each theme, to evaluate its application and to assess how well its expectations match up to my findings. Reflexively working through each approach allows me to develop ideas and to suggest new trajectories. My objective is to reflect critically on tenure and develop new ways of thinking about the subject.

My second aim, as stated above, is to create a new interpretation of Dartmoor in later prehistory. Dartmoor was selected for this project because of its special importance in accounts of prehistoric tenure. The history of land use on Dartmoor has allowed extensive preservation of prehistoric settlement, so that landscapes of exceptional importance for studies of ancient land division are now found across the region. Previous work by Fleming used this evidence to produce influential accounts of prehistoric tenure (Fleming, 1984; 1985b; 1988). However, since the main period of his work on Dartmoor, new surveys of these remarkable landscapes have revealed more of the detail of these landscapes (Butler, 1997b and unpublished work by English Heritage). New interpretations of Bronze Age sociality have emerged (e.g. Brück, 2000; 2001a), and some of Fleming's early conclusions have been challenged (Johnston, 2005). To address my second aim I use diverse methods, including GIS analyses, metrological analyses, experimental reconstruction, studies of lithics and metalwork and synthesis of palaeoenvironmental and excavation data. My objective is to use the approaches developed through my first research aim, to generate a new interpretation.

Methodology, Ethics and GIS

Expansion of GIS in the 1980s and 90s has lead to an increasingly polarised debate concerning its ethics and validity. Two positions emerged: On the one hand were those who considered GIS neutral tool of 'positivist' science (Openshaw, 1991; 1998; Kvamme, 1997; 1999). On the other critics of GIS who characterised it as ideologically loaded and environmentally determinist (Pickles, 1995; Curry, 1998; Gaffney & Van Leusen, 1995). Between these two poles GIS practitioners have increasingly established a middle ground, acknowledging that GIS technology is influenced by its 'social context' while expanding techniques to explore issues like perception and non-visual sensory experience (Coucelis, 1999; Gillings & Goodrick, 1996; Wheatley & Gillings, 2000; Witcher, 1999). Recently, Thomas has attacked this middle ground, arguing that there is no place at all for GIS in archaeologies of the 'distant past' (Thomas, 2004: 198-201). GIS, he argues, manufactures '*simulacra ... divorced from any context of human involvement*' (Thomas, 2004: 200 his emphasis). GIS is '*distinctively modern*', he insists, and its use in archaeology is 'anachronistic'. Attempts to 'humanise' GIS are doomed.

I take a different view. I begin from the now well-established observation that archaeology does not describe or discover a pre-existing past 'out there', but involves more or less precarious efforts to hold together, stabilise or construct multiple pasts in the here and now. Studies of physical and social sciences (Latour, 1987, 1993; 1999; Law, 2004) as well as recent examinations of archaeological methods (Lucas, 2001; Yarrow, 2003) have shown how methodologies construct 'realities'. GIS, like any methodology, participates in transforming reality (Law, 2004). GIS, therefore, does not 'merely' construct simulacra, illusions or 'appearances' of a 'distant past' from somewhere else (cf Thomas, 2004: 198-201). It actively participates in constructing the 'reality' of the past in the present.

It is certainly the case that GIS is ideologically loaded, but so is everything else that participates in producing knowledge. Many technologies, not just GIS, play an active role in constructing archaeological realities, from Harris matrices and typologies, to thin sections, trowels and theory. The question is whether GIS - in and of itself – is more or less malign than other things? Thomas favours humanistic 'experiential' methods based on bodily immersion in landscapes. He implies that these methods are less malign than GIS. But is this really the case? As Thomas himself points out, bodies are mutable (2004: 214-16). The notion that bodies are essentially unchanging and ideologically pure, is a major flaw in the 'experiential' methods Thomas prefers (Brück, 2001b; cf Thomas, 2001). Why should the body be any less 'anachronistic' in studies of the 'distant past' than GIS? One could argue that the 'human' body is at least as anachronistic, and as malign (Haraway, 1991, 1992).

The predicament of any knowledge practice is that realities must be made within ethically compromised networks. Some networks within which GIS participates are unconscionable (see uses of GIS in the 'War on Terror', Crampton, 2004; Cutter et al., 2003). However, some of the networks which used Heidegger's writings were equally unethical (see Thomas, 1996). The answer does not lie in laws of methodological hygiene. Blanket prohibitions are just as unhelpful whether they come from the 'positivist' school of GIS studies or a 'humanist' branch of archaeological theory. It is much more helpful to bring methods into new networks, and to allow them to cross-fertilise productively with other ways of making knowledge. This process, (described by Law as 'method assemblage') (Law, 2004) has the potential to change what we can know from these technologies. For this reason I believe the GIS 'middle ground' is an important space: Its significance does not lie in 'humanising' spatial studies, but in the way it can expand and transform the 'human' in the course of constructing knowledges.

In this study I do not foreground GIS. I use a range of methods to explore particular themes, integrating 'harder' scientific methods with 'softer' interpretative approaches, and allowing both to inform each other. I deploy methods that help me think through and visualise ideas, building on how different facets of the research interconnect. GIS is part of my methodology, but only one part, and GIS findings are interwoven with the results of other kinds of enquiry to generate interpretation.

This approach is partly directed by my chosen subject of tenure. Law's study of methodologies in the social sciences points to how traditional methodologies attempt to stabilise realities that are definite, singular and coherent (Law, 2004). However, the subjects of social sciences seldom resemble these kinds of reality; they are often not definite and singular but 'messy' ephemeral and heterogeneous. Tenure epitomises the way people produce one dimension of social life as a context or idiom for the expression of others, it thus connects different realms of life into heterogeneous realities (Strathern, 2004). Detailed studies, from Malinowski (1921) onwards, emphasise the multi-dimensionality of tenure. Any firmly delineated single method is perhaps unlikely to grasp the heterogeneous reality of tenure with great success, and may risk reducing the subject. I build my methodology through a process of method assemblage, integrating GIS with other techniques in a series of analyses. I then work between the findings of these analyses to build the interpretation.

Structure of the Monograph

The thesis is in nine chapters. It starts with a history of existing approaches and interpretations, the middle section is taken up with analysis and interpretation, then the final two chapters summarise how I have achieved each of the two aims of the research, outlines their contribution, and suggests directions for future work.

Chapter one begins with a conceptual history of tenure. Through this review I group previous approaches to tenure into four themes:
1. 'Classical' Theories
2. Labour Theories
3. Tenure as territorialisation
4. Tenure as part of the Constitution of Identity

Of these four themes, three have a long history in archaeological interpretations. The last is an emerging approach, incipient in some recent archaeology, although relatively well-established in the philosophy of property law and anthropology of tenure. The rest of the text examines and develops these themes.

In **chapter two** I discuss previous interpretations of Dartmoor, particularly the seminal work of Andrew Fleming. I discuss how archaeologies of land division elsewhere in Bronze Age North-west Europe have changed since Fleming produced his interpretations. I then introduce the data sources that are now available, including new palaeoenvironmental, excavation and survey data. I set out a chronology based on recalibrated dates, and outline the creation of several databases used in the analysis.

The next five chapters (3 - 7) analyse Dartmoor to explore the themes identified in chapter one. **Chapter three** examines the 'classical' theories of property common in mainstream law and economics. These characterise land tenure as a legal institution with a functional role allocating resources and managing scarce goods. I assess Dartmoor's prehistoric landscapes to investigate how well they fit the expectations of such approaches.

In **chapter four** I develop labour theories of tenure, exploring approaches based on the idea of intensification. These interpretations have generally taken a rather narrow view of what constitutes productive labour. I develop ideas of intensification through analysis of the Dartmoor dataset, and I introduce a theory of value that broadens concepts of productive action.

Chapter five examines the assumption that tenure grows from a natural urge to territorialize – tenure-as-territorialisation. I assess narratives of territorialisation against evidence for Dartmoor settlement. I argue that tenure implies re/deterritorializing as well as territorializing processes. Maintaining the potential for both is important.

In **chapter six** I approach tenure as part of the constitution of identity. I examine evidence for exchange, mortuary practices, and metalwork deposition, using the findings of my analysis to interpret identity. I discuss how identification relates to what is exchanged and what is kept back from exchange in tenure, and I suggest how tenure might be said to translocate aspects of persons and places.

Chapter seven develops the ideas introduced in chapter six through analysis of land division. I explore the practical mathematics used to lay out land division. I suggest that measuring land was a process of valuing. I link the processes of valuing involved in Dartmoor landscapes to the constitution of personhood.

The final two chapters - eight and nine- return to the two aims of the research. **Chapter eight** reviews my interpretation of Dartmoor. I discuss how this new interpretation contributes to Bronze Age archaeology and suggest new directions for future work.

Chapter nine reviews the contribution of the research to tenure studies in general. At present concepts of property are undergoing dramatic transformation. I discuss the role of archaeology in this rapidly changing field.

In this short introduction I introduced the subject of tenure, and set out the aims and methodology of the research. In the next chapter I investigate concepts of tenure further, what is it, how has it been approached in the past, and what are the trajectories along which it can be advanced?

Chapter 1

The first who bethought himself of saying 'this is *mine*' …
A Thematic Review of Theories of Tenure

On a remote mountainside seventy years ago, two priests were brutally hacked to death. The motive for their murder, a court later found, was to steal back land the priests had bought. But this judgement was only one side of the story. What really caused the murder was a conflict between two understandings of tenure. The priests thought they had acquired 'rights' over the land at the time that they paid for it. They assumed that this was a final sale. However, for the people of Simbu province, Papua New Guinea, obtaining tenure meant becoming a new kind of person. By taking the land the priests had entered into in a sequence of ongoing transactions. Simbu people logically expected that further payments, support in wars against enemies and even marriage commitments would be forthcoming (Brown, 1998: 278-9). The missionaries' refusal to follow through with these obligations outraged the most sacred principles of person and kinship. In this context, assuming that tenure reflected property was a fatal mistake (Gibbs, 2006).

Concepts of property can vary in ways that shape our comprehension of the world and ourselves at a fundamental level. As this example illustrates there is more than one way of conceptualising tenure. In this chapter I discuss existing approaches to tenure in historical context. I group approaches to tenure into four themes. My first theme emerges from a brief history of land and its links to territorialized national identities. Secondly I consider economic and legal definitions of tenure which emphasise exclusion, rights, and the evolution of legal institutions. Thirdly I discuss the labour theory of tenure which makes cultivation a justification for unlimited accumulation of property. My fourth theme involves a range of approaches that connect tenure to personhood, as part of the constitution of identity. The last section develops this fourth theme by discussing how tenure might differ according to different forms of identification.

1.1 Land and Territorialisation

Any history of ideas, Appadurai affirms, 'is an argument in the guise of a discovery' (Appadurai, 1988: 40). In this section I begin just such an argument with a brief history of the idea of land in Britain. I then consider how a notion of traditional land tenure emerged out of reactions to capitalism and modernity. Finally, I argue that contemporary approaches often understand land tenure in ways that refract nationalism. 'Territorialized' notions of land tenure preserve a connection between territory and identity that is homologous to the connection between nation and identity.

A History of Land

'Land' is a concept inflected with sentiments that 'property' lacks. Land's associations are with the vocabulary of kinship (motherland, *Vaterland*, *patria*) and home (homeland, *heimat*). 'Land' conjures permanence and stability, organicism and 'naturalness' senses that fit with what we expect of the ancient and primordial. The significances of land, however, are not given, but made. They can be observed in the way land has been held in relation to the market, and in the senses in which it has been held outside and against that market

for the last three hundred years. Some commentators trace the ability to alienate land as a commodity to the Enclosure Acts of the post-medieval period (Bell, 1998: 33). However, others warn against over-simplifying enclosure, pointing out that this involved a series of changes to the distribution of land and resources, and took place over a very long period between the late medieval period into full modernism (Johnson, 1996). Whilst feudalism was gradually eroded, in most cases, enclosure did not immediately release land into a fully fledged market. Instead, land was held in forms of at best partial alienability. To understand the associations that land retains today, we need to briefly explore what was preserved through the partial alienability of most land in the early modern period. What was preserved, I argue, was an image of sovereignty, of inheritable power and of their permanence.

From the Medieval period onwards tenure in parts of Europe presented miniature models supporting an overarching vision of sovereignty and social order. For several hundred years between the late medieval period and the eighteenth centuries the landowner controlled his local community, exercising judicial, administrative, and (through his ability to bestow livings to clergy) religiously sanctioned authority (Johnson, 1996). (Since women were increasingly debarred from land-ownership the landowner was often both ideally and actually male). Land was an unavoidable resource for social advancement and a route to political enfranchisement for men. In the seventeenth and eighteenth centuries, institutions at different scales retained key similarities: the family, the estate and the nation all held land according to principles of patriarchal sovereignty.

In Britain the principle of inheritable power was preserved in land law. From the late thirteenth century until 1925 land law enacted the principle of primogeniture (Jamoussi, 1999). The law stated that if a landowner died intestate all the land passed to the first born son to the exclusion of all other children and the widow. Laws of primogeniture were backed by widespread customary primogeniture and entail (terms and conditions imposed by wills). Entail usually specified that the recipient of land could not sell it, but signed it over to his male heirs at the time he received it. Although women could sometimes inherit land in Europe (see Goody, 1976, 1998) they did not hold it as individuals in their own right, but as the bearers of the next generation of male heirs (Jamoussi, 1999). The effects of these laws were far-reaching. Even today around a third of Britain's land area is still held by titled families (Weiner, 1992: 39). Furthermore, they extended far beyond the nobility or gentry and were applied even to small plots owned under copyhold. Until very recently most land in Britain was not at the disposal of individuals or corporations, but was indissolubly bound to descent groups.

The 'permanence' of land describes more than a physical characteristic of terrain; it also describes a quality attributed to relations embodied in land. The positive associations of land with sovereignty, inheritable power and permanence refer, of course, to ownership not tenancy. It was land ownership that was idealised and that bestowed power. Renting land was low status, invidious and insecure. Historically, it was considered morally proper to preserve an inalienable connection between family and land. Land objectified the antiquity and respectability of the bloodline. Demonstration of the antiquity of land possession was the pride of families. Land inheritance constructed the family tree as an image of kinship (Bouquet, 1996). The landed gentry evoked a past (libraries, ancient trees, parks, architecture, genealogies) that authenticated the attachment of their bloodline to the land (Lowenthal, 1994).

The tendency to see land as the most stable, enduring form of property emerges from a particular set of historical circumstances. These associations of land were not only 'symbolic' but described the economic conditions enacted by the partial land market that existed throughout the seventeenth, eighteenth and nineteenth centuries. Throughout these periods land was a pre-eminent source of prestige and power, but it was also very hard to come by. The large quantities of land in the hands of aristocratic lineages and the tendency of those that had land to retain it at all costs, meant the supply was restricted. As a result there was a tendency for land prices to remain high. Land was not only symbolic of permanence and wealth it was also the safest form of economic investment until the 1870s (Jamoussi, 1999).

The ideals of sovereignty, inheritable power and permanence preserved in land were nonetheless increasingly challenged on all sides. Throughout the period, individuals had used a range of (technically illegal) legal dodges to get rid of entail and alienate land (Jamoussi, 1999). As the emergence of less regulated markets increasingly required greater liquidity, these legal dodges became more important. At the same time there emerged an increasingly vocal opposition to heritable power, often taking the form of struggles over the rights of Man and Woman, over enfranchisement and slavery. Liberal economists and Utilitarian philosophers envisaged a world of individuals acting rationally on their own behalf, who were free to engage in contractual arrangements with others to ensure the greater good. Theories of property based on 'natural rights' to land emerged (see below). Civil rights, including individualised property rights were enshrined in declarations of state such as the Napoleonic Code and American Constitution (Hann, 1998). Increasingly individual rights to land were being enacted in emerging land markets. The partial inalienability of land was becoming ever more partial.

The Invention of Traditional Land Tenure

The emergence of markets and market individualism stimulated a strong reaction against the erosion of idealised family, moral and political institutions. A nostalgic literature evoking the continuity of communities untouched by commerce developed throughout the eighteenth and nineteenth centuries. Reaction against capitalism and modernity increasingly took the form of myths of the past. In the nineteenth century, a distinction emerged between the original peasant society of Europe and modern society. Traditional societies were seen as self sufficient, communal, based on religion and customary law and growing out of 'natural' affective bonds of blood and land, whereas modern society was alienated, individualistic, based on contract and money. Theorists like Maine argued that society grew from natural ties of blood between kin (Maine, 1891). Gradually, he contended, ties of blood were displaced by ties of land. 'Village Communities' emerged based on communal land tenure (Macfarlane, 1991). It was believed that these village communities existed everywhere in Europe prior to feudalism (cf Hatt, 1931). Past and primitive societies that lacked formal law were understood to be cemented by blood ties and communal land tenure which took the place of legal institutions (Carsten, 2004a: chapter 1).

The distinction between modern commodified property and 'traditional' land tenure conformed to a series of dualistic oppositions developed in the late 1800s. Influenced by Maine, Tonnies developed the contrast between *Geminschaft und Gesellschaft (*Shils, 1991). Elsewhere, Durkheim's distinction between mechanical and organic solidarity involved similar distinctions between communities cemented by affective and land-based ties and those cemented by the modern division of labour (Carsten, 2004a). The distinction between modern individualism and past communitarianism was also reflected in popular romantic constructions of traditional village and peasant life, with its pre capitalist values. This idealised organic village community formed a contrast that could be used to condemn the impersonal, specialised, alienated, and calculating attitudes of modern urban life.

Glorification of primordial attachments to land, coupled with scorn of the vulgar estimation of land as real estate, constructed a polarity that consecrated love of country as a bulwark against all that was bad about modernity. At the very same time that a mercenary view of land was supposedly victorious in the modern West, a form of nationalism was invented based on the very same attitudes to land that were supposedly endangered. Nationalist sentiment was affective, involuntary, and based on ties of shared blood and land (Smith, 2000). Patriotism represented the selfless values of the past, opposed to modern selfish greed.

'The status of land', Evans argues, 'is the main issue that archaeology addresses of direct political relevance' (Evans 1997: 126). Traditional land tenure based on authentic 'dwelling' gave archaeology new political resonance in debates over proper relations to land. Romantic notions of the peasant past increasingly played a part in ideologies of blood and soil in Britain and elsewhere (Matless, 1998, Marsh, 1982). In Germany, archaeologies of field systems played a part in Nazi ideology. The Third Reich enacted ideas of 'traditional' land tenure in policies that prevented the *Bauern* from alienating land, thereby preserving the connection between land and racial purity (Farquharson, 1976). Internationally the evolution of the plough became an arena in which claims to national superiority were played out (Trigger, 1989; Sklenar, 1983: 163). It was proposed that farming in long strips began in prehistoric Germany, and thus the mouldboard plough must have been spread by the Aryans from Nordic Europe (Barger, 1938, cf Curwen, 1929: 24). The importance of traditional land tenure to national identity meant that Archaeologists were increasingly able to use notions of traditional, authentic, tenure to support politically marginalised groups. In parts of Britain, people who had formerly been looked on with horror as 'Britain's internal Indians' were now lauded as islands of authentic being (Evans, 1997: 120-5; Matless, 1998). Through the creation of what Evan's calls 'sympathetic prehistories' archaeologists were able to 'sponsor rights to territory and establish cultural authority' (Evans, 1997: 126). This process, he argues is comparable to the present role of archaeology in 'many Third World states and in the land claims of aboriginal / indigenous populations' (ibid.).

The contrast between modern Western attitudes to land and primitive non Western traditional land tenure remains part of archaeological interpretations. Western attitudes to land are characterised as objectifying and acquisitive - they are commodifying and capitalistic. By contrast, non western attitudes to land are mythical, non-commodified, and inalienable (see Tilley, 1994; Thomas, 1993; Bender, 1993; Abramson, 2000). This dualism ignores the fact that contemporary markets do not rely on the 'purely' economic, but also on romanticised 'non-economic' values created in the 'cultural' sphere.

Nationalism and Territorialisation

Concepts of land tenure, I argue, tend to refract forms of identification that take place within modern nationalisms. The concept of nationalism I employ is that used by Anderson and developed by Smith (Anderson, 1983: 15; Smith, 2000: 796). These writers stress how the nation is 'imagined as both inherently limited and sovereign' (Anderson, 1983: 15). It has 'sacred properties' (Smith, 2000) that are in part performed through archaeology (Smith, 2001). This argument goes beyond the banal nationalism found in some archaeological texts – as, for example, when Fowler describes prehistoric land division as a British 'national achievement' (Fowler, 1983). It goes beyond what Lowenthal describes as the 'scenic nationalism' to which archaeologies of field systems are perennially prone (Lowenthal, 1994, cf Hawkes, 1951; Taylor, 2000). Instead, this argument addresses the forms of identification that are assumed to be at the heart of what tenure is. Archaeologies of tenure, I argue, tend to assume that tenure is a process of 'territorialisation'.

My use of 'territorialisation' is more restricted then Deleuze and Guattari's (1987). I use 'territorialisation' to refer to what Deleuze and Guattari identify as a particular kind of reterritorialisation. In this form of reterritorialisation the territory is organised as a bounded object tessellating within a series of other bounded objects (ibid: 478, 559-62). While Deleuze and Guattari distinguish 'land' as a quantifiable, appropriable resource from 'territory' (ibid: 487-8) they also note that discourse can reterritorialise land as homeland or fatherland. It is in this restricted sense that I use 'territorialisation' to discuss tenure. Archaeologists, I argue, envisage land tenure as identical to this kind of territorialisation, linking it to territorialized identities. In this sense ancient land tenure comes to resemble forms of identification familiar from modern nationalism.

Territorialized tenure presents images of territory as homeland. As Barth observes this image is 'enshrined in [anthropological] models of corporate groups, defined by their exclusive and excluding rights to their respective shared estates' (Barth, 2000: 23; see also Ingold, 2000;

Carsten, 2004a). Both national myths and the corporate descent group of traditional approaches to tenure are based on the 'elementary figure of a farmer and his family on the land they possess' (Barth, 2000: 23). The farmer exercises his tenure against those in neighbouring lands, excluding those not of the same blood. This elementary figure is 'readily projected as a figure of homeland-and-country, with national boundaries demarcating it, and defining the European concept of nation' (ibid). When tenure is understood as territorialisation prehistoric fields become homologies for the nation.

In this section I offered a brief history of how land has been emotionally, morally, and economically constructed.

Land has been made into a permanent 'immovable' ground linked to genealogical roots, homeland and nation. Many approaches to tenure, I argue take land tenure as equivalent to territorialisation. Accordingly land boundaries can be read as defining territorialized identities. The 'traditional' land tenure I discussed here, however, represent only one aspect of existing approaches. Another strand represents the kind 'economic' reasoning that these romanticised approaches sought to resist. These accounts speak less of 'land tenure' and more of 'property'. In the next section I review these legal and economic definitions of property, definitions that treat tenure as a jural institution evolving towards exclusive and individualized privatisation.

1.2 Classical Theories of Property

'There is nothing which so generally strikes the imagination, and engages the affections of mankind, as the right of property; or, that sole and despotic dominion which one man claims and exercises over the external things of the world, in total exclusion of the right of any other individual in the universe.'
(Blackstone cited in Verdery & Humphrey, 2004a:1)

In this section I discuss what Rose calls 'Classical Theories of Property' that were developed in the seventeenth and eightcenth centuries (Rose, 1990). These classical theories have become entrenched in mainstream legal and economic definitions of property and also in what Verdery calls 'western native categories of property' (Verdery, 2003: 14). As was discussed above, the 'spread of the full capitalist market economy', stripped away rights and obligations that circumscribed earlier forms of tenure in favour of 'unlimited rights' of alienation and private property (MacPherson 1978: chapter one). The property relation most valued, and most prominent in classical literature, was the 'sole and despotic dominion' of which Blackstone speaks above. I begin this section with an outline of characteristics of classical theories. I then discuss economic theories of the evolution of property. Lastly, I review the legacy of classical property theories in anthropology and archaeology of tenure.

Characteristics of Classical Theories of Property

The first characteristic of classical theories is an emphasis on exclusion. Property is defined as 'an exclusive individual right' (MacPherson, 1978: 2). This definition sees property as consisting of two sorts of relation, firstly a relation between the owner and a right, and secondly a relation between the individual owner and all others in society who are excluded from the owner's right. For most economists and legal scholars the 'institutional' sanctions that enforce exclusion are the essence of property. This definition leads directly to the second characteristic of classical theories – because exclusion is enforced by legal sanction, property is understood as a legal entity. 'The origin of justice' as Hume put it 'explains that of property' (Hume, 1896: 491). Property is seen as a jural institution to the extent that some writers imply it cannot exist without written law (Hunt, 1998, Bell, 1998). For classical theorists legal institutions emerged logically from natural law and the social contract. According to natural law the world consisted of rational individuals able to contract with one another. It would be in every rational individual's self-interest to contract with other individuals to respect property. As Hume put it; 'I observe that it will be for my interest to leave another in possession of his goods, *provided* he will act in the same manner with regard to me' (Hume, 1896 [1739]: 490 his emphasis).

Classical theory assumes that property is naturally motivated by scarcity. Economists like Malthus pointed to the profound consequences of scarcity and to the significance of laws of supply and demand (Malthus, 2005, Smith, 1776: chapter VII). Ricardo investigated the special circumstances of land as a commodity, observing that the value of rent depended on the scarcity of good land (Ricardo, 1821: chapter 1). It was presumed that property resulted from the individual's desire to maximize personal wealth, a desire that would be intensified in times of scarcity.

Property, classical theorists believed, functioned to resolve what Gregory calls 'the economic problem'- 'the problem of understanding how universal economic man allocated his scarce resources among his competing, and unlimited wants' (Gregory, 1982: 26). Property served to 'identify authoritatively that claims that any given person has to any given resources' (Rose, 2004: 276). Enforcing identification by law functioned to make trade possible. 'When owners are known, all parties can negotiate for resources instead of fighting for them' (ibid.). Property was supposed to reduce conflict, and eventually increase the wealth of all (Smith, 1776) . It would be in every individual's self-interest to create legal institutions of property in order to avoid a Hobbesian war of all against all that a world of scarce resources would otherwise naturally promote.

The main characteristic of classical theories of property is the insistence on singularity. As an 'exclusive individual right' property relates singular subjects to singularized 'rights'. Modern economic definitions of tenure recognize that the owner is not always the sovereign individual of seventeenth century natural law. Nonetheless they still configure owners as singular bounded entities, the owner of property rights might be a group, a state, an institution or corporation but it must still be a single whole (see Demetz, 2002, United Nations, 2005: chapter 3). This characteristic of mainstream property theory is based on the legacy of the notion of the 'liberal-democratic' rights-bearing person who arrived 'with the spread of the full capitalist market from the seventeenth century on' (MacPherson, 1978: 7). Classical property theory is thus based on a model of the individual, who was understood as owning themselves as well as property (self-possession). Private property is thus powerfully connected to totems including 'rights', 'democracy' and the liberty of the 'individual' (Verdery, 2003: 14-17).

These characteristics are so well established within the 'western native category' of property that it can be difficult to see that they actually offer a very limited description of tenure. Classical theories assume that all property everywhere is private property, and to the extent that tenure does not display the characteristics of private property it is simply ignored (see Demetz, 2002: 653-4). Property, classical theory supposes, originated not from other forms of tenure, but from a state of no property, a 'waste' or *terra nullius*, like that which existed at the dawn of time (cf Locke, 1690). In this context evolutionary accounts are important in explaining how private property institutions emerged.

Evolutionary and Economic Theories

The Origins of Property came to be one the great debates of nineteenth century political economy. The concept of social evolution arose through agricultural images of 'improvement' and self 'cultivation', which shaped ideas of 'culture' in the seventeenth and eighteenth centuries (Trigger, 1989). Cultivation was positively valued as the 'highest form' of subsistence (Pluciennik, 2001). Cultivation was the badge of civilized land husbandry and the model of labour which entitled man to ownership. It was considered that early people must have possessed intimate personal possessions, food and certain resources, but only the civilized had property in land. Accordingly in the nineteenth century evolutionary schemes were developed that systematically classified societies according to stages in property arrangements corresponding to social forms and levels of substance

(Morgan, 2005 [1877], Engels, 2005 [1884]). Within such schemes cultivation was the evolutionary benchmark and most important form of production. Society, Morgan argued, moved from the early stage of Savagery, with no private property in land, to Middle-Later Savagery and Older Barbarism in which land was owned within descent groups based on matrilineal succession. After the domestication of animals, land ownership switched to the patrilineal descent group in the periods of Middle and Later Barbarism. Finally, civilized societies evolved in which private property might be owned by individuals or the state. Marx and Engels also saw cultivation as a benchmark in the evolution of private property, although they linked it to evolution of oppression. As Childe explained, 'the plough … deprived women of their monopoly over the cereal crops and the social status that it conferred' thereby removing from them the right to property (Childe, 1942: 72). The evolution of the plough was the first oppression of one class by another.

Evolution remains an important concept to property theorists (Earle, 2000, Demetz, 2002). Property is observed to exist at a range of levels of excludability, from 'bands' to 'tribes' to 'states', and agriculture is still understood as an evolutionary benchmark that 'opens the door' to privatization (Demetz, 2002: 667). Tenure is assumed to be absent among groups which do not practice agriculture (see Ingold 1986 for critique). Even where social evolution is eschewed its ghost survives in the way that tenure is customarily classified as continuum between two poles, with variations progressing from common property towards increasingly restricted individualized private property (Smith, 1988:245). Commons represent a state of nature, from which property emerges as progressively greater social control. Private and common property are always opposed to one another.

In recent approaches evolution is explained using notions of economic efficiency (Demetz, 1967, Neale, 1998, Demetz, 2002). These studies compare the functional efficiency of different property institutions (Merrill, 2002: 33). Economists focus on the ways that these institutions deal with externalities (the effects of economic actions on those other than the actor). They argue that private property evolves because it is functionally superior in;

i) creating incentives for improvements
ii) reducing negative externalities (e.g. environmental decline)
iii) reducing transactions costs (because fewer decision makers are involved).

For example, Demetz argued that the Montagne Indians of Quebec developed more restricted property rights because the fur trade created negative externalities (over hunting) that were reduced when land was parceled up (Demetz, 1967). Cost-benefit calculations like these are used to explain the emergence of land division.

Boundaries, it is argued, arise in situations where the cost of land division is less then the benefits of constructing it (cf Casimir, 1992).

Traditionally economic accounts have offered wealth-maximization motives or social efficiency models to explain long term changes in tenure. Recently, Demetz has offered an economic history of property that does not centre on externalities, but on efficiency in trade (Demetz, 2002). He argues that western societies have evolved towards increased scale of economic networks, productivity and technological advancement. The 'socio-legal system' of private property ultimately triumphed over earlier common property and 'socialism' because it was more efficient in facilitating economic trade between strangers in situations of 'organizational complexity' (see also Shennan, 1999).

Archaeologists have not been immune to valourising their subject matter in evolutionary terms. As Bowen suggested, ancient fields marked a development between the ages of the 'savage' and the 'barbarian' (Bowen, 1961:1). The discovery of prehistoric land division confirmed the expectation that '...the areas occupied by the chalk were probably in prehistoric times, and even much later, the most settled and highly civilized parts of Britain' (Clement Reid cited in Curwen & Curwen, 1923: 63). National and racial types of land division indicated property forms that were more or less advanced, so that 'celtic' fields initially denoted not only an ethnicity, but also a more 'communist' and 'primitive' form of tenure (Seebohm, 1926 [1883]). Land division marked the triumph of economically superior cultivation over stock raising (Curwen, 1946, Fowler, 1984). Later large scale rectilinear land division (called 'coaxial') were described as evidence for 'technical competence' and 'elements of high organisation' (Fowler, 1983). 'To bring order out of chaos' asserted Bowen, 'is a process of civilisation' (Bowen, 1975: 55). Historically, evidence for land division has been interpreted as evidence for evolutionary advance.

The Legacy of Classical Theories in 'Social' Approaches

Anthropologists have underlined many times the point that *'property relations are social relations'* (Godelier, 1986, his emphasis, see also Hann, 1998). However, these 'social' approaches have often approached tenure using classical definitions of property. Classical theories, as was described above, see property as consisting of two sorts of relation, a relation between the owner and a right, and a relation between the owner and everyone else in society who are excluded from the first relation. 'Social' approaches emphasise the second part of this definition. Property as Godelier puts it, is not to be considered as 'a relation between people and things', but as 'a relation between people and people with reference to things' (Godelier, 1986). Likewise many 'social' approaches to

property follow classical theories in seeing tenure as a jural institution and structure of 'law'.

The structural conception of tenure involves approaches based on jural notions of 'rules' or 'rights'. This notion of property derives from classical theories of property developed in legal scholarship. Law scholars have traditionally broken down full title into singularised rights - for example into rights of *usus* (use), *usus fructus* (gains from use), *abusus* (transformation) and transfer (alienation and inheritance) (Niederle, 2004). The lawyer Henry Maine, for example, approached ancient and 'primitive' tenure as a 'bundle of rights' some or all of which might be possessed by particular individuals at particular times (Maine, 1891; Macfarlane, 1991). Subsequently many studies have produced their own catalogue of 'rights' singularised in particular ways (see Boserup, 1965: Chapter 9, Sahlins, 1972: 92). For example, Netting argues that tenure comprises the following:

1. 'rights of use, including hunting, grazing cultivation, water, wood, mineral, passage, building, and residence rights (the accompanying rights of disuse may include those of fallow, or of the holding of reserves for future family expansion);
2. rights of transfer, including those of inheritance, gift giving, lending, swapping, mortgages, rentals, sales, and other contracts; and
3. rights of administration, including allocation or withdrawal of use, dispute settlement, regulation of transfer, management of land for public uses, and 'reversionary' or 'ultimate rights' (e.g. to collect royalties, tributes, or taxes)' (Netting, 1993: 157).

Rights of 'control' are generally placed at the top of abstract hierarchies of rights, as 'over rights' (Sahlins, 1972: 92, see also Hatt, 1939, Boserup, 1965). However this tendency reflects the assumptions of classical theories that 'ownership' is the most important kind of tenure, taking precedence over usufruct or customary transactions (see Agarwal, 1994, Cummings et al., 2001, Whitehead & Tsikata, 2003 for critique).

The 'bundle of rights' approach has been attractive to anthropologists and archaeologists because, as Strathern points out, they are very frequently confronted with multi-dimensional, unstable and overlapping tenurial arrangements (Strathern 1988: 104). Frequently people are found to have attachments with things that are not in the classical legal sense their property, and relations are often devolved between parties in ways more complex the classical theory allows. Within the classical legacy that archaeologists inherit these multi-dimensional aspects of tenure can only be understood by breaking down monolithic 'property' into a more flexible realm involving multiple interests. The traditional approach in anthropology, as Alexander observes has been to begin with a 'bundle of rights' and go on to 'unpick that bundle, examining for instance, how membership in kin groups may give a person particular rights of access, or the means by which different rights to, and relations through an object are determined and managed' (Alexander, 2004: 252). Breaking property down into a series of rights goes some way towards dealing with complexity, allowing the analyst to grasp the way that tenure appears to be multidimensional in terms of both its subjects and objects (Carrier, 1998; Verdery, 1998; Johnston, 2001a). However, such approaches perpetuate the assumptions of classical theories by singularizing 'rights'.

Classical theories define property as individualised rights of exclusion. The history of property is one of the evolution of institutions that enforce exclusion. In this section I reviewed narratives of evolution and economic explanations for these transformations. Approaches in anthropology and archaeology are influenced by classical theories to the extent that they see tenure as a jural institution and aspect of social structure. In the next section I turn to an important part of classical theories – the labour theory of property. I show how the 'natural rights' of the creator to his property have been seen as the authentic source of property, justifying its unlimited accumulation. Claims about how such rights have, or have not been expropriated, continue to enflame political debates over property relations and land. Archaeologies of tenure have implicitly and explicitly participated in these debates.

1.3 The Labour Theory of Property

In the fervent atmosphere of mid-seventeenth century England it seemed that the second coming was nigh. Radical groups, like the Diggers, encamped on the commons, laying out fields. The earth, they declared, had been given by God 'as a common treasury for all' (Winstanley 1649, cited in Bradstock, 2000). Each man was entitled only to what he could cultivate. Inheritance of land, and the hereditary rights of Kings and nobles, was against God's law. In this chaotic period the puritan John Locke spent his youth. Locke went on to devise a theory of property that would both appeal to protestant morality and justify unlimited appropriation by the rich and powerful. In this section I discuss the labour theory of property and its legacy. I begin by outlining the theory and its effects. I review how the labour theory has been drawn on in political struggles over tenure. Lastly I discuss how archaeologies of tenure have been influenced by ideas of natural rights and their expropriation.

The Labour Theory and its Legacy

Locke's labour theory asserted a biblically authorised possessive individualism. Every Man, Locke argued, had been given his own body as his property. Through the capacities given him by God, man (sic) was able to appropriate land 'through the labour of his body and the work of his hands' (Locke, 1690). The holding of land was linked to the morally correct life, and the improving quality of hard work. Indeed, Locke used the words 'property' and 'propriety' interchangeably, linking rights of ownership to the moral person. Like Hume, Locke saw civil society and law as emerging naturally from the functional necessity of protecting private property rights.

It is difficult to underestimate the influence of the labour theory. For the first time, a case had been made for 'an individual right of unlimited appropriation' (MacPherson, 1978:12), a case which differed profoundly from the 'divine rights' of primogeniture and hereditary power. The labour theory supplied justifications that could be used to support an extremely wide range of causes. Locke himself was interested in justifying colonial conquest, specifically, colonial expansion by the British (who developed agriculture on land taken from indigenous owners) rather then the French (who traded with them) (Verdery & Humphrey, 2004a:4). Locke's theory went on to play a role in the new form of colonialism that emerged after 1700, colonialism distinguished by large scale land-taking (Gosden, 2004). The labour theory was also useful to large land-owners. Land-owners justified their extensive estates by pointing to the 'improvements' that they made. In the eighteenth century the landlords were opposed by political economists who also used the labour theory. The economists argued that the rents imposed by unproductive land-owners limited the 'productive' labours of capitalists (e.g. Ricardo, 1821). Landlords, it was argued, were actively detrimental to the production of wealth; loving to 'reap where they never sowed' (Smith, 1776). Liberals like John Stuart Mill, used the labour theory to argue for a free land market, liberating land from primogeniture so it could become more 'productive'. At the same time the labour theory was also useful to the radical cause. Radicals argued that land belonged to the workers, not to the landed elites (Paine, 2004 [1795]). Inherited property, they proclaimed, was nothing more than unjust expropriation.

In the eighteenth century the labour theory of property was developed into a labour theory of *value*. This theory of value explained the most basic laws of economic life. The exchange value of a commodity was largely determined by the labour necessary to acquire the commodity. Even in the 'early and rude state of society' if it took twice as long to kill a beaver as it did to kill a deer, one beaver would naturally be worth two deer (Smith, 1776: chapter VI). Therefore, in primitive societies, naturally, 'the whole produce of labour belonged to the labourer' (Smith, 1776: chapter IV). Marx developed the labour theory of value into a critique of capitalism and private property (Marx, 1976). In early societies, Marx believed, private property had been 'personally earned' through labour which conjoined the 'working individual with the conditions of his labour'

(Marx, 1976: 928). Under capitalism however, the commodity presented labour as abstracted from the labourer ('socially necessary labour'). Labour became an undifferentiated quantity, 'the equal of every other sort of human labour' (Marx, 1976: 155). Under capitalism labour had become 'inauthentic' and the labourer 'alienated'. Mass production, Ruskin argued, stifled the potential of labour to improve the moral self - replacing 'men' with mere 'segments of men' (Ruskin, 2004[1853]). The alienated condition of capitalist workers could be contrasted with the authentic, non-alienated relations that had once existed in the past (Engels, 2005).

The labour theory of value even entered into arcane debates over measurement of ancient fields. Marx noted that 'among the ancient Germans the size of piece of land was measured according to the labour of a day' (Marx, 1976: 164). Here, he showed, labour was not only an act of producing value but a means of measuring its value. This form of measurement may indeed have been used to measure some kinds of fields (including some English acres). However, the power of this image was the way that it associated the labour theory of value and the labour theory of property. For some writers field systems were associated with authentic unalienated labour (Hammond & Hammond, 1911). For a long time it was assumed that the size of prehistoric fields was decided by the amount of land that could be ploughed in one day (Seebohm, 1926, 1914). Entire typologies of prehistoric fields were built on this premise, with sizes and shapes of fields determined by plough technology and labour time (Curwen, 1927; 1929;1932; 1938; 1946; Hatt, 1931; 1949; Crawford, 1953; Bowen, 1961). The notion continued to appear in archaeologies of land division into the 1980s (Reynolds, 1979; Fowler, 1971; Fowler, 1984).

Among the most enduring legacies of the labour theory in archaeology is Esther Boserup's intensification theory. Boserup argued that as populations rise labour input is increased to produce higher agricultural yields. Agriculture therefore evolves from hunting and pastoralism to forest fallow to long fallow to short fallow cultivation. Intensification in European prehistory, Boserup argued, had lead to sedentarisation within permanent field systems. Long-term tenurial rights which could be inherited within lineages emerged from territorialisation (Boserup 1965: 56-59). In fact, archaeology has some claim to have originated Boserup's account of tenure, which owed much to work by fellow Dane Gudmund Hatt (Hatt, 1939, 1949). The concept of intensification has been used widely in archaeological interpretations of prehistoric land division (Welinder, 1975; Waterbolk, 1995; Widgren, 1989; Kristiansen, 1998). Later writers have rejected the demographic pressures in Boserup's concept of intensification, but continue to reproduce her account of how tenure arises from sedentarisation and territorialisation (De Hingh, 1998; Barrett, 1994; Barrett, 1999). The labour theory thus continues to play an important role in archaeologies of tenure.

The Labour Theory and Expropriation

'The first man who, having enclosed a piece of ground, bethought himself of saying 'this is mine', and found people simple enough to believe him, was the real founder of civil society.'
(Rousseau, 2005 [1754])

If labour creates 'natural rights' in land and its products, then removing them (or part of their value) from the labourer is an act of expropriation. Marx argued that the 'pre-history of capital', lay in the ruthless and deliberate 'expropriation of the great mass of the people from the soil, from the means of subsistence and from the instruments of labour,' (Marx, 1976:928). Only by such brutal means could the proletariat – a class with nothing to sell but its labour – be forcibly created. Expropriation from the land was characteristic, not just of capitalism, but of all societies with private property: 'In private property of every type the slavery of the members of the family at least is always implicit since they are made use of and exploited by the head of the family' (Marx, 1976: 1083 emphasis removed). Property, as Proudhon famously proclaimed, was theft.

The labour theory supplies a moral right to ownership on both left and right. 'On this head' as Veblen observed, 'the socialists and economists … are substantially at one' (Veblen, 1898: 352). Expropriation therefore ferments powerful emotions across the political spectrum. Expropriation relies on the conviction that 'we' have been (or are going to be) robbed. For the right, collectivization represents expropriation. It is a 'theft' of wealth from those who laboured to create it, and a violation of 'natural' 'human' rights. Social conservatives believe that society should respect the moral boundaries of property and propriety. While libertarians feel that private property represents individual freedom, and that privatization actually restores to the individual liberties compromised by society. For the left, all landed property was once held in common. Private property formed through aggressive expropriation by self-interested. 'The theory of the Communists' wrote Marx and Engels 'may be summed up in a single sentence: Abolition of private property'. A ringing phrase qualified as the abolition of 'modern bourgeois private property', or property 'based on the antagonism of capital and wage labour' (Marx and Engels 1999: 11-12). The left sought to establish ownership by and for the workers, restoring the link between labour and property severed in the capitalist labour market. The centrality of the labour theory to political debates means that archaeologies of tenure are inevitability political.

Archaeologies of Expropriation

'Property determines exclusive rights to things. The core of property is the right to exclude … the only pan-cultural

concept of property might be equivalent to 'Keep your cotton pickin' hands off my (whatever)'
(Earle, 2000: 40, citing Neale, 1998).

Archaeologists have tended to follow classical theories, defining property as exclusion. Archaeologies of property thus continue to be influenced by the legacy of nineteenth century social evolutionists, particularly Morgan and Engels. Property changes, these archaeologists suggest, as the social structures (within which economic behaviour is 'embedded') evolve (Gilman, 1998, Earle, 2000, Earle, 2002). An important stage in evolution comes with the emergence of 'stratified' (or 'class') societies. At this time rights in land previously created through labour are seen as being expropriated by elites. Elites mobilize the surplus labour of the masses to accumulate wealth. Archaeologies of property thus resemble nineteenth century histories of expropriation (e.g. Marx, 1976: Part Eight).

The period when stratified societies first flourish on a large scale in Europe is the Bronze Age (Kristiansen, 1998; Earle, 2002). Archaeologies of property represent the Bronze Age as the age of 'chiefdoms' and of wholesale expropriation. Elites control the economy, manage the distribution of land, and guarantee the rights and security of land holders. The emergence of large scale land division is seen as reflecting 'direct control over staple production' by chiefs, 'through carefully delimited ownership of land' (Earle, 2002: 346). Elites are seen as a 'centralized decision making hierarchy' responsible for the coordination of the construction of boundary systems. Following Morgan, it is even been suggested that separate patri-clans were allotted 'specific demarcated land sections' within Bronze Age land division (Earle, 2002: 327). Elites are 'strategic', 'competitive' and 'self-interested', in other words their motivations entirely concur with the classical theorists vision of 'economic' rationality.

What, then, explains the ability of elites to assert their self-interest over the equally 'economically' motivated individuals who made up the rest of Bronze Age society? To explain this anomaly, archaeologies of property stress the ideological aspects of property: To the extent that tenure represents expropriation it must be 'legitimized'. 'Legitimation' of tenure explains all the efforts that prehistoric societies expended on constructions with no apparent 'economic' benefit. When those sites are seen as legitimating tenure they are immediately understandable as the outcome of 'economic' motivations. Tombs and mortuary sites are traditionally interpreted in just this way as 'signaling land claims'. Much as Morgan suggested societies are seen as forming patrilineal corporate descent groups with lineal inheritance rights where land is scarce (Goldstein, 1981). Bronze Age barrows offer opportunities for manipulating personal genealogies, as well as ideologically reinforcing the prestige of elites. Beneath the façade of ritual pomp the cynical strategies of self-interested *Homo economicus* operate. Archaeology, especially in the Bronze Age, reproduces the legacies of classical and labour theories of property. It therefore continues to produce evolutionary narratives. In this literature we can see how fundamental concepts of tenure are to archaeological interpretation.

In this review of the labour theory and its legacies I have discussed how this theory of property, presented a moral image of productive work. This morality created 'natural rights' that could justly be used to exclude others. It justified unlimited accumulation of private wealth and colonial occupation. However, it was also developed into critique of private property. The notion that histories of property are histories of expropriation still influences archaeological approaches to tenure. The power of the labour theory rests in the way it constructed a moral personage, a person of 'propriety', who 'combined himself', in Locke's terminology, with things (including abstract things like 'rights'). In the next section I develop this aspect of approaches to tenure. I explore a range of alternative approaches based on concepts of identity and personhood.

1.4 Approaching Tenure through Personhood

'Ownership', Veblen argued, is 'too external and colourless a term' to describe the relations between people and things (Veblen, 1898). 'The unsophisticated man, whether savage or civilised' he avowed 'is prone to conceive of phenomena in terms of personality'. People have intimacy and fellow feeling with possessions, which are sensed as a 'quasi-personal fringe' or 'penumbra' of the person. The phenomenology of possession presents alternative approaches to tenure, approaches less closely linked to theories of law and civil society: The penumbra of personhood, as Veblen observes, may extend into entities that are not legally owned just as much as those that are.

In this section I begin to develop a new approach to tenure bringing together studies from a range of disciplines. I review evidence for 'self-extension' in human and non-human development. I then present a theoretical foundation that can be used to understand this evidence for self-extension. These theoretical approaches, I suggest, can be developed into an approach to tenure, and I review some previous studies which consider tenure in a similar way. Finally I discuss how approaching tenure through personhood is connected to studies of the ethics of property.

'Self-Extension'

Evidence for 'self-extension'- personal intimacy or communion with objects of the kind Veblen describes – is now well established across a range of disciplines (see Kleine & Baker, 2004 for review). 'Self-extension' through objects is found in animals as well as humans from laboratory rats to primates (Ellis, 1985). Primates differ from other species only because they rely more on visual and social markers to denote possession then they do on olfactory markers (Ellis, 1985: 123-9). Psychologists have long documented the patterns of attachments between people and objects, in human development. A complex body of theory has emerged concerned with how infants develop sense of self in conjunction with their sense of objects. This is a process that continues throughout life; relationships with objects changing alongside concepts of selfhood during life transitions (Kleine & Baker, 2004: 12-6). 'Self-extension' has been found cross culturally: Belk catalogues a range of practices that reveal the literal bodily incorporation of objects at the moment of possession. These include: 'licking new possessions, burying the umbilical cord on tribal land, inserting removed foreskin beneath the bark of a personal tree, eating or taking the name of conquered enemies, burying ancestors on sacred tribal land, and claiming ownership of new land or artefacts by toughing them, naming them for a part of the person's body, leaving a lock of hair on them, or shedding blood on them' (Belk, 1988: 144).

In America and Europe the diminished sense of self experienced following loss of possessions has been widely documented (Belk, 1988: 142-4). This produces some effects that confounded the classical expectations of *Homo economicus*. Economists have consistently found that people are irrationally 'loss averse'. We put more emphasis on avoiding losing what we already have, than we do on gaining what we don't (Novemsky & Kahneman, 2005). This loss aversion has been found to vary according to how much people see possessions as 'me' or 'not me' (Kleine et al., 1995). Loss aversion is the focus of ongoing studies in marketing. Companies are keen to encourage us to overcome our aversion to throwing out items to which we are attached, and to attach us to new items (Kleine & Baker, 2004).

When tenure is assumed to be a variety of law much of what is important about the phenomenology of possessions is missed. Studies suggest that changing legal institutions alone is not enough to develop 'psychology of ownership'. For example, many firms in America follow economic explanations of property, believing that property is an incentive to greater investment (see Demetz, 1967 and discussion above). Therefore firms attempted to increase productivity by giving workers share ownership in the firm. This, it was supposed, would 'incentivise' workers to increase production. However, many firms found that the predicted productivity increase did not materialise (Pierce & Rodgers, 2004). Formal legal ownership does not necessarily lead to 'possession' or to effective tenure (see also Verdery, 2003).

Forms of 'self-extension' vary according to sense of 'self'. For example, studies show that ownership differs consistently according to gender. In American populations, men generally see property as expressing their 'rights', and speak of objects in terms that emphasise individual autonomy and exclusion. Women, on the other hand, tend to express self-extension in terms of relations of responsibility and affiliation with objects (Kleine & Baker, 2004). Self-extension also changes with age: Older people and those who are dying express interpersonal ties through possessions more frequently; extending their personal efficacy after death through objects.

These studies imply dimensions of tenure that are largely unexplored in approaches derived from the classical and labour theories of property. Classical theories envisage a world which individuals and things enter fully formed. But studies of self-extension suggest relations with entities surrounding the self may actively shape personhood.

Objectification and Personification

> 'The person has for its substantive end the right of placing its will in any and every thing, which thing is thereby mine; [and] because that thing has no such end in itself, its destiny and soul take on my will. [This constitutes] mankind's absolute right of appropriation over all things.'
> (Hegel cited in Radin, 1982: 973).

Hegel's dialectical materialism has supplied the philosophical basis for a range of approaches which relate property and personhood (e.g. Radin, 1982, 1995; Miller, 1987, 1995a, 2005; Belk, 1988: 145-6; Graeber, 2001: 56-67). These readings of Hegel refute the notion that there is a 'fundamental separation between humanity and materiality' (Miller, 2005: 8). Processes involve acts that create consciousness at the same time as producing form. Action produces the subject as concrete, realised existence through its externalisation in the outside world (Miller, 1995b). Humanity is thus a by-product, as it were, of particular materialities. Existence is not prior to processes of creation but emanates continually.

Miller develops his reading of Hegel into a theory of objectification. Objectification describes a circular process of externalisation involving continual displacement of consciousness between the bearer and the world. Processes externalise aspects of consciousness and then reflect the subject back onto itself concretising a particular subjectivity (Miller, 1987: 19-33). This theory enmeshes both subjects and objects, persons and things, so that 'both … can equally be understood as part of the process of societal self-construction' (Miller, 1995b: 277). 'Everything we are and do' as Miller puts it 'arises out of the reflection upon ourselves given by the mirror image of the process by which we create form and are created by this same process ... As we create law, we understand ourselves as people with rights and limitations. As we create art we may see ourselves as a genius, or as unsophisticated. We cannot know who we are, or become what we are, except by looking in a material mirror, which is the historical world created by those who lived before us' (Miller, 2005: 8).

Anthropologists have long been aware of more than one 'material mirror'. Mauss described relations with a material environment animated by a 'pervasive personality' (Mauss, 1970). Objects, he suggested, were not only instruments to be dominated and controlled but could be 'persons', with whom humans entered into a variety of emotional or sentimental relations. Anthropologists have developed an important literature on these processes of 'personification', particularly in the ethnography of Melanesia (e.g. Gregory, 1982; Strathern, 1988). The processes of personification involve '...things that are to some extent persons, and persons and groups that behave in some measure as if they were things' (Mauss, 1970: 11). Boundaries between subjects and objects assumed to be autonomous and separate in dominant discourse break down. Personification involves objects that can act in their own right.

When agency is imputed to objects through personification, artefacts can be understood, as Gell puts it, as elements of a 'distributed mind' (Gell, 1998). The inferred agency of 'persons' distributed across time and space 'translocates' in the way described by Nancy Munn (Munn, 1990, see preface). Distributed mind infers agency along 'protensions' and 'retensions' branching out in 'listening posts to somewhere else' (ibid.).

Tenure and Personhood

Tenure, I suggest, can be approached using Miller's and Radin's reading of the Hegelian dialectic. Different kinds of person are configured differently according to different 'material mirrors', or materialities. As tenure is created persons understand themselves as different kinds of person. Tenure, I argue, can be approached as part of how persons matter.

Radin reads Hegel as pointing to a fundamental link between property and the ontology of persons. 'To achieve proper self-development – to be a *person*', she argues, 'an individual needs some control over resources in the external environment' (Radin, 1982: 957: her emphasis). In fact, she demonstrates this fundamental connection between property and person is implicit in the enactment of American law. She cites numerous examples of legal decisions that are enacted differently according to how objects are felt to be more or less part of the person (Radin, 1982). Radin's reading of Hegel,

importantly, observes that identities configured through the Hegelian dialectic involve more than an 'immediate exclusive individuality' or 'self' as it is commonly understood. Phenomena like 'families' or groups can also be objectified as 'persons' (Hegel cited in Radin 1982: 975).

Ingold has also suggested that tenure should be approached as part of the constitution of identity. His approach is one that sits very well with theories of personification:

> *'Tenure is about the ways in which a resource locale is worked or bound into the biography of the subject or into the developmental trajectory of those groups, domestic and otherwise, of which he is a member. For it is only by virtue of his belonging to the community that a person acquires a relation to a determinate portion of natural space...'*
> (Ingold, 1986: 137).

Ingold suggests tenure allows the extension of persons. It 'prolongs' relations beyond 'the spatio-temporal bounds of the immediate self' (Ingold, 1986: 138). He re-figures Mauss' theory of personification of gifts into an approach that applies to tenure. Tenure, he implies, allows land, trees, rivers and other resources to be seen as persons and transacted as persons or parts of persons.

Personhood and the Ethics of Property

Theories that relate property and personhood create opportunities for ethics of property. Legal scholars observe that classical theories of property embody ethical contradictions. Classical and labour theories justify the unlimited right of individual's to appropriate property, but, this unlimited right contradicts the abilities of others to fulfil their needs: 'Property as a human right needed by all to enable them to express their human essence' is contradicted by property based on the individual right to exclude and alienate (MacPherson 1978: 205). Legal scholars have sought to re-envision property in ways that are less ethically compromised. They do so by invoking notions of 'rights' attached to human persons.

MacPherson argues that property should be based on inclusive rather than exclusive rights (MacPherson, 1978). Ethical theory property would be enacted as 'a right to what is needed to be human'; a right to access to 'the accumulated means of labour and capital' and to be included in 'the income for the whole produce of society' (MacPherson, 1978: 205-6). This ethics is based on an historical analysis of concepts of property. The emphasis on exclusion in classical and labour theories, MacPherson argues, is inherited from the ages of slavery and serfdom. He suggests that common property, neglected by classical theorists, offers alternative basis from which property can be re-imagined: Common property involves rights to be *included* rather than rights to exclude. An ethical property would emphasise the rights of individuals to be included in the communal good.

Radin's ethics of property and personhood, also involves notions of 'human rights' and limited property rights. The law, she argues, should strive to create 'healthy' human persons, not obsessed with material things, but with property rights limited to possessions necessary for personal development. Accordingly, her notion of what property should be is based on a 'cross-culturally' applicable theory of what is necessary for the proper development of the human person (Radin 1984). Radin bases her ethics around what she calls 'good' and 'bad' identification with objects. These are distinguished on the basis of a 'moral consensus' which allows 'us' to 'tell the difference between a healthy person and a sick person, or between a sane person and an insane person' (Radin 1982: 969). 'Bad' identification involves 'fetishism' or 'materialism'; living 'only for material objects'. This is a way of life that 'works to hinder rather then support healthy self constitution' (ibid.).

Ethics of property developed from notions of personhood are arguably constrained by the kinds of 'human person' that they envisage. Radin's approach fails to grasp the full possibilities of Hegel's dialectic as it has been developed in theories of objectification and personification. As Radin herself notes, Hegel's theory 'carries the seeds of destruction' of the idea of 'liberal rights attaching to individuals' (Radin 1982: 976). But legal ethicists envisage personhood in much the same way - as that of individuals bearing 'human rights'. Accordingly, Radin's anxiety is that moral boundaries be maintained between people and things - people must not be treated 'like things', and owners must control possessions, rather then possessions controlling the owner. These are just the kinds of boundaries, however, that anthropologists discover are transgressed again and again in situations described using theories of personification. Arguably, re-envisioning tenure requires a reconsideration of identity and personhood.

In this section I reviewed evidence for 'self-extension' into possessions. I then offered a theoretical basis for understanding this aspect of possession, using concepts of objectification and personification developed in anthropology. I then discussed how these theories could be used to approach tenure. Lastly I showed that theories of property and personhood had ethical consequences. However, I suggested that this ethics of property may have been limited by the legacy of classical approaches which involved a rights-based concept of 'humanity'. In the next section I develop this last point by exploring alternative concepts of identity and personhood. I discuss approaches to tenure based on concepts of 'relational' identity. Ethnographies of tenure which employ notions of relational identity and personhood show how these approaches might be developed in archaeologies of tenure.

1.5 Tenure and Relational Identity

If tenure involves 'self-extension', how are we to understand 'self'? In this section I discuss different notions of the person, concentrating on approaches that understand identities as relationally constituted. I begin by discussing some of the different kinds of person described by ethnographic studies. I discuss recent archaeologies that have built on these concepts of identity, and address some of criticisms of this literature. Lastly I review tenure studies of situations where identities are relationally composed. What differences might be expected when identity is configured relationally?

Kinds of person

Concepts of how persons are made, of procreation, vary cross-culturally. Analyses of American kinship have shown how, the 'individual' is made (Schneider, 2004 [1972]). Individuals are seen as having a natural biogenetic essence bestowed at birth. The uniqueness of each individual is a permanent inheritance that fixes the individual within biologically determined kinship relations. However, anthropologists working in parts of India and Melanesia describe persons made in very different ways. Here identities are not fixed, but may be quite fluid and changeable. In parts of India, interpersonal transactions involving sexual intercourse, food and co-residence transform the substances of which persons are composed, transferring moral and spiritual qualities between persons (Busby, 1997). In Melanesia, identity is continually in flux. Persons are repositories for substances that flow from others and directly compose their bodies (Strathern, 1988). Identities are produced through the absorption of essences from others and the giving out of one's own essences into others (Strathern, 1988: 348). Persons are not thought to be indivisible bounded units but to be 'dividual' or 'partible'.

Understanding identities that are relationally composed requires keeping a network of transactions in view. Whereas the ideology of *Homo economicus* sees the individual as 'owning' her or himself, being innately 'free' of obligation to other entities. Here it is not self-possession, but the condition of being comprised of aspects of others that might just as well appear as the 'original' condition:

> '...relationships do not link individuals. Rather, the fact of relating forms a background sociality to people's existence, out of which people work to make specific relationships appear' (Strathern, 1991: 587).

Relational notions of personhood present a radically different understanding of the locations of rights, powers and agency. Whereas individualism presents these as capacities of single human actors, in this kind of personhood they are best understood as distributed. Rather than being atomistic, essential and unchanging entities are relational, malleable and transactable. Furthermore this understanding of the person does not just describe single bodies, may equally index a group, family or another entity. Since these identities are also multiply composed, identities appear nested or 'fractal' rather then singular. They often appear as homologies and analogies of each other.

Archaeology of Relational Personhood and their Critique

Relational identity and personhood have recently become important subjects in archaeology (Chapman, 2000; Brück, 2004; Fowler, 2004; Jones, 2004c) although this literature makes little use of the idea of tenure. Chapman approaches identity using evidence for fragmented objects and composition of 'sets'. He observes how enchainment and accumulation of objects influences the way that identities are composed. In prehistory, objects were detached and circulated as parts of persons. The most sustained studies of personhood focus on the Late Neolithic and Early Bronze Age periods, and on analysis of human remains and portable objects (Fowler, 2001, 2004; Brück, 2004; Jones, 2004c). These studies argue for identities constituted dynamically and multiply composed rather then fixed and singular.

Archaeologies of relational identity and personhood have not been accepted without criticism, some of which should be addressed here. One criticism argues that relational identity pertains to places like Melanesia and India only; it is irrelevant to European prehistory. Another accuses such archaeologies of primitivism, because they use analogies from the developing world as parallels for the distant past of white Westerners. I disagree with these criticisms. Firstly, concepts of relational identity are very relevant to studies of the west. Secondly, to allege that this use of analogy is 'primitivist' is to ignore its widespread application in studies of modern property networks.

Although alternatives to the sovereign individual first appeared outside the west (indeed it is difficult to see where else they could have appeared given the historical prominence of ideologies of the individual in the west) arguably, it is in studies of modernity that these approaches are now making their greatest inroads. Concepts of relational identity have proved particularly relevant to analysis of emerging technologies. These studies require approaches that can understand dynamic entities which are distributed rather than atomized. Studies by Strathern have shown how approaches using concepts of relational identity can be used to analyze biotechnologies, emerging intellectual property

formations and online publishing (Strathern, 1999, 2001a, 2001b). Cyberspace supplies numerous examples of property objects that are multiply constituted and multiply authored, involving forms of tenure poorly described by classical theories of property. Innovative tenurial forms such as 'creative commons' and 'copyleft' licenses recognize multiple authorship as the basis of future claims on creativity (Coleman, 2004; Brown, 2004). Free / Open Source Software usually comprises multiply authored property. Several writers argue that the creation of this software is better understood using the anthropology of gift transactions than using classical economics (Rossi, 2004; Leach, 2002; Zeitlyn, 2003; Strathern, 2001a).

Following Lipuma, I would argue that the relational 'dividual' can appear in all societies, indeed the tension between 'individual' and 'dividual' personhood is an important element of understanding how identities are configured (Lipuma, 2000: chapter 4). There would, indeed, be error in any approach which classified stable types of personhood and then tried to transfer these wholesale into prehistoric contexts: As Jones argues, 'we must be careful not to totalize the 'dividual' or the individual' (Jones, 2004c: 168). However, the new archaeologies of personhood rarely do this. Instead they use ethnography to open up possibilities for diversity in the kinds of 'self' we are able to describe.

Approaching Tenure and Relational Identity

What difference might relational and multiply constituted persons make to tenure studies? Recent ethnographies address this question (Strathern & Hirsch, 2002; Leach, 2003b, 2003a, 2004; Kalinoe & Leach, 2004; Hirsch & Strathern, 2004). These studies offer ways of approaching 'self extension' when 'selves' are multiply composed. On the Suau Coast of Papua New Guinea (PNG), settling tenurial claims involves finding, not an individual 'owner' who exists prior to or outside a property object, but 'establishing who the land *is* at that particular juncture in time' (Demian, 2004: 40).The person whose relationships can encompass the whole group is able to become land and 'stand for' it. Likewise, in Fuyuge PNG, making a land claim involves summoning all knowledge of entities and persons among a group so that the person making a claim encompasses and *becomes* the place entire. Only once a person has consolidated all these parts within their identity are they able to 'speak for' the land (Hirsch, 2004b). In these examples tenure involves processes that create a person whose relations embody the land. The person identified in this form of tenure is both a single person carrying out a personal project of action, and a collective objectification, embodying wider relations.

The relations that compose identity can include relations with ancestors, supernatural beings and the land itself. Relations with land, like relations with human persons, may involve exchanges of substances. Bodies may appear to be composed from the land. Tenure thus appears more like a relation of kinship, than one of ownership. It may involve nurture as much as the 'despotic dominion' described by Blackstone above. The Are Are, for example, consider birth to be a detachment of substance from the person of the land: 'person (land) thereby *enters into an exchange* with the land (person)' (Strathern, 1991: 589 emphasis hers). This originary gift from the person of the land necessitates return gifts. In the case of the Are Are these take the form of buried placentas, which are understood as second babies born to be given back to the earth. Elsewhere, we might envisage similar transactions with land involving deposition of parts of bodies or special objects.

Cosmological models of procreation are often based on mythical transactions, to which tenure often refers. Tenure is often understood as 'inalienable' because it was given as an originary gift at the dawn of creation (Godelier, 1999). The debt imposed by such imaginary gifts can never be discharged, but become the foundation for ongoing 'returns'. These may take the form of deposits (as with the Are Are) or of performances. Tenure understood as a gift from the gods can never be completely alienated but always retains something of the (imaginary) personage who bestowed it. Transactions of tenure may involve what Weiner calls 'keeping-while-giving' (Weiner, 1992) maintaining relations that make tenure an inalienable aspect of identity.

Where tenure is part of the constitution of relational identities it is inherently inclusive rather than exclusive. Tenure cannot be other than inclusive because entities are multiply constituted. Every relationship is the product of earlier relationship. Theoretically relations proliferate infinitely - although in practice the contexts that would allow infinite proliferation are usually absent (Strathern, 2005a: chapter 6). Where identities are composed relationally economic networks typically include all the persons who have contributed in whatever way to another person's success, and who will later lay claim to their share (Kirsch, 2004). Relationships that are seen to have composed bodies also become the grounds for future claims over them. Claims rely on an extensive network of existing relationships, and in many situations the more inclusive these can be made to appear the better (Leach, 2004, Kalinoe, 2004). It is the generation of future productive relationships that is the object of economic life, not the accumulation of exclusively held wealth. What is held in this situation is not land as such, but knowledge about relationships. It is this knowledge that is the principal source of economic 'wealth'. Such knowledge concerns the relationships that produced multiply constituted entitles, it thus refers to the past. Inequalities in this situation are relational and historical - concerning who one is, and how one is made up.

All this is very different to the economics that predominate in conventional accounts based on classical theories of property. The anonymity, 'freedom' and atomisation presumed to exist in capitalist markets is absent. Whereas classical theories of property emphasise exclusion - cutting networks and foreclosing 'externalities' or obligations the 'economics' described here are based on inclusion and the proliferation of ties and obligations. Whereas classical theory is based on understanding the allocation of goods that are defined through their scarcity, here the key resource – relationality – is not scarce. Indeed relationships can be abundant - the problem, for the relatively wealthy, is how to make such relations, debts and obligations scarce. Approaching tenure through concepts of relational and multiply constituted personhood therefore has considerable implications for tenure studies, pointing to the need for an alternative 'economics' that differs in important respects from classical theories.

Conclusions

Tenure has to do with who you are. It generates expectations of relationships. Two priests in Simbu Province, Papua New Guinea failed to appreciate what was expected, not just of what they did, but also of whom they were - provoking their killers. Indeed, there were innumerable things for them to consider in reproducing the relations that sustained their tenure. A brief (and not exhaustive) list how what was involved might include '…ancestors burial places, the pigs sacrificed, shrines and sacred grounds, the plants and marks at boundaries, houses at traditional sites, the labor invested and crops raised, the trees planted, the pigs browsing in the bush, the wild plants, fruits and building materials that grow, the goods made and stored…' (Brown, 1998: 272). All these elements were evidences of the conditions of persons and their relations, revealing that they observed the obligations that pertained between themselves and others and that relations were properly ordered. In fact, almost any change in the personhood of the priests would have to be considered as a question of tenure. Here, then, is good example of the networked and relational aspects of tenure.

In this chapter I reviewed existing approaches to tenure. These approaches were grouped into four themes. These themes can be summarised as follows:

Theme 1: Classical Theories of Tenure: These approaches see tenure as an exclusive individual right. The innate self-interest of individuals means that it emerges 'naturally' in conditions of scarcity. Property implies the relation of exclusion that exists between the owner and all other non-owners must be sanctioned by a legal institutions. Property thus requires some form of law, which is often seen as being 'embedded' in the evolution of social structures over time.

Theme 2: Labour Theory of Tenure: Approaches which see tenure as created through 'productive' work or land-use. A theory that is implicit in notions of intensification.

Theme 3: Territorialisation and Tenure: Land has economic, emotional and moral values, which are historically linked to models of genealogical roots and ideals of nationhood. Approaches to tenure are influenced by these values, producing narratives that assume tenure arises principally from territorialisation.

Theme 4: Tenure as Constituting Identity: Tenure can be approached as part of how persons matter, or of how identities are constituted. Different kinds of tenure may be connected to different kinds of personhood.

In the chapters that follow, I develop each of these themes reflexively using insights from my analytical work. My analysis begins in chapter three where reassess classical theories and test the notion that organised land division emerges in response to scarcity of good land. I address theme two in chapter four where I discuss the labour theory of value that lies behind this theory, and I assess approaches to intensification, investigating how land division may have influenced farming systems. In chapter five I begin to involve theme four. I analyse the measurement and valuing of land and its connections to the valuing of relations. In chapter six, I assess how tenure is linked to territorialisation (theme three), analysing evidence from prehistoric settlements. In chapter seven I investigate mortuary practices, metalwork deposition and transactions across the region, developing theme four in new directions. In chapter eight I return to these four themes and assess how my evaluation of the approaches that each describes have changed. Before I begin my analytical work, however, my next chapter introduces the area that forms the foundation of my enterprise; Dartmoor and its prehistoric landscapes.

Chapter 2

Dartmoor and Archaeologies of Tenure:
Significance and Potential

'This town's enclosed with desert moors,
But where no bear nor lion roars,
And nought can live but hogs :
For, all o'erturned by Noah's flood,
Of fourscore miles scarce one foot's good,
And hills are wholly bogs.'

(William Browne, Lydford Journey c.1612)

When the higher parts of West Devon are mentioned at all in literature before the 1800s⁴ they are seldom celebrated. Risdon apologised to his readers for detaining them overlong in a place 'so wild', with 'so slender repast' and 'where it is to be doubted whether they have taken the cold or the cold hath caught them' (Risdon c1620 cited in Worth, 1994: 41). It was not until Samuel Rowe brought his Grand Tour home to Devon that 'Devonia's dreary Alps' became scenery of 'grandeur', 'magnificence' and 'subliminity' (Rowe, 1985 [1828]). It was at this time that the region emerged as an object of nature-historical, archaeological and folkloric interest. At the same time tourism and an associated literature of guidebooks and travel writing began in earnest. New ways of producing and circulating knowledge, made it possible to compose an entity called 'Dartmoor' through interactions with the hills, rocks, rivers, plants and animals of this place. In the twentieth century this entity became a National Park, an administrative territory, marked by definite boundaries (Beeson & Greeves, 1993).

2.1: Location of the Study Area(© Crown Copyright/database right 2002. An Ordnance Survey/EDINA supplied service)

2.2: Reave on Rippon Tor with tor cairn on skyline (© Author)

26

To study Dartmoor is thus to engage in networks that construct the area as a separate object of knowledge. The work of this construction depends on the special quality of the area, which today stands out from its surroundings. Dartmoor is currently the largest area of open country in southern Britain, covering 368 sq miles. Its topography comprises two plateaux, a north moor (highest point 621m OD) and a south (539m OD). More then half the area is over 300m ASL. Trees, roads and buildings are very few on the higher moors, which are used mainly for rough grazing. Peat has been growing here since at least the end of the ice age and today covers the tops of the high hills and many valley bottoms. The most common habitat is acid grassland, lending the landscape the poetic resonance of a wilderness (Carrington, 1826). Geologically, Dartmoor sits on a granite batholith, differing only in the coarseness of the grain of the rock. Deposits of gravelly head accumulate at the tops of its many rivers, material rich in cassiterite (tin ore). Among the remarkable features of this landscape are its weirdly shaped granite tors, (called 'rock idols' by earlier writers). These are accompanied by other curious natural features - rock basins, logan stones, tolmen - as well as scatters of boulders and waterfalls. Archaeological sites are seen as part of this 'natural wilderness' and, historically, Dartmoor preservationists have emphasised that these remains are part of what they desire to protect (Collier, 1894, Griffiths, 1994). Prehistoric monuments have contributed to images of a haunted landscape, a land of death that might literally consume the unwary traveller by sucking him into the mire (cf Conan Doyle, 1996 [1902], Agatha Christie (1931), and Dorothy L Sayers (1930). The integrity of Dartmoor as a study region builds on a range of networks which rest on how the natural and the cultural interact.

Dartmoor is exceptional for its number of prehistoric sites. The National Park claims to contain the greatest density of Bronze Age sites anywhere in Europe (Dartmoor National Park Authority, 2004). Archaeological remains are visible as stone constructions and earthworks across the open moorland, especially on the edges of the high plateaux. Sites form extensive archaeological landscapes with remains of prehistoric buildings and ceremonial sites found alongside abundant evidence for prehistoric land division. A lattice of collapsed dry-stone walls - known locally as 'reaves' – can be traced on the ground and from the air. Reaves form enclosures of various sizes and shapes and landscapes of enclosed fields. The extent of these remarkable traces make Dartmoor an important location for studies of land division and tenure.

In this chapter I aim to show the potential Dartmoor has for investigation of the themes identified in the previous chapter, and the significance it has within previous archaeologies of tenure. I begin with a review of previous accounts of prehistoric land division in the North West Europe. I argue that this is an important juncture for interpretations of land division, and suggest that Dartmoor is a good region in which to explore current concerns. I then discuss previous interpretations of tenure on Dartmoor highlighting some issues emerging from previous work. Next, I examine the regional datasets, their problems, and new data now available for study. Lastly, I discuss the chronological framework and databases I created for my analysis.

2.1 Archaeologies of Land Division in North West Europe

Across North West Europe from Finland to France and from Ireland to Estonia, traces can be found of ancient land enclosure. These traces take various forms including ditches, earthen banks, walls, hedges, fences and cairns. They were built at different times, from the Neolithic into the historical period. The oldest include third millennium BC land division from parts of Ireland and Scotland (Caulfield, 1978, Caulfield et al., 1998, Barber, 1997). An important florescence in construction occurs in the second millennium BC in the Middle Bronze Age of southern Britain and the Netherlands where extensive regular land division was laid out. This was followed by later construction in the Late Bronze and Iron Ages of the Netherlands, North Germany, Jutland, Sweden and parts of northern Britain (see reviews in Müller-Wille, 1965, Bradley, 1977, Fleming, 1987a, and Johnston, 2000). Southern Britain is increasingly emerging as a region dominated by such landscapes, which have been discovered from Scilly in the West to the Thames valley in the East. Although some of this evidence has proved to post-date the second millennium BC (Ford et al., 1994) most seems to date to the mid-second millennium, or, as recent work at Heathrow indicates, even earlier (Framework Archaeology, 2002). The appearance of regular land division across large parts of southern Britain coincides with an era of expanding connections between distant parts of Europe. Communications and exchange networks widen, and objects, knowledge and persons move long distances. The fluorescence of land division in southern and south western Britain during the second millennium BC is thus potentially associated with wider transformations happening at this time.

I begin this section by reviewing previous interpretations of land division. I discuss how these interpretations envisage tenure as an aspect of sedentarisation and a process of territorialisation. Lastly I point to recent analyses that suggest landscapes of land division may not have been settled in the manner that was once supposed. These new findings have implications for existing interpretations of tenure.

Competing Interpretations of Land Division

From the 1960s onwards, interpretations of land division have adopted what might be called 'commonsense' assumptions. They assumed that field systems reflected the evolution of more efficient forms of (principally arable) farming. Land division was simply a matter of becoming 'better farmers' (Fowler, 1971: 30). This functional 'economic' view continues to be influential. For example, Fowler and Blackwell, interpret land division as the 'rational reaction' to an economic crisis which necessitated the creation of a 'reliable mechanism' for feeding a 'growing population' (Fowler & Blackwell, 1998: 54). Since land division was assumed to maximise productivity it was treated as *prima facie* evidence for intensification (Brongers, 1976, Welinder, 1975, Fowler, 1984, Hedeager, 1992). Intensification was supposed to be driven primarily by land scarcity resulting from population growth.

From the 1970s onwards the evolution of social hierarchies increasingly supplemented functional explanations. Influenced by the institutional economics that emerged in the 1960s and 70s (e.g. Sahlins, 1972) the economy was now seen to be 'embedded' in social structures. Bradley suggested that the impetus behind land division was provided by the growth of new elites (Bradley, 1977: 276-7). Bronze Age land division indicated 'stratified societies' defined by the presence of 'chiefs and kings' that 'set themselves apart from the agrarian substratum' (Kristiansen, 1998: chapter 3). Echoing the evolutionary narratives of property produced by nineteenth century writers including Morgan and Engels, land was supposed to be owned inalienably by chiefly lineages (Gilman, 1998, Earle, 2000, 2002). Elite were motivated by self-interested desire for 'prestige' and 'prestige goods'. Desire for prestige goods stimulated intensification, which required a new architecture of land division (Yates, 1999, 2001). Chiefs were then able to skim off surpluses from agricultural production to fund the acquisition of more 'prestige'. In a related power strategy chiefs are also seen to control the allocation of shares in land. According to this view land division involves parcelling land for periodic redistribution. Through control of redistribution chiefs further confirm and legitimate their authority (Earle, 2002: chapters 12-4).

Alongside these elite ownership models another kind of interpretation focuses on relations within groups and management of land at a more local scale. This has been termed the 'Communal Ownership of Property Model' (Chapman & Shiel, 1993). Andrew Fleming's interpretations of Dartmoor supply some of the most influential accounts of this type (Fleming, 1984, Fleming, 1985b). De Hingh has extended this approach using a Europe wide perspective (De Hingh, 1998). In 'egalitarian prehistoric society' De Hingh argues, there would have been 'no 'land owners' in our sense of the word (De Hingh, 1998: 12). Instead 'the identity of the individual is derived from belonging to the group, to the communal land, and also to the economic advantage involved in participating in this system' (De Hingh, 1998: 14). Land Division thus relate to changing concepts of

tenure that emerge from the social dynamics of small scale communities.

Territorialisation and Tenure

In Southern Britain the advent of extensive land division is seen as signalling the arrival of a truly sedentary way of life - a population fixed in time and space. In the Later Neolithic, landscapes contain few permanent settlements. Instead the record contains large ceremonial gathering places. Societies seem to be more mobile involving larger groups with spatially widespread social connections. The 'Middle Bronze Age transition' is held to mark the time when mobile gives way to permanent settlement. The period is seen as one of 'social fragmentation' - larger mobile groups break down into smaller extended families each with their own buildings, fields, common lands and cemeteries.

Narratives of the Middle Bronze Age tend to assume that tenure is a form of territorialisation, (see chapter one). Sometimes tenure-as-territorialisation is explicitly naturalised, as, for example, when Pryor states that land boundaries 'express a fundamental human and animal motivation - what Desmond Morris called the Territorial Imperative' (Pryor, 2001: 314). In other accounts territorialisation is not seen as innate, but tenure is seen as part of the territorialisation of social identities. Accounts which focus on identity offer theoretically sophisticated approaches to change in which the Middle Bronze Age transition is seen as a transformation in subjectivities (e.g. Gosden, 1994, Barrett, 1994). These accounts draw mainly on evidence from the Wessex region. Here, the construction of land division is linked to changes in the way that space and time are lived (Gosden, 1994: 84-100). More precise spaces are inscribed into peoples being through activities taking place within smaller bounded spaces and connections that are more localised. Barrett expresses the transformation in subjectivity between the Late Neolithic/ Early Bronze Age and the Middle/Late Bronze Age as a difference between 'being' and 'becoming' (Barrett, 1994). 'Being' signifies territorialized identities, linked to two important processes: firstly, the development of 'lineal histories' and 'genealogical reckoning'; secondly the intensification of agricultural production.

Barrett's evidence for the emergence of lineal histories is based on the 'individuating' mortuary rites that emerge at the end of the third millennium BC. These changes lead to lineal inheritance of land and long term occupancy of the same place. 'Households and household clusters', he states 'were the products of a lineal history in which their individual identities were fixed historically and also in relation to the land' (Barrett, 1994: 147). This account of lineal inheritance is taken up by subsequent work in South west Britain and on Dartmoor (e.g. Owoc, 2001, Johnston, 2005). Interpretations that link land division to land inheritance have long been important in North West Europe. Evidence for subdivision in coaxial land division is sometimes seen as indicating partible inheritance in the Bronze and Iron Ages (Hatt, 1939; Müller-Wille, 1965). However, the evidence for 'individuating' mortuary rites now seems much less secure (Jones, 2004c, Brück, 2004). What Barrett interpreted as the symbolic construction of lineages through positioning of primary and secondary burials (Barrett, 1990) has been shown to be a much rarer practice than was formerly assumed (Woodward, 2002). These new assessments of mortuary evidence suggest grounds for re-examining Barrett's interpretation.

Agricultural intensification, especially shortening of the fallow period is the second factor in Barrett's account of the Middle Bronze Age transition. Short fallow cultivation, Barrett argues, allowed claims to land to endure over time, as farming activities were focused on the same areas of land (Barrett, 1994: 149, 1990). However recent soils studies in Cranbourne Chase, Wessex, show that what was previously thought to be evidence for intensification is nothing of the sort (French et al., 2003). Both before and after the construction of land division, land uses were predominately pastoral. Again, this suggests that changes in identity be rethought.

Whilst interpretations of the Middle Bronze Age transition that focus on the constitution of subjectivities have proved to be productive approaches, the evidential basis of these interpretations has changed. This is especially true of the evidence for sedentary settlement patterns, to which I now turn.

Settlements, Sedentarisation and Tenure

The assumption that tenure is linked primarily to territorialisation means that tenure is emphasised when permanent sedentary settlements and bounded territories appear in the record. The appearance of substantial 'houses' surely indicates 'increasing attachment to place' as Barrett puts it, and a process of settling down in the landscape. However, analyses of the lifecycles of Middle Bronze Age houses demonstrates that settlement is much less permanent and sedentary in this period than might at first appear (Brück, 1999a, 2000). In southern Britain, Brück's work shows that many Middle Bronze Age roundhouses 'were occupied for only a single generation'. Settlement architecture did not monumentalise or legitimise 'a long term relationship with place'. Instead the evidence suggests a 'neolocal residence pattern'. This pattern might involve the construction of a new house on marriage with the settlement cycle ending on the death of the household head. In the context of this shifting settlement pattern, 'land rights may not have been invested in the individual household but were perhaps held communally by lineage, clan or community groups' (Brück, 1999a: 160). This form of tenure would entail a certain amount of flexibility; with tenure 'redistributed as new households formed' (ibid.) Brück's account thus fits with interpretations like those of Fleming that emphasise

management of tenure at levels above that of the individual household.

It is instructive to compare the situation in southern Britain with interpretations of land division from the southern Netherlands. Here, studies have shown that Late Bronze and Early Iron Age buildings were only occupied for one generation. After c.20 years old houses were abandoned and new houses rebuilt elsewhere in the surrounding landscape. Studies suggest that 'the bond of individual families with specific plots of land seems to have been very loose, and was probably not inheritable'. Farming was predominately pastoral, with tenure based 'entirely on collective ownership and forms of land use' (Roymans & Theuws, 1999: 14). Tenure seems to have involved a 'set of overlapping claims' (Gerritsen, 1999: 94). Gerritsen suggests that tenure might have been held by the group, but exercised flexibly by households. Plots would be claimed 'for the duration of the life cycle of house and household, and that after the house was abandoned those rights reverted to the local community' (Gerritsen, 1999: 95). This interpretation of later prehistoric tenure is similar to that developed by Brück.

Although I have emphasised the contrast between Brück's neolocal residence pattern and Barrett's vision of a Middle Bronze Age transition marked by sedentarisation and permanent settlement Johnston's recent account of Dartmoor landscapes reconciles both these positions (Johnston 2005). Johnston follows Barrett in seeing cairns and barrows as 'visible expression of the lines of descent and inheritance through which access to resources and social status was maintained' (Johnston, 2005: 13). He argues that this interpretation of cairns can also be extended to houses. Barrows were 'physical markers of a community's attachment to an area of the landscape' and 'houses represented a continuation of this process' (Johnston, 2005: 13). The practice of abandoning houses meant that the ruins of houses were visible in the landscape long after occupation ceased (see also Bradley, 2002). These houses, like cairns, materialised the memory of genealogical forerunners from whom tenure was inherited. Even though the locations of houses might change, Johnston implies that territorialized identity, lineal histories and 'being' are still important aspects of Bronze Age subjectivation.

I have pointed to several sources that suggest previous accounts of the Middle Bronze Age transition may have over-emphasised the importance of what Barrett calls 'being'. Firstly I pointed to reassessments of Bronze Age cairns and barrows, which new interpretations suggest show mortuary rites that are neither individuating, nor aimed at the manipulation of genealogical connections (Brück, 2004, Jones, 2004c, Woodward, 2002). Secondly I showed that evidence for intensification in central southern Britain has now been overturned (French et al., 2003). Thirdly I discussed evidence that the transition did not mark a switch to long term occupancy of fixed locations, but seemed to involve a short-term shifting settlement pattern (Brück, 1999a, 2000). Barrett invokes subjectivation based on fixity, territorialized identities and lineal histories. Recent accounts of landscapes in the south-west have tended to follow this view (Owoc, 2001, Johnston, 2005). However, taken together the new sources of evidence suggest grounds for reassessing current views of subjectivation associated with the appearance of land division. It may be that the fixity and territorializing aspect of 'being' have been over-played. Alternative forms of identification that are more fluid, plural and changeable might be more appropriate. These forms of identification might be linked to a view of tenure that is less reliant on territorialisation.

Archaeologies of land division are at an interesting juncture. It is now widely recognised commonsense notions of economic efficiency and function do not explain enough. Interpretations need to address the issue of tenure. However, at the same time, archaeological evidence is emerging that dislocates land division from the traditional grounding places in which tenure is sought (i.e. from territorialisation). Land division is not necessarily associated with long term occupancy of the same structures or with intensification, but may be associated with shifting settlement patterns and mainly pastoral land uses. Fleming's accounts of common property regimes have an important place at this juncture. However, the main body of analysis on which these accounts are based is now around twenty years old. It may be that new work can produce interpretations that are even more pertinent to the current scene. The next section reviews previous work on Dartmoor, focusing in more detail on Fleming's ideas and identifying directions in which it might be developed.

2.2 Previous Archaeologies of Tenure on Prehistoric Dartmoor

Dartmoor is an important location for archaeologies of tenure world-wide. This is both because of the exceptional extent of its prehistoric landscapes and because of the work of Andrew Fleming. Although Fleming did not 'discover' Dartmoor's prehistoric land division (see Gawne & Somers Cocks, 1968; Fleming et al., 1973, 1975, 1978a) he can rightly be said to have discovered their significance for archaeologies of tenure. Fleming's survey, excavation and analysis introduced the category of 'coaxial' land division (Fleming, 1987a), and produced a large body of interpretation on Dartmoor landscapes and prehistoric tenure (Fleming, 1978b, 1979, 1982, 1983, 1984, 1985b, 1988, 1994b). His researches took more than twenty years and during this time his interpretations underwent changes of emphasis. Here I review Fleming's work in the context of previous literature. I summarise his model of land division on Dartmoor and I discuss how his interpretations have been used and reassessed in other work on Dartmoor. This review highlights several issues that emerge from the current literature.

Fleming's Work in the Context of Dartmoor Studies

Fleming's work demonstrated the centrality of commons even within enclosed landscapes. Nineteenth century evolutionary accounts cast a long shadow. Many writers were predisposed to take the emergence of land division as a sign that society had left barbarism and common property behind, as it evolved towards private property and civilization (Curwen & Curwen, 1923; Bowen, 1961; cf Hatt, 1939). Fleming's work considered commoning as more than an evolutionary stage in which property was absent, showing that commoning was land tenure in its own right. Consequently his research has shown how common property can take different forms, and can coexist with other tenurial arrangements (Fleming, 1998b, 1998a). His use of ethnographic and historical analogy opened a space for thinking about land tenure as part of social organisation.

Within the archaeology of Dartmoor, Fleming's work fits within a twentieth century tradition concerned with spatial distribution and the environment of sites. Although it had long been known that the dwelling of the moor's ancient inhabitants were spread most profusely around its lower slopes (Ormerod, 1876, Rowe, 1985) the systematic interpretation of spatial patterning was lacking until the twentieth century. The work of Aileen Fox was important in stimulating this kind of work. Fox examined the morphologies of enclosures to identify types of settlement that were correlated with environmental variables (Fox, 1954a). She suggested that sites could be divided into 'pastoralist' pounds, rectilinear 'arable' field systems and 'mixed' settlements with field that were not rectilinear (Fox, 1954a). She argued that Dartmoor could be divided into the drier east, dominated by arable, and the wetter west with pastoral land use. Simmon's later study suggested that soil type was also a factor in this distribution (Simmons, 1969). Within the same tradition is Hamond's analysis of the distribution of settlements and environmental characteristics of the region (Hamond, 1979). Hamond's early computerised spatial analysis found that the highest parts of the moor were characterised by unenclosed settlements whereas the steep valley slopes were densely strewn with pounds. Field systems were found on the 'best' land with gentler slopes at lower altitudes. As a result of this work Fleming was able to draw on, and react to, a body of observations concerning spatial distribution, environment, and land use, which he could relate to his sustained investigations of tenure and social relations.

Fleming's Models of Landscape and Social Organisation

Fleming proposed that the distribution of settlements was related both to land use and to the coexistence of different tenurial systems. The high moors, Fleming suggested, had been an open access commons used seasonally for intercommoning by different groups from the Neolithic onwards (Fleming, 1983: 196). These groups came from a very wide area - possibly the whole of Devon (Fleming, 1994a). The densely clustered very large unenclosed settlements suggested seasonally occupied gathering places linked to the interaction of incoming groups (Fleming, 1987b). Further down the valley slopes were seasonally occupied pounds. These were inhabited by groups originating from each valley territory. The surrounding land was demarcated by reaves and rivers into 'group owned' common land (Fleming, 1978b: 107). At the lowest altitudes were rectilinear 'parallel reave systems'. Tenure in these field systems was more 'individualised' and 'privatised' then in the commons but was 'controlled or 'owned' 'at the level of the community' or 'neighbourhood group' (Fleming, 1979; 129-30, 1984, 1985b).

Fleming's spatial model was based on ten river based territories. Each river valley territory was bounded by reaves running along the watersheds of the valley or, in some places, by watercourses. 'Group owned' commons were divided from open access pastures by 'contour reaves' running between higher and lower altitude zones. Permanent settlement was situated within the 'parallel reaves' in the lower reaches of each valley. Parallel reaves made up 'coaxial' landscapes. This word was developed from Bradley's distinction between 'planned' and 'unplanned' land division (Bradley, 1977). Fleming divided land division into planned 'coaxial' systems (with a dominant axis) and unplanned 'aggregate systems (which lacked such an axis) (Fleming, 1987a). Coaxial field systems were laid out so that parallel reaves formed 'axial reaves' running parallel to one another along an axis. Axial reaves usually ran uphill, against the contour. Land division was thus 'terrain oblivious', paying careful attention to the topography so that the axis ensured most of the system ran uphill (Fleming, 1988).

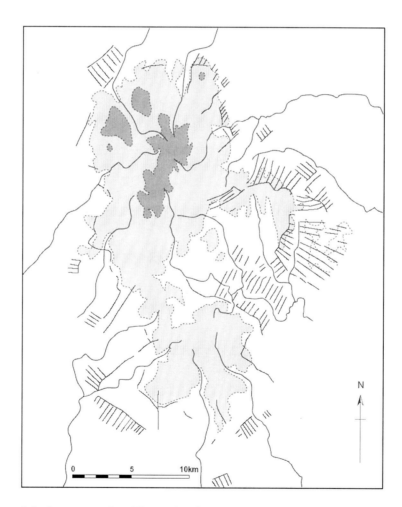

2.3: Reaves used in Fleming's 'diagrammatic representations' of land division (redrawn from Amesbury et al 2005)

The spatial model relates to another model of social organisation. This social model comprised a series of 'levels' of social structure. At the highest level, each territory formed a 'community' 'responsible for coaxial systems and their associated pasture land' (Fleming, 1984: 11-12). The lowest level was the 'household', but, (influenced by Sahlin's discussion of Chayanov), Fleming argued that the household was not an independent unit (Sahlins, 1972; Fleming, 1984: 132-3). Between the highest and the lowest level were clusters of buildings that represented 'neighbourhood groups'. These close-knit groups were linked by kinship and exchange relationships. Neighbourhood groups were 'able to use labour flexibly and to share certain kinds of resources' (Fleming, 1984; 11). Facilities available to households through the neighbourhood group and territorial community included access to marriage partners, to labour (e.g. the communal shepherd), to technology, to communally owned resources, (especially the open access commons) and shares of redistributed agricultural products.

Fleming made extensive use of ethnographic analogy to support this model. He suggested that tenure may have been administered by joint decision making bodies analogous to the St Kilda parliament or the *cuaird* of County Clare (Fleming, 1985b: 133-4). Analogy showed that existence of common property regimes did not preclude the possibility of inequality between individuals, households and communities. Indeed, as Sahlins (and Chaynaov) suggested, inequalities integrated households and groups in relations of gift exchange, and in pooling labour and resources (Sahlins, 1972) .

The contradiction between household and group is at the heart of Fleming's account of how tenure systems developed. In the Late Neolithic, he argues, tenure was entirely collective. However, in the Bronze Age the increasing prominence of households led to 'an attempt to maintain collective economies' in the face of fragmentation (Fleming, 1985b: 142). Land division and tenure were a way of overcoming the tensions that resulted from the appearance of households. The emergence of households themselves, however, is not fully explained.

This account begs the question of how the levels of Fleming's social model are constituted. Fleming's interpretation is strongly structural. His levels are nested inside one another and their relations involve contradictions between already stabilised forms. Fractures between levels correspond to distinctions between privately exercised and collectively held tenure. A problem of such structural approaches is that they make change difficult to explain. In the chapters that follow I will argue that these social levels might be better understood not as structural categories, but as moments in processes that constitute identities. When tenure is seen as part the constitution of relational identities, common Recent critical attention has focused on the Boundary Making Episode (BME) that was a feature of Fleming's

and private collapse into one another in ways that dynamically integrate the levels held apart in Fleming's models. For the moment, however, I will leave this issue and move on to other issues emerging from Fleming's work and its place in subsequent literature.

Issues of Synchronicity

Fleming created an image of Dartmoor as a structure of static, tessellating territories (see 2.3 above). In his earlier work he developed the notion that reaves were laid out simultaneously in one 'Boundary Making Episode' (BME) (Fleming, 1983, 1988). 'Most of the Dartmoor land boundaries' he avowed, 'were laid out around 1300 bc as part of one grand plan' (Fleming, 1983: 223). Reaves were 'the consequence of a single political decision' (Fleming 1983: 222). The strong emphasis on synchronicity in this work produced mismatch between the reaves viewed at a regional level – where they could be represented in diagrams as an integrated system – and the reaves viewed at a local level – where the idiosyncrasies of each landscape were apparent. On the one hand, Fleming remarked, 'one feels a society of conformists, whether one sees them as bending to the will of one of Colin Renfrew's chieftains, or hammering out an obsessively egalitarian system after some interminable meeting of fellow commoners'. But, on the other hand, 'when one gets down to detail, it seems that they were rugged individualists, living in quite small face-to-face groups little bigger than hunting bands, arranging their own affairs according to their needs' (Fleming, 1982: 54-5). Fleming's work attempts a compromise between both perspectives, arguing for regional synchronicity whilst detailing evidence for variability and chronological depth (Fleming, 1978b: 102, 111).

In his more recent work Fleming stresses lengthy processes of territorialisation behind the regional territorial pattern. In this interpretation the BME is no longer a single phase construction event, but merely an idea; the '*conception* of the grand plan' only gradually implemented on the ground (Fleming, 1994b: 72-3 his emphasis). The reaves themselves, he suggests, might emerge from gradual stone clearance. The territories within his spatial model, he suggests, might have Neolithic origins. This idea was developed in Barnatt's study of ceremonial monuments (Barnatt, 1989). Barnatt argued that stone rows and cairns formed 'foci' for communities exercising tenure within distinct river valleys. These Neolithic territories then went on to be demarcated by boundaries in later centuries. In his latest contribution Fleming uses Barnatt's analysis to argue that territorialized identities evidence by boundaries have great chronological depth. Each river valley territory, he argues, formed a self-consciously separate identity from the Neolithic onwards, 'river, people and zone perhaps bearing the same name, as they often did in Anglo-Saxon England' (Fleming, 1994b: 67).

earlier work. Johnston has re-examined the record of excavated reaves from Shaugh Moor, and studied the layout of the coaxial landscape at Shovel Down (Johnston, 2001b, 2005). He shows that the excavated reaves possess long sequences of multiphase constructions, suggesting that they were built piecemeal over a long period. Even coaxial landscapes were the outcome of 'unconscious coordination' based on the distribution of existing monuments, particularly the site of abandoned houses (Johnston, 2001b, 2005). However, this critique of Fleming's BME still leaves the striking layouts of coaxial land division to be explained. Even if this architecture was not planned and built in a single synchronous episode these landscapes have still be constructed with some care. The unusual qualities of this architecture still require interpretation.

Issues of Hierarchy

Fleming argued that the BME, (or the idea behind it) must have been conceived by 'some form of political authority' (Fleming, 1988). This authority was either an individual chief or, Fleming suggests some more democratic institution, such as a 'council of commoners'. The central authority was responsible for the decision to enclose territories, their demarcation, and the co ordination of labour and construction processes (Fleming, 1983:195; 1984: 13). Diagrammatic maps combined with a synchronic model of spatial organisation, create the misleading impression of a ruthlessly ordered landscape, one which must have been heavily controlled. Subsequent work has seized on this image of order, on 'terrain oblivious' layouts, and on the idea that an authority 'planned' the system, to argue that Dartmoor society was dominated by a chiefly elite.

Assimilation of Dartmoor within literature on Bronze Age chiefdoms was promoted by Pearce's discussions of the relationship between land division and exchange of metalwork (Pearce, 1979, 1981, 1983, 1999). Exchange of prestige goods Pearce argued, demonstrated the existence of powerful individuals. The production and acquisition of such objects was linked to increased agricultural prosperity 'to which the land organisation of fields and grazing land represented by the Dartmoor reave system bears witness' (Pearce, 1999: 69). Chiefs accumulated hoards, which 'supported the position of leading men, whose superiority may have been bound up with the control of land and of the metal supply' (Pearce, 1999: 70). Land division, Pearce argued allowed elites to obtain surpluses that could be channelled into the acquisition of 'wealth' and 'prestige'. Later writers draw on Pearce's work to depict Dartmoor as an economy planned and controlled by chiefs (Kristiansen, 1998: 367-8). Earle, for example, sees Dartmoor as a typical 'staple finance' chiefdom society with elites periodically redistributing tenure to consolidate and legitimate their power (Earle, 2002: chapters 12-4). Pearce's work highlights the issue of how land division relates to exchange networks. Throughout the second millennium

BC long distance exchange seems to be increasingly important evidenced by increasing rates of deposition of metal objects (Bradley, 1998a; Pare, 2000). Existing literature envisages that transactions in prestige goods were controlled by elite individuals.

Fleming believed the main significance of Dartmoor's exceptional landscapes did not lie in furnishing another instance of the evolution of chiefdoms. Instead, Dartmoor's potential lay in the 'empirical evidence' it supplies for 'the size of face-to-face communities and of the collective use of land' (Fleming, 1982). His archaeology of tenure stressed small scale 'bottom up' as much as large scale 'top down' decision making. The strength of his approach was the way that he drew on ethnographic studies of tenure, describing how it might emerge from gift exchanges, marriage alliances, and the practical basis of kinship relations (Fleming, 1979, 1982, 1985b). It is this contribution to theory of tenure in the Bronze Age that has been taken up by recent workers (e.g. Brück, 1999a; De Hingh, 1998). Aspects of Fleming's work that have been subject to criticism are his insistence on synchronicity and the need for a central authority behind the reaves (cf Johnston, 2005).

Four issues have been identified in this review:

1   The issue of how the different levels of Fleming's social model are constituted. Fleming discusses these as structural entities, which makes it difficult to incorporate dynamics of social change into his model.

2   The synchronicity of Fleming's spatial model, which has been challenged in recent work. If coaxial layouts were not planned according to a template, how is coaxial pattern to be explained?

3   Previous accounts see Dartmoor as an example of a Bronze Age chiefdom. But Fleming remained equivocal on this point (Fleming 1982) , and later writers have rejected this model (Brück, 1999a; Johnston, 2004). Was land division a way of intensifying production in order to satisfy elite demands for surplus? Did an elite plan coaxial landscapes in order to control the distribution of tenure and legitimise their power?

4   Related to this issue is the question of how land division on Dartmoor relates to wider transformations in exchange networks. Could agricultural surpluses be 'converted' into prestige goods to be exchanged by elites?

These issues are addressed in the analyses that follow and I will revisit them in chapter 8. Now I turn to the regional datasets available for Dartmoor and the opportunities these present for new work.

2.3 The Archaeology of Dartmoor

Reverend Baring-Gould was an extraordinary man. Folklorist, theologian and writer of nearly a hundred books, it would be unfair to call him eccentric – although his habit of lecturing with his pet bat on his shoulder is a matter of record. Conan Doyle's son considered he may have inspired the character Sherlock Holmes, indeed, *The Hound of the Baskervilles* was written after one of Conan Doyle's visit to his home. Today he is best remembered as the writer of the hymn, *Onward Christian Soldiers*, and for a scholarly study of werewolves. However, his contribution to the archaeology of Dartmoor was also extraordinary. Together with his curates Burnard and Anderson, and other members of the Dartmoor Exploration Committee he was involved in a prodigious number of excavations. In this section I review existing sources for archaeological studies, including the writings of Baring-Gould and his accomplices. I begin with the history of excavations, assessing the quantity and quality of existing records. I then consider the available survey and remotely sensed data. Lastly I review existing palaeoenvironmental sources. I conclude with an appraisal of these data and their potential.

Archaeological Excavations

Excavation on Dartmoor was something of a craze in the late 1800s. As a result, a great many sites with the region have been excavated, but the records of this work vary considerably in quality. Butler records that 130 cairns, 338 roundhouses and 25 stone rows have some recorded excavation (Butler, 1997a). This corresponds to a sizable proportion of some kinds of site – for example, Butler estimates that at least 12% of the cairns and 9% of the prehistoric buildings have been the subject of some sort of investigation (Butler, 1997a: 118). However, the vast majority of these interventions took place before 1950 and many sites lack what would now be considered full reports.

The history of archaeological excavation on Dartmoor is dominated by the work of the Dartmoor Exploration Committee (DEC). Founded in 1893, this institution excavated an enormous number of sites between the 1890s and the First World War. Baring Gould in particular supervised numerous reconstructions of archaeological sites. A great many of the moors most popular 'prehistoric' monuments are in fact hybrid constructions; built by prehistoric people, but 'improved' by Victorian restoration.

Despite the obvious problems of using data from early excavations there is still information that can be obtained from this data. Members of the DEC were punctual in ensuring their work got into print and there appear to be few sites for which there are no reports. A comprehensive review of early archaeological literature has been carried out by Butler (1997b). Antiquarian literature is also the subject of ongoing work by Jane Marchand at Dartmoor National Park (Marchand pers comm.). Butler's work in particular compiles useful data from these sources that, because of the sheer number of sites excavated at this time, supplies an important insight into settlement archaeology in the region.

Relocating where excavations took place is an important first step in using this material. Using early archaeological literature, the DEC reports and Butler's review I have relocated previous excavations in the region (see 2.4). Excavations of settlements are analysed in the research, and therefore these are also mapped separately (Appendix A). Some sites excavated before 1950 cannot now be relocated. For example I have not been able to find two roundhouses 'near the Dewerstone' excavated 1893, nor 'some explored at Assacombe' mentioned in 1894 (Baring-Gould et al., 1894: 117). Details of excavations that cannot now be relocated are given in Appendix B.

The excavation record is dominated by early archaeological excavations (see 2.5). Among relocated interventions only 7% took place after 1950, when modern methods were available. Within each site, some reports lack the details needed to relocate trenches. Other reports do not specify which buildings were excavated. Appendix B distinguishes sites where locations of excavated buildings can be firmly established, and those for which this is not now possible.

Making use of records of early excavations has involved researching the methods and quality of the fieldwork. My assessment of this work suggests that it still has some value. For instance finds recovery seems to have been quite good because the DEC routinely sieved deposits. Appendix C reviews the methodology of early excavations. This review has also found many instances of buildings where excavation was left incomplete. There is clearly scope for further work on these already damaged sites, which could enhance the information currently available for these sites (see Appendix Z).

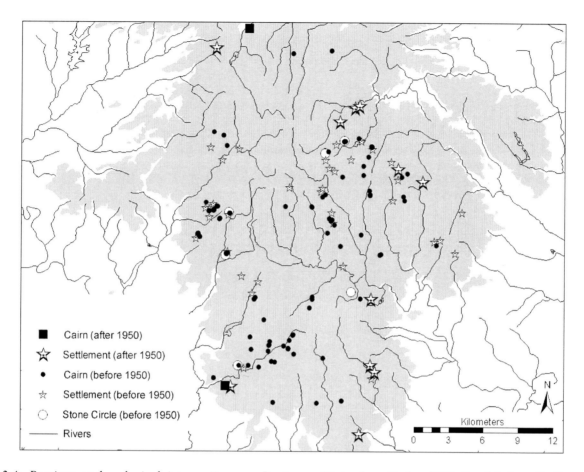

2.4: Previous archaeological interventions on Dartmoor (Data from Butler 1997, Spatial data © Crown Copyright/database right 2002. An Ordnance Survey/EDINA supplied service).

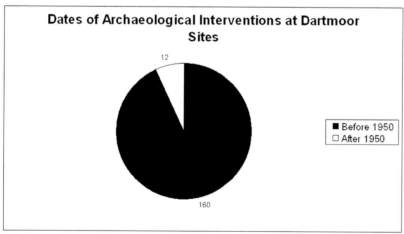

2.5: Dates of archaeological interventions

The work of Aileen Fox marks a milestone in the literature, separating the often brief reports of the DEC from the more comprehensive excavation reports of later periods. Fox's reports contain site plans, section drawings, and specialist contributions including environmental analyses and finds reports. Her work certainly compares favourably with some contemporary reports: For example the report on excavation of three buildings near Gripper's Pound is only three sentences long (Hurrell in Fox, 1961) and the notes on excavations by a pupil at Plymton Secondary School at Owley Gate are less then one page in length (Hurrell in Fox, 1961). The locations of fourteen excavation projects which have taken place on Dartmoor since 1950 are shown in 2.6. Apart from Fox's excavations at Kestor and Dean Moor, (Fox, 1954b, 1957) another important post-war excavation was carried out at the Cholwichtown stone row (Eogan, 1964). This report is detailed and includes environmental work (Simmons in Eogan, 1964).

Important excavations took place in the 1970s at Shaugh Moor and Holne Moor (Smith et al., 1979; Wainwright & Smith, 1980; Smith et al., 1981; Fleming, 1988). The focus on a landscape perspective, environmental work and 'off-site' archaeology was a particular strength of these projects (Balaam et al., 1982; Maguire et al., 1983). The last twenty years have seen much less excavation work take place on Dartmoor - although Gibson's excavation and survey at Gold Park, and Gerrard's work at Teigncombe have been notable exceptions (Gibson,

1992, Gerrard forthcoming). Excavation, survey and environmental work is ongoing at Shovel Down (Brück et al., 2003, 2005). A particularly important insight of this later work has been the extent and importance of the buried archaeology. Early excavations tended to chase walls and concentrate on the interiors of buildings, but later work revealed much evidence for cut features. A world of prehistoric timber structures suddenly appeared, including buildings, fence lines, and other structures. It was no longer possible to proceed as if the survey data were a complete record of prehistoric activity. These discoveries show how essential excavation is to advancing understanding of this region.

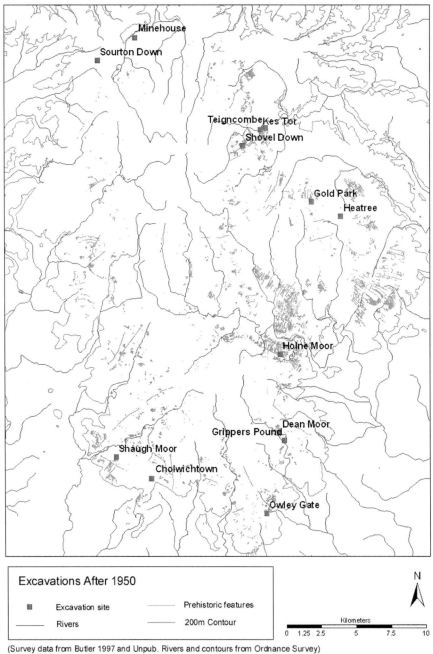

(Survey data from Butler 1997 and Unpub. Rivers and contours from Ordnance Survey)

2.6: Locations of excavations after 1950 (© Crown Copyright/database right 2002. An Ordnance Survey/EDINA supplied service).

Unfortunately several sites excavated since 1950 lack full published reports. These sites include excavations in advance of the A30 (including the site at Minehouse) and at Enclosure 25, Shaugh Moor and the full details of the Holne Moor work (English Heritage, 1987; Fleming, 1988). Details of other sites are available in unpublished reports, such as excavations in advance of pipelines at Batworthy Corner and Dousland to Rundlestone (Gibson, 1990; Reed, 1994). Some sites left unpublished by the original excavators have been written up by subsequent workers as with excavations at Heatree and at Sourton Down (Quinnell, 1991; Weddell & Reed, 1997).

Despite a large number of archaeological interventions the record of excavation is not as good as it could be because most excavation took place at an early date. Early excavations, which make up the larger part of the record, missed the subtle traces of cut features and confined themselves largely to the interiors of visible stone architectures. Extensive 'off site' sampling has been carried out only since the 1970s at Shaugh Moor, Holne Moor and at Shovel Down. The excavations of the 1970s and 1980s at Shaugh Moor, Holne Moor and Gold Park remain extremely important because they are among few sites with absolute dates, and because no more recent excavations of comparable ambition and extent have yet been published.

Survey and Remote Sensing

Some of the most extensive, and in places, the most detailed, archaeological survey in Britain now exists for Dartmoor. Measured survey has a long history in the region, starting with a focus on notable monuments, such as Shillbeer's 1828 plan of Grimspound, and Hamilton-Smith's 'Birds-Eye view of Merrivale' (Pattison & Fletcher, 1994; Baring-Gould et al., 1895). Ormerod's plans of large scale coaxial land division at Kestor were an early example of the mapping of a landscape rather than a site (Ormerod, 1864, 1876). In the 1920's E.C. Curwen spent his honeymoon surveying on the moor, leading to publication of seminal maps of field systems (Curwen, 1927, 1929, 1938) which became the basis for later work (Fox, 1954b; Price & Tinsley, 1976). Fox produced surveys of Dean Moor and a detailed plan of the settlement at Gripper's Pound (Fox, 1957, 1955). Land division close to quarrying activity at Shaugh Moor and Crownhill Down has been intensively surveyed (Price, 1973; Collis, 1978; Smith et al., 1981; Pye et al., 1993; Probert & Newman, 1998).

Until Fleming's observation of large scale relationships between reaves, survey remained largely piecemeal, but after his work the first region-wide mapping campaign was initiated. The Royal Commission's 'Archaeology of Dartmoor' project transcribed aerial photographs of the whole area taken by the RAF soon after the Second World War. The resulting transcriptions provide a useful starting point for subsequent work, but have never been checked by ground survey and must be interpreted with

caution (Simon Probert pers comm.). They have never been published but are available from the National Monuments Record. Other unpublished sources include surveys of the Plym valley by University of Edinburgh (Robertson, 1991) and extremely detailed work on Duchy of Cornwall land-holdings available from the National Park Offices. New aerial reconnaissance programmes surveyed selected parts of Dartmoor periodically since 1980 (Griffith, 1990).

The most extensive detailed surveys are by English Heritage and Jeremy Butler. Butler has surveyed large areas, including almost all unenclosed land and all the major archaeological landscapes. His five volume Atlas of Antiquities includes 63 maps covering of large areas of the region (Butler, 1991a, 1991b, 1993a, 1994, 1997a, 1997b). The survey was initially compiled from aerial photographs, followed by ground survey. Butler found many previously unrecorded sites. The number of recorded cairns was increased by 60%, and six new stone rows were discovered. Five additional settlements have been recognized since the first edition was published (these are included in the second edition). More detailed plans of cairns, stone rows and stone circles were all produced at scales between 1:100 and 1:500. Field systems were planned at 1:4000. Gazetteers of cairns, stone rows, stone circles and settlement sites are included in the atlases. Butler's thesis also contains catalogues of excavations featuring types and numbers of finds (Butler, 1997b). English Heritage (formerly the Royal Commission) has carried out detailed ground survey of large areas including several important areas of land division.

Of course, a problem of survey data is that, no matter how excellent, it is inevitably partial. Excavation demonstrates timber structures were also an important part of this landscape. At the same time, however, excavation will only ever offer tiny windows on particular areas, whereas survey data now covers vast landscapes. Geophysical survey should offer a way to mediate between these two perspectives, however it has been very little applied in the region until recently. Magnetometry was first deployed only recently at the Langstone Moor stone circle (Carey and Dean 2001). Resistivity survey was first attempted, apparently without success, at Shaugh Moor (Smith et al., 1981 see microfiche). Geophysical survey on a large scale was applied recently at Shovel Down, and the results verified by excavation (Johnston & Wickstead, 2005). Resistivity and magnetometry were tested, and the results suggested resistivity might be applied more widely in the region to enhance and extend the survey record.

Palaeoenvironmental Studies

The acidic soils and peat of Dartmoor preserve ancient pollen and plant macrofossils. The region contains valuable resources for learning about prehistoric environments and has a high profile in the study of past environments, partly because of comparatively early pollen studies by Simmons (Simmons, 1963, 1969). Several regional summaries have appeared recently (Evans, 1999: 26-34; Simmons, 2003: 297-305) and detailed reviews have been regularly compiled by Caseldine (Caseldine & Macguire, 1981; Caseldine & Hatton, 1994, 1996; Caseldine, 1999). The reputation of Dartmoor is such that it is often supposed that environmental changes are fully understood however as Caseldine makes clear, there is still work to be done in this area (Caseldine, 1999).

Since Caseldine's last review new sources have enhanced the available dataset. This can be seen in 2.7 which locates currently existing palynological sequences (key to 2.7 in Appendix D). Caseldine's most recent review recorded 38 sampling locations, to which it is possible to add six (Caseldine, 1999). Some of these sequences are

from rescue excavations (nos 39, 42, 43 and 44 - Gibson, 1990; Reed, 1994; Straker in Weddell & Reed, 1997). Other sites are from recent research projects (nos 40, 41, 45 and 46 - Thorndycraft et al., 2004; Amesbury et al., 2005; Brück et al., 2005). The number of cores with absolute dating has also increased since Caseldine's review. Dates have been supplied for the core at Tor Royal (West, 1997). And recent work, with radiocarbon chronology, has been undertaken at Ermington, Aveton-Gifford, and Taw Marsh (Thorndycraft et al., 2004). Cores with high resolution C14 dating are becoming available from the Shovel Down excavation project in the north east of the moor, which previously lacked securely dated sequences (Amesbury et al., 2005). Key sequences with relatively good dating have been published for Pinswell, Bellever Tor, Royal Ermington and Shovel Down (Caseldine & Hatton, 1996; West, 1997; Thorndycraft et al., 2004; Amesbury et al., 2005).

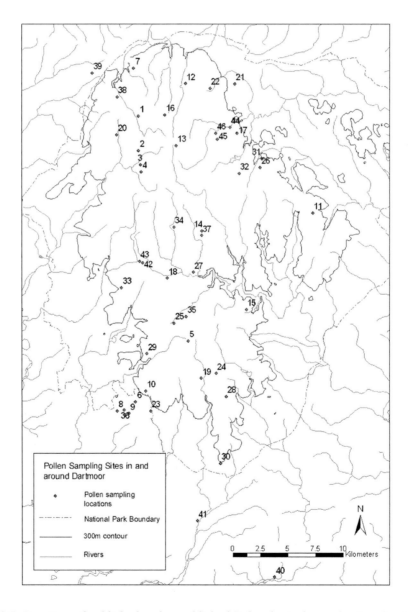

2.7: Location of published and unpublished Palynological samples (see key in Appendix E)

These new palynological sources, combined with the high sampling density (although poor dating) of earlier work, reveal a region whose palaeoenvironments are better understood than many others. Although, as Caseldine observes, the Neolithic landscape has very few dated pollen evidence, the Bronze Age and later periods are relatively well covered. There have also been innovative approaches to data on prehistoric atmospheric pollution and sedimentology, data that may provide a proxy-measure for the intensity of construction activities or mineral extraction (West, 1997; Thorndycraft et al., 2004). In comparison with surrounding lowland Devon, environmental sequences are very well understood indeed. This lack of information from lowland Devon has recently begun to be addressed. Excavations along the A30 around Honiton have supplied data from charred plant assemblages (Fitzpatrick et al., 1999), and some well dated palynological sequences have been published (Caseldine et al., 2000; Fyfe et al., 2003). This work is making apparent the diversity of the lowland environments, a mosaic of woods, heaths and grasslands which extended into the moor fringes (Straker in Weddell & Reed, 1997). The diversity of these environments reinforces the point that the differences between Dartmoor and its surroundings are relatively recent constructions. In later prehistory heathland habitats and moors were also distributed around lower altitudes (Fitzpatrick et al., 1999).

Regional datasets offer both opportunities and limitations. Major limitations follow from the lack of recent excavation. Although the area has been extensively excavated, most sites were explored without modern methods. The result of this work is a large excavated database lacking in good dating or stratigraphic detail. The challenge is to make use of this material in ways that complement the new excavation projects currently being undertaken at Teigncombe and Shovel Down. By contrast the survey data are now outstanding, especially for the extent of the landscapes covered. In the interim since the main period of Fleming's work, new and more detailed surveys have been produced. Good survey data now exists for most of the region including all the major archaeological landscapes. This data can now be used for advancing new analysis and interpretation. Lastly, although the acidic soils of the region do not preserve bone, and even corrode ceramics and metals, the peat does preserve ancient pollen. The region has been the subject of a great deal of palaeoenvironmental study. As a result environmental change is comparatively well understood – particularly for periods after the second millennium BC. While more work directed at increasing the chronological resolution of existing narratives would be useful, recent studies supply well-dated sequences. The new data that I have focused on in this review, particularly from new survey and palaeoenvironmental work, furnish a new standpoint from which to reconsider previous archaeologies of tenure. In the next section I discuss how I organised and amassed databases for this project and the chronological frameworks within which the data were understood.

2.4 Databases and Frameworks for Analysis

'Seeing as these things are beyond us, let's pretend to be the organiser of them'
(Jean Cocteau)

There is a sense in which data organises our thought, rather then the other way around. In this section I describe the databases created for my analyses, their limitations and the steps that I took to address them. I go on to develop a chronology for the dataset, recalibrating dates where necessary, and setting them within current understandings of the dating of Bronze Age land division within southern Britain.

Databases for Analysis

The high quality and substantial body of survey data formed an important resource for my researches. Two datasets formed the backbone of the work:

i) Detailed ground surveys produced by English Heritage
ii) Aerial photographic transcriptions and ground survey by Jeremy Butler

The English Heritage surveys, as yet unpublished, were licensed to the study in digital form. The surveys were initially produced by Total Station and subsequently manually digitised and integrated with later surveys produced using a Differential Global Positioning System (GPS). Butler's data were produced as paper maps. I therefore manually digitised them from Butler's unpublished surveys. I am grateful to Dr Butler for allowing me to work directly from the latest version of his unpublished ongoing surveys, which allowed me to obtain better calibration points than are available on the published maps. The resulting databases contain information on numerous sites. The Butler survey contains 802km of reaves, (nearly 500 miles) - 979 cairns and 3818 prehistoric buildings. The coverage of the English Heritage surveys is less (245km of reaves) but is a very detailed and accurate dataset. I am grateful to Simon Probert and Martin Fletcher of English Heritage Exeter for arranging my access to this data.

Data for the Digital Terrain Model (DTM), the location of physiographic features, modern roads and buildings were obtained from Ordnance Survey data made available digitally through the Digimap service. The DTM data was of low resolution, recorded at 1: 50,000. The survey data was draped over this surface to allow the dimensions of surveyed features to be measured. At an early stage in the project it was suggested that physically measuring coaxial boundaries on the ground would be more accurate than measuring using this DTM (Frances Griffith pers com.). An experiment was devised to test the accuracy of this process compared to that of tape survey (see appendix E). The results, somewhat surprisingly, showed that the digital model was more accurate than the tape survey. To supplement the OS DTM another higher resolution DTM was produced from ground survey in the area of the Shovel Down excavation project. An area of 6.65 sq km was sampled intensively (5m transects) using differential GPS. This high resolution DTM is suitable for modelling tasks that could not be applied to low resolution data, such as viewshed analysis.

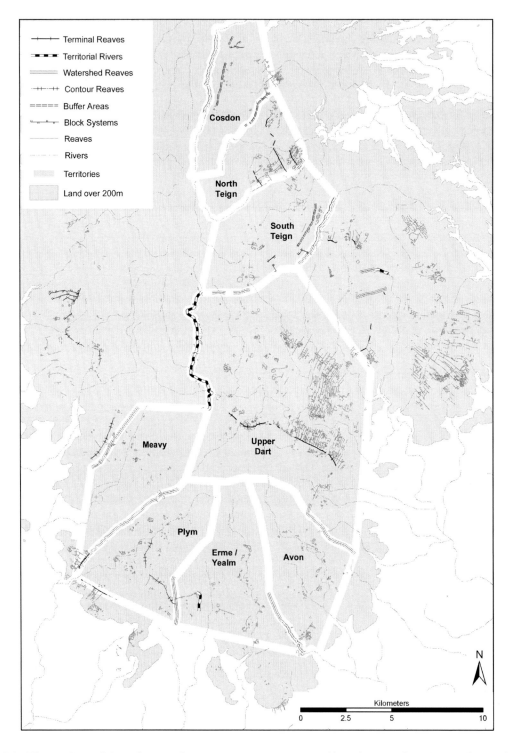

2.8: Fleming's model implemented using most recent surveys (data from Butler 1997 and Unpub., Fleming 1988 and Digimap, © Crown Copyright/database right 2002. An Ordnance Survey/EDINA supplied service).

The survey databases were classified using the terminology given in the National Park chronological framework (2.9 below). This classification imposes general chronologically based distinctions although it does retain the distinction between 'aggregate' (or 'irregular') and 'coaxial' (or 'regular') land division (Fleming, 1987a). Previous writers have gone on to devise finer typologies dividing these categories, for example those distinguishing different cairn architectures (Turner, 1990), and numerous schemes for classifying settlements (Ralegh Radford, 1952; Fox, 1954a; Hamond, 1979; Gerrard, 1997a; Butler, 1997a). There comes a point where there is little to be gained from building site typologies, when it may even be a distraction from understanding the processes that construct landscapes. Furthermore, the detailed data now available makes the true complexity of the record clear. Settlements are characterised by diversity, and by interaction with particular qualities of their surroundings. These processes are often poorly captured by site typologies. A possible exception is the designation 'coaxial', which attempts to describe a process of construction. Managing the databases in GIS allowed the data to be flexibly classified. This made it possible to implement a range of existing classifications on Butler's detailed and extensive survey. Among the models implemented in this way was Fleming's model of territorial organisation. This mapping exercise revealed much more of the complexity, diversity and potential diachrony of the landscape than Fleming's diagrammatic maps allowed (see 2.8). The compression of temporal depth must be kept in mind in any analysis based on survey data. The next section develops chronological frameworks within which the processes that are hidden in these representations must be integrated.

Chronological Frameworks

Despite the abundance of prehistoric sites the lack of recent excavations means very few absolute dates are available. Even when sites were excavated in the radiocarbon age they did not always retrieve suitable material for dating (as with Eogan's excavation of the Cholwichtown stone row (Eogan, 1964). The best sequences currently available are on peat cores taken for palaeoenvironmental studies. Even today the most useful sequence of absolute dates from an excavation is that produced by the Shaugh Moor Project (Balaam et al., 1982). Radiocarbon dates have been published from excavations at Holne Moor, but no comprehensive excavation report was ever published for these excavations and the dates therefore lack full contextual information (Burleigh et al., 1981). The platform building at Gold Park has absolute dates for both phases, but dating samples from four other structures were lost by the British Museum (Gibson, 1992).

Sampling procedures in the late 1970s and 1980s mean dates from this period are prone to certain problems

(Jordan et al., 1994). The dating techniques used at this time required large samples and that often had to be made up of composite materials - as with some of the dates from Holne Moor. Dates were often taken on less than ideal materials, for example, on species with a long growth date effect, like the oak charcoal used at Shaugh Moor. The effect of these techniques meant that dates were few, and resolution was less good than it might be today. Ongoing excavation work on Shovel Down is increasing the available database using multiple dates and high resolution sequences on peat fractions, which should improve the available dataset (Brück et al., 2005).

Several recalibrations of dates from Dartmoor have been published. Dates from the Shaugh Moor Project were recalibrated as part of a review of English Heritage excavations (Jordan et al., 1994). The Holne Moor dates have also been revised (Walker et al., 1991). Dates from reaves have been recalibrated for recent studies (Johnston, 2001b, 2005; Amesbury et al., 2005). For this study I have recalibrated all available dates in Oxcal 3.10 (appendices F-H). The many early excavations mean that artefactual associations are the only chronological information available for many sites. Material from the DEC excavations is kept in Plymouth Museum and this material is currently the subject of ongoing work by Quinnell, who is re-examining the ceramics and sampling charcoal residues for dating (Quinnell, 1994a, 1996). Metalwork typologies were developed by Pearce (Pearce, 1983) but since her studies typological schemes have been comprehensively revised (see Needham et al., 1997). Forthcoming work by Fay Stevens will update current typologies for metalwork across the South West. The paucity of chronological information combined with the enormous database of survey evidence has prompted attempts to unravel 'horizontal stratigraphy' from the ways that different types of site are related in the field (e.g. Fleming, 1978b, Butler, 1997a). It is difficult to determine such relationships without excavating. Furthermore some excavations have contradicted the relationships previously assumed from surface archaeology (Fleming, 1988).

The lack of dating information means that building a chronological framework inevitably involves making links between excavations within the region and information from elsewhere. The chronological framework currently used by the National Park Archaeology service is shown in 2.9. The validity of this process depends a great deal on the integrity of the categories used, some of which are not very precise. For example, the category 'cairn' encompasses everything from simple piles of stones to round cairns with elaborate architecture. Excavated cairns include one at Minehouse from which Neolithic ceramics were retrieved (English Heritage, 1987), and several at Gold Park which may post-date the Later Iron Age (Gibson, 1992). There are currently no dates at all from excavations of stone rows and stone circles, and this means that the assumption that these sites pre-date reaves is not secure. Elsewhere in

Britain evidence is coming to light of lengthy sequences at stone settings; even of stones erected in the Late Bronze Age (Bradley & Sheridan, 2004). There is certainly no reason to assert conclusively that all stone rows pre-date all buildings and reaves. This urges caution in applying frameworks like that in 2.9, which imply 'successive periods of prehistoric societies which may not be relevant to Dartmoor' (Quinnell, 1994b: 49). The best that can be done is to treat these frameworks as provisional tools that may be overturned or undermined by future work. Existing frameworks are deployed here provisionally, in the hope and expectation that future work will transform them.

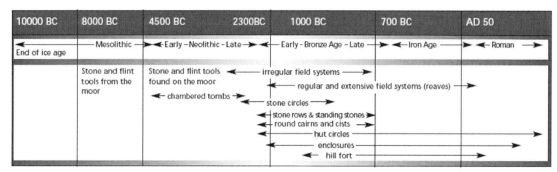

2.9 Chronology of Prehistoric and Roman sites (From Dartmoor National Park 2004) © DNPA

There has been a tendency in some previous work to assume that landscapes of boundaries and buildings post-date and replace earlier landscapes of ceremonial sites. Following this 'Middle Bronze Age transition' perspective, it is widely assumed that reaves belong in a post-transition Later Bronze Age after c.1500 BC. Reaves are here assumed to be analogous with field systems in parts of Wessex and the South-East. The recalibration undertaken for this study shows that this assumption is incorrect. Recent reassessments of the phasing and dating of excavated reaves underlines the long sequences involved in their construction, showing that they began to be built at the same dates returned from deposits in cairns (Johnston, 2005). The overlap between dates currently available for buildings and reaves and dates from cairns is shown in 2.10 and 2.11 (based on the recalibrations in appendices F-H).

The richness and extent of the survey data is such that the dating of sites may never fully match it. Strategies must be found to deal with these limitations, including extrapolating between Dartmoor and similar sites elsewhere. At Patteson's Cross in lowland Devon the ditch of a coaxial boundary contained a deposit of 22 chert flakes and blades. The lithics could be refitted and must have resulted from a single knapping episode. The flakes were of an Early Bronze Age type, suggesting that the ditch had been filled in at an early date, and this combined with the palaeoenvironmental record suggested that the field system may have gone out of use before the Middle Bronze Age (Fitzpatrick et al., 1999: 90). At Brightworthy near Exmoor changes in environments and sedimentology suggested 'extensive clearance' and 'the probable laying out of field systems' beginning c2270-1940 cal BC (Fyfe et al., 2003: 178). Elsewhere in Britain, palaeoenvironmental studies and OSL dating of boundaries in the Stonehenge landscape also suggest early dates (Allen, 1997) and recent excavations at Heathrow have revealed even earlier dates, with boundaries constructed around 2000 BC (Framework Archaeology, 2002). Coaxial landscapes across southern Britain may begin to be laid out earlier than is sometimes appreciated.

The dates recalibrated here indicate that reaves begin to be built as early as Needham's period 3, contemporary with the emergence of cremation, the elaboration of rites of deposition and the deposition of new objects (Needham, 1996). The dating of the end of occupation is much less easy to determine. It has been argued that reaves were abandoned after c1350 BC (Amesbury et al., 2005). However, excavations immediately to the east of the moor reveal boundaries with Iron Age dates, and it is clear from excavations at Gold Park and Teigncombe that occupation of the Dartmoor landscape continued throughout the Iron Age (Gallant et al., 1985; Silvester, 1980; English Heritage, 1987; Quinnell, 1994a - also see appendix F). At a minimum I assess that the chronological envelope of reave construction begins around 1850 BC (Needham's period 3) and continues throughout Needham's periods 4 and 5, until c1150 BC. However it is quite likely that dates will be forthcoming in future that extend this range into both earlier and later periods.

According to the minimum range I offer here, the inception of reaves coincides with several important transformations in the record. Entire landscapes of land division emerge at around the same time as substantial roundhouses begin to appear. Mortuary rites are also undergoing a process of gradual change with much more emphasis on cremation than in earlier periods. New metalwork types are appearing in the record at this time and the circumstances of deposition are changing, so that metalwork is increasingly deposited away from cairns. At the same time there are indications that the nature of transactions themselves is undergoing important transformations. Across Europe bronze may be being used as a 'proto-currency' and commodity exchange may be more important than formerly, possibly accompanied with a new intensity in gift exchanges (Sherratt, 1993; Pare, 2000). At the same time that these landscapes are becoming established the evidence seems to imply that identities are also changing, through processes that would have profoundly influenced tenure.

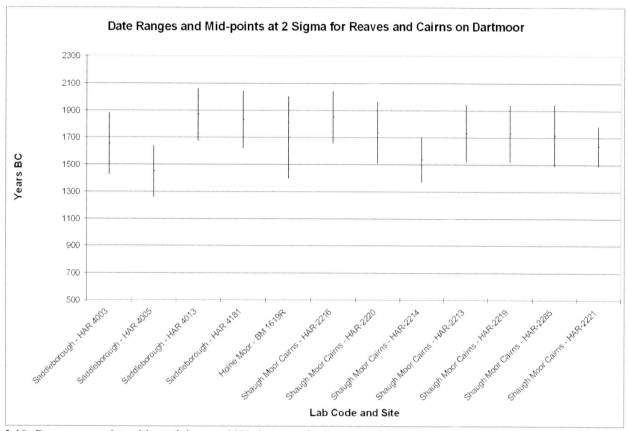

2.10: Date ranges of recalibrated dates at 95%, 2 sigma, for Reaves and Cairns

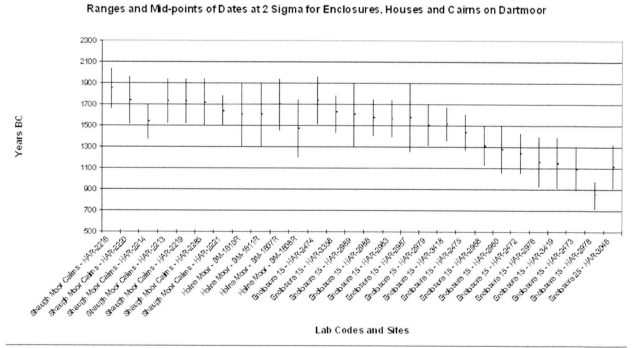

2.11: Date ranges of recalibrated dates at 95%, 2 sigma, for Enclosures, Houses and Cairns

This section outlined the various databases created for my research and the currently available chronological information. Databases used in the analysis include geographical and survey data, for which an appreciation of chronological parameters is important. However the chronological resolution is limited because of the lack of absolute dates. Despite this limitation it is important to maintain a perspective that can interpret survey databases diachronically. My study integrates spatial analyses with other types of method to maintain appreciation for the diachronic. Working between the results of different kinds of analyses allows findings from the analysis of survey data to be integrated with other kinds of approach.

Conclusions

In this chapter I aimed to show the significance of Dartmoor for archaeologies of tenure and the potential of the region for further research. I began with a review of archaeologies of land division in North West Europe. I showed how accounts that rooted tenure in intensification, sedentarisation and territorialisation are challenged by new evidence. I argued that this was an interesting juncture for archaeologies of tenure, with recent reassessments of evidence for mortuary rites, intensification and the lifecycles of buildings offering opportunities for new interpretations of landscape change in southern Britain. Next, I reviewed interpretations of tenure on prehistoric Dartmoor, especially those of Andrew Fleming. Several issues emerge form Fleming's interpretations and later reinterpretations and criticism: Firstly there was the issue of how levels in Fleming's structural models were constituted; secondly, the need for an interpretation of coaxial landscapes that could explain their striking pattern without resorting to a 'top-down' plan; thirdly, the question of the extent to which it is appropriate to incorporate Dartmoor within models of Bronze Age chiefdoms; and lastly, the issue of how transformations in landscape relate to wider changes in exchange networks. I then reviewed sources of data that might be used in the study. Although excavations have been few since Fleming's analyses were published, the palaeoenvironmental record has steadily advanced, and detailed, accurate and extensive survey data is now available. Lastly, I discussed how I produced the databases that form the basis of the analyses, and the chronological framework that I use in the interpretation.

I began this monograph with an extended investigation of theories of tenure. I argued that tenure is polyvalent, bound up with the constitution of identities or the procreation of persons. It is what Mauss called a '*total social phenomenon*' that 'contains all the threads of which the social fabric is composed … religious, legal, moral and economic' (Mauss 1970: 1 his emphasis). Because tenure requires an understanding of multiple different threads of evidence, detailed studies of particular locations are necessary. This chapter aimed to demonstrate the value of Dartmoor as one such location, as a case study for the investigation of tenure as a subject. The archaeology of Dartmoor, while limited by the lack of recent excavations and absolute dates, has a wealth of survey data, good sources of palaeoenvironmental information, and an important interpretative literature that relate the data to theory of tenure. This makes Dartmoor an area of great potential for addressing the question that guides this study – the question of how archaeologists might approach tenure. The next chapter begins to answer this question. Here I will take up the classical theories of property discussed in chapter one. I will approach Dartmoor using approaches derived from these classical theories to interpret landscapes of the second millennium BC and also to reflect on the wider questions of how tenure should be approached.

Chapter 3

'A Post-hoc Explanation':
Classical Theories of Property

'We wish to escape from imaginary worlds! We no longer wish to have this autistic science imposed upon us!' (Fulbrook, 2000). Economics students at the *Ecole Normale Superieure*, Paris, issued a petition in the year 2000 calling for a 'post-autistic economics'. In the years that followed similar petitions have been circulated in Cambridge and Havard, calling for more teaching of 'Heterodox Economics' (Alcorn & Solarz, 2006). Archaeology is not a parallel for the economics criticised by the 'Post-Autistic Economics' or 'Heterodox Economics' networks. However, some archaeological interpretations depend on a reductive 'commonsense' economics that might be seen as having inherited a few 'autistic' tendencies. In this section I examine classical theories of property in archaeologies of tenure. These approaches, as discussed in chapter one, assume that property is an exclusive individual right. Property is understood as a jural institution emerging from the self-interested 'economic' motivations of individuals in the world of scarce goods. Some archaeological interpretations, influenced by classical theories, see land division as increasing efficiency, maximising yields and increasing benefits to the individual.

I begin this chapter with a discussion of 'economic' accounts of property, based on concepts of maximisation, efficiency and scarcity. I then address functional explanations of land division and I assess the extent to which reaves heralded increased productive 'efficiency' or maximisation of yields. Next, I analyse the extent to which land division on Dartmoor was driven by land scarcity. Lastly I assess how well coaxial landscapes fit interpretations which suggest they result from the self-interested maximisation of elites.

3.1 Maximisation, Efficiency and Scarcity in Classical Theories

In this section I discuss the history of 'economic' accounts of property in archaeology and the background to concepts of maximisation, efficiency and scarcity in narratives of the origins of property. I begin with a brief history of 'economic' approaches, and I then discuss how these have informed interpretations of prehistoric land division. I then examine concepts of maximisation, efficiency and scarcity in narratives of property origins. Lastly, I review critiques that underline the limited application of these concepts.

Brief review of 'economic' approaches

'Classical' theories of property emerge from writings of political economists of the seventeenth and eighteenth centuries (Rose, 1990). These texts introduced fundamental premises of 'natural law', which included the premises of scarcity (Malthus, 2005) and of the self-interest of individuals (Hobbes, 1660; Hume, 1896). It was a natural law that the rational individual would want to continue to live, and would prefer the continuance of his own life over that of others (Rose, 1990: 41). The exercise of reason would result in the calculation of rational self-interest by each individual. Individuals would contract between one another to create civil governance (including property institutions) (e.g. Hume, 1896).

As Rose has observed, there is a contradiction here between the selfishness ascribed to individuals and the collaboration that is demanded in the process of building social institutions (Rose, 1990). Classical theories tend to presume that individuals switch suddenly between a state of nature and an authoritarian state of social order, in ways that are already present in Hobbes' classical account of the social contract (Granovetter, 1985; Hobbes, 1660). The ongoing problem for those following in the wake of classical theories has been the impossibility of imagining individual behaviour as *both* self-interested and social determined. It has become impossible to approach the subject from both perspectives in the same moment.

Aspects of 'classical' theories were continued in the 'Neoclassical' economics that emerged in the 'second quarter of the nineteenth century' (Arnsperger & Varoufakis, 2006). Recent commentators characterise this school through its ongoing adherence to three 'crucial meta-axioms' – individualism, instrumentalism and equilibration (the imposition of equilibrium). In neoclassical models individuals tend to pursue goals instrumentally, and the results of these activities are then represented as equilibria (general rules or patterns). In neoclassical narratives of property, individuals have historically tended to maximise food or wealth yields, and property emerges as a way to accentuate the positive and eliminate the negative 'externalities' accruing to each individual as they instrumentally pursue these goals (e.g. Demetz, 1967, 2002). These explanations tend to rely on the idea that private property is more optimal than common property in terms of the sum of each individual's instrumentally pursued goals.

From the 1940s onwards there has been a strong reaction against neoclassical or 'formalist' economics, particularly in disciplines that assert the power of the 'social'. The 'substantivist' school emphasised the way that economies were 'embedded' in social institutions (Polanyi, 1944; Wilk, 1996: chapter 1). Within more mainstream economics there also emerged a new interest in institutional regulations and socially determined norms (see Williamson, 2000). While the New Institutional Economics concentrated on modern institutions like the firm. Substantivists described pre-modern 'embedded' economies, which they argued, were different to modern 'market' orientated societies. They argued that individuals might maximise socially-determined 'prestige' as much as rational 'utility': People *are* 'rational' in their economic aims, as Wilk puts it 'but they do not seek wealth or leisure like 'we' do. Rather they seek status, rank, and power in their community' (Wilk, 1996: 119).

In the stand-off between formalist and substantivist, neoclassical and 'New Institutional' approaches the tendency for approaches to 'lurch directly from an under-socialised to an over-socialised state' continues (Granovetter, 1985: 485). In 'under-socialised' neoclassical accounts individuals are atomised and their behaviour is determined by the 'narrow utilitarian pursuit of self-interest' (ibid.). In the over-socialised institutional approaches individuals are still atomised but now their behaviour is determined by a social code or structure that has been internalised. As Graeber points out, *Homo economicus* is still present in substantivist approaches, except that his self interest is now 'embedded' within a static social-structural edifice. The individual remains a self-interested maximiser, except that the object that he is trying to maximise is now called 'prestige' instead of utility (Graeber, 2001). Whether the individual is motivated by internal desires arising from nature or by internal desires inculcated from society, 'economics' remains the generalised outcome of individual's instrumentally pursued goals.

In recent years a range of alternative approaches have emerged. Particularly important have been the 'network' and 'relational' approaches of the 'New Economic Sociology' that have attempted to overcome the traditional 'division of labour' between the disciplines of Economics and Sociology (Granovetter, 1985; Swedberg, 1997; Velthuis, 1999). These have been developed by Callon, who seeks to replace the emphasis on 'social' construction in such accounts with a focus on technology and the material world (Callon, 1998). Recently some of these approaches have begun to filter into more mainstream economics via *'Post-Autisme'* and 'Heterodox' literature (Alcorn & Solarz, 2006).

Given the vast array of approaches within Economics (which can only be glossed here) it is important to distinguish between Economics, neoclassical economics and commonsense 'economics'. It is the latter that most often appears in 'economic' interpretations in archaeology. 'Commonsense' economics tends to assume that rationality, utility and individual's preferences are always represented by the same kind of measures: For example, it assumes that greater utility is represented by greater agricultural yields or 'efficiency'. Today, even 'neoclassical' economists are cautious about such generalising assumptions. For instance, game theoretical studies have shown that co-operation actually increases utility for the individual over the long term (Axelrod, 1980a; 1980b). Experiments using economic 'games' show that cross-culturally, a majority of people prefer to co-operate - splitting goods nearly equally – rather than to act 'selfishly' (Henrich et al., 2001: 74). Economic models increasingly involve concepts of 'bounded rationality' in which agents are given imperfect information and even act altruistically and/or irrationally. Neoclassical approaches may allow agents to adapt their preferences in response to past outcomes and beliefs about the expectations of others (Arnsperger & Varoufakis, 2006). For some neoclassical economists, therefore, it is possible that *Homo economicus* might display unselfish behaviour, when that will result in greater long term benefit. Commonsense economics, on the other hand, supposes that individual will always prefer greater 'wealth' (or 'social' proxies like 'prestige') Commonsense 'economic' explanations do not reflect neoclassical economics, still less the discipline of Economics, but represent what we might (after Verdery) call a 'western native category' of economics (Verdery, 2003: 12-14).

'Economic' interpretations of Prehistoric Land Division

> *'...the existence of a property regime is not predictable from a starting point of rational self-interest; and consequently, from that perspective, property needs a tale, a story, a post-hoc explanation'* (Rose, 1990: 52).

Classical theories and nineteenth century evolutionary narratives of the origins of property have long supplied ready-made 'stories' within which archaeologists can interpret prehistoric land division. For many commentators land division has been seen as the outcome of greater efficiency, maximisation of food production, and the 'achievement' of higher forms of economy (Curwen, 1946; Bowen, 1961; Fowler, 1983). These accounts have direct precedents in historical justifications of enclosure, which valorised enclosure as increasing 'efficiency' and maximising yields (Johnson, 1996; Evans, 1997). Indeed, some archaeologies make the connection between prehistoric coaxial land division and historical enclosure explicit (Fowler, 1971, 1984).

The notion of economic rationality is sometimes evoked in such 'economic' accounts. For example, Fowler argues that the emergence of land division in the second millennium is a 'rational reaction' to the 'ultimately pointless and wasteful' Neolithic, when too much attention was paid to building extravagant monuments rather then food production (Fowler & Blackwell, 1998:54). Elsewhere, coaxial landscapes are seen as representing more efficient solutions to the to the need to enclose land (Caulfield, 1978, 1983; Fleming, 1984). The question becomes one of which style of enclosure allows most land to be enclosed for least calorific expenditure.

Archaeologies influenced by substantivist economics present 'Bronze Age Economics' in a rather different setting. Here it is understood that 'economic' motivations are distorted by the social structure within which they are embedded. Property – which classical theories characterise as a legal institution – suits the vision of over-arching structure here very well (e.g. Hunt, 1998; Gilman, 1998; Earle, 2000). Motivated by self-interest, elite individuals strategically and rationally redirect agricultural surpluses to obtain goods that will maximise 'prestige'. Agricultural efficiency retains its importance here, because chiefs are concerned to maximise production so that they may accumulate more wealth and hence more social 'power'. Land division thus continues to be interpreted as a token of increased 'efficiency'. Property is interpreted as a jural institution, with chiefs imposing the necessary legal sanctions. This function 'legitimates' their position in the hierarchy. Coaxial land division divides land into evenly sized parcels ownership of which can easily be redistributed by elite administrators (Earle, 2002).

Maximisation, Efficiency and Scarcity

Evolutionary narratives chronicle how societies move towards ever more efficient ways of maximising food production. Historically, at the top of these evolutionary hierarchies, stood cultivation – supposedly the most productive and efficient furtherance of life. For some commonsense economic approaches to land division there is little need to inquire any further than this simple maximising function (Fowler, 1984: 30). More sophisticated explanations, however, point to the balance between benefits and costs that makes land division more or less 'efficient' under different circumstances. Where goods are abundant, property is 'uneconomic'. Building boundaries is only worth the effort when resources are scarce (Casimir, 1992).

Maximisation of food production is thus not the same thing as efficiency. Increases in the latter do not necessarily produce the former. Furthermore, both efficiency and maximisation are different from intensification. Intensification is sometimes incorrectly discussed as increased efficiency and/or maximisation, but it is neither. In fact intensification actually reduces efficiency, leading to declining productivity per labour

hour (Boserup, 1965). (Intensification is discussed further in chapter four).

The concept of scarcity is important in both 'commonsense' and neoclassical explanations of property. As land becomes scarce, neoclassical approaches argue, maximising efficiency inevitably leads towards ever more restrictive property regimes – and ultimately to private property (Demetz, 1967). Common property regimes are inherently inefficient because they tend towards 'Tragedies of the Commons'. The idea of 'Tragedies of the Commons' can be traced back to Thomas Malthus, who pointed out that while the capacity to reproduce is common property, food is a scarce good. Self-interested individuals have little incentive not to breed regardless of the wider consequences to society, and famine is the result (Malthus, 2005 [1778]: chapter 1). The necessity of avoiding Tragedies of the Commons is a motif common to both classical to neoclassical approaches. It continues to be important today in policies from pollution reduction schemes (Hardin, 1968; Rose, 1998), to the worldwide land reforms advised by the World Bank (Deininger, 2003). In these examples economists argue that privatisation will ensure that the costs of depletion fall in the same place as the benefits of exploitation. Private property is thus functionally beneficial. Fleming's early work argued that reaves resulted from a Tragedy of the Commons: Soil deterioration and peat encroachment following deforestation reduced the amount of good grazing land and reaves were built in response (Fleming, 1978b).

In conditions of scarcity, unrestricted common property is seen as a cause of 'uneconomic' conflict. As Rose expresses it; 'if there were no property rights in the berry patch, all of us would just have to fight all the time for the berries' (Rose, 1990: 40). Property functions to reduce conflict, and this function is widely referenced in archaeological interpretations of land division. It assumed that conflict will be something prehistoric people wish to avoid, and therefore boundaries were introduced to minimize it (Adler, 1996; Stone & Downum, 1999; Stone, 1997). Fleming argues that reaves were 'conflict-reducing devices' (Fleming, 1978b: 110) built in 'an atmosphere of increasing aggression' (Fleming, 1994b).

Such are the strength of 'commonsense' associations between land division, property restrictions and scarcity that scarcity has more often been assumed than demonstrated. How can we begin to investigate whether land actually was a scarce good at the time that land division was built? Studies of land scarcity indicate that where people report high scarcity the morphology and distribution of land division tends to express certain characteristics. 'Involution' or 'impaction' occurs. These situations describe landscapes that have been more and more subdivided by farmers attempting to extract every last scrap of excess productivity from the system (Geertz, 1963). Features like boundaries, terraces, and ridges, proliferate (Netting, 1993: chapter 1). Analyses of landscapes under pressure from scarcity suggest the following indicators of scarcity:

1. Land division will cover every possible area;
2. Boundaries will be uniformly dense

Instead of assuming that land division is driven by scarcity, these features indicate the extent to which scarcity predominates in each landscape.

Critique of 'commonsense' Economics and Classical theories

Empirical evidence for conditions of scarcity leading to entirely new property regimes is actually almost non-existent. Indeed, commentators increasingly argue that scarcity is not the cause of property but the reverse – property leads to interests in resources that provoke scarcity (Rose, 2004). Sen suggests that the study of scarcity should start with tenure rather than the other way round: Famines cannot be understood without an account of how societies produce the 'entitlement' of individuals or group – their existing 'endowment' and their 'exchange entitlement' (Sen, 1983: 753-5). The way that persons matter differently in tenure and exchange networks, determines whether they live or die regardless of the absolute scarcity of goods.

The commonsense assumption that private property is more 'efficient' and less prone to 'Tragedy' than common property has been widely contradicted by economic studies. Common property regimes can be even more 'efficient' than private regimes (Berkes et al., 1989). A number of empirical studies show common property to be more 'optimal' where goods cannot be easily parcelled, are unpredictable, or where use of one resource has a potential detrimental effect on an adjacent resource (McCay & Acheson, 1987). Among groups without formal courts or written texts collective management may be more administratively 'efficient' than individualised land titling and registration (Ostrom, 1990; McKean, 2000). Fleming's later archaeologies of tenure on Dartmoor stressed the advantages of communal property regimes over privatisation (Fleming, 1985b, see also 1998b, 1998a).

Not only has it been shown that common property can be 'efficient' but economists have documented situations in which private property is inefficient. 'Tragedies of the Anti-Commons' occur when legalistic property institutions create so many 'rights' that it is impossible for anyone to use a resource productively (Heller, 1998).

These accounts reverse the traditional justifications of private ownership, and also supply evidence for how property persists even when it is non-optimal and debilitatingly 'uneconomic'.

Classical, neoclassical and commonsense approaches can all be criticised for assuming 'universals' that anthropology suggests are 'specifics'. This debunking approach has proved an important means of countering what some analysts describe as 'economic imperialism' in the social sciences (Velthuis, 1999). Anthropology describes countless examples of situations in which individuals do not maximise 'wealth' nor utility (Malinowski, 1921; Sahlins, 1972; Wilk, 1996; Graeber, 2001: chapter 1). Malinowski observed an economy in which production was not directed towards maximising gains to the individual. The labourer acquired no 'rights' over the products of their labour, which belonged from the outset to others in specified relationships to them. As a result, he observed, the economy 'enmeshes the whole community into a network of reciprocal obligations and dues, one constant flow of gift and counter-gift' (Malinowski, 1921: 8). 'Everyone is working for somebody else' rather then acting self-interestedly (Malinowski, 1921: 8). Sahlins challenged the assumption that 'savages' were impoverished compared with cultivators; in contrast to the toil of the cultivator, the life of a hunter-gatherer was one of unparalleled leisure, leaving ample time aside from food production to engage in social activities and sleep (Sahlins, 1972: chapter 1). These studies reinforce Substantivist's arguments that 'maximisation' and 'efficiency' are culturally specific.

Scarcity is just as culturally specific as maximisation and efficiency: For example, Munn records how gardening magic in Gawa is not only concerned with increasing productivity, but also ensures that people will not want to eat much. The Gawans do not see hunger as caused only by scarcity; it is also caused by an excess of desire for food - if people ate less then there would be more food in the stores (Munn, 1986: 80-89). Resources and people must grow and adapt concurrently to avoid scarcity. In many parts of the world, studies suggest, responses to scarcity mirror responses to abundance: Both scarcity and abundance increase the velocity with which people and goods circulate (Strathern, 2005a). In either case people make extra efforts to propagate relationships, increase the flow of transactions, engage in rituals, and organise exchanges, marriages and feasts. In many contexts scarcity does not lead to more restricted property rights but to increased activation of productive social ties.

3.2 Maximisation and Land Division

'There is no mystery about our great extents of prehistoric landscape' avowed Fowler, 'the people who were using those areas were quite simply trying to be better farmers' (Fowler, 1984: 30). By 'better' farmers

Fowler means more efficient 'economic' maximisers of food production. In this section I review evidence for land use in Dartmoor landscapes and functional explanations of reaves. I assess the evidence for cultivation and / or pastoralism. Then I discuss the range of possible purposes that reaves may fulfil.

Land use in Dartmoor landscapes

For producers who aim to maximise calorific output cultivation is almost always the best option in the short-term, even on comparatively unfertile ground (Tivy, 1990). Traditionally, economic approaches have seen cultivation as the best, and most 'economic' kind of land use (for an account of this view applied in development policy see Boserup, 1965). Traditional interpretations of prehistoric settlement on Dartmoor see cultivation or pastoralism as explaining settlement morphology (Curwen, 1938; Fox, 1957; Ralegh Radford, 1952; Butler, 1997a). 'Types' of settlement were related to types of agriculture. Curwen related different settlement types on Dartmoor to different plough technologies (Curwen, 1938). He suggested lynchets in pounds evidenced prehistoric hoe cultivation in pounds, while field systems were based on plough agriculture. Fox argued that pounds were primarily livestock enclosures and field systems indicated arable land use (Fox, 1954a). Similar distinctions between field systems / cultivation and pounds / pastoralism have recently been made by Butler (Butler, 1997a). Here, I assess this distinction between pastoral settlement and arable settlement using the evidence from palaeoenvironmental studies (see section 2.3). I investigate the extent to which land division heralds adoption of cultivation and maximisation of food production.

Soil studies on Dartmoor, initially seemed to confirm Fox's distinction between pounds and field systems. Pounds, it was observed, were mostly found on peaty gleyed podzols while field systems were more often found on more fertile brown earths (Simmons, 1969). However it was soon pointed out that some sites reversed this pattern: At Trowlesworthy pounds were located on 'deep, well drained clay loams of the acid brown earth group' whereas in the nearby coaxial fields land was 'degraded acid brown earths' with secondary podzolisation and gleying (Price & Tinsley, 1976: 151). It is now known that the distribution of modern soil types does not represent soils present in prehistory. Distribution of brown earths and podzols has more to do with cultivation taking place in the historic period than with prehistoric land use. Brown earths will develop into stagnopodzols when left unploughed for a long period (Clayden & Manley, 1964; Ralph 1982): Surface soil characteristics on Dartmoor 'largely reflect the intervention of historic and modern farmers' (Ralph, 1982: 425). The correlation of pounds and field systems with certain soils does not indicate 'that prehistoric communities chose to farm in places with soils especially suited to cultivation … but that medieval and modern farmers chose the same locations' (Ralph, 1982: 425).

Evidence for lynchets on Dartmoor relate largely to historic period reuse of prehistoric landscapes. Lynchets in pounds at Trowlesworthy seem likely to represent medieval cultivation (cf Curwen, 1938; Price & Tinsley, 1976). An idea supported by evidence for cereal pollen in the medieval period around Trowlesworthy (Balaam in Smith et al., 1981: 265). Lynchets within field systems are also related to historic period cultivation. 'Lynchets are quite marked' within the Kestor field system (Curwen, 1927: 283). But Fox's excavations here found no evidence for prehistoric arable. Stratified peat contemporary with occupation of the field system contained pollen with a high percentage of grasses but no cereals (Blackburn in Fox, 1954b: 62). Later palaeoenvironmental work at Kestor showed 'a mainly pastoral Bronze Age phase … with a later activity involving arable activity at c AD 1000' (Wier in Gibson, 1990: 20).

Stratified prehistoric soils *do* provide evidence for prehistoric soil conditions. These studies suggest soil conditions vary considerably within field systems. Soils sealed beneath prehistoric structures on Holne Moor were more fertile than modern soils. Buried soils had no peat, no iron pan, and little evidence of leaching. Moles and earthworms, which do not survive on unfertile soils, were present in prehistory. Ditches were filled with silt rather then peat. On the other hand, sites along the Saddlesborough Main Reave revealed stratified stagnopodzols and stagnogleys. Peat profiles were preserved beneath the banks of the reave and some parts of the ditch were waterlogged (Balaam et al., 1982). At site 15 on the Wotter Common Reave 'severe soil deterioration had occurred by the Bronze Age' suggesting that land within these field systems was not good for long term cultivation (Keely and Macphail in Balaam et al., 1982 1982: 219).

Phosphate studies on sub-surface and buried soils strongly suggest that land use within coaxial landscapes was predominately pastoral (Ralph, 1982). At Holne Moor the intensity of this pastoral land use varied. Samples of the soils across abandoned fields showed that a considerable mean increase in soil phosphorus (c.60%) was associated with a single large prehistoric field. The spatial distribution of soil phosphorus within this field conformed to the pattern of nutrient redistribution associated with sheep (Ralph, 1982: chapter 2). Comparison with medieval fields showed that the prehistoric field had much higher net increases; suggesting that pastoral land use was more intense in the prehistoric field then in surrounding medieval enclosures. This field also appeared to have been more intensively grazed then other prehistoric enclosures. Two other enclosures showed an 'absence of clear phosphorus anomalies, positive or negative' (Ralph, 1982: 428). However, excavation showed that they had been cleared of stone (Fleming, 1988; 105). The possibility of a 'balance between crop removal and manurial addition of phosphorus' was explored perhaps indicating harvesting of hay from the fields; another possibility is that these enclosures were cleared but were never used for either cultivation, intensive grazing, or hay making (Ralph,

1982: chapter 5). Extensive phosphate studies at Shaugh Moor showed no difference in land use or grazing intensity between areas within the coaxial landscape and areas within and surrounding pounds (Balaam and Porter in Balaam, 1982; 215). The construction of a coaxial landscape here did not lead to major transformations in land use. The landscape was dominated by grazing both before and after the building of coaxial landscapes.

Pollen studies support the evidence from soils, indicating little evidence for cultivation anywhere in the landscape. Extensive pollen sampling at Shaugh Moor showed 'evidence for arable farming, by the presence of pollen grains of cereals and … arable weeds … is either totally absent … or very scarce' (Balaam et al., 1982: 262). Nonetheless, charred grains indicate that cereals and beans were finding their way into buildings within coaxial field systems. Charcoal from sealed contexts at Holne Moor contained seven cereal grains (4 of barley, 1 of wheat and 2 of uncertain species), twelve *Vicia faba* beans (Celtic bean) and seventeen seeds of species that may be weeds of cultivation or pasture (Maguire et al., 1983, Ralph, 1982). These need not have been grown locally, but the evidence for occasional cereal pollen suggests that cultivation cannot be entirely dismissed (Staines, 1979; Caseldine, 1999) . Pollen studies suggest that pastoral land use was primary in both coaxial landscapes and pounds. At Shaugh Moor, it was concluded that evidence for pastoral farming was present across the whole area regardless of different settlement morphologies (Balaam et al., 1982: 262).

In summary, evidence for land use does not suggest a straightforward progression towards efficiency and maximising calorific output in the short term. There is no evidence to suggest that the construction of coaxial landscapes heralded a great transformation in farming life. Disconcertingly the construction of land division in some places seems entirely without an 'economic' explanation. Around Shaugh Moor, the density of boulders in some coaxial enclosures would have made them unsuitable for either cultivation *or* grazing (Price, 1973). Examples of enclosures filled with boulders are not uncommon on Dartmoor (Butler, 1997a), and are difficult to account for in functional terms.

The Purposes of Land Division

It is often assumed that land division has a 'commonsense' explanation – 'they were simply trying to be better farmers'. But when it is examined in more depth land division becomes more complex. The idea that a field functions to keep animals away from crops belongs to a modern period of agriculture: To a time and place when agriculture is dominated by the cultivation of cereals on an annual basis and arable fields are in near continuous use. This high intensity agriculture is, in fact, highly unusual. Across world farming throughout history, most land has lain fallow for most of the time (Boserup,

1965). Familiar images of farming and fields conjured by the term 'field system' are misleading.

The functions of reaves are far from clear. Reaves alone seldom formed walls that could exclude animals. Topped with a hedge, however, they could have made effective barriers (Fleming, 1988). There is some evidence for hedges contemporary with reaves outside Dartmoor: Palaeoenvironmental evidence from ditches of a late Bronze Age field system at Castle Hill, lowland Devon, suggested that the banks had been topped by hedges (Fitzpatrick et al., 1999: 194). Evidence for hedges has also been found associated with boundaries in East Anglia and Cambridgeshire (Pryor, 1998; Evans & Knight, 2001). If hedges were used the functional life of the barrier would be determined by upkeep of the hedge rather than non-living parts of the boundary. It seems very likely that reaves went into and out of use as potential barriers. Indeed, they have done so throughout Dartmoor's history until their preservation as monuments prevented farmers using them. A barrier that can be used flexibly is an advantage. When enclosures are kept fallow between cultivation episodes it is beneficial to encourage animals to wander over them distributing fertiliser, whereas at other times it would be better to exclude them. Archaeologists should beware, however, of assuming that fields are primarily used to protect crops. Walls, ditches and hedges are extremely useful in stock management. They exclude wild predators, prevent diseases, enforce breeding regimes, enable better calculation and control of stock food requirements and allow future productivity to be predicted more easily (Pryor, 1996, 1998). There are also many non-barrier technologies that can be used to constrain the movements of animals and that may be combined with land division. Animals may be 'hobbled' or tied, and, in small-scale societies, it is more usual for animals to be watched by shepherds than not (Caulfield, 1983). Some writers focus on the 'symbolic' rather than economic functions of reaves. According to this view land division has a 'symbolic' function; 'to establish lasting property rights, written on the land in ways not unlike deeds' (Earle, 2004: 155). Reaves are interpreted as unambiguously referring to land titles defined and regulated by institutional elites. This interpretation is considered further in section 3.5, but for now it is worth noting that 'symbolic' functions, like economic functions do not exhaust the possible meanings of reaves. Land division does not have a single function, and it is very unlikely that any functional explanation will adequately sum up all the potential significances of reaves.

In this section I have begun to show how land division evades commonsense economic explanations. Reaves are not a straightforwardly 'maximising' innovation. Furthermore there are no grounds for supposing that reaves in prehistory had a single purpose or function. The findings of this section thus open up potential for alternative ways of understanding land division. In the next section I evaluate another common approach to prehistoric tenure – the notion that it emerges from land scarcity.

3.3 Coaxial Land Division and Land Scarcity

Within classical theories of property scarcity is assumed to promote property. Increasing scarcity leads to increasingly restrictive and privatised property regimes, simulating the construction of boundaries. In this section I examine the extent to which coaxial land division on Dartmoor was influenced by sustained land scarcity. Earlier studies of land division, as discussed above, suggest that long-term scarcity causes land division to become 'impacted' or 'involuted'. Landscapes under pressure display the following characteristics:

1. Land division covers every available suitable area;
2. Land division is highly and evenly dense across suitable land.

According to the first of these expectations sustained pressure from scarcity motivates land division and leads to landscapes with land division packed into every suitable and available niche. If land scarcity was a major factor driving enclosure, we might expect land division would be present in every available suitable area, so if gaps in good land remain unoccupied it seems likely that the landscape is not arranged solely around responses to long-term land scarcity.

In this section I assess how much the coaxial landscapes of Dartmoor meet this first expectation. I do so by analysing the distribution of existing traces of coaxial land division. From this I suggest characteristics of land judged 'suitable' by the builders. I then investigate the region to discover how much of it might be 'suitable' in these terms. Lastly I assess how much of this theoretically suitable land was actually taken up with coaxial land division. Finally I compare the findings of this modelling exercise with environmental evidence, looking for indications of sustained pressure from land scarcity.

It should be emphasised that the methodology pursued here is not 'predictive modelling' in any sense. GIS is not used to make positive assertions about site preservation or location. Instead, a simple and low key model is used to gain purchase on a wider interpretative problem – the issue of how we explain the origins of prehistoric land division, and of how this explanation relates to wider assumptions concerning the origins of property.

Factors influencing Land Quality

Previous writers have suggested that builders of coaxial landscapes selected locations with particular attributes. Fox argued that land with comparatively low annual rainfall was preferred by builders of coaxial enclosures (Fox, 1954a). Simmons suggested that brown earths were preferred over podzols (Simmons, 1969). Hamond showed that coaxial landscapes were located on gentler slopes then other types of settlement (Hamond, 1979). Others argued that coaxial landscapes were built at lower elevations to take advantage of longer thermal growing seasons (Fleming, 1978b, 1983; Butler, 1997a; Gerrard, 1997a). Variables known to influence the quality of land, which might influence locations used for coaxial landscapes, include thermal growing seasons, rainfall, elevation, slope, aspect, and pedology.

Studies of modern habitat distributions show that climate strongly influences vegetation, and is especially important in determining quality of upland grazing (Harrison et al., 2001; Simmons, 2003). Bioclimate analysis suggests that most variation in species distribution is linked to changes in rainfall, closely followed by temperature (thermal growing season) (Harrison et al., 2001; Chapter 2). Although the climate of Dartmoor has changed considerably since the Middle Bronze Age (Amesbury et al., 2005), many climatic variables vary isostatically related to topographic features, so that areas of comparatively high or low readings are likely to remain so. The influence of temperature is especially important in upland regions. In Britain, thermal lapse rates are among the steepest in the world (Simmons, 2003: 13). This produces rapid fall off in thermal growing season length in upland areas. Length of the thermal growing seasons is closely linked to elevation. The growing season shortens by about 12 calendar days for every 100 metres gained in elevation (Simmons, 2003: 13). Because of this link, elevation is often used as a general proxy for growing season length (Tivy, 1990).

I obtained data on modern climate from the UK Climate Impacts Programme (UKCIP) in 5km grid tiles (see 3.1 and 3.2). The low resolution of this data means that it relates to the scale of the digital dataset in a highly discontinuous manner. Some of this discontinuity can be overcome by converting grid tiles into contours, but this does not remove the disparity in scale between the climate data and other data sources used in the analysis. Given the strength of the relationship between elevation and growing season length, and the poor resolution of the growing season data I decided to use a finer resolution DEM as a proxy growing season map. Rainfall intensity does not follow elevation in the same way, and therefore the low resolution UKCIP data had to be used for this variable.

Aspect and slope may also influence site location. Variability in modern habitat distributions is linked to sunlight exposure during the months of January to July - a variable that is related to aspect – though this accounts for much less variation than rainfall and growing season (Harrison et al., 2001; Chapter 2). Slope has already been shown to influence the distributions of different types of land division on Dartmoor. Hamond observed that coaxial sites tended to be located on gentler slopes (Hamond, 1979). This finding corresponds with studies of livestock behaviour, which show that cattle will not graze slopes of more then ten degrees (Bailey et al., 1996). Surfaces showing aspect and slope were generated from the DEM used in the analysis.

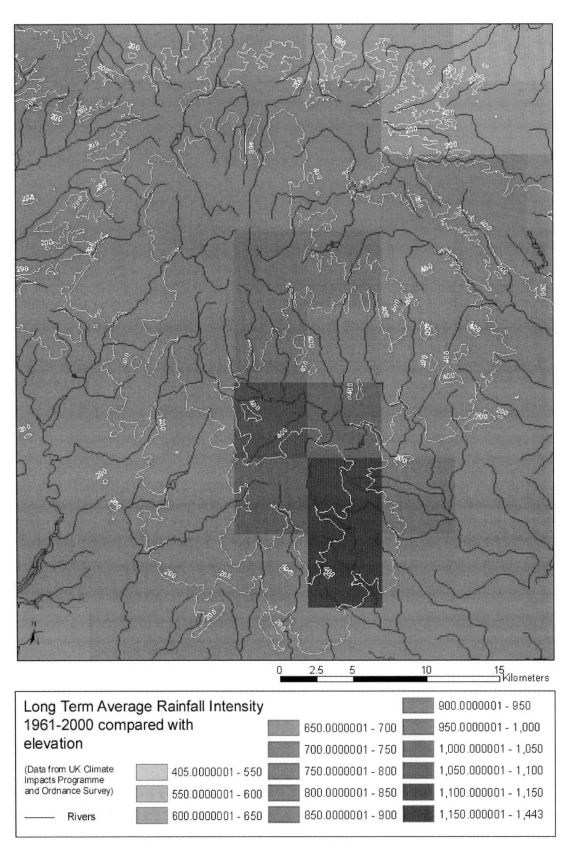

3.1: Rainfall intensity compared with elevation (Data from UK Climate Impacts Programme and Digimap © Crown Copyright/database right 2004. An Ordnance Survey/EDINA supplied service).

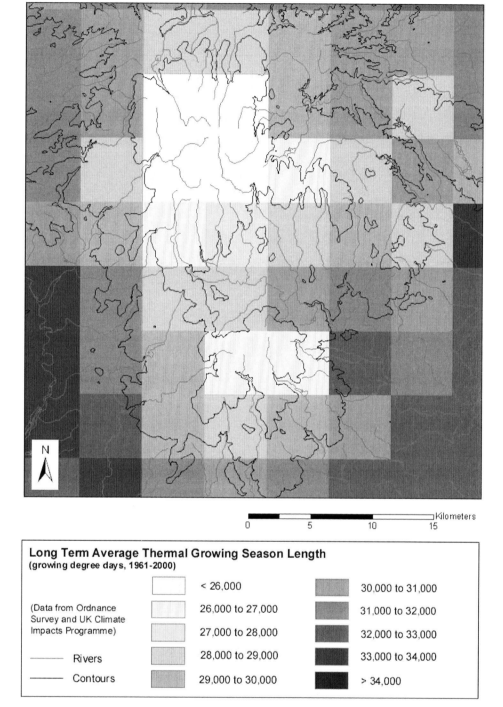

3.2: Growing season length compared with elevation (Data from UK Climate Impacts Programme and Digimap © Crown Copyright/database right 2004. An Ordnance Survey/EDINA supplied service).

As already discussed, pedological studies demonstrate that soils have changed considerably in the last four thousand years. Brown earths have become podzolised, and, in some places, historic period land use has converted podzols back into brown earths (Ralph, 1982). Peat has spread in many areas (Caseldine, 1999). Consequently, data like the modern Land Capability for Agriculture (LCA) Indices, (which use modern pedological surveys) are unsuitable here. Furthermore maps of hard geology are of little explanatory value, since coaxial landscapes are all found on the granite. Since no adequate proxy data for prehistoric soils could be found it proved impossible to include pedological data in the analysis. Variables used in the analysis thus comprised elevation (a proxy for growing season), rainfall, slope, and aspect.

Constraining the Study Region

Survival of coaxial landscapes is largely due to the history of low-intensity of farming in the region. Because higher parts have been used for rough grazing throughout history, prehistoric landscapes remain intact. In those places where land has been 'improved' sites have been comprehensively destroyed. Butler's survey reveals that extensive destruction has been wrought inside modern enclosed land and within the walls of the now abandoned post-medieval newtake enclosures (Butler, 1997b: chapter 1). Because agricultural practices are a pervasive influence on preservation across the region, the edge of modern and historic enclosures can be used to exclude places with the worst preservation. Although constraining the analysis does not prevent differential preservation having an effect on the model, it does take account of one of the most important. The edges of historic and modern enclosures were digitised and used to constrain the sample subjected to analysis (see 3.3).

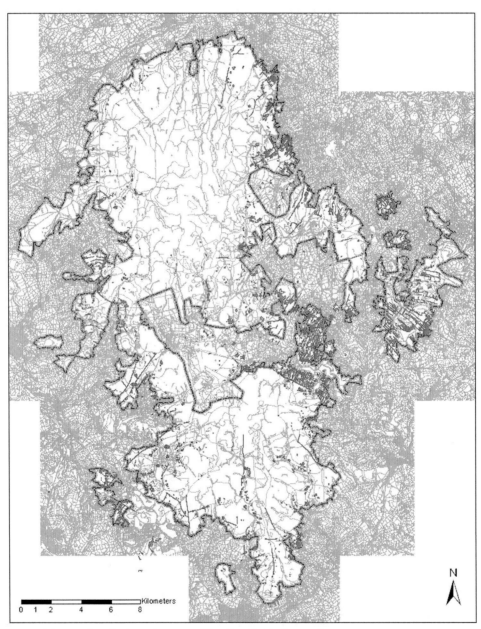

Edge of Present Day Enclosed Land with Sites identified in Recent Survey

| Sites mapped by Butler 1997 and Unpub. | Edge of study control | Ordnance Survey 1: 10,000 Landline Map |

(Data from Ordnance Survey and Butler Unpub.)

3.3: Edge of enclosed land and distribution of survey data (Data from Butler Unpub and Digimap © Crown Copyright/database right 2002. An Ordnance Survey/EDINA supplied service)

Location Analysis of Coaxial Land Division

How does the distribution of coaxial landscapes relate to elevation, rainfall, slope and aspect? To answer this question a 100m grid was generated around all coaxial reaves. The frequency of grid cells within each class of elevation, aspect and slope was then counted. Elevation and slope presented high resolution cardinal data. For data of this type I took the interquartile range of the distribution as that most preferred by the builders of coaxial land division (see 3.4 and 3.5). Unlike elevation and slope, aspect varies ordinally around the compass. Here, a more flexible approach was adopted. The results in 3.6 evidence a 'least preferred' aspect at 225-270 degrees and a 'most preferred' between 45 and 90 degrees, but between these directions are a range of aspects that seem 'OK' – being neither more nor less common than expected. Taking into account the relatively slight impact of this variable overall, (as 3.6 shows, few points of the compass are completely avoided), I decided to include all but the least preferred aspects in my model of land suitable for coaxial land division.

My treatment of rainfall intensity allowed for the low resolution of this dataset. Firstly I converted the 5km grid cells into 50mm contours. Coaxial areas were here represented as points generated from the 100m grid used above. I then counted the frequencies of these points within polygons representing each contour draped over the DEM. The results (3.7 and 3.8) reflect Fox's observation that coaxial enclosures avoid the wettest parts of the region (Fox, 1954a). Given the low resolution of the data the interquartile range was too proscriptive a marker. It excluded too much land as 'unsuitable' without taking into account the fine variations in microclimate often found in upland regions (Simmons 2003). I decided to exclude the land that experienced very high rainfall intensity (above 1100mm) as unlikely to be suitable for coaxial sites.

The results of my location analysis suggest that land preferred by the builders of coaxial land division possessed the following characteristics:

1. elevation between 250m and 400m OD
2. slope between 2 and 10 degrees
3. any aspect apart from that between 248 and 23 degrees
4. Annual average rainfall intensity currently below 1100mm contour.

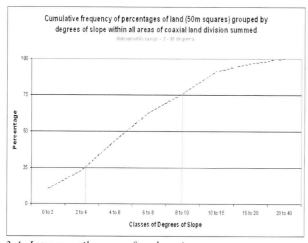

3.4: Interquartile range for elevation

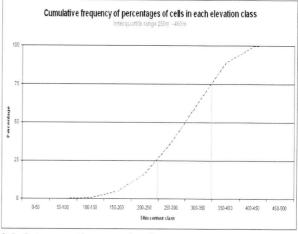

3.5: Interquartile range for slope

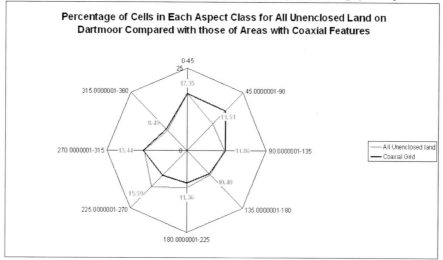

3.6: Frequency within aspect classes

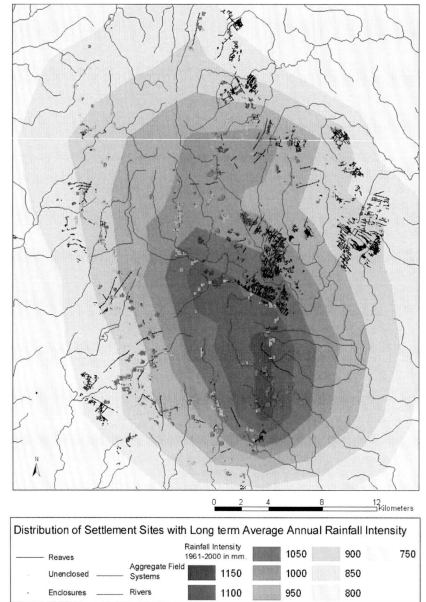

3.7: Long-term rainfall intensity (50mm contours) compared with distribution of settlement (data from UKCIP, Butler 1997 and Unpub., and Digimap © Crown Copyright/database right 2004. An Ordnance Survey/EDINA supplied service.

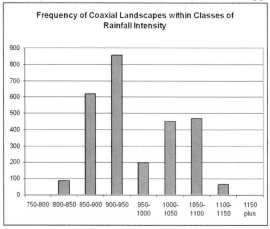

3.8: Frequency of coaxial land division within rainfall contours

3.9: Map Calculations and Reclassifications used to Model Results of Location Analysis

**Step 1: Elevations
of unenclosed
areas reclassified**

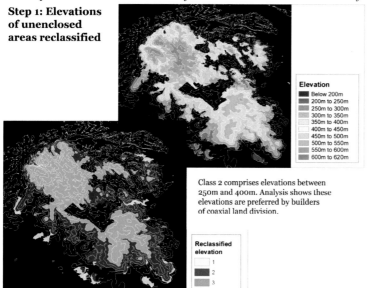

Elevation
- Below 200m
- 200m to 250m
- 250m to 300m
- 300m to 350m
- 350m to 400m
- 400m to 450m
- 450m to 500m
- 500m to 550m
- 550m to 600m
- 600m to 620m

Class 2 comprises elevations between
250m and 400m. Analysis shows these
elevations are preferred by builders
of coaxial land division.

Reclassified
elevation
- 1
- 2
- 3

**Step 2:
Degrees Slope
of unenclosed
areas reclassified**

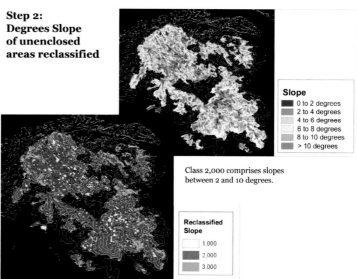

Slope
- 0 to 2 degrees
- 2 to 4 degrees
- 4 to 6 degrees
- 6 to 8 degrees
- 8 to 10 degrees
- > 10 degrees

Class 2,000 comprises slopes
between 2 and 10 degrees.

Reclassified
Slope
- 1,000
- 2,000
- 3,000

**Step 3: Reclassified
elevation map
added to slope map
(calculation one)**

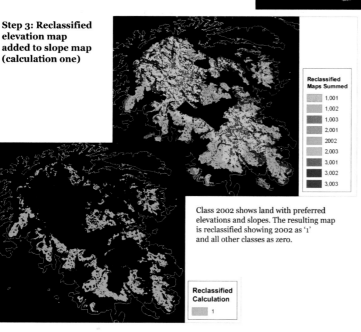

Reclassified
Maps Summed
- 1,001
- 1,002
- 1,003
- 2,001
- 2002
- 2,003
- 3,001
- 3,002
- 3,003

Class 2002 shows land with preferred
elevations and slopes. The resulting map
is reclassified showing 2002 as '1'
and all other classes as zero.

Reclassified
Calculation
- 1

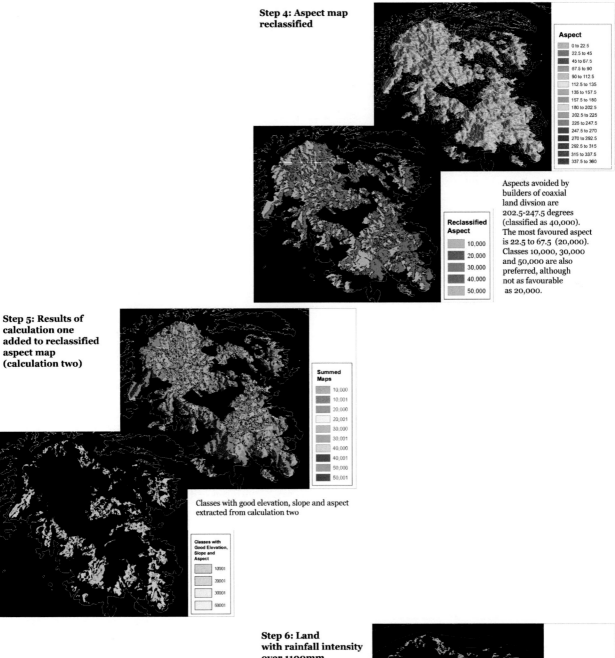

Step 4: Aspect map reclassified

Aspects avoided by builders of coaxial land divsion are 202.5-247.5 degrees (classified as 40,000). The most favoured aspect is 22.5 to 67.5 (20,000). Classes 10,000, 30,000 and 50,000 are also preferred, although not as favourable as 20,000.

Step 5: Results of calculation one added to reclassified aspect map (calculation two)

Classes with good elevation, slope and aspect extracted from calculation two

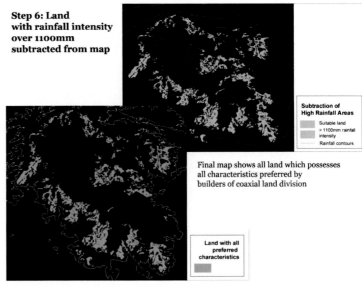

Step 6: Land with rainfall intensity over 1100mm subtracted from map

Final map shows all land which possesses all characteristics preferred by builders of coaxial land division

Modelling Land Potentially Suitable for Coaxial Land Division

This analysis suggests characteristics of land theoretically suitable for coaxial land division. If coaxial land division reflected sustained pressure from land scarcity, then, following the expectations of previous studies, one would expect that all suitable land would have once been occupied by coaxial sites. To test this expectation I built a model of the distribution of suitable land. Maps of elevation and slope were reclassified, identifying the 'good' land that fell within the interquartile ranges for coaxial frequency. Next, these maps were summed, creating a new surface in which land good for both elevation and slope could be identified. The aspect map was reclassified identifying 'good' and 'bad' aspects, and this map was added to the results of the first calculation. Lastly, the wettest areas were subtracted from the map. Figure 3.9 represents all the analytical steps within the modelling methodology.

The results comprise a map of terrain which, according to the variables I have examined, is 'suitable' for coaxial land division. Comparing this model with the actual distribution of sites it is clear that not all suitable terrain is occupied by traces of coaxial land division. In 3.10 several 'empty' areas are evident. However, 'empty' areas are seldom completely devoid of archaeological remains – in many places there is a low density scatter of monuments, especially of cairns and stone rows. (see 3.11). For example, in the south-east (around Butterdon Hill) a large tract of land is occupied mainly by cairns and stone rows. In these cases, land may not have been seen as available for coaxial landscapes (although, there are examples of stone rows and ceremonial complexes within coaxial landscapes, as around Yar Tor, for example). This distribution is difficult to explain in conventional 'economic' terms. Ceremonial sites represent land use which, Fowler and Blackwell argue, is 'uneconomic' (Fowler & Blackwell, 1998: 54). Yet the very fact that these 'uneconomic' sites were allowed to take up large expanses of the best terrain suggests this was not a landscape dominated by 'economic' scarcity. Other areas empty of coaxial landscapes contain pounds and unenclosed settlement. Examples include the Plym valley in the south west where large expanses of good quality grazing exist. Medieval land division was constructed here when the climate was considerably wetter and colder than in the Bronze Age (Amesbury et al., 2005). This suggests the Upper Plym could easily have supported land division in the warmer and drier Early to Middle Bronze Age. Nonetheless, in this area, and in other places without coaxial landscapes, extensive tracts of grazing land were left unenclosed. This is not the 'involuted' settlement pattern expected for a landscape impacted by scarcity.

Even allowing for areas given over to other kinds of site, there are still relatively 'empty' landscapes. Of course, absence of evidence is not evidence of absence: Some empty areas may once have contained sites which have subsequently been destroyed. However, many such areas do contain thin scatters of prehistoric features. For example, in the north-west suitable land contains sparsely distributed cairns and cairnfields. The likelihood of destruction that left only ceremonial sites is remote. Differences in preservation factors, therefore, do not seem to account for all the absences. Another possibility is that some empty areas contained coaxial landscapes built entirely of wood. Timber fences are known from the coaxial landscapes (Smith et al., 1981; Fleming, 1988). However, where such fences are found, they are usually interspersed with stone features. Furthermore, they generally become stone features over time because stone tends to be cleared against them (see Fleming, 1988, 1994b). The possibility of extensive landscapes built only of timber cannot be ruled out, but it seems unlikely, given the stoniness of the terrain. Therefore, the possibility remains that within this region of extensive, well preserved, prehistoric landscapes, there are areas that were not occupied intensively. Not 'absences' exactly, but not the pattern expected of a region enduring sustained land scarcity.

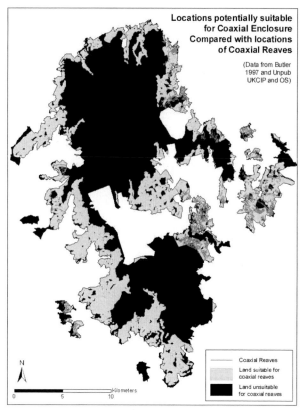

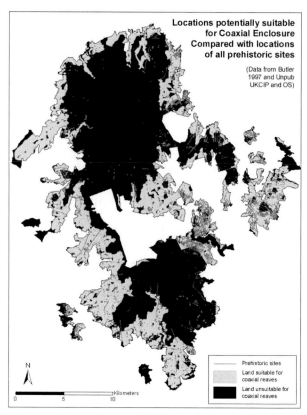

3.10: Land with characteristics preferred by builders of coaxial land division compared with locations of known coaxial sites (Data from Butler 1997 and Unpub. and Digimap © Crown Copyright/database right 2004. An Ordnance Survey/EDINA supplied service).

3.11: Land with characteristics preferred by builders of coaxial land division compared with locations of all known sites (Data from Butler 1997 and Unpub. Digimap © Crown Copyright/database right 2004. An Ordnance Survey/EDINA supplied service).

Land Scarcity and Environmental Evidence

Palaeoenvironmental evidence confirms the impression that the region was not subject to scarcity pressures. There are two moments in which scarcity might be assessed here, firstly, immediately before reaves were built, secondly, during their occupation.

Before the reaves there is no evidence for the kind of wholesale decline in grazing quality that might cause a 'tragedy of the commons'. Palynological information shows that the removal of the canopy did not immediately provoke podzolisation and peat formation (Caseldine, 1999). Instead, peat onset seems to have occurred at different times, caused by a combination of changes in land use and climate (Amesbury et al., 2005). Decline in soil quality often occurs only after palaeosols were buried by structures (as in the soils under house F at Holne Moor (Maguire et al., 1983: 65-6; see also Staines, 1979). Soils under field boundaries at Holne Moor showed no evidence for peat development (Maguire et al., 1983; Ralph, 1982) or for iron pan formation (Ralph, 1982; Fleming, 1988). However, some samples beneath the Saddlesbrough Reave had peat (Balaam et al., 1982) and one profile beneath the Wotter Common reave showed 'strong soil degradation' prior to the building of the reave (MacPhail in Balaam et al., 1982: 18). Despite these examples, the picture of land use immediately before the

reaves does not suggest scarcity. This was not, Caseldine reports, an era of 'great climatic / environmental pressure' (Caseldine & Hatton, 1996: 60).

During the occupation of coaxial landscapes there is likewise little indication of scarcity pressures. As has already been observed, ditches running alongside reaves at Holne Moor were infilled with silt, not peat, and there is evidence that earthworms were common (Fleming, 1988). The brown earth progenitor of Dartmoor soils did not suffer widespread decline until after reaves went out of use, probably in response to climatic impacts combined with land use that left soil profiles undisturbed (Ralph, 1982; Maguire et al., 1983; Amesbury et al., 2005). There is little evidence to suggest land division was either stimulated by scarcity, or that scarcity followed on from construction.

In his early work, Fleming suggested that environmental decline of common grazing land caused land scarcity – a 'tragedy of the commons' – which prompted reave construction (Fleming, 1978b). Here, I have argued that coaxial landscapes are not 'impacted' or 'involuted'. They do not resemble landscapes in which scarcity is a major long-term pressure. Archaeological data however, are limited, and a model which identifies absences can only take interpretation so far. Further analyses are necessary to corroborate the conclusions I have drawn from my modelling exercise and palaeoenvironmental studies. In the next section I turn to the second expectation of landscapes under pressure from scarcity. This second expectation suggests that in 'involuted' landscapes areas of land division will all be more or less uniformly dense. Here is an expectation that relies on positive aspects of known data rather than identifying absences. How much do coaxial landscapes meet this expectation?

3.4 Settlement Pattern, Scarcity and Maximisation

I begin this section by assessing the extent to which Dartmoor meets the second expectation of 'involuted' landscapes; that there is a high density of boundaries across field systems. I compare settlement density between different coaxial landscapes. I then move on to investigate what dynamics might cause this kind of settlement pattern. I suggest that land division is not motivated by land scarcity but involves 'scale-free' growth. Lastly I discuss the implications of my findings for approaches based on the classical theory of property, on scarcity and maximisation.

Density and Scarcity

A landscape impacted by scarcity should have density distributed boundaries within all areas of land division. The density of land division within coaxial landscapes can be measured as the length of reaves per hectare. I selected fifteen different sample areas to compare using Butler's catalogue of coaxial landscapes (Butler, 1997b see 3.12). Most of these areas contain well preserved coherent systems, the area around Cox Tor, however contains a series of more or less isolated reaves connected only by shared orientations. The area of each system was generated from a 100m buffer drawn around the reaves. The total length of reaves within each area was measured and then divided by the area in hectares. The results are shown in 3.13 below.

Areas of coaxial land division are not equally dense. While some areas contain many closely packed walls (e.g. Throwleigh Common, Kestor) others contain large empty blocks (e.g. Buttern Hill, Cuddlippton Down). Differences in reaves per hectare are considerable; the most dense area has nearly three times as much reave per hectare. Butler's reports on each area, and my own field visits, suggest that the differences in density between systems are not due to differential preservation. Robbing of walls usually leaves fragmentary traces, as demonstrated by excavation on Saddlesborough and Wotter Common (Smith et al., 1981). Walls in the less dense landscapes are not generally fragmentary; they do not stop and start, as would be expected of reaves built partly of timber, like reaves excavated at Holne Moor (Fleming, 1988). Usually they are similar to reaves in other areas. The exception is the Cox Tor area, where reaves traverse long distances but do not make a coherent pattern. However, other systems made up of large empty blocks have walls that are usually fairly intact and well preserved (e.g. Buttern Hill, Cuddlipption Down, Easdon Down). Differences in density between landscapes of this very extensive scale, are unlikely to reflect different preservation factors. Instead they reflect observable differences in landscape morphology. Landscapes that are less dense are comprised of large blocks of pastureland, whereas denser areas comprise lattices of smaller enclosures.

Prehistoric land division on Dartmoor does not suggest an impacted or involuted landscape: In impacted landscapes it is expected that land division is found in every suitable available area. In section 3.3 above, I suggested that this was not the case on Dartmoor. In involuted landscapes it is expected that land division is highly dense wherever it is built. But as I have just indicated, on Dartmoor it is highly dense in some places, but much less dense in others. These spatial characteristics are complemented by the evidence of palaeoenvironmental studies which offer no evidence for a landscape under sustained pressure from scarcity.

The variable density of coaxial landscapes on Dartmoor is also found in coaxial landscapes elsewhere. Similar 'patchiness' has been recorded in Middle and Late Bronze Age land division on Salisbury Plain and the Berkshire Downs (Bradley et al., 1994; Ford et al., 1994). Like Dartmoor there appear to be empty areas without any evidence for land division: As Bradley reports for Wessex, concentrations of field systems in some regions exist alongside 'other regions in which such evidence is limited or absent altogether' (Bradley et al., 1994: 138). As on Dartmoor, environmental studies suggest that the extent of arable cultivation was 'limited'; pressure on grazing land was 'modest'; and there is 'no reason to suppose' land scarcity or population pressure motivated construction (Bradley et al., 1994: 142, see also environmental studies of Cranborne Chase (French et al., 2003). Overall there is little evidence to support the notion that the emergence of prehistoric land division in southern Britain was stimulated by a 'Tragedy of the Commons' and/or increasing land scarcity. Classical theories of property – which depend on the idea that scarcity motivates ever more exclusive property – are perhaps unlikely to supply useful approaches for studying tenure in these cases.

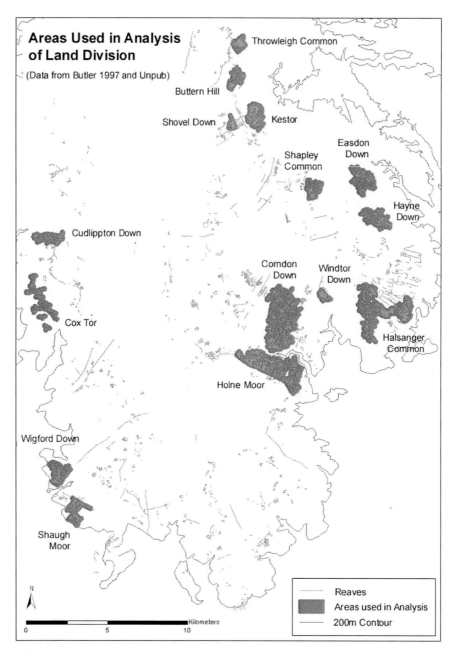

3.12: Areas of Coaxial Land Division used in analysis (Data from Butler 1997 and Unpub and Digimap ©Crown Copyright/database right 2004. An Ordnance Survey/EDINA supplied service).

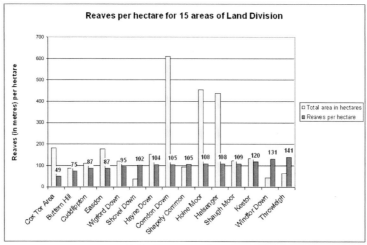

3.13: Reaves per hectare

Of course, it is possible that 'patchy' density of land division reflects localised scarcity acting on small regions. If this were the case, scarcity pressures would vary within such short distances that they are unlikely constitute the Malthusian pressures that are traditionally envisaged within classical theories (i.e. 'population pressure' or reduction in environmental 'carrying capacity'). Instead one would have to envisage 'socially' motivated scarcity within strongly delimited social territories. Population increases would have to be very localised and contained by strong social boundaries. If this were the case, we might expect to see areas of dense land division showing indications of environmental pressure. However, as discussed above, there are few such indications. In fact, for reasons that I now turn to, I do not consider that the settlement pattern on Dartmoor was divided up in this way. Instead I suggest that the variation in densities between areas results from an alternative dynamics.

Scale-free Settlement Growth

If not scarcity, what dynamics are expressed in the settlement patterns of Dartmoor? Interestingly where walls are densely packed, buildings also tend to be densely distributed. As Fleming has observed, this gives coaxial landscapes a 'clustered' aspect. Land division contains distinct clusters of buildings surrounded by clusters of yard areas and smaller enclosures (Fleming, 1988: chapter 2). Fleming called these clusters 'neighbourhood groups'. This property of coaxial landscapes can be illustrated at a gross scale by comparing reaves per hectare with houses per hectare for each area. As can be seen in 3.14, areas of denser boundaries like Throwleigh Common and Kestor, also have denser buildings. The significance of this relationship can be measured using Spearman's Rank Correlation Co-efficient, which reveals a weak positive correlation between boundaries per hectare and buildings per hectare ($Rs = 0.507$).

It is likely that clusters of buildings and reaves formed over time, rather than being built all in one go. New buildings and boundaries seem to have been located next to older pre-existing and abandoned sites (Johnston, 2005). In some areas occupation continues for centuries, as the history of reave construction around Shaugh Moor suggests (Smith et al., 1981; Johnston, 2005). Elsewhere, however, there is evidence for small clusters of one or two houses being occupied for only a short time, before both buildings and boundaries rapidly go out of use, as at Patterson's Cross, East Devon (Fitzpatrick et al., 1999). Although not all houses were occupied simultaneously it seems likely that at least some were, as Fleming argues, occupants would value relationships with neighbours, taking advantage of opportunities for reciprocal exchanges of labour, goods and services between households (Fleming, 1984, 1985b). These factors would encourage clustering among houses occupied contemporaneously as well as successively.

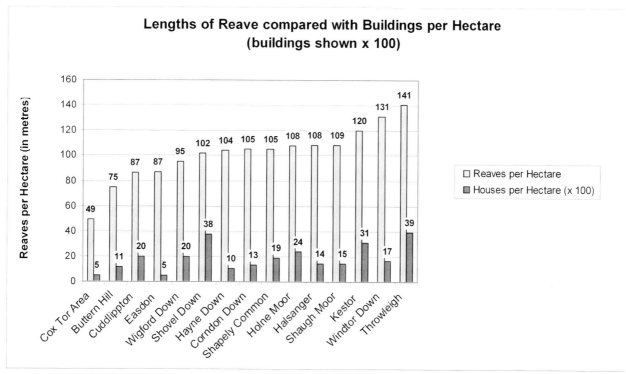

3.14: Reaves per hectare compared with buildings per hectare

Clustering in settlement is, if anything more marked outside the coaxial landscapes. Clustering within the settlement pattern can be analysed by simply recording the frequencies of buildings within a set distance from each other. First for the landscape as a whole, and then just for the coaxial landscapes, I counted the numbers of buildings within 100m of each other. I described a 100m radius around each building and counted the numbers of buildings within. Once again areas of poor preservation within modern and historic enclosures were excluded from the analysis. The results are shown in 3.15 and 3.16.

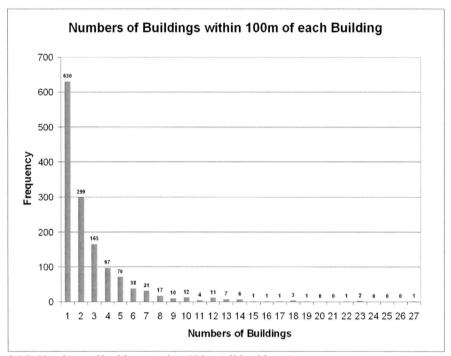

3.15: Numbers of buildings within 100m (all buildings)

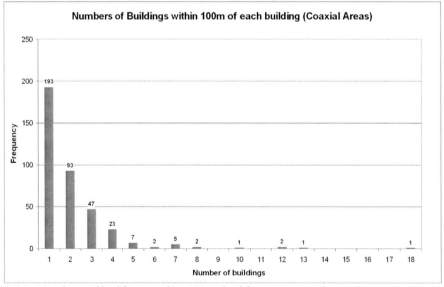

3.16: Numbers of buildings within 100m (buildings in coaxial areas)

The results show a very considerable range in the sizes of clusters both within and outside coaxial landscapes. Although most buildings are found more than 100m from other buildings, there are a small number of clusters where very many buildings are found together. This frequency, in fact, indicates very distinctive kind of distribution pattern. It does do not exhibit the bell curve that characterises most distributions. Instead it suggests a 'power law'. Power laws occur where there is a very large proportion of small frequency readings and a few very large frequency readings. Furthermore the disparity in frequencies is proportional, so that, for example, the first rank tends to be twice as big as the second, which tends to be twice as big as the third, and so on.

The significance of the power law is that it characterises processes of 'scale-free' growth. Power laws appear to be ubiquitous among phenomena that are 'networked, for example, they characterise, links on the internet, citation in academic papers, even frequency of sexual liaisons

(Bentley & Maschner, 2003; Bentley et al., 2005). Networks that are not subject to constraints (that are not 'scaled') will develop inequalities in frequencies over time, so that nodes with many connections will tend to acquire even more. The result is a network with many comparatively poorly connected nodes and a few that are very highly connected. When such a pattern characterises settlement, we would expect that settlement dynamics involve a few settlements that are well connected within a network. Over time, these well connected settlements become even better connected. They act as attractors, encouraging even boundaries and buildings to be built in the same area.

To see whether the frequencies of buildings within clusters do represent a power law distribution the frequencies were cumulated and then graphed on a log log plot (3.17, 3.18). The results do suggest a power law-like distribution for buildings within coaxial landscapes. For buildings as a whole, however the distribution is less power-law like except in the tail. Each of distribution spans more then two orders of magnitude on the y-axes so the results are reasonably robust, and the samples, in archaeological terms, are large (1408 and 377 buildings).

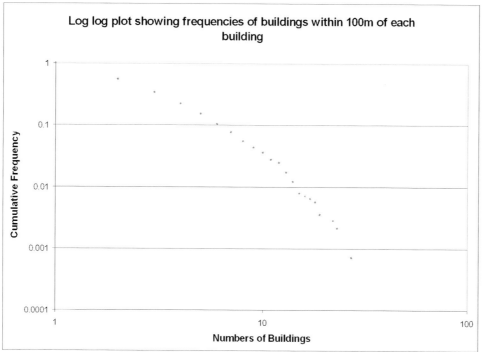

3.17: Log log plot of numbers of buildings within 100m (all buildings)

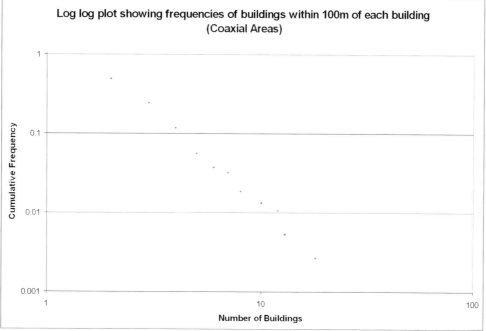

3.18: Log log plot of numbers of buildings within 100m (buildings in coaxial areas)

The power law-like distributions of settlement clusters on Dartmoor point towards a networked dynamic of settlement, a scale-free dynamic very different to the scaled processes evoked by land scarcity-based narratives. This scale free property is relevant even over short distances (100m). Even localised scarcity within social territories would not explain such a pattern, since this would suggest some kind of scaling over short distances. Land availability does not seem to have been important in settlement growth. Instead builders chose locations according to networks of relationships. Buildings already occupied attracted further settlement, and already large clusters became even larger. This settlement dynamic fits well with Fleming's account of social relations in the Dartmoor landscape. Settlements were successful, Fleming argued, to the extent that they were able to mobilise social relationships, through kinship, alliance and reciprocal transactions. Only by mobilising social ties could agricultural tasks be accomplished, creating a network 'above the level of the household' (Fleming, 1985b). This network, Fleming argued suggested tenure held 'communally' at the level of the 'neighbourhood group' and the 'community' (Fleming, 1984). The analysis I have offered here confirms the importance of networks, and presents an alternative to approaches based on scarcity and resource maximisation.

Implications of Scale-free Settlement Growth for Classical Theories

Traditional 'economic' accounts treat land as a species of wealth. Individuals attempt to maximise productivity and access to this good. Anything which makes the supply of land scarce, therefore, exacerbates the urge to exclude others and thus produces more restrictive property. All the land-wealth should be taken up, although the ability to accumulate is limited by costs of enclosing and defending ownership (Demetz, 1967; Casimir, 1992). Occupation would be orientated around maximising exclusive ownership of quantities of land-wealth. It would therefore be strongly 'scalar'. Ideally the settlement pattern of classical theory would contain a mosaic of individual smallholders, each attempting to make their own plot productive, much as was visualised by Locke (Locke, 1690).

3.5 Property and Hierarchy

In this section I turn to approaches that see prehistoric property as a legal institution evolving alongside social hierarchy (Gilman, 1998; Earle, 2000). These interpretations see land division and tenure as the outcome of self-interested maximisation by elites (Pearce, 1983; Kristiansen, 1998; Earle, 2002: chapters 12-4). In this section I evaluate these interpretations against features of Dartmoor landscapes.

My findings here, contradict this vision. In the first place there is little evidence that land scarcity motivated enclosure. Furthermore settlement was not spread out to maximise quantities of land contained within individualised land-holdings. Instead, land division is densely concentrated in some areas, less dense in others. Settlement patterns are clustered. They do not indicate 'single family farms', but networks of relations (Fleming, 1984, 1985b). Settlement growth is not scalar but 'scale free'.

These findings suggest an economy orientated along different lines than the common sense 'economics' evoked by approaches to tenure which emerge from classical theories of property. What is maximised here is not food production, or land, but relationships. Land does not have value as an abstract quantity; instead relationships are essential to processes by which land acquires value. Occupiers of new houses wish to be located with respect to productive relations, and land is part of how these relations are accessed. Relationships, in themselves, are important in creating value. When approaching this kind of scenario the classical definition of property – an exclusive individual right – is of very little use. Instead tenure needs to be understood as *inclusive*. To be effective, tenure must include social relations productively rather than defining and excluding others (Verdery, 2003). Approaches based on the classical theory of property, and on commonsense 'economic' concepts of scarcity and maximisation are unlikely to advance archaeologies of this kind of tenure.

In this section I concluded that there was little evidence that scarcity drove the construction of coaxial land division. I argued for an alternative settlement dynamic in which new buildings and reaves were attracted to places because of the productivity of previously existing relationships, rather than on the basis of land availability. This suggests an economy organised along different lines than those envisaged by classical theories of property. However, there is one more archaeological approach where classical theories of property are still widely used: 'social' approaches in which property institutions are directed by the interests of elites. It is to these approaches that I now turn.

Tenure from the 'Top Down'

Bronze Age Dartmoor has been interpreted as a 'redistributive chiefdom'. In an economy of this type production is controlled by centralised elites and their entourage. Elites redistribute goods among the populace creaming off the surplus to support their lavish habits. As was discussed in chapter two, Fleming was equivocal about this kind of approach preferring 'bottom-up' to 'top-down' dynamics (Fleming, 1982). However, other writers have shown little hesitation when it comes to incorporating coaxial land division on Dartmoor within accounts of hierarchically organised economy and social structure (e.g. Pearce, 1983, 1999; Kristiansen, 1998). One account that has been particularly influential is Earle's interpretation of Dartmoor as an example of a chiefly economy organised around a 'staple finance' strategy (Earle, 2002; chapters 2, 13). This approach is especially interesting because it focuses on the distribution of tenure.

'Staple finance', according to Earle, is a strategy pursued by elites who focus on controlling 'the ownership of and restricted access to productive resources, most importantly land' (Earle, 2002:61). Land in such societies is the inalienable property of chiefs, who redistribute use rights to the lower orders. Food may also be accumulated and redistributed: The emergence of staple finance systems on Dartmoor and Wessex is linked to 'the Age of Hill Forts' when, Earle argues, field systems were constructed along with centralised facilities for the storage of grain (Earle, 2002: 335-346). Earle sets out the landscape features which characterise 'chiefdoms' as follows:

1. Firstly, chiefdoms have 'a centralised decision-making hierarchy coordinating activities among several village communities ... the chiefs are central directors and centrality is the clearest indicator of chiefdoms' (Earle, 2002: 54-5). Central places with centralised storage facilities should therefore be present.
2. Secondly, chiefly landscapes should display evidence for having been 'regionally organised' or planned from above (Earle, 2002: 54).
3. Thirdly, on Dartmoor and Wessex, chiefdoms are associated with 'carefully delimited ownership of land' (Earle, 2002: 346). A 'new system of land ownership' in which, 'land, given over to the chiefs, served as their income estates. Use rights to individuals were given in return for household labour on chiefly land and other projects' (Earle, 2002: 330).

Using evidence from Dartmoor it is possible to assess these point by point.

The first problem of the redistributive chiefdoms approach is the lack of any feasible central places in the Dartmoor landscape. Unlike Wessex, where construction of some hillfort sites may have begun in the Middle Bronze Age (Needham & Ambers, 1994), construction of

hillforts in Devon begins much later than current dates for construction and occupation of reaves (Fox, 1996). Fleming made efforts to distinguish 'dominant settlements' or 'Major Enclosures' that might act as central places of elite power (Fleming, 1978b: 109-10). But he found he could not relate Major Enclosures to his 'territories', larger or more impressive sites simply do not spread out evenly as exploitative central places should (Fleming, 1978b:110). In fact central places and storage facilities are entirely absent.

Earle, makes much of the 'planning' behind reaves, which he sees as 'evidence for their politically motivated design from the top' (Earle, 2002: 346). However it is increasingly difficult to support this idea of a synchronous system planned by a central authority (cf Fleming, 1984). Excavations and survey data reveal evidence for chronological depth and piecemeal accumulation in reave layouts, not consistent with the idea of a regionally organised landscape (Johnston, 2005). Whenever landscapes are studies in detail they reveal evidence for having been laid out, maintained and altered over a long period (see Brück et al., 2005).

Earle's concept of staple finance is based on cereal cultivation, for which, as I have pointed out, there is very little evidence in the Dartmoor landscape (see section 3.1). His account of food redistribution does not fit the evidence. However Earle's idea that *tenure* might be redistributed is not so easy to dismiss. Coaxial land division does indeed suggest a landscape that has been 'carefully delimited'. It is even possible, as Earle suggests that land was regularly allotted into a series of standard units for ease of redistribution by chiefs. Coaxial land division divides land in two ways; a) into individual enclosures; b) into long strips. Conceivably either of these attributes might have been used to standardise tenure so that it could be redistributed a central elite power.

To evaluate this idea, I first examined the extent to which enclosures on Dartmoor were of standard area. Enclosures from nine coaxial landscapes were selected for the study. Area was measured only where sides of an enclosure were marked by archaeological features on all four sides, either completely or partly. All enclosures that did not have four sides were excluded from the analysis. The areas of more than six hundred enclosures (640) are shown in 3.19 (for areas within each system see Appendix J). The interquartile ranges are given in 3.20.

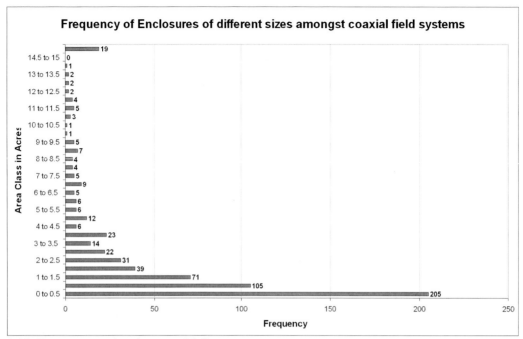

3.19: *Frequencies of enclosures of different sizes*

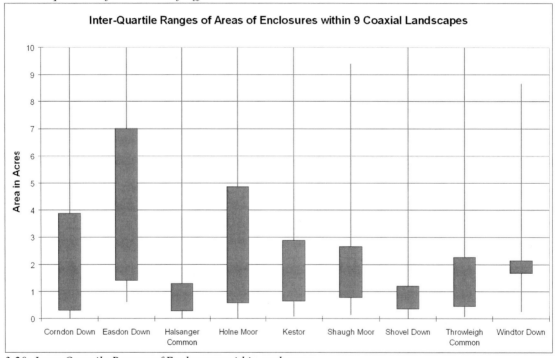

3.20: *Inter-Quartile Ranges of Enclosures within each area*

As these results make clear, the areas of enclosures are very little standardised. There is an enormous range - from small enclosures of less then half an acre up to more than 68 acres for an enclosure on Corndon Down. Most enclosures are very small (94% are less then 10 acres in size) but there are a few extremely large enclosures as on Corndon Down, Shovel Down, and Easdon Down. These are not landscapes with the kinds of regular allotment that facilitates the redistribution of tenure from the top down.

Could coaxial landscapes have been standardised using the long strips that make up coaxial layouts? Unfortunately previous work has demonstrated that there is no standard strip width common to all field systems (Butler, 1997a: 89). Regularity in strip widths appears only over short distances. The longest 'run' of consistently sized strips is on Holne Moor where Fleming observed a series of large blocks of roughly equal width each of which had been subdivided in different ways (Fleming, 1988: 64-5). Table 3.21 lists examples of short runs of similar width strips recorded by Butler.

3.21: Strips of similar widths (from Butler, 1997a)

Area	Approximate width of similar strips
Throwleigh Common	c. 115m
east of the Rowbrook as far as Corndon Tor	c. 60m
opposite bank [of the Rowbrook] at the south end of the North Dart system	'slightly less' then c60m
'blocks' in the Rippon Tor system	c. 400 – 500m
south side of Mountsland Common	c. 50-60m
Wind Tor	c. 30m

I studied widths of strips in detail for five coaxial landscapes - Windtor, Shaugh Moor, Throwleigh Common, Kestor and Holne Moor. Rather than measuring the 'gaps between widths (as Butler does in 3.21) I measured the lengths of actual reaves between strips. The results of this exercise are given in Appendix K. These results confirm the idea that builders made efforts to maintain regular strip width only over short distances. Lack of standardisation in areas of enclosures and widths of strips would have made redistribution of tenure difficult to implement.

In fact the absence of standardisation within coaxial landscapes strongly suggests flexibility in land use and tenure, arrangements more likely to have been decided from the 'bottom-up' than from the 'top-down'. Most coaxial landscapes contain a few very large areas that are most plausibly interpreted as restricted access commons (Fleming, 1998a, 1998b). However, it seems likely that a degree of communally organised access was possible in many different enclosures. Large blocks are not sharply differentiated from other sizes of enclosure, nor are larger enclosures always located on the periphery of intensively subdivided areas (see examples in 3.22). As these examples show very large enclosures are present at Halsanger and Horridge Commons and Shovel Down, where they seem to be separated from other sizes of enclosures, but large enclosures are also present amongst other sizes of enclosure at Throwleigh Common and Holne Moor. Extremely large commons are not sharply differentiated from other larger enclosures. In fact there is a diversity of larger enclosures that might have involved some degree of commoning at different times, accompanied by many smaller enclosures suitable for penning and separating stock, small scale horticulture, hay-making and other land-uses.

3.22: Five Coaxial Landscapes from Dartmoor Showing Varying Plot Sizes. Data from Butler 1997 and Unpublished, and (at Holne Moor) from English Heritage.

1. Horridge and Halsanger Commons

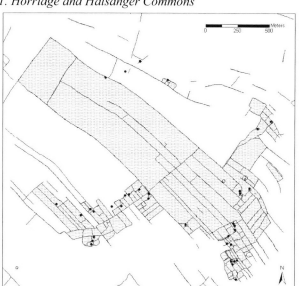

2. Holne Moor

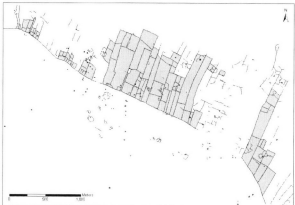

3. Throwleigh Common

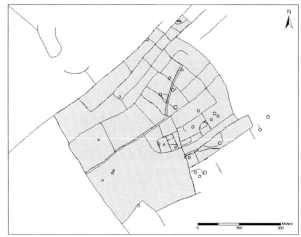

4. Kestor

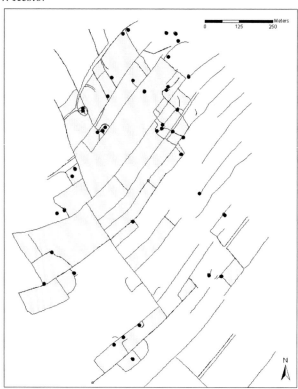

5. Easdon Down

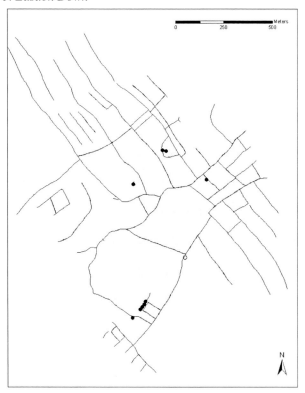

Variation in enclosure sizes suggests tenure was flexible and worked-out locally from the 'bottom-up'. Indeed, this would have been the most suitable strategy for the mainly pastoral agriculture that palaeoenvironmental evidence suggests was taking place. It is unlikely that all enclosures were subject to the same tenurial arrangements. Tenure of larger enclosures and unenclosed land was probably managed differently to that of smaller yard areas. It is likely that more than one group had access to certain places simultaneously, and that complementary tenures overlapped in time and space. This kind of tenure fits very well with the networked communities suggested by my interpretation of settlement patterns (see above). However it does not support the idea of a 'staple finance strategy' in which elites legitimised their power by distributing tenure. Land allotment is not standardised into individualised units that can easily be reallocated amongst individuals or households. Instead, tenure seems to have been more flexibly organised. The kind of overlapping tenure that seems likely to have characterised Dartmoor landscapes would have been very difficult to impose from the top-down.

Conclusions

In this chapter I applied approaches that draw on classical theories of property. I began by refining certain conceptual aspects of classical theories – especially its reliance on ideas of maximisation and scarcity. I reviewed critique of these concepts. I argued that archaeological approaches which employ maximisation and scarcity tend to employ the more commonsense elements of economic thought, rather than exploring economics in a wider sense. Having refined these conceptual points, I reviewed 'economic' explanations of prehistoric land division. Within such accounts land division heralds better ways of maximising food production, notably cultivation. Such maximising explanations are of little use in understanding the Dartmoor reaves, which, I demonstrated are not linked to dramatic transformations in land use and do not seem to have a single functional role. I then examined the Dartmoor landscapes to see how well they supported narratives of property based on scarcity. Using the results of a range of analyses, I argued that coaxial land division was not driven by land scarcity or a 'Tragedy of the Commons'. Instead, I observed evidence for scale-free settlement growth. These patterns suggest that social connections were more important than land availability in the dynamics of settlement on Dartmoor. Land holdings were not individualised but relied on networks of sociability.

Classical theories, I argued, tend to lurch from an under-socialised to an over-socialised conception of the individual. In the last section of this chapter I assessed 'over-socialised' conceptions of property based on Bronze Age social hierarchies. Archaeological approaches to the Bronze Age see elites as the administrators, arbiters and enforcers of jural property. Emphasis on enforcement springs from the classical definition of property as a right to exclude (see Earle, 2000). I argued that accounts of redistributive chiefdoms do not fit the landscape evidence, which suggests more flexible localised arrangements.

The analyses presented in this chapter highlight several limitations of approaches derived from classical theories. Firstly, the under-socialised aspects of classical theory are dependant on assumptions about economic motivations, maximisation and scarcity that are challenged by a growing body of recent and not so recent studies from social sciences and increasingly from economics. Secondly, the over-socialised element of classical theory supports heavily structural models of social and jural institutions. Within these over-socialised accounts it is difficult to understand the mechanisms that link individual behaviour and the overarching structural 'code'. This means that it is difficult to envisage how tenure changes over time. Thirdly the analyses presented here underlined just how little classical theories have to offer the analysis of inclusive tenure. Where classical theory encounters common property it simply singularises the subjects of property into land-holding groups that can be made to resemble 'individuals' holding singular 'rights'. Once property subjects have been individualised in this way it then becomes possible to 'explain' tenure using the effects of maximisation and scarcity. As a result of these limitations, classical theories of property are not very useful for approaching cases where tenure is non-individualised, resources are plentiful, and individuals cannot be assumed to maximise along commonsense 'economic' lines. My findings suggested that Dartmoor might be just such a case.

In this chapter I looked in detail at one of the themes identified in chapter one. Through the application of approaches derived from classical theories I highlighted the limits of these theories. In the next chapter I move on to develop another theme, historically related to classical theories: It is to labour theory of property which I now turn.

Chapter 4

Labour isn't working:
The Labour Theory of Property and Intensification

When two people from the interior of East New Britain meet, they are in the habit of engaging in an act that, from the perspective of the labour theory of property and value, is inexplicable. At the exact same moment they will exchange the same quantity of the same thing. For example they will swap an identical amount of betel nut, or, before cooking a meal, they will go to their neighbours and swap with them an exactly equivalent quantity of food to that which they are about to eat (Graeber, 2005b: 39-40). Neither party profits from these transactions, nor does anyone come away with a debt owed to them, nor is any 'prestige' obtained in these everyday exchanges. Here is an example that apparently confounds the logic of 'productive' activity. In this chapter I present a theory that explains this apparently pointless act. In doing so, I attempt to broaden the conventional notion of what is productive labour. This notion, as I will explain, is at the heart of labour theories of property and value, and is what makes the labour theory of property so difficult to apply to studies of prehistoric tenure.

I begin with a discussion of the labour theory of property and its legacy within theories of intensification. These theories have been important in archaeological interpretations of land division and tenure. However they bring with them problems, both practical and theoretical, due to narrow assumptions concerning what is meant by productive labour. Recent approaches which integrate intensification within broader concepts of innovation and flexibility in agricultural change are introduced. Next, I apply conventional intensification theory to the Dartmoor dataset, underlining some of the practical difficulties with this approach. An alternative perspective follows, that makes use of the concept of flexibility in agricultural change. Lastly, I return to the problem of the narrow definitions of productive 'work' encouraged by the labour theory of property. I review new theories of value that have the potential to develop existing theories of tenure along new trajectories.

4.1. The Labour Theory of Property and Intensification Theory

Property comes about, according to the labour theory, through productive labour, even if that labour is simply the labour of appropriation. The origins of this idea are present in English common law, but were developed influentially by Locke (see chapter 1). The labour theory supplied the first justification for unlimited individual accumulation (MacPherson, 1978). It is difficult to underestimate its significance in systems of thought over the last three centuries. In this section I discuss the development of the labour theory within theories of intensification, and the use of intensification in interpretations of land division. I discuss two types of problem in intensification theory - problems of identifying intensification correctly, and problems linked to the narrow definition of labour as productive 'work'. Lastly, I suggest an alternative approach to the dynamics of agricultural transformation.

Intensification and Prehistoric Land Division

Esther Boserup developed her theory of intensification citing the archaeological studies of ancient agriculture carried out by Danish archaeologist Gudmund Hatt (Hatt, 1949). Hatt's investigations into prehistoric agriculture

seemed to illustrate the labour theory in action; in prehistoric Jutland, he suggested, agriculture evolved from Neolithic shifting cultivation associated with cairnfields, towards permanent settlement associated with coaxial land division in the Iron Age (Hatt, 1931, 1949). Increasing investment of labour in cultivation led to sedentarisation, increased territoriality and thus to the individualised ownership of land that could be inherited within lineages (Hatt, 1939). Boserup developed an account that envisaged similar evolutionary trajectories in agriculture around the world (Boserup, 1965). She argued that the principal force in agricultural change was labour input. Her argument countered Malthus' notion that population always outstrips food production. Instead Boserup suggested that knowledgeable actors were capable of reflection and of changing their practices accordingly. However, the price of increased production was a life of increased toil. Boserup surmised that people would avoid intensive regimes unless absolutely forced to adopt them. Intensification would only occur when compelled by land scarcity, population pressure or social hierarchy (Boserup, 1965: 54). According to Boserup, agriculture progresses along an evolutionary trajectory from long fallow systems, to short fallow, and finally to annual or multi-cropping.

Boserup envisaged an evolution towards private property that fit both Locke's labour theory and associated classical theories of property (see also Hatt, 1931). In systems of forest fallow, all members of a 'tribe' had 'general rights' allowing them to farm somewhere within tribal territory, and had 'specific rights' over the plot of land they were cultivating at any particular time. Rights were 'inalienable' - only lost by being expelled from the group. With the change to short fallow agriculture land scarcity and increasing investment of labour meant cultivators became more territorial. They became permanent occupiers of bounded land plots exclusively owned by each family. Just as Locke had suggested property rights were linked to productive labour.

Boserup's theory has been widely adopted and extended as part of a raft of 'Neo-Boserupian' approaches. Subsequent revisions have opened up the range of possible causes for intensification. Brookfield argued that 'social production' might be just as important, if not more important, than production to meet subsistence needs. In Chimbu Province, (PNG), he found people investing labour in ways that were that were 'wildly uneconomic'. Huge efforts were expended raising pigs, which were not eaten by the producers but given away in feasts and ritualised exchanges. At any one time less than one fifth of the land was given over to foodstuffs eaten by the group itself (Brookfield, 1972: 37). 'Social production' Brookfield suggested, stimulated intensification just as much as population growth (Brookfield, 1972: 38). Following Brookfield, Neo-Boserupian approaches have steadily increased the catalogue of factors that might cause intensification. Such factors now include:

- production for feasting and gift exchange (Brookfield, 1972; Sahlins, 1972);
- production for growing markets (Netting, 1993: 288-294);
- risk reduction through storage (Winterhalder, 1990; Hegmon, 1989);
- and production to create solidarity among larger communities who can protect tenure 'security' (Adler, 1996).

In fact, approaches that base intensification on 'social' factors are now more common than those that emphasise population growth (Bayliss-Smith, 1999: 323).

Intensification theory has been important in interpretations of land division. Boundaries are widely seen as evidence for intensification in their own right, even without evidence for changes in fallowing period. Many accounts see land division as evidence for a shift from long fallow mobile agriculture to short fallow settled production (Welinder, 1975; Harding, 1989; Parker Pearson, 1993; Barrett, 1994). Whilst earlier accounts stressed population pressure or land scarcity, more recent narratives emphasise 'social' factors, especially social hierarchy. In North West Europe, Bronze Age land division is seen as reflecting intensification driven by the demands of elites (Bradley,

1977; Kristiansen, 1998). Recently discovered coaxial landscapes in the Thames Valley are interpreted as evidence for 'social intensification' generated by the demands of competing elites (Yates, 2001). Barrett interprets land division in Wessex, as evidence for intensification linked to sedentarisation, and the emergence of territorially 'fixed' identities (Barrett, 1994: 139-141). 'New forms of tenure' emerged whereby land 'passed from one generation to the next' (Barrett, 1999). However, as was noted in chapter two, the evidence for intensification in parts of Wessex is no longer sound (French et al., 2003). Intensification cannot be assumed without a firm evidential basis. Archaeologists need to be sure what exactly they mean when they use intensification theory. It is to this problem of identifying intensification that I now turn.

Problems of Intensification

The most common mistake made by archaeologists is to assume that intensification is equivalent to maximising production. Boserup's central thesis was that intensification was *not* increased productivity, but usually meant a fall in productivity, when productivity was measured per hour of labour imput (Boserup, 1965: 41). Increases in absolute productivity are achieved only at the price of increasing toil, so that as productivity increases, productivity per labour hour decreases after a certain level. Boserup's main target was development economics, where she sought to explain why it was entirely sensible for people in developing countries to resist the imposition of western-style cultivation by colonial governments and development agencies. Intensification is properly defined as the 'increase in the input of labour hours per unit area' (Stone, 1993). Identifying intensification requires that the analyst demonstrates an increase in productive labour.

Unfortunately, this is what most archaeological applications of intensification theory do not do. Intensification is a process, but rather than identifying this process most analysts look for *causes* of intensification (e.g. population growth, land scarcity, or expanding social networks), or indicators of a *state* of intensity (productive farming, many labour hours expended in agriculture) (Morrison, 1996, her emphasis). To identify intensification as a process the analyst must show increase in labour per unit area of land. However this is not at all easy to demonstrate archaeologically. Firstly it requires that the productive land area of an earlier and later system are known and compared. Secondly it requires that hours were expended in productive labour can be extracted and divided into land area. Archaeological data seldom allow productive land area and labour to be quantified with great certainty (Leach, 1999).

It is often assumed that land division demonstrates intensification by its very existence (Stone, 1994; Adler, 1996; Gilman, 1998; Pryor, 1998; Yates, 2001). Building land division is seen as productive work which must therefore entail labour imput. But this is not enough. What is required is an overall comparison of labour hours per unit area in agriculture before and after land division. It is entirely possible that the construction of land division might indicate a fall in labour input, rather than an increase, if, for example grazing was more extensive in the new landscape, or less labour was expending in watching and tending to livestock. Land division alone is not *primie facie* evidence for intensification, it may equally represent de-intensification or diversification (Leach, 1999).

Boserupian and Neo-Boserupian theories both define productive labour in very narrow terms. Indeed, if they did not intensification would become meaningless. Effectively the narrower the definition of productive 'work' the easier it is identify intensification. In both Locke's theory of property and intensification theory the model for productive work is plough cultivation. Some analysts, for example, argue that intensification is only shortening of the fallow period, and nothing more or less (Stone & Downum, 1999). Although Boserup argued that the fallow period could be either shortened or lengthened, (evolution could go backwards as well as forwards), her work was part of an evolutionary tradition in which cereal cultivation was associated with the rise of private property (Morrison, 1996; cf Stone & Downum, 1999). The emphasis on cultivation led intensification theory to underestimate the significance of livestock and agroforestry, and failed to engage with the dynamics of these important components of many farming systems (Brookfield, 2001).

The narrow definition of productive labour within the labour theory of property and intensification theory is rooted in Protestant moral values. The ideology of 'work' separates 'subsistence production' from supposedly non-productive activities like art or ritual. These 'uneconomic' practices may be explained as 'social production' but it is not always clear where to draw the lines between 'social' and 'subsistence' work. As Gardner puts it:

> *'If ... lowlands Telefol can only sustain themselves as a viable population by ensuring the co-operation of powerful high-altitude Telefols in raiding other groups for women and children and deterring those who would raid them, is the production that is necessary in order to sustain these relationships, social production or production of 'normal surpluses'?'*
> (Gardner, 2001: 202-3).

Effectively, and for most people, social production *is* subsistence production. Many analysts find the separation between productive and non-productive realms increasingly difficult to impose. Identification of intensification requires measurement of labour inputs neatly separated from other sorts of activity. But differentiating the productive from the non-productive introduces all kinds of assumptions that may not be appropriate to every case. The assumption that we known which activities properly constitute 'work' lies behind intensification theory, the labour theory of property and, more profoundly, the labour theory of value which underlies these ideas.

Alternative Approaches to Agricultural Change

Analysts of agricultural systems are increasingly finding alternatives to intensification. Studies of real world farming show that it invariably deploys a range of strategies – intensification, extensification and diversification – simultaneously rather than relying on only one at a time as Boserup's model would suggest (Boserup, 1965: Chapter 6; Leach, 1999). Critics argue that intensification fails to accommodate the multiple trajectories and multiple starting points that characterise agricultural life (Morrison, 1996). Concentrating only on one dynamic - the cultivation fallow period, reduces and distorts the multiple dynamics involved in most farming systems. Alternative approaches thus concentrate on the management of more than one dynamic.

Alternatives to intensification emphasise innovation and flexibility in agricultural systems (Brookfield, 1984; Adams & Mortimore, 1997; Brookfield, 2001). These recent studies suggest that the main agent of agricultural change is not necessarily ever-increasing labour for ever-decreasing returns. Instead agricultural change involves innovation within realms of flexibility constructed by society, environments and technologies (see Table 4.1). The main agent of change may not be labour but the ability to bring 'the factors of production together in new ways' (Brookfield, 2001: 189). These approaches point out that intensification is not necessarily the best nor the most likely response to the causes of intensification. There may even be a trade off between intensification and flexibility, since increasing labour inputs might impede the capacity to innovate, increasing risk (Brookfield, 2001: 189). Because theories based on innovation and flexibility do not require the measurement of labour input per unit area, they are much easier to apply in archaeological contexts.

4.1: Possible Realms of Flexibility in Agricultural systems (from Adams & Mortimore, 1997)

1.	Flexible use of grazing resources;
2.	land rotation;
3.	use of diverse crops;
4.	use of wild and 'off-farm' resources;
5.	deployment of labour;
6.	flexibility in livelihood strategies (off-farm incomes from trading and labouring elsewhere).

Another aspect of flexibility, involved in most of these realms, is the ability to transact tenure flexibly. The difficulties that arise when tenure is inflexible have been described by economists as constituting 'Tragedy of the Anti-Commons' type situations (Heller 1998, see chapter three). Increasingly economists are interested in 'sharing' as an aspect of flexibility in everyday economic life (Benkler, 2004). Studies suggest that 'sharing' will emerge when tenure of entities is bundled in ways that include spare capacity, and where tenure is broadly distributed among many parties (ibid.). The ability to transact and negotiate tenure - 'sharing' at times and not sharing at others - is an important realm of flexibility in agricultural systems, as in other areas of life.

In this section I described how the labour theory of property and its development within Boserup's theory of intensification influenced interpretations of prehistoric land division. I identified two main sets of problems. The first set comprises practical problems of application; intensification is very difficult to evaluate archaeologically. The second set are more theoretical, emerging from the narrow definition of production in the labour theory of property: The assumption is that productive labour resembles the kind of 'work' bought and sold in the classical era of capitalism. Lastly I reviewed some alternative approaches to the study of agricultural systems which may ameliorate some of the practical difficulties of applying intensification theory. In the next section I examine the extent to which evidence from Dartmoor can be interpreted as intensification. In this way, I illustrate the practical difficulties entailed in approaching prehistoric land division as intensification.

4.2. Assessing Intensification on Dartmoor

Verifying intensification requires that labour inputs be shown to increase per unit area of land. To demonstrate Boserupian intensification on Dartmoor one would need to know labour input per unit area in the landscape before the reaves, and to be able to compare it with labour input per unit area afterwards. In this section I explore the practical problems of applying intensification theory. I begin by looking at the evidence for Dartmoor landscapes 'before the reaves' - in the Late Neolithic and Early Bronze Age periods. I discuss the extent to which this evidence can be used to assess intensificatory narratives. I then discuss the processes involved in building reaves: How useful is it to represent these processes of construction as intensification? I conclude by returning to the problems of intensification and the labour theory of property.

Before the Reaves

Evidence for agricultural life on Dartmoor derives from three main sources; environmental sequences, the distributions of various kinds of architecture (stone circles, stone rows, cairns etc.) and gradual changes in the locations of lithics findspots. Existing accounts interpret these sources as indicating economy based around transhumance with group tenure of seasonally occupied pasturelands (Fleming, 1983: 200-2; 1988: 98-100; 1994b; Barnatt, 1998). Here I discuss each of these

sources before assessing their value to narratives of intensification.

Lithic Findspots and Occupation

The distribution of lithics offers some evidence for changes in the occupation of 'upland' and 'lowland' landscapes emerging gradually throughout later prehistory. The distribution of findspots compiled from Miles' review (Miles, 1976) and from Devon Sites and Monuments Record (SMR) (see 4.2 and Appendix L) suggests differences in the locations of findspots containing lithics of different dates – differences that have also been identified by previous studies (Miles, 1976; Gerrard, 1997a). At higher altitudes a large proportion of Neolithic and Bronze Age findspots are associated with Mesolithic material. However, at lower altitudes, findspots often contain only Neolithic and Early Bronze Age types. At least some of this distribution is probably due to the circumstances in which lithics are recovered. Many finds are made by ploughing, which is absent at higher altitudes. It seems likely that where ploughing is scarce only the larger scatters containing flints of a wider range of dates are likely to be found (see 4.3 and 4.4). Nonetheless, when viewed in association with palaeoenvironmental evidence and the emergence of new kinds of monument there may be some evidence here for changing patterns of occupation with a new spread of occupation across the lowlands from the Neolithic onwards (see Miles, 1976: 5).

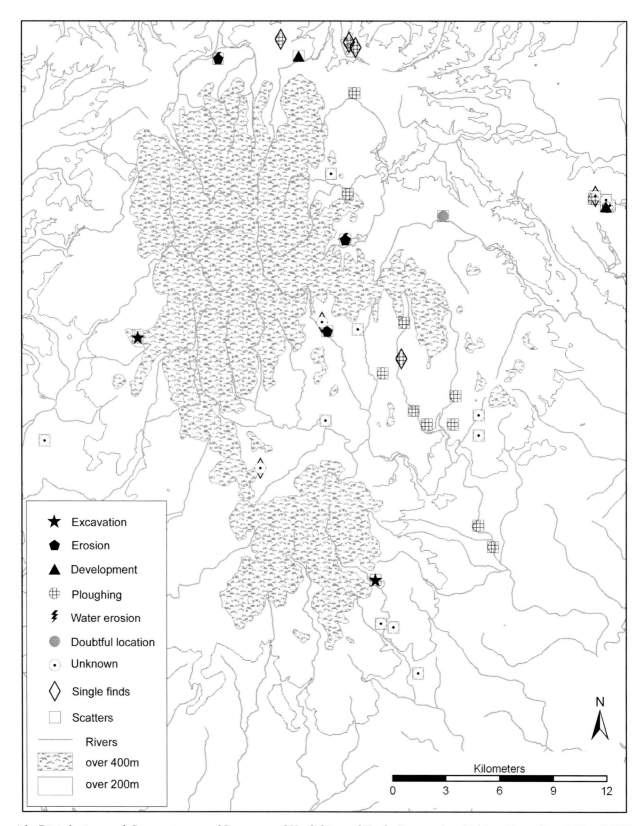

4.2: Distribution and Circumstances of Recovery of Neolithic and Early Bronze Age Lithics (Data from Miles (1976), Devon SMR and Digimap ©Crown Copyright/database right 2004. An Ordnance Survey/EDINA supplied service).

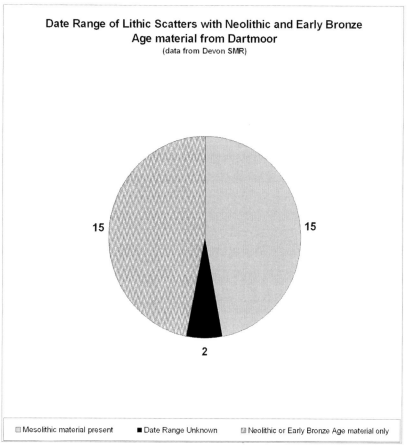

4.3: Dates of Lithics Found at each Findspot

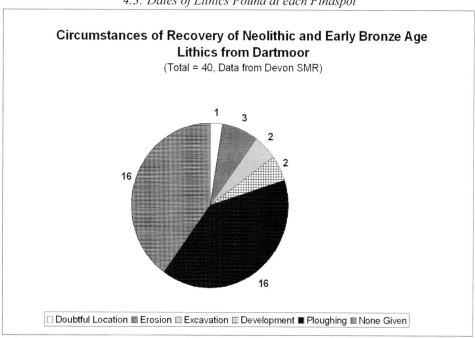

4.4: Circumstances of Recovery of Lithics

Analysis of the topographic locations of findspots offers some support for this idea, suggesting that, from the Neolithic onwards, a contrast began to emerge between upland and lowland occupation patterns. Findspots which contain both Mesolithic and later types tend to be found at higher altitudes but on gentler slopes (see 4.5 and 4.6). This would support the idea that in the later periods a greater range of places in the lowland landscape were inhabited, while, at higher elevations the most forgiving locations continued to be revisited (see Miles, 1976: 5). It seems likely that this reflects broader changes in economies and environments as lower altitudes become more focused on pastoral agricultural and tenure of pastures (Barnatt, 1989, 1998; Fleming, 1988, 1994b).

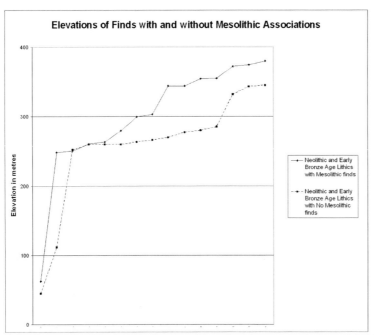

4.5: Elevations of Lithic Findspots with and without association with Mesolithic material

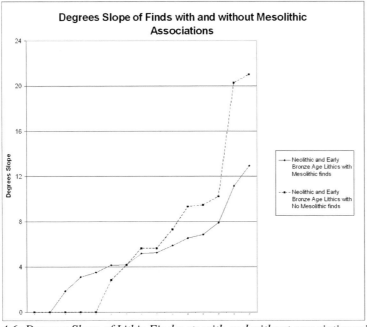

4.6: Degrees Slope of Lithic Findspots with and without association with Mesolithic material

Environmental Change

The main transformation in Dartmoor landscapes does not occur with the construction of land division, but actually takes place centuries before with the 'opening up of the upland landscape' in the Late Neolithic and Early Bronze Ages (Caseldine & Hatton, 1996: 59). Palaeoenvironmental evidence suggests large tracts of grassland were present several centuries before the current dates for reaves. Pollen sequences show that forest clearances became more frequent and widespread throughout the Neolithic, while weeds of intensive grazing including *Plantago lanceolata, Rumex,* and *Pteridium* begin to appear (Simmons, 1964, 1969; Balaam et al., 1982). However, the main period of clearance, seems to have occurred centuries before

coaxial landscapes were constructed at the end of the third and beginning of the second millennium BC (Caseldine & Maguire, 1981; Caseldine, 1999: 580). There was no sudden or significant reduction in arboreal pollen in diagrams at the time that reaves were built (Caseldine & Hatton, 1996) because there were extensive tracts without tree cover before land division came about (Balaam, 1982; Maguire et al., 1983). Confirming this picture, a study of atmospheric pollution across the region has revealed a peak in the centuries 2400 to 1780 BC. Pollution from heavy metals around this time was caused by soil disturbance from agriculture, burning of vegetation and possibly even mining for mineral deposits (West, 1997).

Once trees were cleared something prevented the woodland regenerating. Although the factors that maintained open grassland undoubtedly varied, peat formation and acidification were probably not major factors: In most places peat had not yet formed, and grasslands were for the most part good pastures with little evidence for decline in soil quality (Caseldine & Hatton, 1996: 60). Grasslands may have been opened by deliberate burning at times, as evidenced by atmospheric pollution studies (West, 1997). However, sustained grazing pressure appears to have been an important factor in keeping the grasslands free of mature woodland. Browsing by ungulates (deer and domesticated animals) has a major impact on woodland regeneration (Harmer & Kerr, 1995; Harmer & Gill, 2000). Environmental sequences are thus indirect evidence for an expansion in grazing pressure either by domesticated or non-domesticated ungulates (Caseldine & Hatton, 1996: 59). At the same time, an emphasis on these species would also supply the reason for the 'opening up' of the landscape: Clearing woodland is an effective way of reducing attacks on grazing animals, especially by wolves (Ostereng, 2004). The centuries before reaves were constructed thus involved changes in environments that point to changing relations between people and animals.

Bones do not survive on Dartmoor, and understanding human-animal relations therefore depends on indirect sources of evidence. Phosphate studies suggest that sheep/goat were an important presence in the landscape both before and after reaves were built (Maguire et al., 1983: 97; Ralph, 1982). After reaves were built there is some evidence for domesticated animals in the form of footprints preserved alongside the Saddlesborough reave. These prints were almost all of domestic stock - mainly cattle and goat/sheep, but also some horses (Balaam et al., 1982: 272). Evidence from phosphate surveys supports the idea that sheep/goat and cattle were the dominant species within the reave landscapes, and probably also before reaves were built (Ralph, 1982). It thus appears that the Late Neolithic and Early Bronze Ages were marked by an increasing emphasis on grazing domestic stock.

Monuments and Tenure

Accounts of 'pre-reave' landscapes generally assume that reaves are an exclusively Middle Bronze Age phenomenon, to be separated from the earlier 'ceremonial' landscape. However, there are good reasons to be cautious about this distinction. In chapter two I argued, on the basis of recalibrated C14 dates, that reave construction begins c1850 BC, and could well begin even earlier (see Gibson, 1992). Some ceremonial sites could well have been built at the same time as reaves were being constructed. The notion that these sites are definitively 'before the reaves' thus awaits revision from future work. That said there are a number of studies which argue that the changing environments and economies of the Late Neolithic and Early Bronze Age are reflected in the distributions of ceremonial monuments. Several studies have argued that the spacing

of 'group foci' including ceremonial complexes of stone rows, cairns and stone circles indicates a series of bounded territories distributed in the valleys surrounding the higher moors (O'Neill, 1982; Barnatt, 1989; Fleming, 1994b). At the same time movement around and between these territories is suggested by the ways that sites like stone rows form 'axes of movement' across the landscape (Barnatt, 1998). The kinds of movements envisaged fit expectations of traditional pastoral regimes with tenure over known blocks of terrain, and seasonal movements between them (Fleming, 1979).

In conclusion then evidence for occupation 'before the reaves' suggests:

- Gradual emergence of a contrast between upland and lowland occupation (possibly evidenced by distribution of lithics);
- Increased emphasis on domesticated stock, accompanied by important environmental changes and the 'opening up' of extensive grasslands before c2000 BC (Caseldine & Hatton, 1994);
- Emergence of distinct pastures possibly associated with stone rows and other ceremonial sites and the identity of distinct groups of people.

It would not be impossible to approach this evidence using a narrative of intensification. However it would be more difficult to present a firm basis from which to verify the nature of intensification. As has already been pointed out verifying intensification requires that labour inputs be shown to increase per unit area. But it is very difficult to evaluate what 'unit area' might be in this context. One possibility would be to use Barnatt's 'group territories' in this way. However, we then face the problem of differentiating sites that are before the reaves from those that are contemporary with land division. Probably the evidence that is most amenable to intensification theory here is that for increased clearance associated with greater grazing pressure. Here there does seem to have been a major transformation in the character of landscapes and land uses.

Intensification and Reave Construction

Does the construction of reaves represent an increase in labour inputs per unit area of land? Perhaps, but this is far from certain. It is possible to make general estimates and approximations, but these tend to beg more questions than they answer. For example, it is possible to estimate how many labour hours might be involved in building land division on Dartmoor: Experimental reconstruction shows that 2.3 metres of reave can be constructed per hour (1.15m per person) (see 4.7). However, this experiment did not involve digging for stone. Obtaining stone may have been relatively straightforward where hillsides were strewn with boulders. Nonetheless it would probably have taken at least as long as building the wall. Therefore it seems sensible to halve the time and allow circa one metre of wall per one hour for two wallers or c.0.5m per person. This calculation can be coupled with Butler's estimates of population on Dartmoor to produce estimates of labour hours per person (see table 4.8). The surprising results of this exercise are that Butler's population could have constructed all land division on Dartmoor in less than two months.

4.7: Reconstruction of a reave on Shovel Down. (Following excavations at Shovel Down a reave was reconstructed as originally built by two professional Dartmoor wallers (see Brück et al., 2005).Photography by Fay Stevens

4.8 Estimates of Labour Hours involved in Reave Construction

	Total Length of Reaves	Total Labour Hours	Butler's Population Estimate (Butler, 1997a: 141)	Labour hours per person	Labour Days (5 hr day)
All Reaves	802121m	1,604,242 hrs	6029 people	266 hrs	53 days
Coaxial Reaves	331410m	662,820 hrs	1309 people	506 hours	101 days

The usefulness of this kind of exercise is questionable. Population estimates are notoriously difficult to determine archaeologically and experimental reconstruction is fraught with problems. Building projects in real world agricultural societies are usually enmeshed in a range of other activities. In a pre-monetary society it seem very unlikely that labour would have been the kind of concentrated 'work' or socially undifferentiated labour that this calculation implies - This kind of 'work' is a peculiar characteristic of capitalist societies (Marx, 1976: chapter one). It is far from certain how long construction of reaves actually took, but available dates suggest it took many centuries rather than days or years (see chapter two). It seems likely that reave construction involves numerous projects spaced over as much as a thousand years or more. It is thus difficult to find a coherent horizon before and after reaves to compare.

Previous interpretations have seen the construction of land division as, in itself, evidence for intensification. However, to demonstrate this point, archaeologists need to show that labour investment represented an increase per unit area on that which existed before land division. This is difficult to achieve with current evidence from Dartmoor. Although at a gross level building land division clearly represents some kind of labour input, it is difficult to prove that this input is greater than that involved in, say clearing trees, maintaining herds, moving between pastures or building ceremonial sites before the reaves. Gauging the differences between before and after the reaves requires that 'labour' be defined in narrow terms – as subsistence practices, rather than, say ceremonial activities, only in this way can reave building be represented as a development separate from building cairns and stone rows.

In this section I assessed the use of intensification theory to approach land division on Dartmoor. I found that the major transformation in environments actually preceded the dates of excavated reaves by several centuries, taking place in the Late Neolithic and Early Bronze Age, when large tracts of grassland were kept open by clearance and grazing pressure. Assessing the labour hours involved in reave construction yielded figures that were difficult to evaluate. It proved impossible to demonstrate that land division represented increase in labour inputs per unit area (intensification). My efforts to implement intensification theory here ultimately underline the practical problems involved in applying intensification to archaeological datasets. In the next section I turn to alternative ways of describing changes in agricultural systems. I approach coaxial landscapes on Dartmoor using the concept of flexibility introduced by analysis of agricultural systems as an alternative to intensification theory. How might this kind of approach develop narratives of intensification?

4.3 Flexibility, Agriculture and Land Division

Recent approaches integrate intensification within broader understandings of agricultural change. These studies emphasise innovation and the study of flexibility in agriculture (Adams & Mortimore, 1997; Brookfield, 2001). In many agricultural systems land division increases flexibility; allowing for intensification, extensification or diversification, or all three simultaneously (Leach, 1999). Land division enables land rotation, strategic planning of grazing regimes, increased control of breeding, and opportunities to experiment with new animals and plants (Morrison, 1996). In this section I use this concept of flexibility to approach Dartmoor land division. I identify the realms of flexibility that are likely to have been important in Early-Middle Bronze Age agriculture. I then analyse coaxial landscapes to assess how land division may have improved flexibility in pasture rotation and use of grazing resources. Lastly I interpret how these agricultural regimes may have promoted flexibility in tenure.

Identifying Realms of Flexibility

Evidence reviewed here and in chapter three suggests that farming Bronze Age Dartmoor involved raising livestock; there is much less evidence for cereal growing. Phosphate surveys suggest that sheep/goat were important, while footprints preserved at Shaugh Moor show cattle were also present. This picture is supported by evidence from Middle Bronze Age sites elsewhere in southern Britain which have bone assemblages. On these sites bones are overwhelmingly of sheep/goat and cattle, while other species, like deer and pig are rare (Legge in Barrett et al., 1991: 203; Hambleton, 1999). Within this kind of agriculture the following 'realms of flexibility' (see 4.1 above) might be particularly important:

i)   land rotation;
ii)   flexible use of grazing resources;
iii)   use of diverse crops;
iv)   deployment of labour.

As discussed above, flexibility of tenure is an important aspect within these realms of flexibility. Each of these realms supplies a perspective on agriculture in Bronze Age Dartmoor.

Land Rotation and Flexible use of Grazing

In livestock farming, one of the principle methods of increasing productivity is to use land *extensively* rather than intensifying by rotating herds between pastures (Leach, 1999). Land rotation benefits farmers because it allows pastures to be fallowed. Vegetation has a chance to recover from grazing pressure. When grazing is concentrated within a system of bounded fields, fallowing is important in breaking the cycle of infestations and diseases (Pryor, 1998). The most extensive form of land rotation comprises nomadic pastoralism, but land rotation is also practiced at a localised level, with animals periodically moving between permanent enclosures. On Dartmoor most commentators propose that farming life was structured around seasonal land rotation and transhumance (Fleming, 1979, 1988, 1994b; Gerrard, 1997a; Barnatt, 1998). Pounds and unenclosed settlements on the higher ground are seen as summer grazing settlements, with lower lying settlements occupied all year round (Fleming, 1988, 1994b). Sheep come on heat in late autumn and penning animals around houses at this time would allow breeding control and extra care of pregnant animals over the winter (Hambleton, 1999: 70).

Evidence from faunal remains elsewhere in southern Britain suggests similar patterns of regional land rotation. Where bone is preserved, assemblages show that birth generally occurred away from settlement sites. Slaughter, however, took place close by. This suggests that lambing took place in seasonally occupied pasturelands away from settlements (Hambleton, 1999). At these sites there was a single lambing each spring, and lambs were kept in the year-round settlements over their first winter. A seasonal cull seems to be usual in the autumn, with additional animals slaughtered intermittently over winter.

The construction of land division can have both positive and negative effects on the productivity of grazing land. Grazing introduces selection pressures onto vegetation (Bailey et al., 1996). Left to their own devices herbivores graze down the best vegetation and then move onto pastures new, leaving the less palatable fodder to thrive. In these circumstances grazing selects against good fodder and for bad. However, where animals are confined within enclosures they will graze on bad as well as the good fodder. Enclosures can encourage progressively better quality fodder by 'grazing out' poorer vegetation and spreading manure. To achieve this kind of 'positive feedback' enclosures must parcel good and bad grazing patches together. If enclosures parcel good and bad vegetation separately they will instead cause progressive deterioration and 'negative feedback' on overall grazing quality (Bailey et al., 1996). Knowledge of the effects of land rotation on pasturelands is not confined to modern farmers, but is also widespread within small scale farming systems worldwide (Abu-Rabia, 1994).

Use of Diverse Crops
One important source of variability in pastoral farming is in the proportion of sheep/goat and cattle grazed. It is likely that proportions of sheep/goat to cattle varied across the Dartmoor landscape. Cattle will not graze on slopes of over 10% and they require watering regularly (Bailey et al., 1996). Sheep/goat are more adaptable and hardy. Cattle require good quality pasture, ready access to water, and prefer gentler climates, while sheep can tolerate poorer quality pasture. Susceptibility to foot rot and liver fluke means that sheep are better suited to higher well drained land (Hambleton, 1999: 42). Across southern Britain during the Bronze Age, a lower proportion of cattle bones is common where sites are further from water sources (Maltby in Gingell, 1992: 141). Survey of faunal assemblages reveals that Bronze Age sites with peat in their vicinity tend to have a very high percentage of sheep/goat bones (Hambleton, 1999: 48). On Dartmoor we might expect that cattle would tend to be grazed in damp valleys with sheep on the higher ground (although not on blanket bog).

Another realm of flexibility is in the extent to which animals gave meat or dairy produce. Cattle dairying was important at many Bronze Age sites in southern Britain (Legge in Barrett et al., 1991: 205; Maltby in Gingell, 1992: 142) and sheep/goat dairying also took place at many sites including on the field systems of the Marlborough Downs (Maltby in Gingell, 1992: 142). Growing meat requires much more pasture than dairy, because males are kept to maturity. Commentators suggest that dairy farming is more likely where pasture is scarce, whereas meat is preferred where pasture is plentiful (Maltby in Gingell, 1992: 141-2). The sheer abundance of grazing on Dartmoor might imply that more meat was grown here, in contrast to areas further east.

Deployment of Labour and Flexible use of Grazing
In pastoral agriculture shepherding allows some scope for flexibility. Given the presence of predators (including wolves) on Dartmoor, the watching of animals would have been 'a necessity' (Fleming, 1978b: 108). Shepherding, both with or without reaves, would be 'consonant with traditional practice in the British highland zone' (ibid.). Fleming suggests that Dartmoor communities used communal shepherds and shared labour in ways that bound communities together (Fleming, 1985b). Studies of traditional shepherding suggest herding would have required only small numbers of people most of the time, but that some tasks would have benefited from larger groups, possibly accompanied by dogs (Pryor, 1998).

Shepherding is a knowledgeable practice based on familiarity with herds and pasturelands. Shepherding practices demonstrate that pastoral farming is not just a matter of humans imposing their will on 'nature'. Growing animals involves understanding and working with the ways that animals inhabit terrain – what Lorimer calls 'animal geographies' (Lorimer, 2004). Studies show that sheep, goats and cattle produce 'home ranges' comprising 'camps' and paths between them (Jewell & Grubb, 1974; Ralph, 1982). Cattle have well-developed long term spatial memories, remembering details of terrain for at least twenty days, probably more (Bailey et al., 1996). Even where there is no human involvement, Soay sheep live within consistent, seasonally adjusted home ranges (Jewell & Grubb, 1974). In the absence of humanly constructed boundaries Soay create 'boundaries' for themselves that they routinely observe as the peripheries of their home ranges (Jewell & Grubb, 1974: 179). Such natural 'boundaries' include breaks of slope, boulder streams and watercourses. The way that animals make attachments to places is known as 'hefting' (Gray, 1999). Engaging with the ways that animals 'heft' would have been an important aspect of shepherding, and would have influenced how humans inhabited and constructed landscapes.

The architecture of reaves modified the way animals produced camps and home ranges. Reaves seldom represent an entirely artificial pattern imposed on 'nature'. More often, reaves elaborate on existing topography (see Fox's account of the Grippers Hill enclosures, Fox, 1955). In many part of Dartmoor reaves were combined with topography and watercourses to define large 'blocks' of pastureland. These large blocks of pasture are common to both coaxial and non-coaxial landscapes (see appendix M). For shepherds, visibility of camps and home ranges preferred by animals would have been crucial (Gray, 1999; Lorimer, 2004). It is likely that stock visibility influenced where and how reaves were built (Pryor, 1998; Gray, 1999). The larger 'blocks' defined by reaves often comprise areas of good visibility, and exclude areas of poor visibility. This morphology would have allowed herders to control animals without having to retrieve them from steep, awkward terrain.

Land Rotation and Coaxial Landscapes

Palaeoenvironmental data from coaxial landscapes offer some evidence that these landscapes involved localised pasture rotation. Evidence indicates that grazing pressure varied within and between coaxial landscapes: At Holne Moor grazing may have taken place on a 'permanent or near permanent basis'. *Plantago lanceolata* (here described as a 'pastoral indicator') comprised 5-10% of the pollen sums (Maguire et al., 1983: 96-7). Phosphate studies showed that some fields were 'intensively' grazed by sheep (Ralph, 1982). However, there is evidence that some land was fallowed; values of *Taraxacum* type pollen around a timber house at Holne Moor showed it was built on fallow land (Maguire et al., 1983: 92). All soil pollen samples showed high levels of *Pteridium* (bracken) indicating that land which was either fallow or not grazed intensively was a significant component of the pollen catchments across the area (Maguire et al., 1983: 92).Likewise on Wotter Common a 'grazing pressure' was found 'that has only been exceeded in very recent times' (Beckett in Smith et al., 1981: 262). Nonetheless phosphate studies suggested that soil nutrients had been replenished by fallowing (MacPhail et al, (microfiche) in Balaam et al., 1982).

Palaeoenvironmental information is supported by the distinctive layouts of coaxial landscapes. Strips running against the contour group together a variety of habitats spread between different elevations. This kind of land parcelling could have created 'positive feedback' in the selection pressures operating on vegetation. Over time,

pasture rotation could have improved grazing-quality within the enclosures. It is possible to compare this characteristic of coaxial enclosures with other kinds of layout. Coaxial enclosures should contain a greater range of elevations than enclosures in non-coaxial landscapes, or random land parcels.

Elevation ranges of 232 coaxial enclosures were compared those of a random sample and of a non-coaxial area (see 4.16). The sample of coaxial enclosures was drawn from nine coaxial landscapes. Within these landscape were a number of small enclosures (less than 1.5 acres) which may not have been regularly used for grazing but seem more likely to have been enclosures for buildings, animal pens or yard areas. To exclude enclosures of this kind, the sample only used enclosures greater than 1.5 acres. Finding an appropriate non-coaxial landscape was difficult. Aggregate land division enclosures are often only partially bounded by reaves so their original extent is difficult to measure. The well preserved landscape at Riddon Ridge was selected (see 4.16). The random sample was obtained by from a tessellating surface of shapes that were randomly aligned (cf Cederholm, 2005). Shapes had an edge length based on the approximate average length of the coaxial sample (c200m). The surface was then cropped to select only those shapes that fell within areas with environmental characteristics preferred by coaxial builders (see chapter three). From this constrained population 232 random shapes were selected using a random point generator. The resulting sample of randomly aligned and randomly generated quadrangles is shown in 4.10.

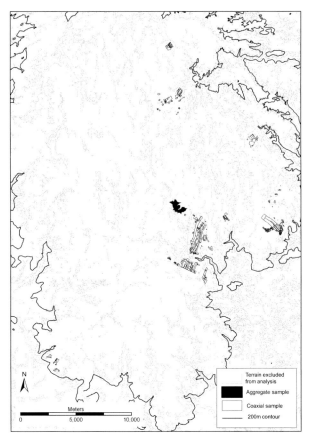

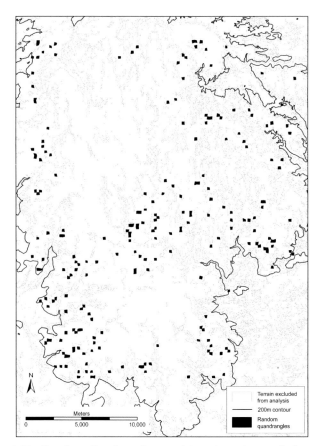

4.9: Enclosures used in orientation and slope analysis (Data from Butler 1997, Unpub and Digimap ©Crown Copyright/database right 2004. An Ordnance Survey/EDINA supplied service)

4.10: Random Quadrangles used in orientation and slope analysis (Data from Butler 1997, Unpub and Digimap ©Crown Copyright/database right 2004. An Ordnance Survey/EDINA supplied service)

Within each of these samples elevation ranges were measured. Elevation range was then divided by the area of each enclosure to prevent the different sizes of enclosures affecting the results. The findings are graphed in 4.11 and the frequencies of coaxial and random samples are cumulated in 4.12. Comparing the random quadrangles with the coaxial enclosures shows that the

coaxial sample has greater elevation range. A t-test confirms that there is less than 1% probability that the random sample mean elevation matches the coaxial distribution. A small-sample t-test (see Hutchinson, 1993: 122-4) showed that the aggregate sample was not a match for the mean of the coaxial sample although the difference was less decisive than with the random sample.

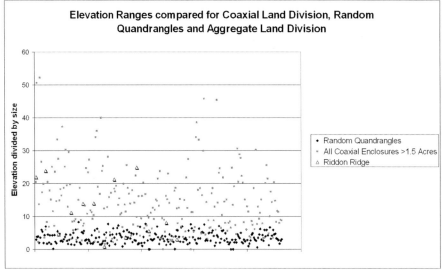

4.11: Elevation Ranges of enclosures in each sample compared

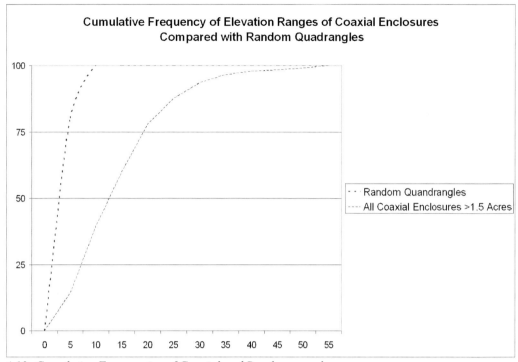

4.12: Cumulative Frequencies of Coaxial and Random samples

Coaxial layout, it has sometimes been claimed, 'does not consider topography and specific local conditions' (Earle, 2002: 346). Actually coaxial layouts show the builders to have been highly responsive to topography. What Fleming calls the 'terrain oblivious' character of these landscapes does not mean that terrain was neglected by builders, but that the landscapes are laid out so that the main axis of the system runs against the contour (Fleming, 1988). Here, I have suggested that this layout might have enhanced the flexible use of grazing. Enclosures in coaxial land division are more likely to group together both good and bad fodder than other kinds of enclosure. Within a rotation and fallowing regime this kind of parcelling could lead to gradual increases in pasture quality, or at the very least, would avoid the progressive deterioration of areas which lacks this kind of parcelling. It is very possible that this kind of landscape involved more intensive grazing. However, it could also have allowed for diversification and even extensification at times. Rather than emphasising only the intensificatory possibilities of these landscapes, it is important to keep in sight the capacity for flexibility they introduced. Unlike earlier landscapes, coaxial layouts could have increased flexibility at the level of the small group or 'household' increasing their ability to make decisions about management of their own animals.

Flexibility and Tenure

Flexibility within pasturing regimes is enhanced when animals can be managed either collectively or separately, and can be redistributed between pastures. The layout and wide range of enclosure sizes within coaxial landscapes suggests that access to pastures was flexibly negotiated.

Large 'blocks' of pasture - both within coaxial landscapes and in other areas – within these landscapes are interpreted as commoning areas (Fleming, 1983, 1985b). Such larger enclosures tend to be located at higher elevations (see 4.14) comprising areas of grassland that would have been better used more extensively. This supports their interpretation as shared-access pastures. The range of sizes of enclosures within coaxial landscapes and the likelihood of shared access to at least some of the largest, suggests that grazing systems included spare capacity within enclosures. This spare capacity suggests tenure may have involved the loaning, sharing, and transacting of access to grazing and shepherding resources.

The kinds of flexibility discussed here for Bronze Age Dartmoor are premised on the ability of farmers to negotiate access to grazing and exclusions over enclosures at various times. Innovation in tenure may have been the fundamental innovation upon which all the other realms of flexibility described here depended. Forms of tenure were required that were communal *and* individual, sometimes exclusive and at other times inclusive. Flexible tenure is suggested by the layout and sizes of coaxial enclosures, by evidence for land rotation and for seasonal transhumance. Shepherding arrangements and access to pastures were probably subject to negotiation and transaction within and between groups. People and groups may have maintained personal connections with and interests in animals that were 'theirs' but this would have also necessitated contributions to the upkeep of shared resources. This kind of tenure allowed groups to innovate without excluding them from the benefits and obligations of wider communities.

85

4.13: Possible Commons within Coaxial Landscapes

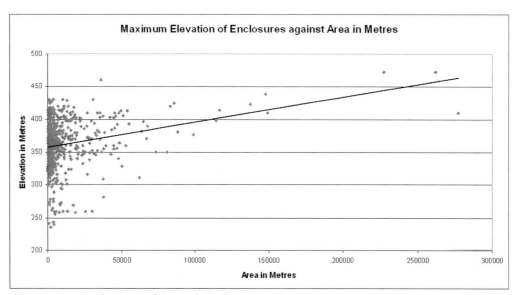

4.14: Maximum Elevation of Coaxial Enclosures against area

I identified several realms of flexibility in Bronze Age Agriculture on Dartmoor in this section. I suggested how land division on Dartmoor might have allowed greater flexibility in certain areas, particularly in the more flexible use of grazing resources, land rotation, and deployment of labour. Coaxial land division, I suggested might be linked to localised land rotation systems, which could have improved the productivity of pastures over time. By stressing flexibility rather than intensification, I have suggested that the dynamics of agriculture within these landscapes were not set on an evolutionary trajectory towards cultivation and private ownership, but could have included extensification and diversification at times, as well as intensification. Flexibility of tenure, involving both inclusive and exclusive arrangements would have been required for these kinds of agricultural strategies.

4.4 Production, Value, and the Labour Theory

The labour theory of property depends on assumptions concerning what does and doesn't constitute 'labour'. Locke formulated an image of labour based on the enclosing and cultivation of land. Subsequently, the development of intensification theory led to labour being read very narrowly, as subsistence agriculture, principally cultivation. Property, according to these theories, should be produced by 'productive' work. But the narrow definition of what is productive means that much evidence from real-world tenure systems contradicts the theory. In the real world - as Veblen archly observed more than a century ago - the distribution of property is seldom correlated with hard toil: people who own a great deal of property don't seem to do that much more work than the rest of us (Veblen, 1898). It has given the classical economists 'no end of bother', Veblen commented, 'to explain how the capitalist is the 'producer' of the goods that pass into his possession, and how it is true that the labourer gets what he produces' (Veblen, 1898: 352). Looking towards economies organised along different lines (in 'small-scale' societies) it is clear that production and property here is no better a reflection of the labour theory (Graeber, 2001: 38). Ethnographies supply numerous examples of tenure transmitted in ways that have little to do with 'labour'. In New Ireland, for example, tenurial arrangements are organised around people's capacity to memorise carved motifs displayed on effigies of dead ancestors (Kuchler, 2002). It is difficult to fit this kind of tenure into the conventional labour theory. In most cases tenure has little to do with how much work an individual puts into producing goods for their own use (see Malinowski, 1921). Instead tenure emerges from kinship and lifecycle events, initiations, exchanges and ritualised performances that effect changes in identity and personhood. The application of approaches that use the labour theory of property and intensification theory is limited because of the narrow definition of productive labour which they employ.

In this section I develop the labour theory of property using a theoretical framework that overcomes narrow assumptions concerning what is productive. In the first part of this section I outline Graeber's work on production and value which radically broadens conventional definitions of productive action. In the second part I demonstrate how this approach might contribute to developing existing theories of tenure in archaeology.

Value and Production in the Labour Theory

It is generally observed that 'the sorts of activities that 'we' would define as economic' (i.e. subsistence production) are by no means those on which the peoples of such societies 'spend the greater part of their time or creative energies' (Graeber, 2005b: 38; see also Malinowski, 1920; Sahlins, 1972). Far from being engaged in a relentless struggle to increase agricultural production, the people of stateless societies overwhelmingly direct their creative energies towards the socialization of new kinds of persons. Intensification theory is thus asking the wrong question; the question is not a matter of how labour is directed towards agriculture by the urge to acquire more, but of how the activities of shaping people become embodied in value-forms, some of which may be produced through agriculture, others through other kinds of activity. To understand these kinds of activity it is necessary to broaden out the conventional view of what is 'productive'.

Recently Graeber has produced a body of work that rethinks the labour theory of value (Graeber, 2001, 2005b, 2006; Sutton, 2004). The labour theory of value is based on the idea that 'productive' work produces the value of objects, just as the labour theory of property is based on the idea that productive work produces property rights. In order to produce what he calls 'an anthropological' theory of value, Graeber begins by re-envisioning production in a much wider sense than is conventionally allowed in the labour theory. When actors engage in projects of action they not only fulfill perceived needs, they also recreate the wider network within which action takes place, as well as reflexively reshaping and redefining their identities, and producing new needs to be fulfilled. What is entailed in productive action is so encompassing that it is almost impossible for any actor to envisage the whole process completely. Actors acquire a 'partial consciousness' of the implications of productive activities through socialization. Social learning allows actors to become aware of and coordinate different perspectives. But to understand productive action, Graeber argues, 'one would have to be able to coordinate the subjective points of view of everyone involved to see how they all fit together ... or don't' – an impossible task (Graeber, 2005b: 34). In place of a full awareness of what is productive, Graeber argues, value emerges as a way that actors can make sense of the importance of actions.

Value, for Graeber, is a process. It is the way that 'people assess the importance of what they ... do as they are doing it'; the way that they 'see their own activity as meaningful' (Graeber, 2001: 47). To be meaningful, Graeber argues, activities must be coordinated by what he calls 'social totalities'. These totalities are, of course, themselves constructed through projects of meaningfully directed action. To understand the role of these totalities Graeber points to the disjunction between the moments and activities where value is produced, and the moments in which it comes to be realized within a 'totality'. The importance of actions must be integrated within a 'social whole' in a public context. Value must be realized through totalities, which, in some instances, include socio-technical equipment able to measure and produce particular value-forms. Realization occurs when value is embodied in what Graeber calls 'concrete circulating media of value'. Such media are sometimes objects, but are also 'intangibles' (performances, knowledge, rumours and reputations). Value forms all have the propensity to act as both media of value (allowing value to be realized in a wider sphere) and measures of value (through their presence/absence, ranking and proportion). The propensity to fulfill both these roles often leads value forms to be seen as 'ends in themselves'. However, ultimately, value is nothing more than the reflected importance of actions. It is 'the false coin of our own dreams' (Graeber, 2001).

Graeber's theory makes sense of actions that conventional economic thought leaves unexplained. Consider the example with which I opened this chapter – East New Britain, where people are in the habit of exchanging identical objects. This activity seems pointless because neither party comes away with any profit. However, what if value is seen as the importance of the act of giving? From this perspective the customs of the people of New Britain make much more sense. Value does not inhere in the objects used in the transaction, but in the act itself. It is the importance of action that is significant, so that, 'if one gives another person food and receives a shell in return, it is not the value of the food that returns to one in the form of the shell but rather the value of the act of giving it' (Graeber, 2001: 45). The meaning of actions like these tends to emerge from what Graeber calls 'theories of creativity' that ramify more widely. For example, on the island of Gawa, (PNG), the act of giving food is meaningful in itself just as in East New Britain. Munn's work showed how the act of giving food is the most elemental level of a wider value system on Gawa. Giving food makes sense as part of a 'value-template' (a 'theory of creativity') that is also found at the highest level of the economy in kula exchange. Food gifts not only materially provision kula (e.g. by supporting those who manufacture canoes), but also provide a 'model in miniature' of actions involved in kula expeditions. Canoes or kula shells at the highest level of exchange are:

> 'value-forms of food transmission (not simply of the medium food) which exhibit the food donor's capacity to transform intersubjective space-time to a more encompassing expansive level'
> (Munn, 1986: 148 emphasis removed).

The importance of actions reflects not only their local meaning but can also 'translocate' within a much wider landscape of significance.

What effect does Graeber's work have on how we understand what is 'productive'? The impact of his work is to underline how activities that are not conventionally understood as 'economic' are still productive. Subsistence agriculture is not categorically different to other kinds of activity; it is not more 'productive' than, for example, singing and dancing or making artworks. Radically broadening conventional assumptions

concerning productive 'labour' Graeber's theory allows a much wider range of evidence to be included in the labour theories of value and property. Because Graeber emphasizes projects of value as *meaningful* action his theory usefully unites 'value' and 'values' (see Sutton, 2004). Traditionally value has been divided into:

i)   its 'economic' sense (as what others are willing to give up for something);
ii) its structural-linguistic sense (as 'meaningful difference' within a social code) and;
iii) 'values' in the sociological sense as 'what is ultimately good, proper or desirable' (Graeber, 2001: 1).

Graeber shows how value in all these senses can be integrated and understood within a labour theory – but only when all the dimensions of 'labour' are embraced by that theory.

Graeber's 'anthropological' theory allows 'small-scale' societies to be viewed within the same analytical frame as 'western' societies. The theory can be applied to gift *or* commodity exchange, 'embedded' *or* 'disembedded' economies. Commodity exchange becomes just other instances of valuing, not an entirely different order of economic life. As Graeber points out, although capitalist societies usually see value as circulating in commodities, value may also circulate in other ways; even within capitalist societies (see Carrier, 1995). As well as circulating value in commodities other forms of circulation are possible. For example 'one might be able to realize the value of an heirloom shell only by giving it away' or 'by displaying it in a public ritual' or 'by hiding it somewhere (but making sure others know that you have done this)' (Graeber, 2005b: 51). It also becomes possible to consider a range of ways in which different sorts of value might circulate simultaneously, so that, for example, gift exchange may exist alongside and interact with commodity exchange

Developing Theories of Tenure

Graeber's work suggests ways in which the conventional labour theories of value and property can be moved on. Value and tenure are intimately connected: as Verdery points out 'no one wants to establish property relations with other people over something they do not value' (Verdery, 2003: 21). Hirsch has recently advocated an approach to landscapes that shows how an 'anthropological' theory of value can be used to interpret land division. He approaches the construction of landscapes as producing both environments and economies. Landscapes or environments are 'created artefacts' through which people realize values (Hirsch, 2004a). The values concerned include both economic 'value' and moral 'values'. Just like artefacts, environments may act as media of value that allow people to assess their relations with one another. For the value of landscapes to be realized they must be constructed appropriately. Hirsch uses the example of a neatly laid out yam farm, which is described as 'gladdening the heart' and as evidence of 'living well'. 'It is this quality or quantitative value of 'living well,' Hirsch observes, 'that is as much the product of the appropriate allotment of land, as the land arranged and perceived as an appropriate landscape' (Hirsch, 2004a: 436-7). The construction of landscape takes place through projects of value, which create valued artefacts, which are then experienced in terms of values. The productive activities of learning place, maintaining cleared land and access to water and constructing boundaries build both environments and economies simultaneously. In pastoral landscapes, Hirsch observes, shepherds produce and value herds economically, but the value realised in animals 'cannot be separated from the landscape and places formed' (Hirsch, 2004a: 447). In another example, the construction of dry-stone walls in contemporary North Yorkshire realises values of 'neighbourliness', embodying transactions of materials, tools and labour (Phillips, 1984). Hirsch's approach, demonstrates how theory of value might contribute to archaeologies of tenure.

In archaeology, intensification theory has encouraged approaches that evaluate agricultural efficiency in terms of productivity or labour hours per unit area. The 'subsistence economy' is seen as the economic 'base'. Activities that materially provision people are separated from superstructural and ideological practices (like art or ritual performance). Archaeologies of tenure, even when they do not explicitly evoke Boserupian intensification, continue to relate tenure more closely to agricultural practices than to other activities: Land tenure frequently crops up when archaeologists discuss land use, stone clearance or boundary construction, but relatively seldom in discussions of transactions or long distance communications. (The exception is in archaeologies of mortuary practices which are often interpreted using notions of land inheritance). In recent years archaeologists have begun to break down the distinction

between 'subsistence' and 'ritual' activities, showing how agricultural practices have ritual and political as well as economic dimensions (Sherratt, 1999; Brück, 1999c; Williams, 2003; Bradley, 2005). However they have little explored the differences broadening the significance of agricultural activities makes to the labour theory of property. If 'labour' has more than conventional 'economic' significance then we can no longer suppose that labour is self-interestedly disposed towards creating 'property'. Instead agricultural activities might involve all kinds of theories of creativity. Projects of value might be realized in many different forms – not only in tenure. Furthermore there is nothing that necessarily prioritizes agricultural activity among many other varieties of 'productive' actions which might conceivably play a part in tenure. Tenure is just as likely to emerge from performances, exchanges and art practices as from agricultural practice. I do not mean to imply that agricultural activities are not at all important to archaeologies of tenure. But I do argue that activities are not necessarily more important because they are agricultural or 'economic'. Activities like herding and care of stock are important, but these actions are 'productive' only because they contribute to the socialization (feeding, nurture and procreation) of kinds of persons, and the reproduction of social worlds. Developing existing theories of tenure in archaeology requires that the narrow concept of production inherent in the labour theory of property and intensification theory be broadened out to encompass all the other kinds of activity that are productive in this wider sense.

This section has suggested ways in which archaeologists might develop existing theories of tenure away from narrow assumptions of 'labour' inherent in the labour theory of property. I presented recent theories of value, which, I argued could be developed in ways that allow productive action to be read much more broadly. Hirsch's work on constructed landscapes, I argued, illustrates how value theory might be applied to land division in this way.

Conclusions

This chapter developed a critical analysis of the labour theory of property and its legacy within intensification theory. I began with a review of existing thinking in these areas. Review concentrated on two sets of problems: firstly, the practical problems of applying intensification archaeologically; secondly, the assumptions surrounding the idea of production imported by the labour theory. The middle sections illustrated the practical difficulties of establishing a firm basis for intensificatory trajectories. Evidence suggested important changes in Dartmoor environments took place centuries before reaves appeared, and the construction of land division could not be shown to represent an overall increase in labour inputs per unit area taking place across a coherent temporal horizon. To overcome some of these

difficulties I introduced the concept of flexibility. This concept has been developed by analysts to integrate intensification within a range of dynamics found in agricultural systems. This allowed me to suggest how land division may have been linked to pasture rotation and flexibility of tenure. Finally, I returned to the theoretical problems introduced by the labour theory. I argued that theories of tenure could be developed by broadening the kinds of activities that might be considered 'productive' in particular circumstances. I drew on recent theories of value to develop concepts of production in this direction.

In this chapter I examined one of the themes I identified in chapter one – the labour theory of property. This theory is an element of classical theories of property discussed in chapter three. The labour theory of property thus shares classical assumptions such as the assumption of a society composed of self-interested individuals and the assumption that property consists of individual rights to exclude. In this chapter, however, I developed an alternative approach. Whereas classical and labour theories assume that 'labour' resembles the kind of 'work' bought and sold in classical era capitalism, I argued that approaches to tenure in prehistory should read productive action far more widely. Production needs to include activities that fall outside the sphere of traditional 'subsistence' emphasizing the reproduction and socialization of persons rather than the accumulation of goods. I argued that the link between labour and tenure was not best envisaged as growing naturally from individual self-interest, but could be rethought as the importance of action realized as value within social, economic, technical and political totalities. In later chapters I use these ideas to develop an interpretation of tenure on Dartmoor. However, next I turn to another of the themes identified in chapter one – approaches that see tenure as territorialisation.

Chapter 5

Self-Evident Domains:
Territories, Houses and Tenure

On Ponam Island it is usual for the nominal holder of a piece of land to give away permission for use of various aspects of it on behalf of his kin group (Carrier, 1998). The recipient, in turn, often gives away the permission. Consequently Ponam Island is riven with vocal disputes concerning tenure. Normally at least three or four people and their kin stand between the original donor and the tenurial object. Attempts to re-bundle or re-allocate tenure are inevitably contested by someone. Success in these disputes depends on the ability of a person and their kin to retrace all the transactions and interests involved in tenure and recompose them as a source for their claim. Without written land titles this process is complicated, however, it is facilitated by practices observed during ceremonial events. Participants in marriage and funerary exchanges observe specially proscribed routes as they walk between settlements. They may only walk over land in which they or their kin have some claim of interest. To walk across the land on these occasions is to memorize a 'map' of tenurial transactions. Tenure on Ponam Island thus distributes traces of identity across the landscape.

Tenure allows aspects of personhood to be distributed about a network. Even when people are 'sedentary' tenure allows capacities linked to land and people to 'move about'. In this way tenure can be said to 'translocate' along multiple connections. However, conventional approaches to tenure are not always very good at identifying these aspects of tenure. Historically, narratives of tenure tend to see it as a form of 'territorialisation'. Using and occupying land for a length of time is supposed to lead people to feel 'territorial' about it. This 'territoriality' is often assumed to be the origins of tenure, which emerges from it as a way of protecting and regulating ownership (see chapters 1 and 3). Tenure, within these narratives emerges seamlessly from territorialisation, and such approaches may even see land tenure as equivalent to sedentarisation within established territories.

In this chapter I critique approaches that see tenure as principally a matter of territorialisation. I begin with a critical discussion of tenure-as-territorialisation. Here I argue for an approach that can include both territorialisation and translocation. The rest of this chapter attempts to anchor this critique within analyses of evidence from Dartmoor. I review evidence from excavations of buildings and settlements on Dartmoor. As was discussed in chapter two, the emergence of these substantial buildings has been seen as marking a new sedentary way of life, however, recent research has suggested that the lifecycles of buildings often lasts only a single generation. Having reviewed evidence from excavations I assess how much biographies of excavated buildings from Dartmoor may be related to this wider pattern and what this suggests about narratives of tenure-as-territorialisation. Lastly, I analyse the ways locations of buildings relate to boundaries, in the light of recent interpretations of occupancy and tenure.

5.1 Territorialisation, Translocation and Identity

'Possession is nine-tenths of the law' – the implication is that property claims will be settled in favour of those who *occupy*. This adage is not without foundation. Property law in the West really does enforce a connection between occupation and ownership (Rose, 2004). The assumption is that long-term occupation should, by rights, go with ownership. Approaches to tenure often involve similar assumptions that tenure arises 'naturally' from sedentarisation within territory. Once people begin to stay on or make use of land for any length of time, it is assumed, they will begin to feel territorial about it, and hence it will become 'theirs'. According to this conventional wisdom, tenure equals territorialisation.

In this section I examine what I call 'territorializing' approaches. I introduced 'territorialisation' in chapter one. Here I pointed to the links between these ideas of tenure and modern nationalisms. In this section I explore territorialisation at greater length. I discuss the notion of tenure-as-territorialisation. I explore the ways that tenure-as-territorialisation relates to concepts of identity, particularly through ideas of 'roots' and their incorporation into studies of kinship. Lastly, I argue that approaches to tenure need to include the potential for re/deterritorialisation (or 'translocation') as well as territorialisation.

Tenure-as-territorialisation and the 'National Order of Things'

The assumption that tenure comprises only territorialisation leads to accounts of tenure which concentrate on singularised entities. Tenure involves a relation between a singular individual, household or group that is related to a singularised 'block' of land. Land and identity are conceptualized 'in the segmentary fashion of the multicoloured school atlas' (Malkki, 1992: 26). Tenure-as-territorialisation is understood as control exercised over bounded property just as in modern nationalisms where 'state sovereignty is fully, flatly, and evenly operative over each square centimetre of a legally demarcated territory' (Anderson, 1983: 26). The notion of 'boundary' is particularly important here. Territories are created and enforced through boundaries that delimit their extent. Archaeological evidence for physical 'boundaries' and land *division* appeals to this approach. Archaeological 'boundaries' around spaces translate readily into metaphorical boundaries around social identities. The two, it is assumed, will tend towards equivalence.

Tenure-as-territorialisation reflects what Malkki calls 'the national order of things' (Malkki, 1992). Taken-for-granted notions of identity 'in ordinary language, in nationalist discourse and in scholarly studies' tend to be founded in ideas of territory (Appadurai, 1988:39). The project of constructing identity in this fashion is one shared across scientific discourses. The project of geography, for example, has been seen as the disciplining of 'national man' (Foucault, 1980). Military and administrative powers 'inscribe themselves both on a material soil and within forms of discourse' through the images of spatial territory, (Foucault, 1980: 69). Anthropology, through a similar territorializing approach, 'spatially incarcerates' the native, so that even among those groups where motion is a way of life, images of 'tribe', 'culture', 'segmentary lineage' and 'nation' all produce what might be called 'molar' identities mapped onto 'molar', bounded territories (Appadurai, 1988; Deleuze & Guattari, 1987).

I suggest that the assumption that tenure is only, or even mainly, a process of 'territorialisation' reflects forms of identification that are dominant in the modern world – specifically in modern nationalisms. Anderson famously defined the nation as an 'imagined community – imagined as both inherently limited and sovereign' (Anderson, 1983: 15; see also Smith, 2000).It is these characteristics of limitation and sovereignty that are transposed from the identifications between people and nation, tribe and territory, onto those between farmer(s) and field(s) within archaeologies of land tenure. Forms of identification dominant within the modern 'national order of things' are projected back to create narratives of tenure in the past. It is easy to see how territorialized tenure might emerge from the important role archaeology has traditionally played in authenticating historical and 'inalienable' homeland (Lowenthal, 1994; Smith, 2000, 2001). However, it is important to point out that the assumption of tenure-as-territorialisation is not only found in 'nationalist' archaeologies. It is widespread, perhaps because archaeologists lack alternative possibilities for imagining identity and tenure.

Roots, Inheritance and Kinship

The concept of 'roots' is significant within the assumption that tenure constitutes territorialisation. Within the 'national order of things' people and cultures are each seen to form 'a grand genealogical tree, rooted in the soil that nourishes it' (Malkki, 1992: 28). By implication, 'it is impossible to be part of more than one tree'- or, to have more than one identity. The insistence here is on the limitedness of the nation and the way those limits are transposed backwards via inheritance. 'Roots' reinforce correspondences between the 'imagined communities' of nations and the (equally imagined) communities of kinship (Anderson, 1983: chapter 8; Carsten, 2004a: chapter 6).

The notion of 'roots' is at the heart of what is traditionally considered 'biological' kinship. What Schneider calls the 'Western folk model' of kinship – 'biological' kinship - is based on the idea of inheritance of a biogenetic essence transmitted from parents to offspring (Schneider, 2004). Transmission of this essence endows each individual with their unique identity; their individuality. In anthropology 'biological kinship' has traditionally been represented though the genealogical diagram, which in turn derives from the aborescent imagery of 'roots' found in European family trees (Bouquet, 1996). The origins of anthropology's 'genealogical models' lie, as Bourdieu has pointed out, in European property inheritance (Bourdieu, 1977:30-43). The originator of the genealogical diagram in anthropology, W H R Rivers, deliberately drew his imagery from the family trees used to preserve connections between lineage and land among the English upper classes (Bouquet, 1996: 47). Deploying the obsessions of English land-owners to study the social systems of savages, Rivers mocked the snobberies of his age, but he also ensured that the imagery of 'roots' that was so important within English customs and laws of primogeniture would be exported much more widely.

British social anthropology has been particularly concerned with lineages, landed estates and land inheritance (Kuper, 2004). In what Kuper calls the 'classical period of lineage theory' writers like Maine and Morgan described 'village communities' or 'clans with strong correspondences between blood ties and territory. Subsequently, there was a revival of these concepts in the twentieth century when the idea of the clan was replaced with that of the 'lineage'. Within 'lineage theory' tenure assumed great importance providing a structural-functional account of kinship (Evans-Pritchard, 2004 [1940]; Leach, 1962; Kuper, 2004; Parkin, 2004). Lineages were seen as political and jural institutions that articulated and administered tenure. Particularly important was the 'segmentary lineage system', famously described by Evans-Pritchard in *'The Nuer'* (Evans-Pritchard, 2004 [1940]). Within 'segmentary lineages' segments of lineages controlled 'territorial segments' of land. Each lineage segment was affiliated to a 'maximal lineage' encompassing the territory as a whole, so that the entire structure resembled a family tree or genealogical model mapped onto spatial territory.

This structural-functional account of kinship and territorialized tenure - while it places 'land' at base of kinship structures – also displaces it from playing an ongoing role in the constitution of personhood. Within many accounts the 'Western folk model' of 'biological kinship' is understood as the foundation on which the 'social constructions' of kinship in other societies rests. To the extent that the 'genealogical model' guides ideas of what kinship is, what matters for identification is not the ongoing engagement with place, but the inheritance of biogenetic essence. When 'roots' are what matters land becomes 'merely a surface to be occupied' (Ingold, 2000: 133). The connection between identity and land is displaced. Consequently land inheritance becomes one of the most significant (if not the most significant) aspects of tenure.

The functional unity of genealogy and tenure in lineage theory has appealed to many later writers (Leach, 1962; Meillassoux, 1972: 101; Sahlins, 1972; Renfrew, 1976). Within archaeologies of land division, echoes can be found in Fleming's structural models of social organisation (Fleming, 1984, 1988) and Earle's insistence that 'specific demarcated land sections' within coaxial landscapes might be linked to segments of 'corporate groups' (Earle, 2002: 327). However, the basis of the 'segmentary lineage model' has been severely criticized: 'There do not appear to be any societies' reports Kuper, 'in which vital political or economic activities are organized by a repetitive series of descent groups' (Kuper, 2004: 88). 'Even the Nuer', he concludes, 'are not like *The Nuer'* (Kuper, 2004: 93; see also Hutchinson, 1996).

The genealogical model of 'roots' that sustains lineage theory has undergone sustained critique and re-evaluation since the 1960s (Stone, 2004; Carsten, 2004a). The so-called 'biological facts' of kinship now appear as a 'Western folk model' of the way that kinship *should* be rather than an objective 'natural' substrate (Schneider, 2004). Even the Americans studied by Schneider in the 1960s did not base their family life on the supposed 'biological facts' of kinship. 'Why', Schneider asked, 'should this model be granted ontological priority over alternative models?'(ibid).

Alternatives to the genealogical model depart from the genealogical emphasis on a once-and-for-all inheritance of individuality, emphasizing processes of nurture and growth that produce persons gradually. These new ideas of kinship are associated with wider critique of identity theory, which re-envision 'molar' identities as fluid, and non-unitary (Braidotti, 2003). Kinship relations are now sought in the ways that substances circulate through feeding, eating, grooming, talking, sexual and social intercourse (Carsten, 2004a: chapters 3-4). Houses, in particular, have been shown to be important sites in the generation of kinship relations (Carsten & Hugh-Jones,

1995; Brück, 2005). Kinship and identity appear to be less and less about roots and more about processes of becoming, or making persons.

Deterritorializing and Translocating Tenure

'Natives - people confined to and by the places to which they belong, groups unsullied by contact with a larger world - have probably never existed'
(Appadurai, 1988: 39).

The ideas of 'native' and 'territory' depend on the possession of panoptic vision; ironically the very vision that the native, confined within her small world, is supposed to lack. Relating a molar identity to a molar territory requires, in fact, a map, that differentiates one segmentary territory and identity from the next, like the school atlas that Malkki invokes. To identify as a 'native' or a 'national' one must not only distinguish self and other, but must possess categorical notions that also apply elsewhere. What I call 'territorialisation' is actually a form of 'reterritorialisation' taking place *after* the 'deterritorialisation' induced by the map (Deleuze & Guattari, 1987: 12-4). Territorialized identification is based on transgressing the local; it is not a primordial, but is linked to modernity.

Dawson and Johnson argue that all identities – including 'territorialized' national identities - involve imaginative translocations (Dawson and Johnson 2001). Concepts of 'natives' and 'territory', Dawson and Johnson argue, are founded on 'migration diaspora and exile' (Dawson & Johnson, 2001). The 'static, place-based view of people and culture' emerges from, and requires 'cognitive movement' between places understood as bounded coterminous territorial categories. Paradoxically, territorialized identities like nationality and the indigenous, require us to imagine the condition of migration. This imaginative transgression is necessary even, or perhaps especially, when people are 'sedentary' (Dawson and Johnson 2001). In the case of modern nationalisms 'translocations' or 'reterritorialisations' emerge at the same time that mapping delimits national territory. By delimiting territory the map inevitably overspills into delineating other territories (Bradshaw & Williams, 1999). The very act of creating bounded identities can be seen as producing transgressions and overspills.

Concepts of 'boundary' tend to reinforce tenure-as-territorialisation approaches. The English word and concept 'boundary', Barth has shown, conflates three levels of abstraction; the division of territories, the division of social entities, and the separation of 'distinct categories of the mind' (Barth 2000: 17). Although these three phenomena are conflated for English speakers, they seldom overlap like this elsewhere. Whilst English speakers may assume that walls or fences are the natural imagery of social identity and distinction this assumption is not shared everywhere in the world (see also Barth, 1969). 'Impressing boundaries on the world' Barth suggests, does not necessarily express the 'natural' limits of groups, but instead concerns the relationships taking place within groups. We should focus not on the emergence and definition of what is contained by boundaries, but on the boundaries themselves (Barth, 1969). Boundaries, Barth insists, do not demarcate, but connect. They are creative; transforming relations and remaking identities (Barth, 2000).

What I have described here as 'territorialisation', is not the whole of tenure, but is best seen as only one aspect of it. Equally important, I would argue, are the ways that tenure re/deterritorialises. While tenure-as-territorialisation starts by assuming pre-given categories of 'territory' and 'owners'; segmenting the world into what Munn calls 'self-evident domains' (Munn, 1990:2). A more helpful approach would consider the 'translocal' aspects of tenure as well. Tenure does not only, or even principally, concern ownership or 'property'; tenure also allows entities to be transacted and circulated - to be decomposed and distributed among networks.

For an example, we might return to Munn's account of tenure on Gawa (Munn, 1987). On Gawa tenure is attached to exogamous kin-groups, but usufruct is extremely flexible. This element of tenure is routinely lent to people outside the kin-group, including people from overseas (Munn, 1987: 278). The lending and borrowing of usufruct is a tenurial transaction emerging from the 'generalized food giving relationships' that unpin life on Gawa. These relations, Munn demonstrates, are translocated into much wider levels of interaction. In no sense does tenure refer to a predefined 'local' subsistence economy separable from regional trade in portable objects. Instead, usufruct and horticulture are important parts of kula exchange. Generalized food giving relationships initiate 'spatiotemporally extending processes' that are *the dynamic base and condition which underlies kula shell exchange*' (Munn, 1987: 56 her emphasis). In fact tenurial transactions are part of the way that Gawan identity is extended and distributed. Gawan identity is not produced through sedentarisation within a bounded territory (as national identities are) but from connections to distant places and persons. The relations of tenure are thus 'translocating' or deterritorialising as much as they territorialize.

I should make clear that I am not suggesting that Bronze Age Europe is directly analogous with the kula ring. Rather I am suggesting that theories of tenure include appreciation of the ways subjects engage with a range of spatial and temporal horizons in any given moment (Munn, 1990). The task for archaeologists is to distinguish which forms of identification seem most appropriate for each instance of tenure. Tenure-as-territorialisation emphasises forms of identification that resemble those of modern nationalisms, and this suggests caution and encourages exploration of alternative possibilities.

Alternatives are increasingly available as kinship studies move away from 'roots' and 'lineage theory'. While the 'genealogical model' displaced the connection between person and land along chains inheritance (Ingold, 2000: chapter 8) more recent accounts discuss alternative processes of making or 'growing' persons (Carsten, 2004a, 2004b). These alternatives imply that identity is not so much a fixed inheritance, but a moment within processes of becoming. When identity is understood in this way tenure can be seen as an aspect of these processes. Recent examples include Leach's studies of tenure on the Rai Coast (PNG) where tenurial transactions enter into the constitution of identities 'making' men and women in particular ways (Leach, 2003a, 2003b, 2004).

In this section I discussed the assumption that tenure equals what I called 'territorialisation'. I suggested that this assumption reflects forms of identification dominant within modern nationalisms. Tenure-as-territorialisation has contributed to two related tendencies in archaeologies of tenure:

i) disproportionate emphasis on 'roots', sedentarisation, and land inheritance;

ii) less emphasise on transactions and exchanges (pace inheritance).

I argued that approaches to tenure needed move beyond the assumption of tenure-as-territorialisation, considering how tenure has the potential to both territorialize and translocate. In the rest of this chapter I examine the implications of this critique in the light of evidence from Dartmoor. I begin by reviewing the evidence from excavations of buildings.

5.2 Excavations of Buildings

Dartmoor contains a large sample of excavations. In chapter two I reviewed this data-source highlighting its bias towards early excavations before 1950. The relative lack of excavations using modern methods limits interpretation. Nevertheless, reports from excavations of the late nineteenth and early twentieth century can still provide useful insights, particularly given the relatively large numbers of sites that have been examined and recorded. Early investigators spread their effort widely,

excavating in most areas of the moor. Some extremely large settlements have been excavated (e.g. forty-three buildings at Standon Down, ninety-four at Watern Oke). In total, a database of 324 roundhouses can be compiled, of probable later prehistoric date (Butler, 1997a: 269-274). Although most of these sites lack absolute dates or full reports the size of this sample suggests some useful information may be gleaned from examining it further.

The aim of this section is to review evidence from excavations as a whole, statistically describing this large, if limited, dataset. I begin by discussing the kinds of features commonly recorded in excavation reports. I then analyze the distribution of these features between different settlement types.

Features of Excavated Buildings

Review of excavation reports from Dartmoor reveals a relatively consistent repertoire of features, also identified by other commentators (Fleming, 1979; Butler, 1997b; Gerrard, 1997a). Many of these features are connected to the presence of charcoal – a highly visible material even for early excavators. Most excavation reports (72%) record some evidence for burning and heating, in addition, many reports describe formal architecture including what they described as 'hearths' and 'cooking pits'. Other common finds were burnt and fire-cracked granite pebbles called 'pot-boilers' (Baring-Gould et al., 1895; Worth, 1994). In addition there are some curious, and much less common, features described in early reports as 'cooking chambers' or 'troughs'. Each of these features is described here in turn.

'Hearths'
34% of all excavated buildings contain features described as 'hearths'. Early reports characterise this in similar ways to more recent texts as '…large flat stones of elvan, that have been much cracked by fire' sunken into the floors of buildings or surrounded by kerbstones (Baring-Gould et al., 1896: 176). These stone settings show evidence for burning and concentrations of charcoal, and may be improvised using combinations of set stones, naturally occurring boulders and scoops dug into floors. The range of hearth architecture is illustrated in the list compiled as Appendix O. The absence of hearths from some houses has been interpreted as reflecting seasonal occupation of houses outside coaxial landscapes (Baring-Gould et al., 1899; Quinnell, 1991).

'Cooking Pits'
'Cooking pits' are shallow pits containing dense concentrations of charcoal. They are oval, rectangular, kidney shaped or circular, often found close to hearths. The pits may be lined with stone (as at Grimspound) or by ceramic vessels (as at Legis Tor and Raddick Hill) (Baring-Gould et al., 1896: 177). They are very strongly characterised and can be readily identified on recent excavations (e.g. at Shaugh Moor, Holne Moor, and outside Dartmoor at Hayne Lane). 14% of excavated buildings from Dartmoor contain cooking pits.

The purposes of these features do indeed seem to have involved food preparation. Plant macrofossils from pits at Hayne Lane, Devon, support the idea that they were used during the day-to-day habitation of the buildings for heating liquids or slow-cooking meat (Fitzpatrick et al., 1999). A small quantity of burnt animal bone was recovered from one of the pits at this site (Fitzpatrick et

al., 1999: 127). Nineteenth century excavators considered that the main function of cooking pits was boiling liquid using 'pot boilers' (Burnard, 1894: 194): One pit at Legis Tor contained a pot with two stones inside (Baring-Gould et al., 1896: 177). It has been suggested that the cooking holes with linings might relate to the production of dairy products that require careful temperature control (Fox, 1957; Fleming, 1979). Fox also suggested that pits found at Dean Moor functioned as 'ovens … in which joints of meat were cooked amongst heated stones and ashes brought from the hearth', and that others were 'soak-aways'; 'the equivalent of the kitchen sink' (Fox, 1957: 39).

'Pot-Boilers'
Chemical analysis and experimental work has demonstrated that pot-boilers excavated from Dartmoor sites were from the hottest parts of fires, 'heated under reducing conditions' probably on 'the charcoal bed' (Wainwright & Smith, 1980: 106). Pot Boilers from early interventions were similar to those found more recently at Shaugh Moor. 36% of excavated buildings were associated with potboilers.

It seems very likely that pot-boilers were used to transfer heat. However, many finds of pot-boilers are not associated with hearths or cooking pits. Over half of the sixty-five buildings with pot-boilers had no hearths or cooking pits present within the building (56%). Hearths are unlikely to have been missed because they were considered an important element of the expected furniture of roundhouses and were deliberately sought out (Baring-Gould et al., 1898; Harris et al., 1935). Almost the entire settlement of forty-three houses was excavated at Standon Down. Cooking stones were the 'feature of the excavation' but to the bemusement of the excavators no hearths or cooking pits were found (Anderson et al., 1902: 163). The majority of buildings (77%) did not even contain charcoal.

It is possible that heated stones were an important way of sharing heat between houses, especially where pot boilers are found in houses adjacent to those with hearths (e.g. Dean Moor). It is also possible that potboilers were deliberately deposited in buildings after their use, a custom that might be linked to the metaphorical importance of heating. For example at Shaugh Moor, two potboilers were found stratified on the floors beneath fallen walls in house 67, but there were no hearths or cooking pits anywhere on the site (Wainwright & Smith, 1980). It may be that potboilers at some sites come from communal fires outside buildings that remain unexcavated. Alternatively, the potboilers – like the many querns found at Shaugh Moor – could have been brought in from elsewhere.

Deliberate deposition of potboilers is suggested by finds from cairns and barrows. At Upton Pyne, a pot-boiler was placed on a laid deposit of clay before being sealed by the mound (Pollard & Russell, 1969). At Roundy Park a pot-boiler was wedged into a cist wall (Burnard, 1894). The heating and cooling of pot-boilers echoes the heating and cooling of the cremated human remains found at these sites. It may be that heating and cooling were metaphors for transformations between life and death.

Paving and Internal Spatial Divisions

Paving across all or part of the floor is found in 16% of excavated buildings. Fox suggests that paving was used for hard-wearing floors in 'working' areas (Fox, 1957). Fleming argues that paving was evidence for the presence of animals in buildings, either for routine milking, or occasionally for hand feeding or care of sick animals (Fleming, 1979).

Studies of prehistoric houses suggest many contain internal spatial divisions, suggesting distinctions between light and dark, life and death, or male and female (Ellison, 1981; Drewett, 1982; Brück, 1999a; Parker Pearson, 1996; cf Brück, 2005). On Dartmoor internal furnishings and floors within buildings have long been described as forming distinct 'sleeping' and 'living' areas (Baring-Gould et al., 1894). At Round Pound, Kestor, the floor was split into two halves, one 'cleaner' and unpaved, the other more 'dirty', with uneven paving stones. Fox interpreted one half as 'living quarters' and other as 'working quarters' (Fox, 1954b: Figure 10). Floors divided into two halves are found in some buildings, where one half of the floor comprises beaten earth or light cobbling and the other half paving or uneven rubble (e.g. hut 1, Dean Moor and Round Pound (Fox, 1957: 38). Excavations of conjoined buildings at Grimspound and huts 5A and 5B, Dean Moor, found one building had a 'clean' floor and the other a more 'hard-wearing' one (Baring-Gould et al., 1894; Fox, 1957). Buildings 'paired' with others may also have 'paired' floors, as at Shaugh Moor where house 19 was 'clean', with small patches of paving around the entrance, while house 18 contained a hard-wearing paved floor (Smith et al., 1981).

'Cooking Chambers' or 'Troughs'

Some sites contain unusual structures that were difficult for early excavators to interpret, since they were clearly much larger than conventional hearths or cooking pits. For example, excavation of ninety-four structures at Watern Oke revealed 21 structures containing large or multiple 'hearths' (see 5.1). Charcoal was removed 'in considerable quantities, much more than usual' from 'most of the huts' (Amery et al., 1906: 102). Some structures had 'traces of fire all over the floor', 'many traces of fire' or 'fire-places' in more than one place or were packed with 'many burnt stones' (e.g. house no.s 4a, 7, 9). The excavators suggested that some of these structures were not houses but large 'cooking chambers' or 'troughs' filled copious quantities of charcoal and pot-boilers.

Features that may be parallels for these 'cooking chambers' were found on other early excavations. Stone lined troughs were found in the centre of buildings at Hart Tor (no 12 and 14) (Baring-Gould et al., 1896:109-1); The troughs were more than twice the average dimensions for cooking pits (1.1m diameter x 0.4m depth, and 0.9m diameter x 0.4m depth). One and a half wheelbarrow loads of charcoal and potboilers were removed from the first pit, two wheelbarrow loads from the second. The troughs were cut down into the natural china clay, which formed a lining reddened by the heat of materials that had been placed within the troughs. Another large trough (1.2m x 0.6m x 0.4m) containing 'much charcoal' was found in a house at Yes Tor Bottom (no. 5) (Baring-Gould et al., 1898: 103). These features are listed, with their descriptions, in Appendix P.

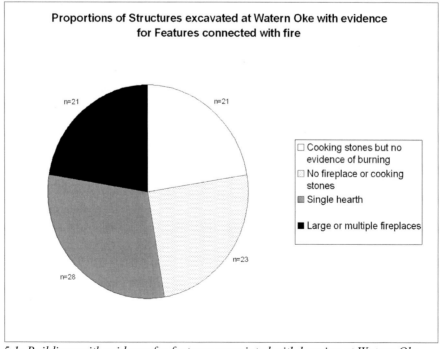

5.1: Buildings with evidence for features associated with burning at Watern Oke

It is difficult to interpret these features because none have been excavated using modern methods. Early interpretations focused on large-scale communal cooking, although Baring Gould also suggested that some 'cooking chambers' may have functioned as 'a primitive Turkish bath, in which water was poured over hot stones to produce a cloud of steam' (Baring Gould cited in Brailsford, 1938: 454). One notable characteristic of all the 'cooking chambers' and troughs excavated is their riverine location. The average distance of these structures from watercourses (83m) is much less then the general average (365m). It may be that some of these features are best paralleled by features from the burnt mound tradition, known from many Bronze Age settlements elsewhere in southern Britain. Burnt mounds can contain masses of burnt stone, sometimes accompanied by charcoal-filled sunken troughs or chambers; they are commonly located close to rivers (Buckley, 1990). These sites are often interpreted as evidence for large-scale feasting activities. However, until comparable features are found and investigated using modern methods, these features remain an ambiguous aspect of Dartmoor's archaeology.

Comparing Excavated Buildings from Different Settlement Types

In chapter two I discussed previous interpretations of Dartmoor settlements which classified them into different types. Using these classifications it is possible to compare the frequencies of different features from excavated buildings. Here I use the classifications devised by Butler and Gerrard (Gerrard, 1997a; Butler, 1997a). The terms of this classification have been explained in chapter two except for the category 'field networks'. Field networks comprise dense clusters with numerous buildings linked by short lengths of walling. Extensive early excavations at Standon Down and Watern Oke are included in this category. Excavations in the past have tended to concentrate on buildings within field networks and pounds. As 5.2 shows, relatively few excavations have taken place in coaxial or aggregate field systems. The small sample sizes for these types make the data difficult to use. For pounds and field networks however represent a reasonable quantity of excavated buildings.

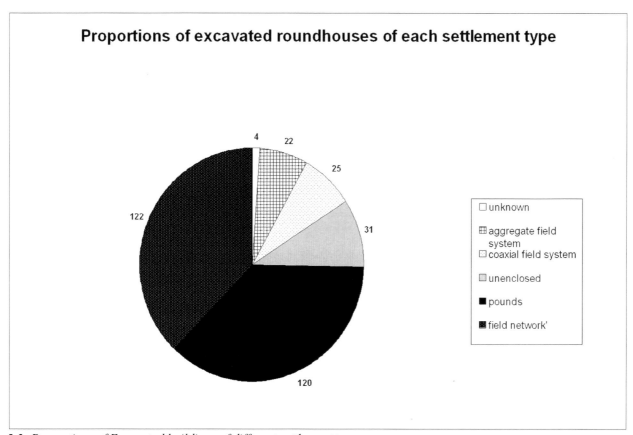

5.2: Proportions of Excavated buildings of different settlement types

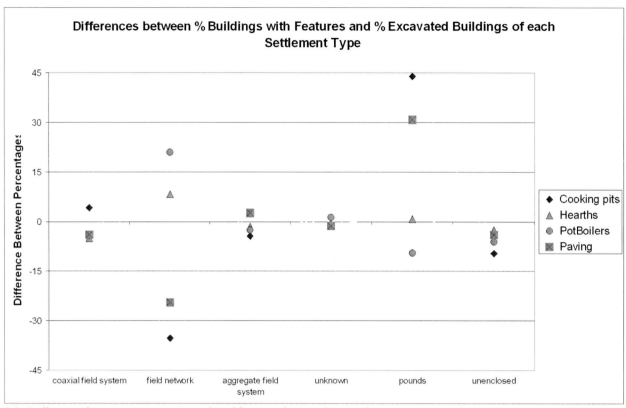

5.3. Difference between Percentages of Buildings with Hearths, Cooking Pits, Pot-Boilers and Paving compared with Percentage of Buildings within each Settlement Type

The difference between percentages of buildings with hearths, cooking pits, pot-boilers and paving and the percentage of all excavated buildings within each settlement type is shown in 5.3. A detailed breakdown of these data including absolute numbers of buildings in each category can be found in Appendix Q.

The results shown in 5.3 may indicate associations between buildings with particular features and certain settlement types. Discounting differences of less than 20%, 5.3 suggests that cooking pits and paving may be associated with pounds, meanwhile field networks show a relative absence of these features. The association of cooking pits with pounds has also been identified in previous work (Fleming, 1979; Johnston, 2001b). Fleming argues that this reflects an emphasis on pastoral agriculture in pounds – with cooking pits used to manufacture dairy produce and paving to protect floors from animal hooves (Fleming, 1979). Previous accounts have suggested that hearths are less common in pounds and field networks, because these, generally, high altitude sites were occupied seasonally over the summer (Baring-Gould et al., 1899; Balaam et al., 1982; Quinnell, 1991). My analysis finds no association between hearths and any particular settlement type. In fact, Appendix R shows that

more, rather than less hearths are found at higher altitudes. Overall, the analysis does not find strongly marked differences between site types, but rather, a continuum of variation with slight differences between buildings in pounds and field networks. It may be that these differences reflect different ways of inhabiting various parts of the landscape – including the seasonal occupation of high pasturelands discussed in chapter four.

In this section I investigated evidence from excavated buildings *en masse*, using information from excavations of the late nineteenth and early twentieth century, alongside the far fewer more recent excavations. There are obvious limitations to what can be inferred from excavations carried out in the absence of modern techniques and absolute dates. However, because the sample of excavated buildings is so large, it is possible to identify some of the key features of Dartmoor settlements, and to compare these between different settlement types. The analyses carried out in this section provide background information that will be explored further in the rest of this chapter. In the next section I use recent excavations with well-documented stratigraphic detail to examine the life-cycles of buildings on Dartmoor.

5.3 Building Biographies

'Until this point ... the people ... lacked that closer sense of attachment which may be given by a substantial and permanent homestead ... Where before the soil had been tilled by hand, the Celts used an ox-drawn plough and with the plough a regular system of fields whose boundaries might have remained constant for centuries. Agriculture of this kind led to the permanent farm and settled village, together with the habits of mind dependant upon generation after generation being born in the same place and even the same house ... Once a way of life was established in which the old expected the young to inherit their houses and fields, there was, I believe, no equally deep change in the feeling of country life until subsistence farming was displaced by industrial agriculture'
(*'A Land'* Hawkes, 1951: 149)

Even at the time Hawkes was writing this account of gradual territorialisation was already well established (cf Morgan, 2005; Engels, 2005; Smith, 1776). The continuity of this territorializing narrative, is remarkable, it has persisted in Bronze Age archaeologies long after other aspects of Hawkes account (Fowler & Blackwell, 1998; Pryor, 2001). In chapter two I highlighted new studies that disrupt these narratives of seamless sedentarisation. In parts of the Netherlands and southern Britain, the earliest land division takes place in the context of shifting 'neolocal' settlement pattern, with houses occupied only for a single generation (Brück, 1999a; Gerritsen, 1999; Theuws & Roymans, 1999). What does this mean for approaches which assume tenure-as-territorialisation?

In this section I assess evidence from Dartmoor in the light of these new studies. I begin with a brief discussion on the significance of houses. I then examine what evidence exists for the lifecycles of Dartmoor roundhouses, addressing their construction, use-life, and abandonment.

The Significance of Houses

'For many people, kinship is made in and through houses, and houses are the social relations of those who inhabit them'
(Carsten, 2004a: 37, her emphasis).

Houses are important to the new anthropologies of kinship. This interest in houses emerges partly as a reaction to a previous tradition that tended to ignore them. Classic 'lineage-theory', concentrated on political, jural and economic institutions assumed to take place outside the nuclear family (Carsten, 2004a: chapter 1).

Inheritance within the 'corporate descent group' provided an explanation of how society could be organised in the absence of the state; the household, meanwhile, concerned only 'natural' reproduction – processes assumed to be the same everywhere. Realising that the genealogical model (in which kinship comprises inheritance of biogenetic essence) cannot be assumed, new approaches look to alternative models of procreation. As a result, there is increased interest in houses as 'engines of relatedness' (Bourdieu, 1977; Carsten & Hugh-Jones, 1995; Carsten, 2004b; 2004b: chapter 2). Ethnographies suggest processes like cooking, heating and eating, which take place in houses, are often understood as producing kin (Carsten, 2004a: 37-41):

'...it is the in the hearth that the different elements that enter the house – meat and vegetable, kin and affine, the like and the unlike – may be said to be mixed and blended, veritably cooked together. Insofar as houses are continually transforming what passes through them, the hearth is both literally and figuratively the site where these transformations actually take place'
(Carsten & Hugh-Jones, 1995: 42-3).

Studies point to the homologies houses evoke with other entities. Houses may be mapped into bodies, onto households, and/or take on forms reflecting the structure of wider society or images of the cosmos (Bourdieu, 1977; Parker Pearson, 1996).

Studies suggest that this distinction between a public/political and a private/domestic sphere is totally inappropriate when it comes to interpreting Bronze Age roundhouses (Brück, 2005). The inception of substantial roundhouse architecture in the Early-Middle Bronze Age is linked to changes in the nature of relations and identity taking place at this time. Houses are seen as heralding 'social fragmentation' –larger groups breaking down into smaller family-based groups (Barrett, 1994; Brück, 2000). In 'western' societies – where the house bounds the private realm and is a supreme property object – it is easy to envisage fragmentation as the loosening of a social contract, and hence the dissolution of society into individualised households each occupying privatised blocks of land. However, evidence from Bronze Age settlements suggests houses provided loci from which wider networks were extended. Evidence for communal cooking and feasting on Middle Bronze Age settlements shows the importance of houses for large-scale gatherings. Brück suggests that feasting was a general characteristic of Bronze Age settlement 'perhaps taking place in the context of visits for exchange or inter-household pooling of labour for tasks such as harvesting crops' (Brück, 2005). These larger gatherings place the roundhouse at the centre of Bronze Age political and economic life, as well as 'domestic' life. The political, public role of Bronze Age houses does not fit well with notions of exclusivity encouraged by the assumptions of tenure-as-territorialisation.

In chapter three I suggested the locations of buildings were linked to the mobilisation of social ties between prospective and existing inhabitants. This interpretation may also be related to the social networks that were necessary for house construction. The construction of a roundhouse would have necessarily involved more then one person. Reconstructions suggest that the optimum number directly involved in building the structure would be three; but many more would have been involved in gathering and preparing materials (Reynolds, 1979: 99). The quantity of resources, including timber, stone, turf, straw or reeds for thatch, would have been considerable. A building would take around six weeks to erect, added to which is the time spent on collecting and preparing materials. During at least some of this time workers would need to be sustained by others. The imperatives of accessing resources and support mean that questions of tenure would have been engaged even before building began. Building a house mobilised a network, so that one could even speak of houses as 'multiply authored' architecture, embodying the relations between new and existing inhabitants.

Assessing Evidence for Lifecycles from Excavations

Unlike many other parts of Britain, the ruins of stone-built structures remain visible on Dartmoor thousands of years after their construction. Most have been subject to various attentions after the period in which they were built. Ruined structures would have been features of the landscape in prehistory too, and, unlike timber structures, left handy locations upon which to set new buildings. it now seems that there may be two different patterns of occupation taking place over the course of later prehistory: in the Middle Bronze Age houses tend to be abandoned after one generation or so, however, a few centuries later, in the Late Bronze and Iron Ages, this pattern changes. In the later period it seems to be important to build houses on top of earlier structures, so that 'successive houses were often superimposed or overlapping' (Bradley, 2005: 54). It seems very likely that, on Dartmoor, where the ruined houses of the earlier period are still visible, these would have become suitable house-sites in the later period. This means that there are real problems determining when the 'life-cycle' of buildings on Dartmoor ends. Dating sequences often lack fine resolution, and the stratigraphic record is seldom able to differentiate a lengthy period of continuous occupation from a series of reoccupation cycles.

To examine what evidence there is for the life-cycles of Early-Middle Bronze Age buildings I concentrate mainly on excavations which took place after 1950 (see Appendix A). Bearing the above problems in mind, I

have divided the lifecycles of houses into three event-horizons - construction, occupation and abandonment – discussing what previous excavators have suggested about these moments in the biography of buildings.

Construction
The way in which houses are constructed may offer clues to expectations about its future. Gerritsen suggests that houses which are occupied for a shorter period tend to be built 'all in one go' whereas houses occupied over many generations will expand and contract incrementally (Gerritsen, 1999). Dartmoor roundhouses display several features which suggest that the major input into their construction took place at the beginnings of their occupation, when they were first built. For example many of the internal furnishing of excavated buildings are integral to the structure of the lower walls, and must have been planned at the outset of the building. Consider, for example, the specially built storage niches and annexes found in buildings at Dean Moor, Kestor and Heatree (Fox, 1954b; 1954b; Quinnell 1991). These 'cupboards' are at low levels in the wall structures and would have been extremely difficult to add to an already standing building. Hut 7, Dean Moor contained a rock cut walled storage pit, built into the fabric of the rest of the house comprising, Fox suggested, a 'cellar' (1957: 50-52). Excavations of conjoined houses at Grimspound and Dean Moor, suggest that these were built as a pair from the outset – rather than being added one to another (Fox, 1954b; Baring-Gould et al., 1894). This does not mean that houses remained unaltered. As I discuss below it is common for features to be altered within already standing structures. Such features are generally entrances or floors. However, these are seldom major architectural transformations. Instead they seem to represent the embellishment of houses that remained inhabitable throughout the alterations.

There is some evidence that the 'event-horizon' of construction was specially marked by the builders themselves. At house 1 at Kestor, the broken pieces of a single straight-sided vessel were found within a post hole 'in positions which showed that they had been broken and placed there deliberately when the hole was open' (Fox, 1954b: 31). Fox argued that this act was a 'symbolic act of libation during the house construction' (ibid).

Alterations, Repairs and Phasing
It is helpful at this stage to separate buildings into two groups:

i) Buildings from area excavations of coaxial landscapes (including evidence for timber structures):

ii) Excavations focusing on stone buildings in non-coaxial landscapes.

Timber buildings in coaxial landscape appear to be relatively short-lived. Several timber structures were found at Holne Moor, site B. Only one house had evidence for repairs including the replacement of the south-western porch support, and the strengthening of the south-western wall. These were minor repairs, however, not suggesting a very long occupation (Ralph, 1982; Fleming, 1985a; Fleming, 1988). Close to Dartmoor, the lowland coaxial landscape at Patteson's Cross included two timber roundhouses each with short sequences and with little evidence for alternations or repairs; the only repairs being replacement of entrance posts (Fitzpatrick et al., 1999). Some stone-built structures in coaxial landscapes are similarly short-lived, including the stone-built house at site B, and house 1 at Kestor, which had no evidence for any repairs, although the life of the house was long enough for the floor to accumulate haphazard paving stones (Fox, 1954b).

Three buildings within coaxial landscapes suggest longer occupation, and/or reoccupations. Firstly, at Site F, Holne Moor, a stone-built house was built on exactly the same plan as an earlier timber house. The timber house proceeded the adjacent parallel reave, but the stone house post dated it. This suggested a gap between the buildings. However, the gap must have been short enough for the remains of the timber house to be visible. The house at site F also has a third phase in which it was reoccupied by a small 'transhumance hut'. Secondly at Round Pound, Kestor, Fox envisaged a lengthy period of occupation from the later Bronze Age into the Iron Age. However some of what was thought to be Iron Age activity within this buildings is now seen as medieval reoccupation (Silvester, 1979; Quinnell, 1994a). Thirdly recent excavations at Teigncombe suggest either several phases of occupation or an extremely long period of continuous occupation. This house has deep floor layers and the ceramics span a considerable period from the Middle Bronze Age to the Romano-British period (Quinnell in Gerrard, 2000).

Outside coaxial landscapes stone-built houses often show extensive alterations. This includes remodelling of entrances, as at Heatree where a rubble 'make up' layer, a step down, and three post holes for doors or porch were added (Quinnell, 1991). At Shaugh Moor the first phase cobbled-way entrances of houses 15, 19 and 67, were substantially rebuilt, narrowed, and resurfaced. In houses 15 and 19 a porch and steps were added. The walls of Shaugh Moor 18, 19, 67 were revetted. The floors of Shaugh Moor 15, 18, 67 consist of an earlier phase of beaten earth and drains followed by later layers of paving or cobbling. At house 15 a drain was extensively re-sculpted after a period of use (Wainwright & Smith, 1980). There is evidence that a lengthy period elapsed between the two occupation phases at house 18 where the earth floor had been gradually worn down into a dished shape before paving was added (Wainwright & Smith, 1980: 79-82).

In some places alterations would have required the organic superstructure of the buildings to have been either dismantled or decayed and they therefore suggest reoccupation rather than continuous use. In house 18,

Shaugh Moor, timber roof supports had either rotted or been removed before paving was added. The paving made it impossible to roof the house, and the alterations suggest dramatic changes in the function of this building.

Abandonment

Across southern Britain and especially in Cornwall the abandonment of houses seems to have been marked by particular practices (Nowakowski, 2001). Abandonment practices include strategic removal of structural elements, packing of post holes to prevent reinsertion of posts, burial and concealment of the house, and the deliberate deposition of special objects within the house. As with construction, 'closing' the house may also have required communal acts, like removing posts, piling interiors with stone and constructing mounds over 'dead' houses.

Some buildings on and around Dartmoor show evidence for abandonment practices: At Shaugh Moor, the entire interior of House 66 was deliberately packed with stone (Wainwright & Smith, 1980). At Riders Rings, sections of house wall had been systematically dismantled (Harris et al., 1935). Across Dartmoor, Butler records numerous instances of buildings converted into cairns, either by heaping rubble infill from part of the walling over another part of the circuit, or by leaving the wall intact and filling the interior with stones (Butler, 1997a: 137). There is one excavated example of a house converted into a cairn just to the east of Dartmoor, at Dainton (English Heritage, 1987). The building, however, contains Iron Age pottery and 'a decorated yellow glass bead dating from the third to first century BC'. I have recalibrated the only date from this unpublished site to 390 BC to 0 AD at Sigma 2 (appendix H).

There are examples of special deposits left on floors of Dartmoor buildings at the very end of their use-lives. At Hut 2, Dean Moor two carnelian beads were left on the house floor: 'These precious objects' Fox notes, 'must have been one of the last things dropped by the inhabitants' (1957: 42). The entire back half of house 1 at Kestor was covered with quartz crystals, which have also been found in considerable numbers at huts 4 and 5B, Dean Moor. Similar finds of quartz have been recovered from c.23 roundhouses excavated before 1950 (Butler, 1997a: 120-1). 'Closing' the house on abandonment seems to have been an important act. Abandonment practices parallel the 'closing' of mortuary sites with mounds and may suggest the 'death' of the house (Brück, 1999a; Jones, 2004a).

The difficulties involved in distinguishing occupation from reoccupation of Dartmoor buildings make it hard to generalise about the length of occupation of these buildings. Add to this the possibility that some of these buildings were occupied within a seasonal round, and this makes interpreting house biography rather more complicated then in some other areas of southern Britain. Timber houses in coaxial landscapes appear to fit Brück's neolocal residence pattern very well, however, stone-built houses outside coaxial landscapes may have longer sequences. Without more excavations, however, no firm conclusions can be drawn.

In this section I explored the significance of houses and evidence for relatively short-term occupations of buildings. I highlighted the problems that these posed for territorializing narratives of tenure. In the next section I challenge territorializing narratives further, exploring the connections between buildings and boundaries.

5.4 Territorialisation and Coaxial Landscapes

Evidence from Dartmoor emphasises the periodic abandonment of prehistoric buildings. These abandoned structures are features of the landscape today, as they would have been in the past. Recent accounts of Dartmoor landscapes have focused on the relation between abandoned houses and reaves, pointing to the ways that land division is orientated by the locations of old house sites (Bradley, 2002; Johnston, 2005). These interpretations envisage a process of gradual territorialisation: Johnston argues that the sites of old houses embodied 'ancestral ties' to land, legitimising tenure by materialising the links between past and present occupancy (Johnston, 2005). Following abandonment of the old house, he argues, the real or imagined descendants of the original occupants would have built another close by. The ruined house would effectively monumentalise genealogical connections, verifying the tenurial claims of the new residents. For this reason, he argues, boundaries tend to link up with abandoned houses, so that coaxial layouts grow from the traces of earlier occupations. A similar argument is advanced by Bradley. He also suggests that coaxial and other landscapes grow gradually as reaves join up abandoned houses (Bradley, 2002: 72-80). Within these interpretations tenure emerges from sedentarisation and territorialisation. Inheritance is taken as the most plausible model for kinship ties, and there is less emphasis on exchanges and transactions.

In this section I reconsider the evidence on which these interpretations are based. I analyse the relations between locations of buildings and boundaries to evaluate the degree to which buildings can be said to determine the layouts of coaxial landscapes. Then I discuss the continuities and discontinuities suggested by previous excavations of these landscapes. My aim is, ultimately, to open up possibilities for thinking about aspects of tenure that are re/deterritorialising in my conclusion.

Buildings and Boundaries

On Dartmoor, it is very common for reaves to incorporate pre-existing features such as cairns, stone rows, tors or roundhouses. Fleming observed how longer reaves used earlier features - especially cairns - as sighting points (Fleming, 1978b). The percentages of different kinds of feature linked to reaves are compared in 5.4. As can be seen from this figure, buildings are the most likely feature to be connected to a reave.

The tendency for buildings to be connected by lengths of reaves is more marked on settlements outside coaxial landscapes than it is within them. Gerrard has produced maps showing how 'agglomerated enclosures' are formed predominately by linking up buildings with short lengths of reave (Gerrard, 1997b, 1997a). Figure 5.5 illustrates this kind of settlement. The relatively high proportion of buildings linked to reaves in this kind of layout can be contrasted with the far smaller proportions of buildings connected to reaves in coaxial layouts (see 5.6 below).

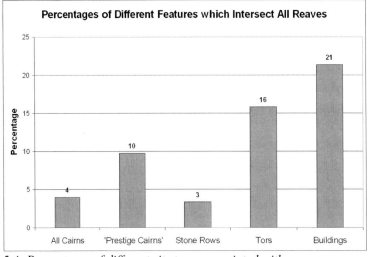

5.4: Percentages of different site types associated with reaves

5.5: Buildings linked to Reaves in Three non-coaxial landscapes.

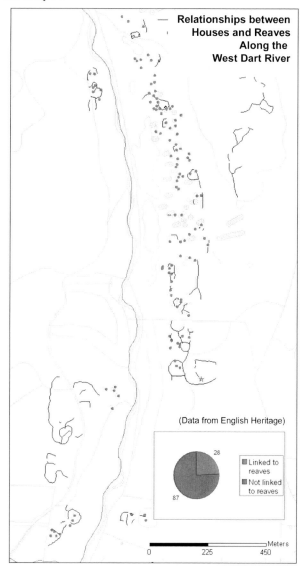

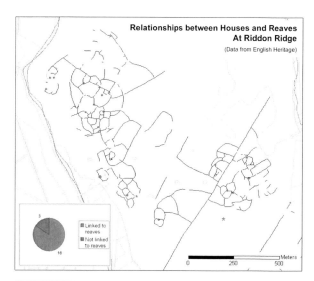

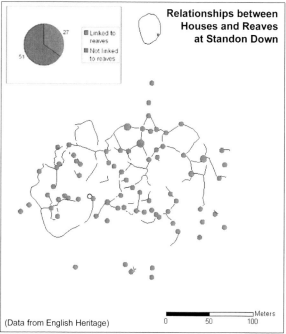

The observation that coaxial landscapes refer to pre-existing structures is not entirely novel; Fleming observed that in certain coaxial landscapes, clusters of houses and small yard areas seemed to precede parallel reaves. He suggested that coaxial 'construction started with the houses and the boundaries near them' (Fleming, 1984: 11). However this is a rather different proposition from suggesting that coaxial layouts were organised to refer to house-sites. Bradley argues that the ruins of older structures, including houses, were used in planning coaxial landscapes (Bradley, 2002: 72-80). He contends that abandoned houses are commonly found in the corners and side walls of fields so that houses provided 'junctions' on which coaxial layouts were based. Johnston makes a similar suggestion based on his analysis of coaxial landscapes at Shovel Down and Kestor (Johnston, 2001b, 2005). He argues that coaxial layouts may have come about through the 'unconscious co-ordination' of building projects, based around the need to legitimise tenure.

I would like to introduce some reservations concerning the significance or degree of relations between houses and coaxial layout. While houses and reaves are often inter-related, there are questions to be asked concerning the degree to which they *determine* coaxial layouts. Coaxial landscapes differ from other areas precisely because the features that supply pattern in the layout do *not* refer to house locations. As was discussed in chapter three, the regularity of coaxial landscapes is largely the result of patterns in the widths between the long 'axial reaves' that demarcate parallel strips (see Fowler, 1971; Bradley, 1977; Fleming, 1987a). As is shown in 5.6, within coaxial landscapes the reaves linked to houses are not, for the most part, these axial reaves. They are mostly shorter lengths of walling delimiting enclosures and smaller 'yard' areas and partitions. The proportion of houses linked to reaves in coaxial landscapes is much smaller than the proportion linked to reaves in non-coaxial settlements (see 5.5 above).

5.6: Axial Reaves within three coaxial landscapes and percentages associated with boundaries

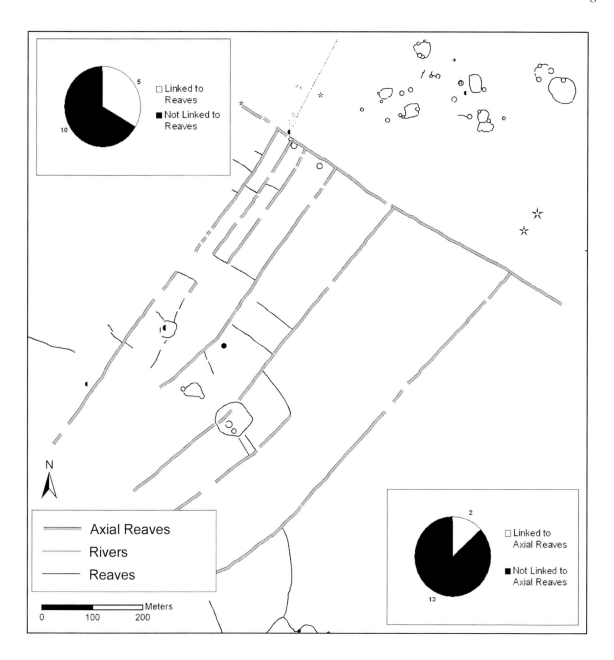

To test the extent of the relationship between axial reaves and buildings I compare the locations of actual roundhouses with those of random simulations. If axial reaves are influenced by the locations of houses they should be significantly closer to buildings than to randomly located points. For this analysis I use coaxial landscapes as surveyed by English Heritage: Holne Moor, Kestor / Shovel Down, and Shaugh Moor. These are the same landscapes discussed by Johnston (2001b; 2005). Axial boundaries in each coaxial landscape were extracted from the other reaves (see 5.6 above). I generated nine distributions of random points. These points were constrained within a 200m buffer drawn around the axial reaves. Random 'houses' were produced based on these points as circles with diameters matching the mean diameters of houses in each landscape. I then measured the proximity of each sample of houses or random simulations to axial reaves.

Analysis found that only two or three buildings linked up to axial reaves in each area. The proximities of simulations and actual houses are compared as cumulative distributions in 5.7. Monte Carlo testing confirms the hypothesis that the actual buildings are no more likely to link up with axial reaves than with the random points. There is no significant relationship between the locations of buildings and axial reaves. The distribution of actual reaves and houses was not significantly different to those occurring by chance alone.

5.7: Cumulative Frequency of Buildings Against Distance from Axial Boundaries at Holne Moor, Shaugh Moor and Shovel Down

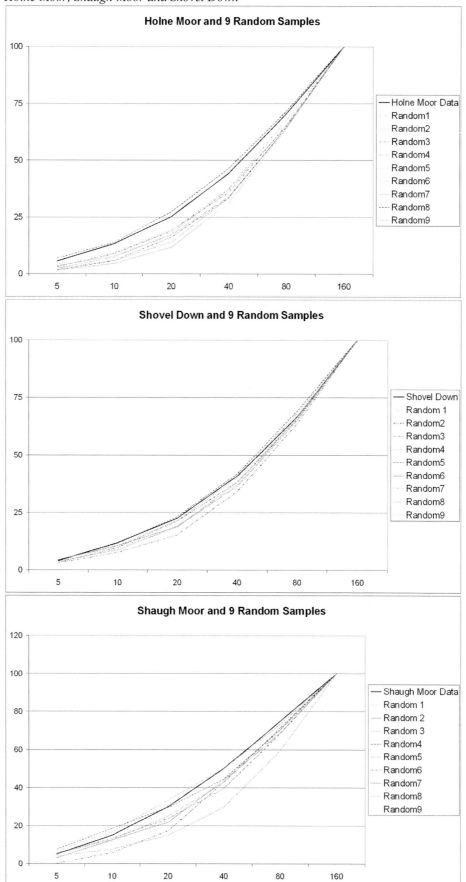

Of course, it is not impossible that the very few buildings joined to axial reaves were all earlier than the reaves, and the others buildings were all built after reaves. If this were so, then the relations between buildings and axial reaves would indeed be significant. In one sample, however, we know that at least one house linked to an axial reave - Site B, Holne Moor – has already proved by excavation to be *later* than the reave (Fleming, 1988). Furthermore, if these houses were a significant influence on coaxial layouts we would expect them to be located at pivotal nodes – at 'junctions' and in the corners of fields, as Bradley suggests (Bradley, 2002: 72-80). However, as is shown in 5.8 only one building – at Kestor, is actually located at a pivotal node, the rest are in locations that are largely incident to the layout of the landscape.

The layout of coaxial landscapes seems unlikely to have been determined by the locations of abandoned buildings to any great extent. However, it is certainly the case that buildings and reaves in general are closely inter-related. Settlement within coaxial landscapes is generally found in dense 'clusters', as has been pointed out by Fleming, and in chapter three (Fleming, 1985b, 1984). While few buildings are linked to axial reaves, many are connected to shorter non-axial reaves. These short lengths of walling tend to form yard spaces in the house vicinity. Frequently these reaves are found in field edges and corners, linking up with axial reaves to form small enclosures. Repeating the analysis carried out above for all reaves – not just axial reaves – does indeed produce a statistically significant relationship between houses and reaves (at 10% probability) (see Appendix S).

It may be that, in the coaxial landscape, axial reaves determine the locations of houses rather more than the other way around. At site B, Holne Moor two timber buildings were located only 2-3m away from the axial reave: Fleming argued that 'the relationship might have been planned' to provide a sheltered area in the lee of the reave (Fleming, 1988: 91-2). It may be that the short reaves around buildings practices that tended to take place in the vicinity of buildings – milking, slaughtering and caring for animals.

It is, of course, impossible to discount the possibility that coaxial layouts were determined by the locations of a large population of timber buildings that have since decayed. Equally the stone-built houses visible today could have been linked to timber axial boundaries, which determined the layout of each system (for example, see the timber fence found at site B (Fleming, 1988: 86). Excavation shows that houses may be earlier, later or contemporary with boundaries – and that survey evidence may be misleading. Survey evidence seemed to show that the building at Site F, Holne Moor was earlier than a reave. However excavation proved that the stone phase of house was actually later then the reave – but beneath it was a timber house that was indeed earlier than the boundary (Fleming, 1985a, 1988: 74-82). Close to Dartmoor excavation at Patterson's Cross showed that the axial boundary here was built before both the buildings excavated (Fitzpatrick et al., 1999: 124). The hidden landscape of timber structures on Dartmoor means that analysis of survey data will always be susceptible to contradiction by excavation.

5.8: Buildings Linked to Axial Reaves in Three Coaxial landscapes (Data from English Heritage and Digimap ©Crown Copyright/database right 2004. An Ordnance Survey/EDINA supplied service)

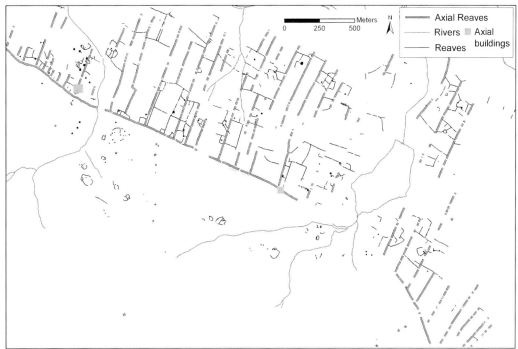

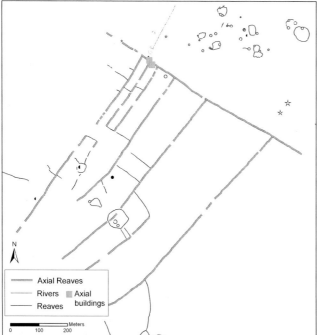

Continuities and Discontinuities in Occupation of Coaxial landscapes

Because Fleming's early interpretations stressed the synchronicity of reaves in order to interpret them as an integrated system of land division, later work has sought to offer a corrective by stressing diachronicity (Johnston, 2005). While Fleming argued that reaves reflected the imposition of a unified plan, or centralised 'mental template' producing coaxial pattern, later writers favour the gradual growth of coaxial landscapes. This corrective emphasis on gradual growth seen in revisions of Fleming's early work by himself as well as others, has led to interpretations that stress continuity. For example, Fleming's most recent contribution argued that reaves were the outcome of gradual processes of stone clearance that formalised boundaries gradually (Fleming, 1994b). Johnston convincingly deploys excavated data to show that reaves are the product of long construction sequences (Johnston, 2005). Continuity and gradual change fit within narratives that see landscape change as gradual progression towards ever greater sedentarisation and territorialisation. By stressing continuity, however, it is easy to create the impression of a seamless narrative of territorialisation.

It is important not to lose sight of evidence for discontinuity and disruption landscape change. Excavations suggest both long sequences of construction, *and* relatively sudden changes; destruction and robbing-out of previous architecture, and even the building of entire new layouts on different axes. For example, at Gold Park an earlier irregular system appears to have been robbed to build a later coaxial layout: One bank and ditch from the irregular system was shown by excavation to underlie a coaxial reave (Gibson, 1992: 32). Excavation suggested that the coaxial landscape on Wotter Common was entirely revamped; an earlier layout was removed, and a new one laid out on a different axis (Smith et al., 1981: 225-6). Traces of the earlier reaves survived as ruined walls on a different alignment to the east of the Wotter reave, possibly stratified beneath the reave itself. Survey data also hints at discontinuity: At Foales Arrishes short lengths of low walling seem to form part of an earlier field system on a different alignment (Butler, 1991a: 57-9). At Stanlake the denuded banks of a possible coaxial system lie beneath a prehistoric agglomerated enclosure (Butler, 1994; cf Gerrard, 1997b: 117).

Just like houses coaxial landscapes may be occupied only for a short duration, before being abandoned. At Patterson's Cross, excavation and palaeoenvironmental evidence shows that the coaxial landscape was abandoned shortly after construction. Cleared ground was rapidly re-colonised with scrubby woodland and ditches filled in (Fitzpatrick et al., 1999). Coaxial landscapes were potentially quite fluid. Granite from earlier structures could easily be recycled, and layouts could be comprehensively redesigned. Narratives of tenure-as-territorialisation, with their emphasis on continuity and sedentarisation, risk suppressing the discontinuities present in some of the evidence.

Territorializing narratives contain implicit assumptions concerning identity and its roots. These are reflected in a preoccupation with 'lineal inheritance' and 'ancestral ties' to land. By criticising the focus on these subjects I am not mischaracterising such accounts by arguing that they require 'real' kinship between inheritors - they do not: It is widely recognised that kinship is remade to suit various purposes at different times (see Barratt 1990, 1994; Johnston 2005). What is at issue here, however, is what such accounts assume kinship is. Following Carsten and Ingold, I would suggest that these accounts presume a 'genealogical model' which takes inheritance and 'biological relatedness' to be the defining ground of kinship (Carsten, 2004a: chapter 1; Ingold, 2000). In this chapter, however, I have discussed alternative models for what kinship is. Kinship is not necessarily defined by inheritance but may be modelled on entirely different dimensions of life – for example in feeding, co-residence of houses, or exchange relations (Carsten, 2004a). Taking these accounts of kinship as my starting point, I would like to re-emphasise the multiple significances of Bronze Age houses. Legitimising tenure through 'ancestral ties' monumentalised in abandoned houses may not be enough to explain Bronze Age tenure; we may also need to consider the flexible and fluid ways in which tenure can be negotiated and transacted.

In this section I re-examined some of the evidence used in recent interpretations of Dartmoor tenure. These accounts envisage the Middle Bronze Age as a period of sedentarisation, and, despite evidence for neolocal, shifting settlement patterns, continue to stress the vertical 'lineal inheritance' of land through 'ancestral ties' (Barrett, 1994; Johnston, 2005). Here, I have questioned the extent to which coaxial landscapes represent the gradual territorialisation of the landscape based on the locations of previous buildings. I have pointed to the evidence for discontinuity as well as continuity of occupation. In my conclusion, I bring together the analyses presented in this chapter to consider the 'translocative' qualities of tenure. Although accounts of the Middle Bronze have traditionally been dominated by narratives of gradual territorialisation, I argue that the evidence from Dartmoor is equally open to alternative approaches to tenure. Tenure does not necessarily emerge seamlessly from gradual sedentarisation within territories and the inheritance of these territories within genealogically modelled kinship. It also involves the capacity to extend relations around wider networks.

Conclusions

The assumptions of tenure-as-territorialisation imply a natural trajectory towards a classical notion of property as an exclusive individual right – except here 'individual' might stand for a singularised household, group, clan, lineage or tribe, as much as a singularised person. The natural trajectory followed, often involves sedentary agriculture, and hence summons the labour theory to explain why people might begin to feel territorial about land.

In this chapter I attempted to disturb the idea that tenure is always equivalent to the creation and preservation of exclusive and inheritable landed estates. Firstly, I explored why territorializing accounts of tenure come so easily to mind. I suggested that seeing tenure in this way results from the influence of modern nationalisms. Nationalisms encourage forms of identification based on 'roots' in territory and shared descent. Next I turned to the analysis of evidence from Dartmoor. I described excavations of buildings. I highlighted the differences between Bronze Age roundhouses and conventional notions of the house as a private domestic realm. Territorializing narratives implicitly imagine the home as a little fortress from which rights to exclude can be extended. However, the role of the Bronze Age house as a nexus for political as well as familial relations implies it may have operated differently; as a locus of inclusion and extension. Next, I considered the biographies of Dartmoor buildings. Evidence is equivocal due to limitations of the excavated record, however, timber buildings within Dartmoor coaxial landscapes do compare with Brück's findings for timber buildings elsewhere in southern Britain which suggests a relatively short-term neolocal residence pattern (Brück 1999). The short lived nature of Bronze Age occupations disrupts the seamless trajectory of sedentarisation often suggested within territorializing narratives. Lastly, I examined recent interpretations which argue that coaxial landscapes grew gradually by incorporating abandoned houses, which monumentalised 'ancestral ties' to land. My analysis found the locations of buildings did not determine coaxial layouts to any great extent.

In chapter three I argued that Dartmoor landscapes were not divided into individualised land-holdings or family farms. I argued that settlement patterns involved the mobilisation of networks of social connections. Subsequently, in chapter four, I suggested that tenure would have been relatively fluidly negotiated and transacted to incorporate flexible use of grazing resources and land rotation. These findings do not fit well with the assumptions of tenure-as-territorialisation. Instead of an inevitable trajectory towards increasing exclusion, these findings imply a concern with various forms of inclusion. In this chapter I suggested that houses might have been places that focused these networked aspects of tenure. Seen as 'engines of relatedness', houses generate intimacy based on sharing food, heat and co-residence. Far from creating separate nuclear families each with their own private domestic realms, these processes may have supplied an idiom of kinship that translocated around wider political, economic and social networks. Houses were built through the multiple contributions of different parties, supplying the grounds for these parties to make later claims on the occupiers. The 'multiple authorship' of the house would have made it immediately an interest distributed among a wider community of interests.

The argument I developed throughout this chapter was that tenure is not solely a matter of territorialisation but also involves processes that de/reterritorialise or extend personhood. These translocal aspects might include (but are not limited to) the way that tenure de/reterritorializes aspects of the person, by enabling the loan, transfer and exchange of various phenomena. This possibility suggests that land division is not so much a signal of fragmentation but way of constructing landscapes to better enable the expansion and mobilisation of networks – distributing aspects of the land among a network of interests. In the next section I will develop these approaches to tenure further as I explore the last of my themes identified in chapter one: – tenure as part of the constitution of identity.

Chapter 6

'Keeping-for-Giving':
Tenure and the Constitution of Identity

A person who has died in New Ireland is considered left unfinished. Evidence for their unfinished condition is distributed across the land, in their unattended fields and unoccupied houses. Gradually the deceased is re-collected through the processes of manufacturing a Malanggan sculpture. This carving becomes a 'skin' for a dead person. It does not resemble the deceased, but is made up of special designs remembered by their family and friends. The revelation of a new Malanggan is a great event. At the time the statue is revealed motifs are broken off as a material reminder of the image. The person who has the right to remember a particular motif also has tenure over part of the land. Much strategic plotting is known to occur around Malanggan fragments 'which entitle their owners to attempt to increase their legitimate share in image and land over time' (Kuchler, 2002: 119). Malanggan fragments enable flexible transactions of tenure across linguistic and spatial boundaries. Rights to remember motifs are exchanged, sold or lent to clan-members who live in different villages, or to different dialect groups. Motifs move about the land as new 'contracts' regarding tenure. In this way tenure is recomposed through exchanges that reconfigure identities.

In this chapter I develop concepts of identity and tenure using evidence from mortuary practices, metalwork finds and studies of exchange. Firstly, I discuss theories of exchange and I review evidence for exchange networks within and without the South-West. I then review previous interpretations of mortuary practices. This review is followed by analysis of evidence for mortuary rites on and around Dartmoor. I then examine the changing treatment of metal objects. Lastly I summarise the transformations of the second millennium BC relating the changing constitution of identities to changes in tenure.

6.1 Tenure and Bronze Age Exchange

Theories of exchange are seldom discussed in archaeologies of tenure. Whereas land in capitalist societies is commodified, elsewhere, it is commonly understood as 'inalienable' (Abramson, 2000). Hence, it is supposed, land is held outside the realm of exchange. But what is meant by inalienability? And how does the inalienability of land come about? In this section I argue that theories of exchange can be used to understand not only what circulates, but also what is kept. I begin with a review of previous theories of Bronze Age exchange and recent critique. I then consider how theories of exchange extend our understanding of the 'inalienable'. I summarise evidence for long distance communication and exchange on and around Dartmoor, and lastly, I review the current picture of exchange networks in the region.

Bronze Age Exchange

In the 1970s and 80s interpretations of Bronze Age exchange transformed: Childe envisaged the Bronze Age as the beginnings of capitalism and commodity exchange (Childe, 1981 [1956]: 117-29). Now a new literature emerged, influenced by Gregory's accounts of 'societies of the gift' (Gregory, 1982) that stressed the opposition between commodity exchange and gift exchange (e.g.

Rowlands, 1980; Gosden, 1985). Bronze Age transactions came to be modelled around an idea of 'prestige goods exchange' (Shennan, 1993; Sherratt, 1993; Kristiansen, 1998). This notion of 'prestige goods exchange' gradually changed the way that gift exchange was represented. Archaeologists moved away from Maussian concepts of the personification of gifts, towards models that emphasised 'strategy' and 'dominance' in gift exchange (Rowlands, 1986).

'Currently' writes Brück 'exchange … is envisaged as an activity which fostered the development of competitive individualism' (Brück, 2006). Starting from a 'general assumption of dominance' (Kristiansen & Larsson, 2005: 5) archaeological accounts represent gift exchange as self-interested. Gift transactions are 'strategies' that allow individuals to maintain dominance through the creation of debts: 'Behind the rules of gift giving' Kristiansen argues, 'the realities of political strategy and of economy are operating' (Kristiansen, 1998: 252). As Brück points out, this prestige goods exchange model, 'implicitly characterises objects as commodities' (Brück, 2006). It represents value as 'prestige' reified in objects so that it can be accumulated as 'wealth' or capital. This implicit commodity economics leads some accounts towards problems of their own making: How, Kristiansen puzzles, do individuals acquire the first gifts (the 'capital' as it were) necessary to enter exchange? His answer focuses how large burial mounds create prestige. Prestige reserves generated in mortuary displays allow relatives to acquire the necessary objects (Kristiansen, 1998: 44-50, 252-3; Earle, 2002: chapter 13). Rendering gifts as pseudo-commodities invokes motivations familiar in common-sense 'economics' – exchange becomes maximisation (of 'wealth' or 'prestige') by self-interested individuals.

This is far removed from Mauss' original vision in *The Gift* (Mauss, 1970). For Mauss, the gift grasped a crucial paradox; the possibility of an economics which was both self-interested *and* altruistic, so that the distinction between these categories was collapsed (Laidlaw, 2000). Gifts circulate as 'persons' and 'parts of persons' (Mauss, 1970; Gregory, 1982; Strathern, 1988). (Remember that the definition of persons here might include not just individuals but families or groups). Parts of persons that are transacted are detached from one entity and incorporated into the body of another (see section 1.5). To the extent that prestige good exchange models fail to grasp the full implications of gifts they fail to engage with the dynamics of exchange fully. Consider the examples of exchange from East New Britain discussed at the start of Chapter four: no party came away having gained a debt and no one accumulated 'prestige' in these everyday exchanges. Despite the lack of 'economic' motive, however, non-agonistic reciprocal exchanges like these are by far the commonest sort of gift exchange (Godelier, 1999: 155). Models that stress dominance, 'strategy' and individual competition cannot explain the ongoing dependencies such reciprocal exchanges engender even after a counter-gift has been returned. They cannot explain why a debt is never cancelled by a counter-gift, why 'to give in return does not mean to give back, to repay; it means to give in turn' (Godelier, 1999: 48). Mauss, however, did explain why; it is because the gift is inalienably part of the giver; 'it still forms a part of him' (ibid: 9) Transactions, as Weiner observes, involve 'keeping-while-giving' (Weiner, 1992). Part of the person travels forward with the gift, and thus, in a sense they 'keep' it. Gift giving does not alienate parties to the transaction, the relationship, and its obligations, are ongoing.

Tenure and Exchange

Archaeologies of tenure may assert that 'traditional' societies treat land as inalienable, but they rarely theorise inalienability. When archaeologists assert that land was 'inalienable', what they usually mean is that a pre-defined 'thing' (land) was understood in the past as belonging to a fixed category of things that were not to be transacted, sold or alienated. Land thus stood in opposition to another fixed category of things (portable objects) that *were* to be transacted, sold or alienated. It is unfortunate that one of the widely cited studies of inalienability (*'Inalienable Possessions'*, Weiner, 1992) tends more towards the definition of the inalienable as a category of things rather than as a process of relating (Mosko, 2000). Other studies of exchange suggest a different perspective – the inalienable is not a category of things but a description of relationships.

Inalienability describes the character of a transaction rather than the nature of a category of things. Anything can be inalienable or alienable depending on whether it is transacted as a gift or as a commodity (Gregory, 1982; Strathern, 1988). The assumption that the inalienable is a structural category of things is based on the 'commonsense' of societies dominated by commodification: Commodity transactions create equivalences between objects and objects. They construct categories of things as if objects were apart from social relations (see critique of commodity fetishism in Marx, 1976: 165). Therefore when the commodity dominates, fixed categories of 'things' emerge distinct from the relations that formed them. One category designates things that are 'not to be sold' (i.e. 'not selling your grandmother'). In situations dominated by the gift, categories of things do not appear in the same way; equivalences are not created between objects and objects, instead, relations are created between persons. Things are seen as parts of persons and/or new persons born of the relation. Anything appropriate to a relationship might conceivably be transacted. The problem in situations dominated by the gift, is maintaining anything outside of the realm of exchange, since all entities are already enmeshed within an inevitable network of relations.

How then, are aspects of tenure kept back from the constant circulation of gifts? The answer, in many societies, lies in the imaginary. Relations with cosmological deities in the imaginary provide an idiom or context for tenure. Tenure expresses both the everyday 'economy' and the 'magico-religious' realms simultaneously (Malinowski, 1921: 15). The origin myths of many societies, Godelier observes, tell how the reproductive forces of society were originally given as gifts by supernatural personages. When this happens 'the exchange object … enters the domain no longer of exchanges between the living, but between the living and their dead, and the living and their gods,' and thus 'the object of trade *becomes sacred*' (Godelier, 1999: 169 his emphasis). We can see how when land is a 'gift from the gods' it comprises a *'certain kind of relationship with the origin'* (ibid.), and this relationship is part of what constitutes identity *relationally*. When land is part of identity people can never be completely detached, or alienated, from it. Land and identity still belong in some sense to gods, ancestors or other supernatural beings.

This does not mean that tenure is kept entirely out of the realm of day-to-day exchange. However, the imaginary does explain what elements of tenure are transacted and what elements are kept. Often, tenure involves 'keeping-while-giving' as Weiner puts it, or 'keeping-*for*-giving' as Godelier prefers (Weiner, 1992; Godelier, 1999: 33 his emphasis). The indissoluble link between sacred objects and identities (their socially reproductive force) is inalienable, but the *effects* of that relation are transacted. In the context of land this may appear as keeping hold of the 'ownership' of land while transacting certain 'rights' in its uses, products, and transfer. However, the words 'ownership' and 'rights' here fail to grasp the way tenure is part of personhood. Relations are less of 'ownership' than of identification. What is ceded are not 'rights' so much as elements of the reproductive capacity of the donor; reproductive capacities that retain something of the sacred.

These observations on the imaginary suggest new perspective on Bronze Age deposition and its possible connections with tenure. Where land is a sacred gift, it entails an obligation that can never be repaid; 'men have no equivalent gift to give in return' (Godelier, 1999: 186). Furthermore the gift is continuously bestowed since reproductive forces just keep on giving. The originary gift becomes the ground of an endless obligation to supply counter-gifts, which cannot repay the gift, but instead offer some return for people's continuing tenure of the original gift. Potent parallels are potentially set up here between the supernatural givers of land and mortals who give away aspects of tenure. 'Gifts to the gods'- deposits in the earth, in water, in caves and in special places - might be expected to occur when relations with sacred objects are changed, such as when tenure changes hands. Through objects, the terms of ongoing transactions might be stabilised; materialised in forms that subsequently acted upon the parties. Such materialisations act on relations in a similar way to modern contract documents (Alexander, 2001) or West African fetishes (Graeber, 2005a). The memory of gifts to the gods might have acted as a sanction, mediating tenurial transactions.

Evidence from South-West England

'Compared with earlier periods' Pare suggests 'the Bronze Age was characterised by a massive increase in exchange' (Pare, 2000: 24). From the late Neolithic and Early Bronze Age the distribution of Beaker-associated items and the swift adoption of tin-bronze indicates a well-established network of regular contact between southern Britain and north-west Europe across the Channel and North Sea (Pare, 2000; Bender, 1986: 37-41). Isotope evidence demonstrates people were travelling long distances between central Europe and southern Britain (Fitzpatrick, 2002). Furthermore, long distance communications may even intensify into the Middle and Late Bronze Age (Bradley, 1998a: chapter 5). Principal sources for exchange networks comprise evidence for:

i) routes and means of communication
ii) materials sourcing
iii) parallels between objects and/or 'exotics'

Devon and Cornwall are dominated by the sea, so that communications here probably coalesced around sea routes. Fragments of sewn plank boats probably used for seafaring are now known from the Severn and Humber Estuaries and at Dover (Clark, 2004; Van der Noort, 2004). Although no fragments of boats have yet been recovered in the vicinity of Dartmoor, metalwork raised from the seabed at Moor Sands, Salcombe, possibly represents the cargo of a sunken vessel (Muckelroy, 1980) although recent discoveries show findspots are widely spread (Maritime and Coastguard Agency, 2005). Finds from Moor Sands are all of types dating c1300-1150 BC with predominantly British or North French affinities. One object, however, represents 'the first secure object of Mediterranean origin and bronze age date to be found in north-west Europe' – a *strumento con immanicatura a cannone* imported from Sicily (Parham et al., 2006).

The south-west contains significant tin sources – materials rare across most of Europe (Harding, 1999). There is also copper ore, and, in Cornwall, small amounts of gold. The levels of tin in objects are consistent across the British Isles suggesting 'consistent, well organised, long distance movement' from 2200 BC onwards (Pare, 2000: 21). Finding objects that can be conclusively linked to Dartmoor, however, has proved difficult. Analysis shows that tin from different sources was mixed suggesting bronzes were recycled (Northover, 1982). One small group of very early objects contained copper from the St Austell area of Cornwall (Budd et al., 2000). The ores, metal or objects had travelled widely, with findspots in Cumbria, Sussex and Wales. Evidence for Bronze Age mining in Devon and Cornwall reveals a curious anomaly. While there is some good evidence for the exploitation of ores in Cornwall, there is much less from Dartmoor. Gerrard suggests that this is due to differences in preservation between the two areas: Dartmoor was aggressively mined in the nineteenth century, possibly destroying much of the evidence, whereas the industrial exploitation of Cornish tin took place in earlier centuries (Gerrard, 2000). Timberlake suggests this anomaly may actually result from regional patterning in gift exchange networks across Britain and Ireland (Timberlake, 2001). He argues that some areas of Britain and Ireland may have been figured as 'givers' and some as 'takers' of various raw materials. Thus, Wales, which has significant evidence for copper mining appears to have been figured as a 'giver' of copper, and Cornwall as a 'giver' of tin and gold. It may be that these 'giving' and 'taking' relationships were also exercised within the south-west region, explaining the strange lack of evidence for Bronze Age mining on Dartmoor (Barber, 2003: 105-7). However, it is still possible that evidence for tin mining on Dartmoor will be forthcoming; recent studies of atmospheric pollution and sedimentology supply some indirect evidence possibly pointing to mining activity (West, 1997; Thorndycraft et al., 2004).

Style, particularly metalwork types, offer evidence for interconnections between regions. From the Early Bronze Age connections with Ireland are suggested by the Early Bronze Age gold lunulae from Harlyn Bay, Cornwall and a flat axe found at Drewsteignton, Dartmoor (Fox, 1973:

94-5; Pearce, 1981: 88). A spectacular amber pommel decorated with gold studs from Hameldown, Dartmoor shows parallels with gold-studded hilts found as grave goods in Brittany (Bender, 1986: 39). Early Bronze Age cups, made of various precious materials, include the gold cup from Rillaton, Cornwall and shale cups from Farway, Devon. These cups are found over a large area from Cornwall to the head of the Rhine. While they seem to be produced locally, they show a distinct maritime distribution, close to the Channel, the Frisian coast and the river Rhine, suggesting interlinked traditions (Needham, 2006). From the Later Bronze Age gold bracelets and torcs suggest either 'Irish imports' or 'someone fully conversant with Irish gold-working techniques'; evidenced in finds from Morvah and Towednack, Cornwall (Todd, 1989: 153). 'Yeovil torcs' are found across south-west and southern Britain, Brittany and Normandy (Bender, 1986: 43). Possible Early-Middle Bronze Age imports with parallels in north-west Europe include 'one, possibly two' axes from a hoard at Plymstock, and another example from Teignmouth both close to Dartmoor (Todd, 1989: 110). On Dartmoor itself, a palstave found in a reave system on Horridge Common derives from Bohemia (Fox & Britton, 1969). Connections with northern France, and possibly further afield, continue in the Late Bronze Age, witnessed in metalwork types found at Mount Batten (Todd, 1989: 154).

Interpretations of Exchange Networks

Existing evidence suggests that, at the time reaves were constructed and occupied, exchange was dominated by gift transactions, although commodity exchange becomes increasingly important after c1600-1300 BC (Sherratt, 1993; Shennan, 1993; Bradley, 1998a; Pare, 2000). In the South West distributions of artefacts and pottery fabrics suggest a series of 'small-scale interlocking exchange networks' (Parker Pearson, 1990:22), orchestrated around 'social relationships of allegiance and affiliation rather than distance and cost' (Parker Pearson, 1995: 98). Evidence for these 'local' spheres of exchange comes from the distributions of distinct regional types of object - Trevisker Ware pottery and Crediton Palstaves. The distribution of these types falls off abruptly at the edge of the South-western region. At the same time certain other artefact types do not pass into the region: 'No Deverel Rimbury styles (or imports)' for example 'passed further west' than Dartmoor (Parker Pearson, 1990: 22). This pattern is not found where objects are traded through competitive market exchange. Instead it suggests gift exchange among related groups. Nonetheless, it is clear that isolated objects could be exchanged outside the

region – for example, one Trevisker Urn was brought all the way from Cornwall to Thanet in Kent, probably by sea (Clark, 2004: 8).

Some accounts distinguish between 'local' and 'regional' exchange suggesting that there is some threshold between either type of exchange network. Pearce observes that exotic imports are quite rare in the interior, and are mostly found in coastal areas (Pearce, 1979; 1981). Bradley suggests trade in bulk commodities on the periphery, with imports melted down to produce types that could be exchanged as gifts in the interior (Bradley, 1984). However, these interpretations do not explain why imports are deposited with ceremony in similar ways to 'local' artefacts (see Barber, 2003). Nor why a region rich in tin needed to import 'scrap' from other tin-rich regions (Brittany and Bohemia), to 'satisfy demand' for raw material (cf Pearce, 1983). Melting down and recasting does not necessarily obliterate the memory of earlier objects and the relationships created through transactions. There are unanswered questions concerning 'commodity' exchanges in the region which await further investigation (cf Brück 2006). For now, it is enough to observe that gift exchange seems to have played an important role in exchange relations.

Fleming's work offered detailed analyses of how small-scale interlocking gift exchange networks might have operated in reave landscapes (Fleming, 1984, 1988). Using ethnographic and historical parallels, he argued that exchanges of labour, technology, and produce played an essential part in social organisation (see section 2.2; Fleming, 1979, 1985b). Fleming's 'Communal Ownership of Property Model' (see section 2.1) goes some way towards explaining a puzzle identified by Clark - how is it that a society without obvious settlement hierarchy, seeming 'fragmented' into small-scale settlements, could organise communal endeavours like the Dover boat, which was surely beyond the capabilities of a single family group (Clark, 2004: 4-6)? Maintaining long-distance communications would have entailed considerable outlay in resources, labour and expertise - as complex undertakings like boat building attest. However, such communal endeavours were not without parallel, the construction of coaxial landscapes provides a model for the organisation of labour and resources on a similar scale.

This review underlines the significance of mortuary sites and metalwork for interpretations of exchange. In the sections that follow I take up these subjects at greater length, examining what they might suggest about tenure and identity. I begin with a review of previous interpretations of mortuary practices.

6.2 Cairns, Territory and Tenure

Barrows are widely seen as property markers - 'written on the land in ways not unlike deeds' (Earle, 2004: 155). Archaeologists have adduced 'territories' from the

distributions of these sites, which they relate to segments of kin groups and social structure (e.g. Barnatt, 1989, 1999, 2000; Fleming, 1971). These accounts put Kitchen in mind of 'some insane system of apian peer polity interaction, each bee policing its own cell within the honeycomb, and occasionally sending the whole colony into a frenzy of activity by the performance of a bee dance' (Kitchen, 2001: 110). Recently, an alternative approach has emerged that focuses on what mortuary practices tell us about the nature of identity. Concurrently, the prominence of tenure has waned. This section reviews previous interpretations. I begin with the notion of burial sites as territorial claims. Next, I discuss barrows and cairns as the graves of high-status individuals. Lastly I review recent approaches focusing on relational identity and personhood suggesting tenure has fallen out of the debate.

Burial Sites as Territorial Markers

In the era of processual archaeology a general 'law' or 'hypothesis' emerged that 'formal disposal areas for the exclusive disposal of the dead' were correlated with exclusive ownership held by local descent groups (Saxe cited in Goldstein, 1981: 59): As land became scarce, it was argued, tenure would be legitimised 'by means of lineal descent from the dead' (ibid.). For example, Fleming argued that barrows on the chalk downlands marked 'seasonally occupied territories ... conceived of as 'home areas' in which the dead were buried' (Fleming, 1971: 159-160). Renfrew's suggested that Early Neolithic megalithic tombs 'served as territorial markers' and that land scarcity stimulated tomb construction (Renfrew, 1976: 208). This functional explanation of burial sites as property markers remains widespread (see Parker Pearson, 1999 for review).

This interpretation has been offered by many commentators on Dartmoor landscapes (Fox, 1973; Grinsell, 1978; Fleming, 1988; Gerrard, 1997a). Fleming argued that 'prestige cairns' were built by groups of graziers from the moor-land fringe to consolidate land claims and signal them to other transhumant groups arriving from afar (Fleming, 1983:216-17). For Barnatt cairns signalled the boundaries of territories, subsequently formalised in the layout of long reaves (Barnatt, 1989). Gerrard observes that although the lower lands of Dartmoor 'were clearly denoted by field boundaries, the upland areas were not'. Therefore, he argues 'claims' on the upland 'may have been indicated at least in part by the building and use of cairns' (Gerrard, 1997a: 61). In these accounts cairns are represented as the functional equivalents of boundaries, marking defined territories, or of deeds, proving proof of exclusive ownership.

The 'owners' envisaged here are local descent groups or lineage heads. The classic model of barrow development involves the death of a local chieftain - the stimulus for building the barrow - followed by 'secondary burials' of individuals of lesser status within the lineage (Woodward, 2002: 22). Linear 'cemeteries' are traditionally interpreted as 'the tombs of a dynasty' in

which each chieftain was interred alongside 'his' (sic) predecessor (Fox, 1948: 3). The positioning of bodies within barrows is seen as indicating the dominance of a lineage 'head' over his (the classic model envisages male leaders) lesser relatives (Mizoguchi, 1993). Barrett argues that the emergence of 'individuating' burial rites at the end of the third millennium BC indicates the emergence of lineal inheritance including inheritance of land rights (Barrett, 1990: 189). Secondary burials represent ideological attempts to manipulate genealogical connections with significant dead personages (Barrett, 1990, 1994: chapter 3). The group that is signalled by barrows and cairns is that of the lineage, symbolised by its headman or chief.

Barrows and cairns are often seen as the first stage of a gradual territorialisation that is subsequently expressed through the construction of boundaries. The 'individuating' burial rite and lineal inheritance of land are associated with a transformation in subjectivities between the Neolithic and Bronze Age. In the Bronze Age, Barrett argues, subjects were 'fixed' temporally within structures of 'lineal inheritance', and situated spatially within coaxial boundaries. A linear directional temporality emerged as tenure configured identity in a new way:

> 'Lines of specific genealogical identity were constructed whose own origins then came to be fixed by mythological images of increasingly more distant times. It was in these distant and mythological ages that the inaccessible and heroic figures had lived and died who now lay buried beneath the massive turf and chalk-capped tumuli...'
> (Barrett, 1994: 127-8).

As symbols of ownership held by the corporate descent group barrows and cairns are the first step towards land division.

'Princely Graves'

Traditionally, burial sites are read in terms of the status of individuals. In the antiquarian imagination barrows were 'princely graves'; monuments to men of great lineages, interred with all the ceremony bestowed on Hector (Homer, trans. Hammond, 1987: 407-8). For the landed proprietor, possessing burial mounds on one's estate conferred glamour-by-association on the landowner's own pedigree (Sweet, 2004: 273-4). Later archaeological interpretations dwelt on grave goods as evidence for the wealth of individuals and their families. A prominent example was found at Hameldown, Dartmoor, where an amber pommel studded with gold pins was excavated: 'It hardly seems extravagant' commented Pearce, 'to see the occupant of the Hameldown barrow as the lord of many herds' (Pearce, 1983: 140). Along with wealth, high-status individuals were seen as possessing good connections. The Hameldon barrow, for example, is one of very few Wessex-style 'fancy barrows' from Dartmoor: - Fox speculated that it was the grave of a chieftain from Wessex (Fox, 1948). Commentators suggest that prehistoric people metaphorically associated height and the ability to command a good view with prestige and domination of territory. Other evidences of 'status' include the size and shape of the mound, and their arrangement within cemeteries. One category of 'prestige cairns' are seen as particularly high status. These cairns 'were built large and sited to impress' on summits, or on ridges, or false crests (Grinsell, 1978).

The 'princely graves' theme persists throughout the Bronze Age, despite the obvious changes that occur in mortuary practices during the period (see Owoc, 2001; Jones, 2005: chapter 6). Commentators present both the Early and Middle Bronze Age mortuary customs as expressing the 'status' of individuals. Fox saw Middle Bronze Age mortuary rites as continuing trends beginning with Beaker graves, comprising 'a tribute to the individual … reflecting his or her importance in the community' (Fox, 1973). Likewise Todd argued that burial sites c1500 BC reflected 'the elevation of individuals above the mass of the population … on the basis of their wealth or status or both' (Todd, 1989: 141). Nonetheless the ways in which mortuary practices on Devon sites differ from the classic interpretations of Wessex sites have long been obvious. Fox observed that barrows west of the Exe generally lacked a central primary burial (Fox, 1948: 13). However such regional 'abnormalities' were traditionally seen as reflecting lack of 'wealth' compared to Wessex, rather then supplying evidence for qualitatively different practices. Throughout the Bronze Age barrows and cairns are described as the graves of notable individuals within 'leading families', who possessed prestigious 'wealth', power and landed territory (Pearce, 1983: 140).

Rethinking Mortuary Rites

Recent analyses of cairns and barrows within the South-West (Jones, 2005) and more generally (Woodward, 2002) have comprehensively overhauled the evidence on which many previous interpretations were based. The emphasis on single primary burials now seems mistaken - a result of 'over dependence on the results of the relatively poorly recorded antiquarian excavations from Southern England' (Woodward, 2002: 23). It has been demonstrated that many barrows contain multiple 'primary burials', or only 'secondary' and satellite' burials and no central grave, or contain no human

remains at all. Some so-called 'grave goods' are not associated with any body (Woodward, 2002: chapter 2). Far from comprising straightforward memorials to heads of lineages, Jones has shown that cairns in Cornwall and West Devon tend to be composite sites, with evidence for lengthy sequences of deposition and elaboration over time (Jones, 2004a). The record suggests a range of diverse practices, implying that cairns are only rarely 'graves'.

Whereas traditional interpretations of Early Bronze Age mortuary practices envisaged 'individuating' rites, more recent accounts argue that bodies may have been understood as multiply composed. Brück points to the manner in which bodies are assembled prior to deposition. Often bodies have been fragmented mixed up together and recomposed. Apparently 'individual' bodies are 'often accompanied by extra pieces of bone belonging to other bodies' (Brück, 2004: 310). Studies of the objects placed in Early Bronze Age burial contexts have also found them to be mixed up and re-assembled from multiple components (Jones, 2004c). For example Early Bronze Age beads are generally not found as complete 'sets', but are often found as 'the remains of several necklaces, dispersed and reconstituted through the mechanisms of inheritance and gift exchange' (Barrett, 1994; Woodward, 2002). Gifts like these, contributed in accordance with relations with the deceased, may have had the effect of recomposing or 'completing' his or her identity (Jones, 2004a). Parallels may be observed with the Malanggan carvings with which I opened this chapter. Several writers suggest that Early Bronze Age treatment of human remains suggests practices that are not 'individuating' but 'dividuating' (see section 1.5; Brück, 2004; Fowler, 2004: 72-76). Bronze Age identities, these writers suggest, are best seen as 'relational', composed of relationships, and hence simultaneously 'individual' and 'collective'.

Just as the focus on identity has advanced in interpretations of mortuary practices, tenure has begun to slide out of view. 'Territorializing' approaches conjure static, structural images that make it easy to map property objects onto social organisation. When identities are understood relationally, however, they are much more fluid, invoking ongoing processes of reproducing kinship and personhood. What do these new ideas of relational identity and personhood mean for archaeologies of tenure? This question has hardly been explored in the new literature. In the next section I begin to investigate this issue through an assessment of evidence for mortuary practices on and around Dartmoor.

6.3 Mortuary Practices Assessed

In this section I examine evidence from excavated barrows and cairns on and around Dartmoor. First I discuss chronology and the limitations of the dataset. Next I evaluate three aspects of previous interpretation:

- 'status' differentiation and 'princely' graves
- primary and secondary burials
- evidence for practices that 'individuate'

Parameters of Available Data

The database of barrows and cairns and the periods when excavations were carried out, are shown in 6.1. As the map shows, the vast majority of interventions took place before 1950. Unfortunately this means that most sites lack adequate reports and absolute dates. The database is further reduced by other factors: The cairnfield excavated at Minehouse has not been fully published (English Heritage, 1987). The cairnfield at Gold Park dates to the Late Iron Age rather than the Bronze Age (Gibson, 1992). Finally the round cairn at the head of the Cholwichtown stone row was badly damaged (Eogan, 1964). This leaves only a single well-recorded Bronze Age site; the group of cairns and ring cairns at Shaugh Moor (Smith et al., 1979).

The lack of well documented sites means that it is necessary to look for parallels outside the region to situate the Dartmoor sites in their wider context. Useful nearby excavations include the Elburton cemetery, which has a good series of radiocarbon dates (Watts & Quinnell, 2001) and the site at Upton Pyne, which has a only a single date but is relatively well recorded (Pollard & Russell, 1969). Two cremations were recovered from a ring-ditch at Exminster (not shown on 6.1), but the site was damaged and no absolute dates were obtained (Jarvis, 1976).

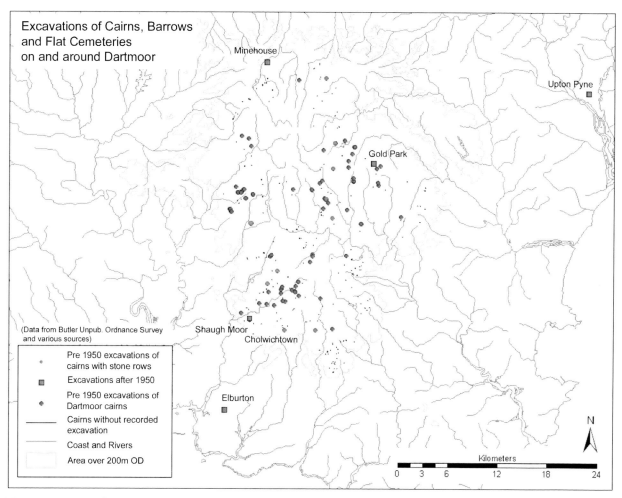

6.1: Excavations of Cairns, Barrows and Cemeteries (Topographic data ©Crown Copyright/database right 2004. An Ordnance Survey/EDINA supplied service)

The lack of recent excavations with C14 dates makes detailed chronology impossible, but some general guidelines can be ascertained. I have recalibrated the available dates from Shaugh Moor, Upton Pyne and Dainton (section 2.4, Appendix H). The main concentration of these dates at (95%, 2 Sigma) begins at the end of Needham's period 3 (c1850 BC) and continues through Needham's period 4 until c1540 BC. This date range is in keeping with the overall distribution of dates from Devon and Cornwall, which suggests cairn building here peaked slightly later than some other regions, with most cairns and barrows constructed between 2000 – 1600 BC (Jones, 2005: 36-8; Quinnell, 1994b). At least four (possibly five) beakers have been recorded from early excavations on Dartmoor (Quinnell, 1996), and some sites may have been built as early as Needham's periods 1 and 2. However, recent analysis of Beakers in Cornwall shows that the most common association of Beaker ceramics is with Trevisker Ware, and suggests Beakers post-date 2000 BC (Jones, 2004a; 2005: chapter 2). This, combined with the lack of pre-2000 BC dates from West Devon, suggests caution in reconstructing mortuary practices of the late third millennium BC.

Reassessing 'Princely Graves'

Evidence for 'high status' objects is extremely rare. The numbers of cairns with artefacts of various materials is shown in 6.2. Most of the materials placed in cairns and barrows are not prestige goods but wood charcoal, flint, or, less commonly, broken pottery. Only five sites contain metal objects.

It is striking how many 'primary burials' in the study area consist only of wood charcoal (see 6.2). This feature of

Dartmoor sites has long been known (Worth, 1994; Quinnell, 1994b). It reflects a wider pattern across the South-West (Jones, 2004a; Owoc, 2001), although the practice is 'most strongly developed on Dartmoor' (Jones, 2005: 128). Wood charcoal deposits are often supplied with 'grave goods' exactly as a burial might be. For example at Fernworthy, excavation revealed a small central pit with an inverted urn containing wood charcoal: 'Not a trace of bone, burnt or unburnt, could be detected' (Baring-Gould et al., 1898: 108-9) but several beaker associated objects; bronze dagger with wooden handle attached, a Kimmeridge shale button, and a flint knife, were deposited. At Two Barrows, on Hameldown, the central deposit was not 'the lord of many herds' as Pearce speculated, but 'one small fragment of charcoal'. The wood fragment was treated with some ceremony, covered with a small cairn of stones. It subsequently became the focus for other deposits including cremated bone, an amber pommel and Camerton-Snowshill dagger (Spence Bate, 1872: 554-7).

Examples of sites with 'primary burials' of wood charcoal include some with dates that place them within the period of reave construction (see section 2.4): At Shaugh Moor primary deposits of charcoal were treated in similar ways to deposits of human remains: At Ring Cairn 2 oak charcoal was accompanied by 'grave goods', including a pot base and a number of segmented faience beads. At Cairn 70 the central deposit of oak charcoal was covered by a capstone. At the centre of Cairn 71 oak charcoal was accompanied by sherds of broken pottery. Central pits containing oak charcoal were also present at Ring cairn 1 and the miniature ring cairn 126 (built into the edge of ring cairn 1) (Smith et al., 1979).

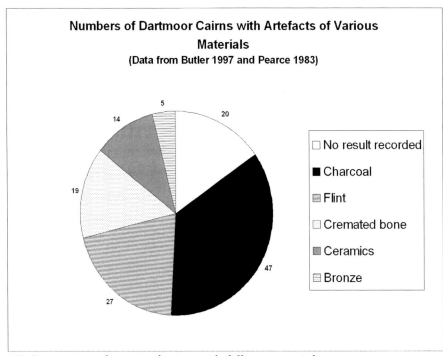

6.2: Proportions of excavated cairns with different materials

The traditional interpretation of sites without human remains has been that they are cenotaphs – burials for individuals or lineage heads whose bodies have been lost (at sea or on the battlefield for example) (Parker Pearson, 1999). More recently archaeologists have begun to look seriously at the treatment afforded to seemingly inauspicious materials - rocks or charcoal - as important practices in their own right (Bradley, 2000). At many Dartmoor sites the central focus is not a burial, but a tor or a boulder. Sometimes an entire rock might be engulfed by a heap of stones, otherwise the tor may be 'referenced' through a ring monument either completely surrounding the rocks (as at Branscombe's Loaf) or a circular segment attached to it (as at High Willhays Tor) (Turner, 1990). There are also at least two examples of cists that make use of natural rock to form one side of the structure (Butler, 1997a: 173). At some sites the centre of the cairn is occupied by a small cairn of stones apparently with nothing beneath it, as at Single Barrow (Spence Bate, 1872) and Shaugh Moor, Cairn 4 (Smith et al., 1979).

The record includes cairns without finds of any description. Cairns 3 and 4 at Red Barrows, despite being 'prestige cairns' within a 'linear cemetery', turned out to be 'mere heaps of stone' (Anderson et al., 1903). Traditionally these sites were separated from 'graves' as 'clearance cairns' (see Gerrard, 1997a). However this distinction is increasingly difficult to sustain. Recent studies have shown that clearance cairns contain a range of special deposits and are sometimes carefully constructed (Johnston, 2001a; Bradley, 2005). On Dartmoor a 'clearance cairn' at Minehouse sealed a deposit of Neolithic pottery (English Heritage, 1987). There is evidence for complex practices at barrows and cairns that never required a human body. Rather then categorising sites into non-ritual 'clearance cairns' vs. ritual 'graves' it is more productive to uncouple them entirely from the idea of 'princely graves'. Barrows and cairns are not always primarily 'funerary' sites for the disposal of the dead. They involve a range of activities which only occasionally made use of human remains.

Assessing Primary and Secondary Burials

The classic model of barrow construction, envisages the 'primary burial' of an adult male lineage head surrounded by 'secondary burials'. These practices have been interpreted as evidence for the manipulation of genealogical connections within lineages (Barrett, 1990). But this classic model is the exception rather then the rule in the South West (Fox, 1973:12-4; Jones, 2004a). Where human remains *are* present their age and sex seldom correspond to the lineage head of the conventional imagination. Analysis of cremated bones from sites across southern Britain has found that female and infant bodies are the main focus of mortuary practices from the end of the Early Bronze Age into the Middle Bronze Age (McKinley, 2001). Female cremated skeletons dominate (51% females compared to 12% males) and of the many

immature skeletons, 75% are infants (McKinley, 2001: 36). This is confirmed by evidence from sites in the Dartmoor area: At Stevenstone Farm, the primary burial was 'probably a woman' or maybe a youth not younger than 12 years old (Fox in Pollard & Russell, 1969: 76). At Brownstone Farm, Kingswear, the primary burial was judged to represent a child, around 10 years old (Fox, 1948: 12). At Burrow Park Tolly, Halwill the 'primary burial' comprised a deposit of 'calcined animal bones' placed within a classic grave pit four and a half feet by three feet and four feet deep (Burnard, 1896). At Upton Pyne, the primary burial comprised the fragmented body of a baby less then a year old, ('perhaps newborn') mixed with oak charcoal. 'Secondary burials' included an urn within a cist containing wood charcoal and burnt organic deposits (possibly grass), another urn containing 'half a teaspoonful of tiny pieces of unidentifiable calcined bone' (ibid: 60), and finally the cremation of another infant. A series of cremations were found at Elburton, but nothing resembling primary or secondary burials: The cremations were of two adult females and an infant around 3 years old. The most complete female cremation contained not only human bone, but also part of the backbone of a cow (Watts & Quinnell, 2001).

The evidence does not support notions of 'princely graves' or 'lineage heads'. Primary burials are generally absent, or where they can be found they are not the 'chieftains' of traditional accounts. It is, of course, still possible that deposits in Devon cairns and barrows were placed to manipulate genealogical connections and secure access to inherited land. But this interpretation requires some other source of evidence.

'Dividuation' and Fragmentation of Bodies

Dartmoor soils are too acidic for bones to survive unless they have been cremated. However the preponderance of cremations may not simply be a matter of preservation. Cremation is a feature of mortuary practices across the South-West, where inhumations are rare even where soil conditions preserve bone (Owoc, 2001; Jones, 2004a, 2005). Nonetheless it is clear that some sites could have contained inhumations. Butler points out that some sites contain cut features large enough to have contained crouched bodies (Butler, 1997a: 208), although most pits beneath cairns are too small to have been graves (Johnston, 2001b).

Where cremated bone is present, it is seldom enough to represent the cremation of an entire individual. As in the rest of the South-West human remains are usually present as 'token handfuls' (Jones, 2004a).

For example, the cairn excavated at Archerton, contained only 'a few ounces of burnt bone' (Burnard, 1986 [1894]). At Upton Pyne, the primary deposit of cremated bone was only 'about two teaspoonfuls' and another deposit was 'less than one teaspoon' (Pollard & Russell,

1969: 58-60). At many sites cremated bone was mixed up with other materials, including earth that seems to have been specially selected to display a different colour to the surrounding matrix (Owoc, 1999). At Elberton the cremations are unusual in representing large parts of the body: Bone from one adult female skeleton was present at about 45% to 72% of the expected weight of an adult cremation. A large part of the infant was present, but the other female burial had been badly truncated (Watts & Quinnell, 2001). A cairn heading of one of the Fernworthy stone rows contained 'masses of burnt bone' which may have been a complete cremated body picked from the pyre (Baring-Gould et al., 1898).

Evidence suggests that whole human bodies – individuals - are not the primary focus of mortuary practices in the South-West. Instead cairns are loci for numerous activities some of which involve deposits of fragmented and partial human bodies. The elaboration of these activites may continue for a prolonged period. The most recent and detailed dating sequence, from Watch Hill in Cornwall, indicates activity over a period of around 300 years (Jones, 2005: 34-6). Owoc has shown that barrows and cairns are composite sites with multi-stage construction processes (Owoc, 2001). The Upton Pyne involved at least five different building phases, four of which were separated by episodes of charcoal deposition (Pollard & Russell, 1969: 62). Many sites incorporate materials that were specially selected for colour and texture (Owoc, 1999). At Upton Pyne the barrow was built on a 'platform' of purple clay deliberately laid across the site (Pollard & Russell, 1969). While the traditional position has been that these monuments were 'erected to mark the passing of the individual' recent analyses show that in the South West they 'were essentially places of communal ritual and ceremony' (Jones, 2005: 142). Like construction of reaves and houses, construction of cairns involved co-ordinated communal efforts, mobilising relationships and engaging questions of access to resources and tenure.

Evidence from barrows and cairns on and around Dartmoor does not suggest 'individuation', but, instead supports recent interpretations that invoke 'dividuation' and relational identities (Brück, 2004; Fowler, 2004: 72-76). Bodies deposited at these sites have been subjected to complex sequences of transformation and fragmentation. Instead of being assembled into 'wholes' bodies were mixed up with other materials or dispersed as 'token handfuls'. It is possible that cremated bone was divided up and exchanged between parties. These practices may reflect identities that were multiply composed, so that death involved redistributing bodies through a series of counter-gifts (including gifts to the gods). The question of what these findings mean for archaeologies of tenure remains to be answered. Before I turn to this question I first compare the results of this analysis with evidence from metalwork deposition. What might this evidence suggest concerning identities in the time of reaves?

6.4 Metalwork and 'Gifts to the Gods'

I have drawn attention to 'gifts to the gods', which, in the Bronze Age, may take the form of deposits placed in the earth, rocks and watery places (Bradley, 1998a). I pointed to the way in which gifts personify things as persons and parts of persons. Following Godelier (1999) I suggested that gifts to gods often constitute counter-gifts given in return for the continuing bounty of socially reproductive forces (which may include land). The effects of these originary gifts permeate each society's exchange relations, influencing what is transacted and what is held back, and providing a model for everyday exchanges.

In this section I review evidence for the treatment of metalwork in the region. I begin with a review of data available for study, its limitations and chronology. I discuss overall patterns in the dataset. Then I assess contexts of deposition in more detail. Lastly, I examine the fragmentation and circulation of metalwork within the region.

Compiling a Database

Data for this review was compiled from published studies (Pearce, 1979, 1983, 1999) and Devon SMR (see 6.3, Appendix T). The data currently available are limited by poor documentation of context; few finds have been recovered through modern excavation techniques. However, work by Stevens is currently revising information on context, chronology and typology within the South-West. This is likely to improve the data available for future studies (Stevens pers com).

Typology and chronology have been developed from Pearce (1999). She uses a simple Early-Middle-Late classification for various typological groupings (see 6.4). The period of reave building spans these chronological categories, beginning at the end of Early Bronze Age - around the same time as Plymstock/Wessex II types enter the record - and continuing throughout the Middle Bronze Age alongside the deposition of Chagford/Taunton types.

6.3: Distribution of Bronze Age Metalwork (Topographic data ©Crown Copyright/database right 2004. An Ordnance Survey/EDINA supplied service)

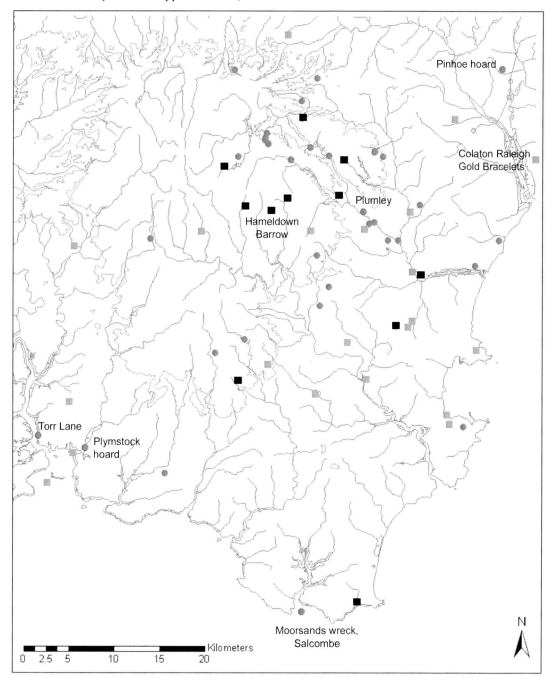

Locations of Findspots of Bronze Age Metalwork around Dartmoor, Devon

● Middle Bronze Age Metalwork	● Late Bronze Age Metalwork	■ Early Bronze Age Metalwork	⋯⋯ Rivers and coast
			☐ Land over 200m

(Data from Ordnance Survey, Pearce 1983, Devon SMR)

6.4: Metalwork Chronology (Adapted from Pearce, 1999)

Period	Dates	Typological Categories
Early Bronze Age	c2500-1600 BC	Copper-Using Harlyn, Trenovissick/Wessex I, Plymstock/Wessex II
Middle Bronze Age	c1600-1200 BC	Chagford/Taunton
Late Bronze Age	c1200-600 BC	Worth/Dainton*, Stogursey/Mount Batten
* Worth/Dainton pieces here placed with LBA to match chronology of reaves		

New chronological information from absolute dating of metalwork suggests that Taunton metalwork of the Middle Bronze Age begins earlier than Pearce appreciated, starting around 1770-1350 BC and ending 1380-1210 BC (Needham et al., 1997: 80). The discrepancies between the typological dating of an artefact and the date of its deposition are obviously an ongoing problem given the limitations of currently available contextual information. Pearce herself exercised some flexibility around this issue: Metalwork from the Plymstock hoard, for example, is typologically of the Early Bronze Age, but Pearce classifies it as Middle Bronze Age because she considers it fits within a Middle Bronze Age tradition of hoards in non-burial contexts (Pearce, 1999: 69).

Patterns in Deposition

Reave construction coincides with important transformations in the history of deposition. At the time that reaves begin to appear deposition at barrows and cairns is reaching its peak in the South West (see section 2.4; Jones, 2005). However during the period and occupation of landscapes of reaves there is a dramatic expansion in deposition of new types of metalwork. There is also a new diversity in the places selected for deposits of metal. The differences in rates of deposition between periods can be compared in 6.5.

Transformations in deposition between the Early and Middle Bronze Age are often seen as indicating a shift in the focus of ritual life from barrows and cairns towards watery places. Metalwork stops being used as 'grave goods' and starts being hoarded. Hoards are then either kept safe by burying them in the earth (so-called 'utilitarian' hoards) or are sacrificed in competitive status-enhancing 'gifts to the gods' as 'votive hoards' in wet places (Bradley, 1998a). The prevalence of findspots in different kinds of location can be compared in 6.6. The decrease in cairn findspots can clearly be seen, but findspots associated with water are relatively few, even in the Late Bronze Age.

In recent work the dichotomy between ritual votive hoards and 'non-ritual' deposits appears increasingly unhelpful. The 'emphasis on votive acts associated with water' Barber argues, has 'led to potentially misleading distinctions being drawn at times between 'wet' and 'dry' contexts' (Barber, 2003: 68-9). Wet contexts have tended to be viewed as 'ritual', whilst dry contexts encouraged functional explanations. 'Utilitarian' deposits, made in the course of everyday 'economic' production and exchange are just as likely to be imbued with ritual significance as 'votive' hoards. Furthermore, even where metalwork deposits were intended to be recovered in the future, the act of withdrawing them from exchange temporarily can still be understood as 'sacrificial' (Needham, 2001). It is increasingly recognised, that metalwork does not need to defy 'rational' explanation in order to be understood as 'ritual' (Brück, 1999b; Bradley, 2005: chapter 5).

Dryland findspots are often found in significant places, and are marked in special ways. For example the Plymstock hoard was also found under a large boulder at the base of a prominent limestone ridge (Pearce, 1983: 433, 452; Barber, 2003: 56). At Plumley eight palstaves were placed carefully in two matching groups beneath a large boulder. Each group contained four palstaves each placed upright in the ground (Pearce, 1983: 433; Barber, 2003: 56).

Dryland findspots yielded only one or two artefacts. Such single finds have often been written off as 'accidental' losses; 'insignificant' compared to the more 'prestigious', 'high-status' hoards. However recent studies point out that the findspots of many single objects suggest deliberate processes of deposition (Barber, 2003: 68-9; Roberts & Ottaway, 2003: 134). Consider, for example, the complete Deverel Rimbury vessel wedged into a crevice high up on the inaccessible rock face of the Dewerstone on Dartmoor (Pettit, 1974: 56). Here, an apparently isolated single find enhanced a place of special significance.

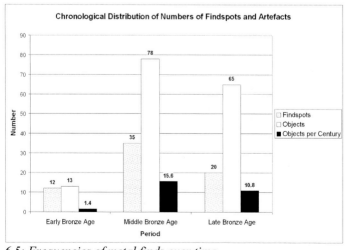

6.5: Frequencies of metal finds over time

6.6: Contexts of Findspots by Period

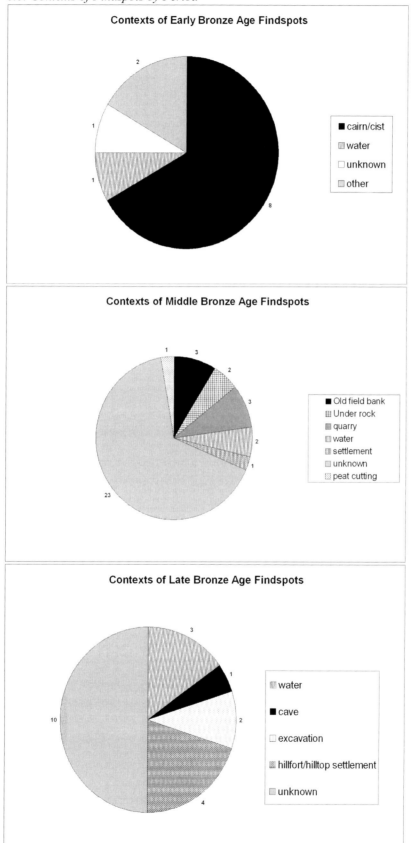

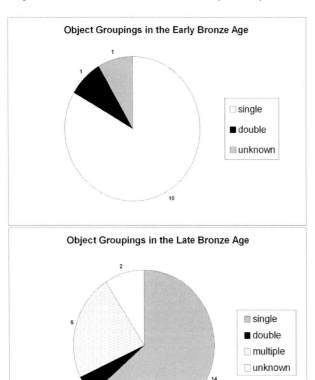

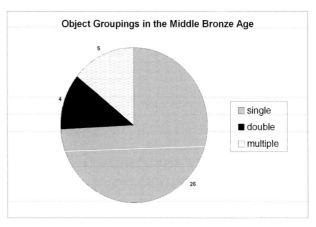

6.7: Numbers of Finds per Findspot by Period

Numbers of finds recorded from each findspot are compared by period in 6.7. Findspots with only one or two bronzes dominate the record. The first 'hoards' appear in the late Early and Middle Bronze Age – as reaves start to be constructed. At the same time, however, there is an even more marked increase in the number (though not the proportion) of finds of single objects. There is a remarkable cluster of findspots, each with two bronzes, around the North-East of Dartmoor (see Appendix U). The large numbers of findspots with only one or two objects suggest that, as reaves began to be built, intentional deposition of metalwork was not the exclusive preserve of elites, but may have been a more widespread practice.

Contexts of Deposition

The distinction between an Early Bronze Age with metalwork associated with human remains and a Middle/Late Bronze Age when it is supposed separated from such contexts is not borne out by evidence from the South-West. Many cairns and barrows were never used as 'graves', thus, metalwork in the Early Bronze Age was often not associated with human remains. On the other hand, in the Middle and Late Bronze Age, metalwork often *is* found in the same places as human remains. For example, antiquarian records document metalwork placed in a series of limestone caves just to the east of Dartmoor (e.g. at Ash Hole, Broken cavern, Kitley Cave, Plateau Rift and Kent's Cavern). At least two of these (Kitley Cave and Plateau Rift) contained not only metalwork, but human remains with Middle Bronze Age radiocarbon

dates (Chamberlain & Williams, 2001). A quantity of Late Bronze Age types have been recovered from Kent's Cavern, this 'hoard', is actually made up from a range of special deposits in different parts of the cave (Silvester, 1986). It seems that caves retained their importance as places where deposits of human remains or metalwork might be placed interchangeably throughout the Bronze Age.

Although finds from cairns decline in the Middle and Late Bronze Age the continuing association between metalwork and cairns is a distinctive feature of the Devon record (Jones, 2005: 133). The Plymstock hoard was close to the edge of an as yet unexcavated barrow, a location that Webster suggests resembles that of many 'secondary burials' (Webster, 2003: 3). A Late Bronze Age deposit of metalworking debris (fragments of moulds, crucibles and bronze) was placed in and around a pit close to the edge of a cairn at Dainton (Needham, 1980).

Many bronzes of Late-Early to Middle Bronze Age types have been recovered from 'old field banks'. Polwhele, writing in the seventeenth century, records that bronzes were found under old walls in Devon, citing one location at Buckfastleigh (Pearce, 1983). A double find of palstaves at Week was located beneath a 'very old hedge bank' (Pearce, 1983: 450). At Torr Lane a hoard of six pieces - rapiers and palstaves - was found in a field bank. The Bohemian palstave from Horridge Common seems to have derived from a prehistoric reave (Fox & Britton, 1969; Fay Stevens pers. comm.). It is possible that at least some of these finds reflect deliberate deposition of bronzes in reaves. Deposition of metalwork in prehistoric boundaries is known in South-West: A double find of axes was found buried in a Bronze Age field bank at Veryan, Cornwall (Pearce, 1984: 34). The Towednack, gold hoard of nine gold neck-rings, armrings and 'unfinished' rods was found beneath a field bank (Pearce, 1981: 123). Further east, bronze was deposited in the enclosure ditches at South Lodge Camp (Barrett et al., 1991). Metalwork was not the only object that was placed in boundaries: at Holne Moor a deposit of broken pottery and charcoal was placed in a reave bank then sealed by more reave material (Fleming, 1988). At Hillfarance in Somerset waterlogged deposits preserved a wooden idol dated to 1410-1080 BC in a pit associated with Bronze Age field boundaries (Webster, 2003). Land division clearly created locations suitable for 'gifts to the gods'.

The record of findspots on and around Dartmoor does not suggest the end of 'grave goods' and the rise of competitive display of vast hoards of 'wealth'. Instead there seems to be a gradual spreading out of activities previously taking place mainly at cairns, to encompass the whole landscape. There is no necessary shift from a concern with human remains to a concern with things: Things and people may have been to some degree interchangeable - 'things which are to some extent parts of persons, and persons and groups that behave in some measure as if they were things' (Mauss, 1970: 11). It is interesting to note that just as metalwork findspots are spreading out into a range of new locations deposits of human remains seem to do the same. Excavations at Honiton, Slapton and at Lower Ashmore Farm indicate 'a little recognised spread' of Middle Bronze Age human remains in Devon, that were never associated with barrows or cairns, but that, like deposits of metalwork, spread out in the landscape in new ways (Watts & Quinnell, 2001: 34).

Fragmentation and Exchange

Rather than drawing a strong contrast between pieces of humans and pieces of metal it may be more helpful to consider Mauss' idea of personification. Gifts may circulate as persons or parts of persons. Bronzes may have been personified, just as much as cremated bone. Chapman has studied the implications of personification archaeologically (Chapman, 2000). He discusses how the circulation of objects distributes personhood around networks. Exchanging objects and fragments of objects allows the 'enchainment' of persons:

'The two people, who wish to establish some form of social relationship or conclude some kind of transaction, agree on a specific artefact appropriate to the interaction in question and break it in two or more parts, each keeping one or more parts as a token of the relationship ... The fragments of the object are then

kept until reconstitution of the relationship is required, in which case the part(s) may be deposited in a structured manner' (Chapman, 2000: 6).

The materialisation of an agreement stabilises the terms of ongoing relations, rather in the same way that the materiality of contract documents stabilise ongoing negotiations (Alexander, 2001).

These processes of circulating materials and substances point to 'dividual' rather than individual identities (Chapman, 2000: chapter 3; Fowler, 2004: 72-6; Brück, 2004). Fragmentation can occur at the level of the single object, but groups or 'sets' also compose multiple wholes that can be dismembered or re-assembled (Chapman, 2000: 44-8). Breaking up 'sets' and reassembling them creates connections between objects that can express, reaffirm or alter interpersonal relationships (Brück, 2004: 314). Bradley argues that many Middle and Late Bronze Age hoards contain deliberately fragmented objects, reflecting the 'enchainment' of people (Bradley, 2005: 154-164).

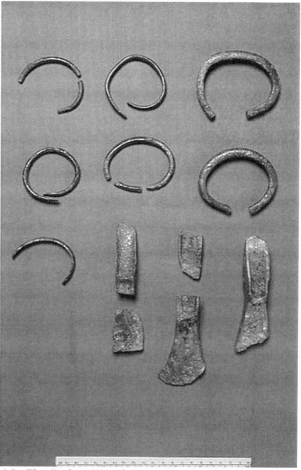

6.8: The Pinhoe Hoard (Reproduced with permission of Royal Albert Memorial Museum & Art Gallery, Exeter, and, acknowledging the finder Mr Jim Cobley OBE)

There are several examples of deliberately fragmented metal artefacts around Dartmoor. The Middle Bronze Age hoard from Pinhoe contained fragmentary palstaves and bronzes armlets (see 6.8). Not only are metal objects deliberately broken, but moulds are often deposited as fragments, as the Late Bronze Age site at Dainton (Needham, 1980). The Late Bronze Age hoard from Colaton Raleigh included three gold bracelets and a small clipped fragment from another. These were carefully placed, nested inside one another within a pit. Their dimensions suggested they were worn by women and some had been worn a long time, probably for whole of an adult life (Taylor, 1999: 214). 'Clippings' from objects of gold are not uncommon finds in graves and hoards throughout the Bronze Age. Taylor links them to changes in identities of the owners; signifying 'membership of a cult' or some other transformation (Taylor, 1999: 214-7).

In this brief investigation, I have suggested that the period in which landscapes of reaves began to be constructed was marked by a diversification in depositional practices. 'Gifts to the gods' might now take place at a wider range of locations, rather than just at barrows and cairns. Newly constructed field banks were among these fresh 'ritual' sites. I argued that, in the Early to Middle Bronze Age, the ability to make gifts of this kind was not restricted to narrow elites engaged in individualistic competition, but may have involved group and 'dividual' identities. Circulation of objects and fragments of objects may have materialised new forms of relations that became important as reave landscapes were emerging.

6.5 Tenure and the Constitution of Identity

'In a society where, in the last analysis, all relations are personal relations, where written contracts do not exist, and where all commitments are made publicly, ownership necessarily appears as an attribute of the person himself and relations of ownership as direct or indirect relations between persons.'
(Godelier, 1999: 91)

I have argued that tenure can be approached as part of the constitution of identities. Although identity has become an important focus of recent Bronze Age studies its connections with tenure have remained unexamined. In this section I return to a question posed above; what do new archaeologies of relational identities mean for tenure? I begin by discussing the implications of my findings concerning mortuary practices. Next I discuss the deposition of metalwork, connecting deposition to exchange relations (including exchanges with the supernatural world). Lastly I discuss how tenurial exchanges can be seen as the necessary basis of long-distance communications, so that tenure was 'translocated' into wider exchange networks.

Mortuary Rites and Tenure

Conventional interpretations of 'burial sites' offer narratives of tenure-as-territorialisation; barrows are seen as property markers signalling territorial claims, and the establishment of such claims is taken as evolution of tenure. In this chapter I presented evidence that suggested cairns on and around Dartmoor were not primarily the graves of high-status individuals. Instead, I found evidence for practices that supported recent archaeologies of relational identities (e.g. Brück, 2004; Fowler, 2004; Jones, 2004c). Previous territorializing accounts envisaged land-holding lineages, often governed by lineage heads. An important source of evidence for these lineages derives from a classic model of the positioning of primary and secondary burials within barrows (e.g. Barrett, 1990, 1994). I found little evidence for this classic model on or around Dartmoor.

My findings have knock-on effects for some recent work. Several writers have suggested that practices formerly focused on barrows and cairns were transferred to houses in the Middle and Later Bronze Age (Brück, 1995; Bradley, 1998b: 152-8; Jones, 2005: 140-1). Johnston has used the links between cairns and houses to argue that the role of cairns in symbolising lineal inheritance became to transferred to houses; houses symbolised ancestral ties to land and thereby legitimised tenure (Johnston, 2001b, 2005). However, I have argued that there is little evidence that cairns on and around Dartmoor ever involved the primary and secondary burials that are taken as symbolising 'lineal histories' (Barrett, 1994). If cairns did not play this kind of role, then it becomes more difficult to argue that houses could have taken it over. Some other sources of evidence are needed if we wish to perpetuate the traditional pre-eminence of segmentary lineages in Bronze Age tenure studies.

If mortuary practices are interpreted using ideas of relational identities what difference does this make to concepts of tenure? In chapter five I discussed how territorializing accounts singularise objects of tenure into territories and subjects of tenure into unitary 'owners'. Even when the owner is a collective group they are still represented as a singular entity. The attraction of this kind of archaeology is the ease with which it allows territories to be converted into images of social structure; physical 'markers' can be identified on maps to produce territories, and these territories can then be read as relatively straightforward indicators of social organisation (for examples see Barnatt, 1989, 1999, 2000; and, to some extent, Fleming, 1994b). As Kitchen observes, this exercise - as an attempt to model *tenure* - misses its object entirely. Conflating Ingold's definitions of tenure and territoriality, it 'fails to grasp the point that it is particular social networks, relevant to tenure, and not territoriality, that must form the focus of our enquiry' (Kitchen, 2001: 111). Behind the identification of territories and the representation of territories as tenure lies the historical influence of classical theories of property. These theories imagine property as an exclusive individual right (e.g. Earle, 2000) and thus demand that, if property is to be identified, property objects and subjects must be singularised and unitary.

When identities are understood relationally, however, a different set of possibilities come into play. Persons are understood as comprised of aspects of relations with others. When personhood is understood in this way, tenure is not best seen as property; as an exclusive individual right. Instead tenure is necessarily be inclusive and distributed, because the subjects at issue are inclusive and distributed. Property does not singularise interests in objects. Instead, tenure multiplies claims over subjects. Land may itself be personified so that it is possible to enter into exchange relations with the land binding land into personal identity.

Exchange and Gifts to the Gods

Moving archaeologies of tenure away from the 'self-evident' domains assumed by tenure-as-territorialisation involves reconnecting tenure with theories of exchange. The theories of exchange that I have used draw heavily on Maussian concepts (see Mauss, 1970; Gregory, 1982; Strathern, 1988). I have criticised previous archaeologies of 'gift economics' that focus disproportionately on the 'strategies' of self-interested individuals trying to establish dominance (cf Kristiansen, 1998; Earle, 2002). Instead I have examined how gifts distribute aspects of personhood, constructing identities relationally.

Current interpretations of exchange in South-West Britain, envisage a society largely dominated by gift exchange at the time when reaves were built. A series of small-scale gift exchange networks operated across the region (Parker Pearson, 1990, 1995). On and around Dartmoor there was a dramatic increase in the rate of deposition at the time that reaves began to be constructed. Deposits at cairns and barrows were at their peak as reaves began to be laid out. Shortly afterwards bronzes began to eclipse other materials, and the rate of metalwork deposition reached its maximum. The transition from charcoal, cremated bodies, pots, axes and daggers towards weaponry and bracelets suggest transformations in the social, moral and economic values congealed in these artefacts. However, there is no necessary opposition between bronzes and human remains. Just as burnt bone may have been exchanged between persons so bronzes would have been personified through gift exchange. Landscapes of reaves may thus be associated with an increase in the velocity of gift exchange and deposition.

Gift exchange does not only take place between people, but can equally take place between mortals and the supernatural. I have interpreted deposition as a way of making gifts to the gods (Bradley, 1998a). The placing of gifts in special places, in cairns, earth and water, contributed to the body of the land. The history of such gifts would have encouraged close identification between land and people, as each became inalienably linked to the other. In the imaginary realm land is often understood as a gift from deities or ancestors (Godelier, 1999). Land thus personifies the sacred. As a result, many societies consider that the bond between people and land is an inalienable relation. This does not necessarily mean that tenure never enters into circulation, however. On the contrary, this may encourage the exchange of certain elements of tenure (especially various aspects of usufruct) within gift exchange networks. The inalienable is thus not outside of exchange networks, but is at their heart, and this is what Godelier means when he writes of 'keeping-*for*-giving'. When tenure circulates as a gift it is an aspect of personhood, but it also refers to that person's connection with the imaginary – to the sacred origins of their identity.

In this chapter I have discussed how deposition gradually moved away from cairns to include a much wider range of locations, after the establishment of reaves began. Places suitable for deposits could now include the newly constructed field banks and boundaries. This 'spreading out' of locations for deposition may reflect transformations in tenure connected to reaves. Deposition of 'gifts to the gods' within the body of the land may relate to changes in tenure. In many societies the act of loaning or giving tenure between people reproduces in the mortal sphere the supernatural acts of giving land that are found in origin myths (Godelier, 1999). Because land is understood as the gift of supernatural agencies it does not belong completely to the person who grants tenure, it still retains something of the sacred. Consequently changes in tenurial arrangements are likely to occasion gifts to the gods. These gifts have the added benefit of materialising the new agreements and acting as a sanction on the parties involved (see Alexander, 2001; Graeber, 2005a). The memory of sacrifices, embodied mnemonically in landscape features, may play a part in stabilising the ongoing relationships that tenure produces.

Tenure and Translocations

Throughout the second millennium BC long distance communications may have become increasingly important, stimulated by exchange of metals (Pare, 2000). While current interpretations emphasise gift exchange within the South-West, there are some indications of a 'threshold' between these smaller-scale networks and long distance exchanges, evidenced by the relatively restricted distribution of 'local' types (i.e. Trevisker Ware, Crediton Palstaves) and by suggestions of greater emphasis on commodity exchange at the perimeter of 'local' networks (Pearce, 1983; Bradley, 1984).

Rather than opposing the local and the regional here it may be more useful to consider how small-scale gift exchange networks were 'translocated' into the realm of long distance communications. I have already referred to evidence for communal activities involved in building boats and supporting crew members on long distance voyages. The exchanges involved in producing boats would have ensured that boats embodied the interests of a wider community (Clark, 2004). There is a parallel here with the construction of land division – another communal activity. In this context the 'threshold' between small-scale exchange networks and long distance exchanges may refer to the ways in which relations were transformed and translocated to allow particular people and objects to travel abroad (see Munn, 1987, 1990). Although Bronze Age travellers may have appeared as 'individual' adventurers they necessarily embodied the relations that produced them. There is no necessary contrast between 'local' land tenure and long distance communications. In fact the elaboration of gift exchange relations surrounding access to land might be seen as a logical outgrowth of the increasing importance of long-distance exchange relations in the second millennium BC. Expanding exchange relations through lending, swapping and giving away elements of tenure would allow groups and persons to develop the social ties that were a prerequisite for long distance exchanges.

Conclusions

In this chapter I reviewed evidence for exchange networks among the groups which built reaves. I investigated evidence from excavations of barrows and cairns and from finds of metalwork on and around Dartmoor. I used these sources to reflect on tenure as part of the constitution of identity. Previous interpretations have tended to focus on elite power, the display of 'prestige goods', and the control of territory. Barrows have been interpreted as property markers signalling territorial claims. Accounts of metalwork have concentrated on competitive displays of chiefly wealth. Here, I suggest that evidence from Dartmoor fits within recent accounts of relational identity and personhood. However, I noted that tenure has slipped out of view in much of this literature. I asked what difference these new ideas of personhood made to ideas of Bronze Age tenure?

Answering this question led me to consider the networks of relations that configured identity, including relations with the imaginary. I considered gifts to the gods as part of wider exchange relations, including exchanges involving tenure. I suggested that deposition confirmed the connection between people and land as an inalienable relation of identification. This did not prevent the exchange of tenure, however: The identity of people/land meant land was kept-for-giving, allowing tenure to be mobilised as a way of extending personhood. Exchanging tenure in this way, I suggested, could have helped form the networks which were necessary for wider communal endeavours, like building boats or constructing land division.

In this chapter I explored the final of my four themes – approaching tenure as part of the constitution of identity. However, it remains for me to relate ideas of identity and tenure that I have developed here to the material form of reave landscapes. Reaves clearly allowed greater flexibility in land uses and in tenurial exchanges, but how does this relate to the striking patterns in coaxial landscapes? The next chapter uses the observations on tenure and identity I have developed here to interpret the layout of reaves.

Chapter 7

Arithmetic of Tenure and Identity:
Measurement and Value in Coaxial Landscapes

The clandestine survey of Tibet by Nain Singh Rawat is amongst the great adventure stories of map-making. Engaged by the Survey of India in 1863, Nain Singh assumed the disguise of a Tibetan pilgrim to penetrate and secretly map what was then forbidden country. Nain Singh's ability to pace exactly 31.5 inches (two thousand paces to the mile) and his retention of all the measurements that would later become the map were crucial. He brought with him ingeniously disguised devices that allowed him to memorise measurements. Every hundredth pace was counted by the dropping of a bead on a 'rosary'; not a standard Hindu or Buddhist rosary of 108 beads, but a specially produced Survey of India rosary eight beads short. Notes and measurements encoded as Tibetan prayers were hidden inside specially designed prayer wheels. Nain Singh repetitively chanted measurements aloud under his breath, in the way that a Tibetan pilgrim might chant prayers. By these means he compiled the information that became the first detailed and accurate map of the Tibetan interior - its vast mountain ranges, rivers and lakes - in an area that had previously been almost a complete blank to colonial cartographers (Allen, 1982: 134-141).

The feats of Nain Singh Rawat illustrate the importance of material things in performing measurement. The capacity to map Tibet was not only that of Nain Singh the individual, it emerged from the intersection of a mathematical idea of space with the landscape itself, via the material equipment that Nain Singh used and his remarkable ability to assimilate a unit of measurement into his habitus. Mathematics is not purely cerebral; it is a practical activity, enacted and materialised.

In this chapter I produce a metrology of coaxial landscapes (metrology is the study of measurement) investigating the practical activities involved in laying out coaxial architecture. I begin with a discussion of mathematics, its materialisation and enactment. Measurement, I argue, is a practical mathematics of valuing. Next, I review previous metrological studies in archaeology. I argue that measurement can be enacted in more then one way – not all of them numerical. Having identified an appropriate methodology, I use it to investigate what kinds of measurement were involved in laying out coaxial landscapes. I go onto interpret the results of the analysis suggesting specific measuring practices. Lastly, I discuss what these measuring practices imply about the valuing of land in coaxial landscapes, and how this relates to issues of tenure and personhood. Ultimately my findings relate tenure to the constitution of identity – developing themes discussed in chapter six.

7.1 Mathematics, Personhood and Value

Mathematics involves practical abilities of grouping and ordering that generate intuitions of space, pattern, rhythm and time. Mathematics represents these processes and produces methods by which analogies, deductions and calculations can be made (Kuchler, 2004: 31-2). These capacities are not confined to 'western' or 'modern' knowledge practices, nor do they consist solely of abstract thought processes. Ethnographies of mathematics emphasise the role of the material world in activating mathematical thought (Were, 2003; Kuchler, 2004). Mathematical thinking has been found to inhere in objects including such examples as knotted strings (Kuchler, 2004), wooden tablets and rock carvings (Bishop, 1995: 72), and especially, in beads (Graeber, 2001). Were argues that mathematics is a form of 'concrete thinking' activated by objects (Were, 2003: 27). Mathematics is commonly learnt through performances or practices linked to material things, for example, in the finger counting of infancy (Mimica, 1988). Studies of maths teaching from classrooms across the world show that material objects are effective vehicles that aid the learning of mathematical concepts (Were, 2003). Ethnographies of traditional arts and crafts in Oceania show how these material practices facilitate 'high level' mathematical performance among those with little or no formal education, particularly in cultures that stress visual knowledge over texts (Were, 2003: 27). These studies emphasise how material practices bring mathematical reasoning about, at the same time that they evoke emotions, embody sacred principles and cosmological understandings, and play a part in constituting identity.

Pattern is particularly important in transmission of mathematical thought. The agency that transmits pattern might be said to inhere not just in an interior world of ideas and mental templates, nor solely in the social acquisition of skills, but also in the forms of objects themselves (Kuchler, 2002: 169). The social 'context' of production is not the only way of accounting for form or pattern in 'material culture'; instead the ways in which material forms are generated through practice tend to involve 'iconic translations' of 'processes that may at first glance have nothing to do with each other' (Kuchler, 2002: 169). Architecture and material objects can be said to 'distribute' capacities like mathematics in time and space, as a 'form of cognition which takes place outside of the body' (Gell, 1998: 232). The spatio-temporal structures of a corpus of artworks might be seen as an externalized, collectivized, cognitive process transcending the individual and the 'co-ordinates of any particular here and now' (ibid: 258).

In this chapter I approach coaxial landscapes as a form of architecture that regenerate and redistribute practical mathematics. Coaxial landscapes contain strong elements of pattern, engaging and embodying mathematical thinking. Building this architecture would itself have activated certain forms of calculation among the builders. In this section I set the scene for this approach. I first describe mathematical systems that may be described as 'fractal', and how these systems relate to apprehension of body and cosmos. Next I discuss how practice mathematics emerges from engagements between bodies and architecture. Lastly I explore the role of practical mathematics in valuing entities within economic networks, according to particular kinds of exchange.

'Fractal' mathematics

> *'The anthropological literature demonstrates, for all who want to see it, that the mathematics which most people learn in contemporary schools is not the only mathematics that exists'*
> (Bishop, 1995: 72)

Mathematics is an extraordinarily diverse dimension of knowledge. If we take counting - the aspect of maths that has assumed iconic importance within what Bishop calls 'western mathematics' - the range of documented systems is astonishing. Nearly 600 different counting systems have been recorded in Papua New Guinea alone (Bishop, 1995: 72). All cultures have generated mathematics, just as they have kinship, or tenure. However, the dominance of so-called 'western mathematics' and its instalment as a form of internationalised, 'culture-free' knowledge, meant that, until recently, alternative systems have been difficult to recognise as mathematics. 'Western mathematics' Bishop suggests, carries with it a 'cultural history' specifically that of imperialism, and hence of power and control. This mathematics perceives a world composed of discrete objects that can be abstracted from their context and accumulated without limit; a world appropriate to the requirements of capitalist economics (Mimica, 1988: chapter 8).

Accounts of other ways of engaging with the world might free us to identify alternative mathematics: For example,

whereas, conventional 'folk maths' imagines the mathematical object as a thing accumulating along a linear extension. In many systems objects are generated through processes that resemble multiplication – number, for example, may appear as multiplication inside the body of an encompassing whole (Verran, 1999). Objects thus resemble fractions, or more accurately, fractals. For example, in Yoruba speaking parts of Nigeria, the world is constituted as a 'sortal entity' or a mode of 'being collected'. In mathematical thinking, Verran relates how Yoruba children learn to measure most successfully using practices that relate to Yoruba language and cosmology. If we imagine English counting practices as proceeding by adding finger to finger, Yoruba counting practices start with a whole body which is then separated into 'sets' that are nested within and mimic the whole (Verran, 1999: 149). The material world (the body) intersects with concepts of cosmology and identity in order to make practices of measurement make sense.

'Fractal' mathematics has been studied at length among the Iqwaye of Morobe Province (PNG) (Mimica, 1988). Whereas number in 'western mathematics' accumulates, amongst the Iqwaye it exponentiates: Counting, for the Iqwaye, is image of reproduction. It is based upon the movement from whole (which is also a one) to a dyad and from the dyad to the birth of another one (which is also a whole). Each whole, in this system, is homologous to a more inclusive whole; wholes are thus 'fractal' entities. Whole and ones are male, and in conjunction with females become twos, that beget more whole/ones. Counting names are the same words as kinship names, referring to child/sibling birth order. Here maths involves iconic dynamics 'symbolically presented as sexual conjunction and reproduction' that concern the reproduction of persons (Mimica, 1988: 124). These dynamics are also contained in cosmological myths explaining the origins of time and the universe. The Iqwaye universe begins with a male 'primordial oneness' within whom sexual opposites are incorporated into an over-arching male whole/one, and from whom other generative entities are generated.

In these examples we can see how mathematics constructs isomorphic relations that permeate many different areas of experience. Mathematics moves from ways of ordering self to ways of ordering the world, so that we can see how, for example, temporality might be ordered either as the accumulation of number along a linear extension or distance (Gosden, 1994: chapter 1, Lucas, 2005: chapter 1) , or as among the Iqwaye, where temporality is grasped 'as a more immediate and pregnant intuition of … bodily dynamics, in short, as generation' (Mimica, 1988: 135). Within anthropology the term 'fractal' has been adapted from its specialised application in mathematics, and is used to describe processes that invoke self-similarity at a range of scales (Wagner cited in Strathern, 1988). The notion of 'fractal personhood' describes the self-similarity of the person both to its interior and exterior worlds (see section 1.5; Fowler, 2004). Just as conventional western mathematics indexes and orders a world of property objects and individuals, so 'fractal mathematics' relates to a world of fractal entities and fractal persons.

Mathematics, Embodiment and Architecture

Corporeal experience is part of what Barth describes as the 'pre-conceptual sources' of cognition (Barth, 2000: 22). The body has both a directly perceived structure of its own and also a role in structuring conceptual and material worlds. It is both 'structured' and 'structuring' as Giddens might put it (Giddens, 1986). Mathematics is not only a matter of conscious reasoning, but is performed unconsciously in everyday practices, as part of what Bourdieu called habitus (Bourdieu, 1977: 78-87). Bodies and mathematical concepts can index one another pointing to the ontology of bodies and their procreation. Mathematics, like discourse, might be said to be part of how things come to 'matter' (Butler, 1993b).

Mathematical capacities emerge from intersections between bodies and architecture. This can lead to what Gell expressed as, the 'isomorphy of structure' between forms of consciousness and 'the spatio-temporal structures of distributed objects in the artefactual realm' (Gell, 1998: 222). Architecture sets up 'isomorphic analogies' in the body that may also embody mathematical capacities (Lopez Y Royo, 2005: 41). These analogies are systematised and indexical. For instance in his first century BC text, *de Architectura* Vitruvius argued that the separate parts and whole design of temples should harmonise with the body of 'a well shaped man' (Vitruvius Pollio, 2005, [90-20 BC]). The male body was envisaged a model of 'natural' metrics. Elsewhere, analogies between bodies and architecture involve systems of movement. For example, Lopez y Royo (2005) discusses how Hindu temple architecture is physically embodied and articulated in dances shown in temple carvings. Isomorphic analogy is set up between the dance movements and dynamics set up by the way the temple orders space. There is a double movement at work here in which the body and its practices produces temple just as the temple produces a bodily ideal.

Mathematics, Value and Economy

Mathematical capacities are materialised and enacted within networks that are economic as well as cosmological. The importance of technologies of quantification (and increasingly, qualification) in capitalist markets has been studied by Callon (Callon, 1998; Callon et al., 2002). He points to the material equipment and architecture that produce economic networks. Formal markets , however, are not the only economic forms to rely on mathematical practices, practical mathematics is also an aspect of configuring non-market exchanges (Callon, 1998: 39). The ways that mathematics is connected to value and exchange can be illustrated by comparing examples of commodity and gift exchange.

In Renaissance Italy societies organised around commodity exchange and proto-capitalism produced a 'commercial mathematics adapted to the merchant' (Baxandall, 1972). The 'mercantile classes' were schooled in a mathematics that emphasised geometry and calculation using fractions. This mathematics also emerged in aesthetic experience. Renaissance painters responded to 'visual skills' valued by the merchants who were their patrons. People 'practiced in manipulating ratios' were sensitive to pictures 'carrying the marks of similar processes' (Baxandall, 1972: 101). The mathematics of proportions also became part of the sacred. Renaissance theology and popular religious writings moralised the mathematics of proportion and geometric perfection. Mathematics was embodied and indexed in the body of Christ. The experience of perfect proportion in Christ's body was among the 'sensible delights' of heaven. Mathematics supplied visual metaphors for moral and social values at the same time as they valued commodities in economic life (Baxandall, 1972: 103-8).

The 'fractal' mathematics of the Iqwaye differs from the commercial mathematics of Renaissance merchants in ways that reflect different ideas of exchange. The Italian merchant used his knowledge of geometry to gauge the quantities of commodities which appeared as ship-loads of containers in a variety of sizes and shapes (Baxandall, 1972: 86-91). Commodities were substitutable for other objects, and made commeasurable using money. Within commodity exchange, a pig is like any other pig; 'attributes such as size, sex and colour may influence the going price, but no longer bear upon the appropriateness of the particular pig to the intended transaction' (Minnegal and Dwyer cited in Strathern, 2005a: 124). Renaissance calculation was thus orientated towards measuring the dimensions and proportions of things to better represent these in abstract terms as price. The quantity and quality of the thing were measured, not the value of the relationships which made it up.

For the Iqwaye, exchange is rather different. Here objects tend to circulate as parts of persons; a pig is not like any other pig – it is brought into exchange as a particular pig, with its own singular history, and it is these relations that make it the only offering appropriate to that exchange (Strathern, 2005a: 124). Here, gifts are valued as extractions from relationships. The fractal mathematics of the Iqwaye thus reflects the economics of gift exchange. In fractal mathematics, mathematic objects, like gifts, are generated from relations in much the same way (and using the same kinship terminology) as persons are generated from relations. Each number has its own singular history, and its own 'kinship' relations with other numbers.

Mathematical practices are valuing processes. Where commodities are important, value might be fetishised as money, and quantified in units of measurement as price – thereby making items commeasurable (Marx, 1976: chapter 3). Price can be represented as a 'universal' possibility. However, where other sorts of exchange predominate it is relationships that are valued (Mauss, 1970). People value claims that they have over the generative potential embodied in specific other persons (Kalinoe & Leach, 2004; Strathern, 2005a). Things circulate as 'parts of persons' (Strathern, 1988). Mathematics is concerned with nested and part-whole relations and objects may be fragmented into fractions allowing parts to be redistributed while maintaining homologies with wholes (Chapman, 2000; Strathern, 2005a: 120-5).

Economic connections between personhood and property are part of what Strathern describes as the 'Arithmetic of Ownership' (Strathern, 2005a). Where images of commodity exchange predominate, concepts of property produce objects and subjects that always count as 'one': One singularised owner must relate to one singularised property object ('right' or 'thing'). However, where gifts are more important the 'Arithmetic of Ownership' is different. Owners may be understood as 'dividuals' and

entities may appear as multiply authored and composed (see section 1.5). Tenure in these situations is concerned with relations between parts and wholes, and with the calculation of shares, fractions and proportions.

Here, I considered mathematics in its widest sense – as an aspect of personhood, embodiment, and economy. I discussed examples of 'fractal mathematics' which differ from the traditional preconceptions of 'western mathematics'. I argued that mathematics is not just abstract thought in the minds of individuals, but is distributed in the material world. Mathematics involves processes of valuing related to different forms of exchange. Where concepts of gift exchange are important fractal mathematics may be appropriate, because it provides ways of valuing relationships and calculating tenure in multiply composed entities. In the sections that follow I develop these ideas by investigating the measuring practices that were used to layout coaxial landscapes. I begin this exercise in the next section with a discussion of previous metrological studies.

7.2 Previous Metrological Studies

In this section I identify three different kinds of measuring, all of which, following on from the above, can be understood as mathematical. One of which, however, has been privileged above all others in many previous accounts. Next I review previous metrological studies in archaeology. I assess available statistical methods. Finally I place the study of measurement on Dartmoor in the context of previous interpretations of coaxial layouts.

Different Elements of Measuring

I propose three different kinds of measuring methods, which I call numerical, analogical and fractional:

- *Numerical methods* use counting devices to make an abstract notation for future action. They might involve a standard unit of measurement or a less formal metric like a pace.
- *Fractional methods* match objects to themselves, fragmenting existing entities into fractions and proportions.
- *Analogical methods* compare attributes of one thing with another. They do not use abstract number, but measure likenesses using metonyms. Analogies may involve nothing more then sizing by eye, matching one entity to the next. One example would be measuring using a length of rope, cut to the length of the object to be measured (but not the counting of lengths of rope which would be numerical. Other, less conventional analogical methods use dance, poetry or song. The Iqwaye use a special rope of shells to measure warriors when they wage war on their neighbours. Prospective soldiers arrange

themselves in a line and a man walks along the line going shell to shell and man to man until he comes to the end of the rope. At the end of the rope the group is regarded as complete (Mimica, 1988: 16).

These methods often overlap and complement one another. It is very unlikely that any group of people would ever use just one of these alone. For example the merchants of Renaissance Italy used a mathematics that was based on manipulating fractions in order to ascertain numerical quantities. If we return to Nain Singh Rawat's ingenious mapping of Tibet, it can be observed that his methods involved disguising numerical measurement making use of technology that acted analogically. For example, Nain Singh's Survey of India rosary was an aid to numerical measurement disguised as a device for the analogical measurement of prayers.

Each of these kinds of measuring involves a different degree of transferability and abstraction. Numerical methods often rely on abstract concepts and technologies (standard units and instruments of measurement) that can be transferred between spaces. Analogical methods may also involve transportable technological and conceptual equipment, but these remain what Gell would call 'token-indexical' - relying on specific reference points (Gell, 1985). By contrast, fractional methods depend on the qualities of particular spaces: A half refers to the whole of which it is a part. A thing divided retains and refers to the specificity of its origins.

Studies of measurement have traditionally regarded analogical and fractional measuring processes as instinctive or uninteresting compared to numerical methods. An implicit evolutionism has led to the supposition that number is the 'best' 'most advanced' or even the only way of measuring (Seebohm 1914). I consider that all of these elements of measuring should be equally interesting objects of metrological study. All constitute aspects of practical mathematics.

Metrological studies in Archaeology

'Man is the measure of all things.'
(Protagorus, 5th BC)

At least since Vitruvius wrote, the male body has been figured as a 'natural' foundation from which numerical measuring should logically evolve. The earliest methods of measurement were thus assumed to comprise 'the *natural* systems of measures – the thumb, the palm, the foot, the step of the middling-sized man' (Seebohm, 1914: 97 his emphasis). The male body is literally seen as a natural standard supplying 'a substratum of common and solid ground extending far back into the past' (Seebohm, 1914: 98). Following this tendency, it is often assumed that the pace, for example, is a 'natural' or primordial method, likely to have been among the earliest used (see Bradley 1984: 77; Pitts 2001: 237-30).

For the measurement of fields, labour offers another 'primordial' unit of measure. It has been widely supposed that the most ancient enclosure sizes would be determined by the amount of land that can be ploughed in one day - just like the medieval acre (Marx, 1976: 164; Seebohm, 1914; Curwen, 1946; Hatt, 1949; Crawford, 1953; Bowen, 1961; Reynolds, 1979; Fowler, 1984). Here the layout of fields fits perfectly with the 'natural law' of the labour theories of property and value.

In the later twentieth century metrological study was overshadowed by debate over the Megalithic Yard (Thom & Thom, 1978). Thom believed he had found a millimetre-precise unit used to lay out stone circles and stone settings, by an elite class of astronomer-priests, responsible for maintaining standard measures. His ideas were enthusiastically taken up on the 'semi-mystical fringe' of archaeology (Fieller cited in Baxter, 2003: 228). The Megalithic Yard debate illustrates the cultural values that surround numerical measuring as a totem of intellectual sophistication and social advancement. The notion of an elite of scientific surveyors does not fit mainstream archaeological understandings of prehistoric society and has been widely, and justifiably, criticised (Bradley, 1984: 77, Pitts, 2001: 227-9).

Several writers have suggested that Thom's megalithic yard is 'actually a megalithic pace' (Bradley, 1984: 77, Pitts, 2001: 237-30). These accounts are written to debunk Thom's notion of astronomer-priests etc., however, it is implied that pacing is a 'natural' or instinctive form of measurement - Pitts even argues that an 'unconscious pace' may have been used (Pitts, 2001: 230). This notion of the pace as a primordial measure seems unlikely. It is more plausible that the pace is

derivative of a standard unit, than that it precedes them. Pacing must be learnt, and this learning transmits a particular sense of the body as an instrument, transformed into an inscription device (see, Ingold, 2004, on the historical performance of walking). In the British Army, Guardsmen are drilled in pacing using a 'drill-stick' and are expected to maintain a pace of exactly 31.5 inches not only while on the parade ground, but even in its vicinity when off duty (Kendall, 1974: 258). Nain Singh's extraordinary ability to pace accurately was acquired only after repeated drilling by a parade sergeant with a measuring stick (Allen, 1982: 335). Given the references that pacing makes to numerical systems of measuring, it is difficult to envisage what an 'unconscious pace' would actually be (cf Pitts, 2001: 230). Pacing *is* a unit of numerical measurement, accurate enough to show up in some types of metrological analysis (Kendall, 1974: 258).

The Megalithic Yard controversy stimulated statisticians to devise new methods for studying ancient metrology (Baxter, 2003: chapter 19). Earlier work had simply matched theoretically reconstructed units to data (Vitruvius Pollio, 2005, Seebohm, 1914) or sized fields to the estimated labour of plough teams (Curwen & Curwen, 1923). Thom's analysis relied on generalisations about frequencies in the data, and ultimately on 'goodness-of-fit'. Now statistical tools began to be used in earnest.

Statistical Methods in Metrology

Metrological analyses test whether, for a given population of measurements, it is true that (up to a certain amount of error), a certain number of them are multiples of some basic quantum (henceforth h). Techniques for identifying h essentially describe the distribution of errors in the measurements. The earliest method developed was Broadbent's 'lumped variance' technique. Prehistoric land division has been subject to relatively few metrological investigations (I am not aware of any previous metrological study of British prehistoric land division) however, the 'lumped variance' technique has been widely explored in Sweden, and applied to prehistoric land division in Gotland (Lindquist, 1974) and Vastergotland (Widgren, 1990). This work suggested use of a prehistoric 'foot', or 'measuring rod'.

A significant drawback to Broadbent's formulation was its requirement that plausible seeming quanta be identified in advance. Swedish studies used units already known from later periods of Swedish history. But in many contexts it is difficult to find appropriate substitutes. A further problem is the question of just how large a peak in the distribution has to be before it is discounted. Simply taking the largest peak (as Thom did) presumes in advance that there must be a numerical unit. To solve this difficulty it is necessary to subject the possible quantum to significance tests. These test the extent to which a particular distribution of results might occur by chance alone.

The problems of Broadbent's methods were solved in a method developed by Kendall (Kendall, 1974). Kendall used cosines to represent the frequency of *h*, (which meant that it did not need to be specified in advance). The resulting graph he called a cosine quantogram. He also developed the use of Monte Carlo tests to gauge the significance of peaks on the quantograms. Kendall's application of his formulation to the Megalithic Yard problem found that significant quanta might arise for the whole of a dataset even when only a subset of the data actually had quantal properties. Furthermore his interpretation suggested that data that responded to the technique did not necessarily imply highly precise standard measures. Therefore he found that even when this method was applied it was necessary to subject the results to further exploratory analyses. Analysing the Megalithic Yard data, Kendall found that a subset of the data had quantal properties, which may have resulted from pacing. Paces should show up using his methods, as a quantum around 0.7 - 0.8m.

Subsequently Freeman developed methods that applied Bayesian statistics. This Bayesian approach has certain statistical advantages over Kendall's method but Freeman's account was constrained by the computational methods of his time, and his method has subsequently proved difficult to apply (Baxter, 2003: 230-235). By contrast, Kendall's formulation has been widely tested using a range of datasets including Athenian temples, Ashanti weights and Mycenaean weights (Baxter, 2003: 234-5; Petruso, 2003). I therefore use Kendall's method here.

Previous Interpretations of Coaxial Layouts on Dartmoor

Previous accounts have interpreted the layout of coaxial landscapes from two basic perspectives: The first of these I shall call the 'mental template' perspective; the second, the 'social context' perspective.

The 'mental template' perspective envisages a 'plan' behind the design of Dartmoor land division. This plan is thought to have been directed by 'some form of social authority'; either a 'chief' (Fleming, 1978b) or a 'council of elders' (Fleming, 1985b). Coaxial landscapes are a 'template' existing in someone's head, and this explains how pattern arises. The 'mental template' perspective contributes to accounts that emphasise the importance of elites (Bradley, 1977; Kristiansen, 1998; Earle, 2002). Associated with this perspective are notions concerning specialised surveyors: Butler observes that the surveying involved in laying out coaxial field systems was of a 'fine precision, rarely, if ever see elsewhere' (Butler, 1997a: 68). He considers that the construction of coaxial land division on this scale:

'could not have been achieved without a well trained body of surveyors, no amateurs who learned as they went, but an already highly skilled workforce familiar with large scale land mensuration who had practiced their craft elsewhere. Specialists certainly ... whose skills had to be mastered rather then empirical' (Butler, 1997a: 68).

Specialists, Butler argues, may have deployed a different unit of measurement to layout each system. The idea of a unit of measurement fits interpretations that see Dartmoor as a redistributive chiefdom controlled by chiefly elites (Earle, 2002).

The second 'social context' perspective reacts against this idea of a mental template or plan (Bradley, 2002, Johnston, 2005). Instead, coaxial land division is seen as emerging from gradual sedentarisation and territorialisation in the landscape. As land-use attaches people to permanent settlement, lineages are attached to houses and land (Barrett 1994; Johnston 2005). Coaxial pattern, Johnston suggests, results from the 'unconscious co-ordination' of activities in relation to the locations of earlier sites (Johnston 2001). The problem of these 'social context' interpretations is that they find it difficult to account for the regular pattern that is so striking in coaxial landscapes. Coaxial pattern seems superfluous to the interpretation. At the same time they offer serious critique of the 'mental template' perspective, pointing out that the chronological depth of reaves suggests that 'there was never a plan' behind coaxial land division (Johnston 2005).

One way around these problems maybe to focus on the practical actions involved in laying out coaxial landscapes and to consider what the actions of constructing these landscapes imply. Rather than beginning with a mental template or an overarching model of society and looking for evidence to support it, this approach starts in the middle and works outwards towards the interactions between people and the material world.

I have described the differences between various aspects of measuring – numerical, fractional and analogical. Previous accounts have tended to focus on numerical methods and, in British prehistory, metrological studies in general have been overshadowed by the Megalithic Yard controversy. Of the statistical methods available Kendall's is the most appropriate. In the next section I apply this method.

7.3 Metrological Analysis of Coaxial Landscapes

The coaxial landscapes of Dartmoor are a non-obvious puzzle, more complex then some of their archaeological interpretations suggest. The most striking aspect of these landscapes is their regular pattern. But this pattern does not produce enclosures that were equal apportionments (see chapter 3). The pattern derives largely from the maintenance of strip widths, while the lengths of strips differ. It is maintained over very extensive areas, a feat that suggests land division was laid out with great care and attention to detail. In this section I investigate the processes used to measure out coaxial landscapes. Was a unit of numerical measurement used, or some other technique? I briefly discuss methodology. I then analyse the widths of enclosures in the eight most important landscapes; firstly en masse, then individually. Exploratory analysis of the results follows, in which I develop the method using spatial analysis to identify subsets of the data with quantal properties. Finally the extent of deviation from the quantum is explored.

Methodology

Figure 7.1 shows Kendall's formula. To recap, h represents the basic unit of which data are multiples (called the 'quantum'). Plotting h against $\Phi(h)$ generates peaks of h on a cosine quantogram. Among these peaks are potential quanta which are assessed using Monte Carlo significance tests.

$$\phi(h) = \sqrt{\frac{2}{n} \sum_{j=1}^{n} \cos(\frac{2\pi x_j}{h})} .$$

7.1 Kendall's Formula

A simple programme which ran this formula was created (CD available on request). The program runs 500 iterations of the Monte Carlo test, so probability can be judged with precision. The Monte Carlo evaluation tests the results against the null hypothesis that the data is a random dataset, based on randomisation from a normal distribution of the same mean and standard deviation. Kendall normalised his function to square root (2n) because he wished to allow for very small values of phi and very large quantities of h, however he recognised that such very large and small quantities would be extremely unusual (a value of phi 'in excess of +4 would only occur with a probability of about 0.000032') (Kendall, 1974: 239). Normalisation to 1 is used here because it makes the output data easier to handle and comprehend. Thus, as the data tend toward quantal, 'phi' tends towards 1, and random data tend towards 0.

The programme allows h to be distributed as series of 'steps' between limits set by the operator. The resolution of steps, and the limits of the analysis, can be changed to facilitate exploratory analysis. Steps of h were assessed initially at 0.01m and then at a range of resolutions to explore the resilience of possible quanta and the possibility of rounding errors. There is no point in looking for quanta that are greater than the mean of the dataset - this result would be effectively meaningless. The upper limits of the analysis were therefore set at the mean of the widths in each population.

The data comprise widths from eight coaxial field systems - Corndon Down, Easdon Down, Holne Moor, Kestor, Shaugh Moor, Shovel Down, Throwleigh Common and, Windtor Down. The data comprised widths measured to three decimal places. The measurements were of actual reaves not virtual lines drawn at right angles between parallel boundaries. 'Virtual' lines have been used in previous work (Butler, 1997a; Fleming, 1988), but, these lines reflect archaeologist's inspection of maps more than practices on the ground. All widths were marked at both ends by intersections with other boundaries, and thus had definite end points. The widths were draped over a DTM, before measurements were taken (see Appendix E). Two datasets were used; data from English Heritage Surveys at Holne Moor, Kestor and Shovel Down and data digitised from Butler's surveys for other areas.

The data contain several potential sources of error. The nature of the sites themselves means that it is unrealistic to expect to find a small unit of great precision. Reaves are collapsed dry stone walls, often quite widely spread, sometimes visible only as indistinct humps. It is likely that the widths surveyed contain errors of location maybe of as much as 1-2m. A second possible source of error lies in the manner in which the data have been digitised. The Butler dataset has been manually digitised from paper maps of scales around 1:10,000. This process inevitably introduces factors of generalisation into the widths. The English Heritage datasets have been recorded differently in different areas, Holne Moor has been manually digitised from a Total Station survey and other areas have been input from DGPS survey, following cleaning of the dataset (see section 2.4). These data imput errors are effectively rounding errors and should be distinguishable in the results as such if they affect results (Kendall, 1974: 243).

Analysis of All Coaxial Landscapes

The first analysis examined the entire population of widths from all coaxial areas. The results are shown in the table (7.2) and cosine quantogram (7.3) below.

7.2: Results from Application of Kendal's Formula to widths of coaxial enclosures

Number of data-points	565
Range of widths	11 - 258
Mean of widths	77.9
Highest value of phi	0.06978
Quantum unit with highest phi	6.2
Monte Carlo result	0.32
Significance level	Not significant

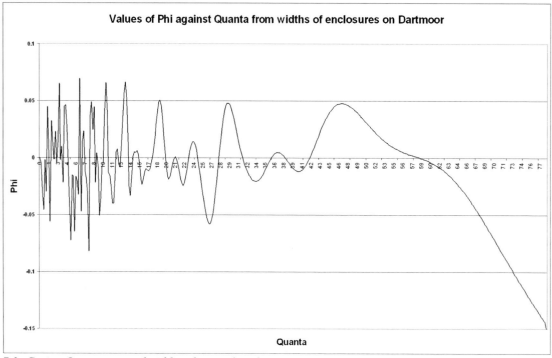

7.3: Cosine Quantogram of widths of coaxial enclosures

The results indicate that there is no overall quantum that might form a standard unit of measurement for all coaxial land division. This result corroborates previous studies which also suggested no overall unit (Butler, 1997a: 89). The analysis does not reveal evidence for a 'coaxial pace'. Experimental work on the accuracy of pacing is presented in Appendix V. This work suggested that regular widths in coaxial systems show the degrees of error that might be expected of pacing. However this work is superseded by Kendall's formulation. If a pace was used it should be visible as a peak around 0.7 to 0.8m in the quantogram. Previous studies suggest that each area may have been laid out using a 'local unit' (ibid). The next section analyses each landscape individually to see if any such units can be identified.

Metrological Analyses of Eight Coaxial Landscapes

The widths of coaxial land division in each area were analysed in turn. The results are given in cosine quantogram (7.4) and table (7.5) below. The quantograms for each area are shown individually in Appendix W.

The results of Kendall's formulation require careful interpretation (Kendall, 1974). The formulation necessarily generates a lot of noise at the lower end of the scale from which genuine quanta need to be isolated. The results indicate that quanta are present at Shaugh Moor and Shovel Down. Here very high values of phi are present in the middle parts of the quantograms at 28.7m and 24.5m respectively. There is only a 1 in 100% probability that these quanta occurred by chance. The statistically significant but small quanta at Throwleigh Common and Corndon Down should be regarded with caution. These may represent rounding errors. Intriguingly, the Throwleigh Common result is in the range expected for paced measures (0.7 to 0.8m). However it has a relatively low probability (5%). At Windtor Down the quantograms shows a large and widely spread bulge at around 46m. This quantum is significant. However, this does not reflect a unit of measurement. Instead, it follows the width of the smallest strip at Windtor Down, which is repeated seven times in the layout.

7.4: Quantogram of widths of enclosures in eight coaxial areas

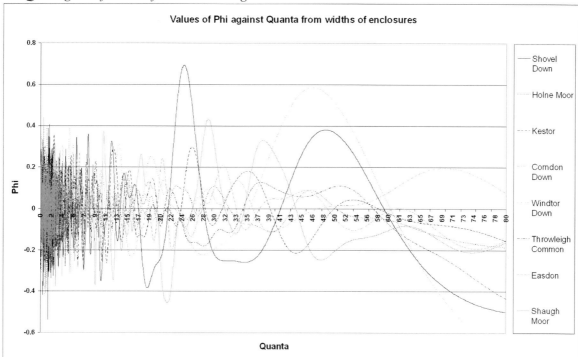

7.5: Results from Application of Kendal's Formula to eight coaxial areas

	Corndon Down	Easdon Down	Kestor	Holne Moor	Shaugh Moor	Shovel Down	Throwleigh Common	Windtor Down
No. of data-points	159	44	39	178	38	18	68	26
range	30.522-199.903	26.349-191.110	25.131-156.282	15.814-228.160	30.428-258.003	25.100-98.771	11.019-214.736	34.227-93.467
mean of widths	91.48	88.11	65.63	78.5	80.67	50.56	63.24	47.622
Highest value of phi	0.225	0.3054	0.3565	0.172457	0.43776	0.69319	0.3012	0.5847
Quantum unit	2.1	3.78	2.29	5.31	27.8	24.5	0.72	46.5
Monte Carlo result	0.01397	0.389	0.1477	0.105788	0.0098	0.003992	0.02395	0.01198
Significance level	1%	not significant	not significant	10%	1%	1%	5%	1%

Exploratory Analysis

The results from Shovel Down and Shaugh Moor suggest significant quanta. It is notable that these are the smaller sample areas containing widths that are mostly from spatially related enclosures. It is possible that quanta were also present in other samples, but that the size of these samples has obscured the results. It is possible that more than one measuring practice was used, and that the juxtaposition of different methods would muddle the data within larger landscapes.

To explore this possibility I examined coaxial landscapes at Kestor and Holne Moor. Here quanta were not significant, or of low probability. However, inspecting the cosine quantograms individually shows both display peaks in the middle of the quantograms. No such peaks are visible in the quantograms for Corndon Down or Throwleigh Common. These peaks might reflect potential quanta within parts of the landscape, obscured by the rest of the dataset.

Spatial analysis allows the deviation from a quantum to be visualised and located. The extent to which each width deviates from a potential quantum can be obtained by dividing each length into the quantum and subtracting the number of times the quantum fits into the width. This gives a measure of the error between -0.5 and +0.5

(which may also be expressed as an absolute error between 0 and 0.5). The spatial distribution of deviation can be mapped in GIS as a simple density surface. This result is obviously affected by the density of the widths, but this affect is obviated by subtracting a density map leaving a surface that shows where the spatial distribution of deviation from the quantum is highest.

The quantogram for Kestor shows a secondary peak at around 25m. Given the similarity between this quantum and those found to be significant at Shaugh Moor and Shovel Down, it was thought possible that this might represent a quantum found in part, but not all of the widths in the Kestor coaxial system. The extent to which each of the widths within the Kestor system deviated from this potential quantum is mapped in 7.6.

7.6 reveals deviation from the quantum concentrated in the northern block of enclosures. The southern block shows much less deviation. Accordingly, the widths from the southern block were isolated and Kendall's formulation applied just to these widths. The results produced a significant quantum of 25.3m.

7.6: Spatial distribution of deviation from quantum

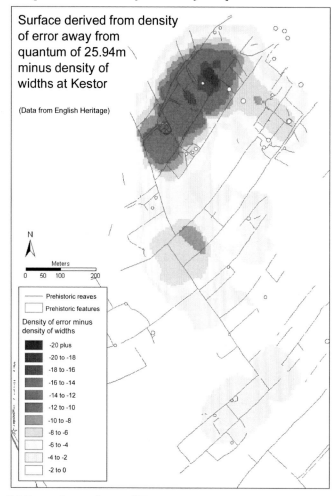

Surface derived from density of error away from quantum of 25.94m minus density of widths at Kestor

(Data from English Heritage)

N

Meters
0   50   100   200

— Prehistoric reaves
▢ Prehistoric features

Density of error minus density of widths

- -20 plus
- -20 to -18
- -18 to -16
- -16 to -14
- -14 to -12
- -12 to -10
- -10 to -8
- -8 to -6
- -6 to -4
- -4 to -2
- -2 to 0

7.7 Re analysis of part of Kestor Area

	Widths from Southern enclosures at Kestor
number of data-points	18
range	27.570-154.867
mean of widths	64.707
Highest value of phi	0.69765
Quantum unit with highest phi	25.3
Monte Carlo result	0.001996
Significance level	1%

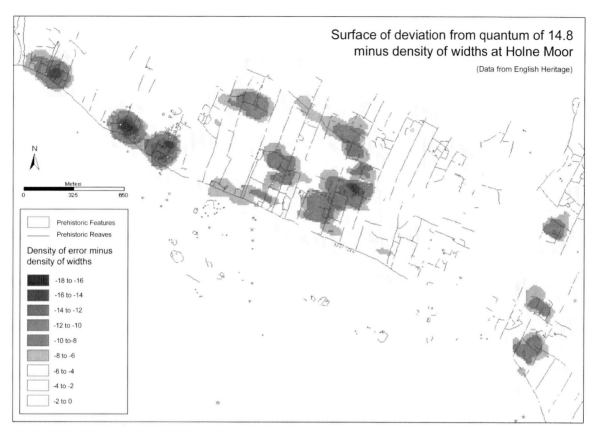

Surface of deviation from quantum of 14.8 minus density of widths at Holne Moor

(Data from English Heritage)

Prehistoric Features
Prehistoric Reaves

Density of error minus density of widths

-18 to -16
-16 to -14
-14 to -12
-12 to -10
-10 to-8
-8 to -6
-6 to -4
-4 to -2
-2 to 0

7.8: Deviation from quantum at Holne Moor

The same process was applied to Holne Moor. Here the quantogram showed a secondary peak at 14.8m. However the surface generated showed no clear distribution of deviation (7.8). Instead, deviations built up wherever there were clusters of buildings and small enclosures. Larger enclosures followed the quantum more faithfully; as did widths along the length of the terminal reave. Overall no uniform block where the potential quantum was followed could be isolated. No new metrological analysis was run on any part of this landscape, although it remains possible that a length of around 14.8m was important in laying out parts of this landscape.

The Range of Deviation from Quanta

Kendall's formulation is very tolerant of deviation. The technique will identify quanta even where some of the sample data are inconsistent. For example , at Shuagh Moor and Shovel Down exploratory analysis shows that both samples include widths which deviate considerably from the quantum. 7.9 and 7.10 show the levels of inconstancy found in these layouts, although both returned highly significant results

The inconsistencies within these datasets suggest that while widths are patterned enough to show definite quantal properties many widths are far from accurate multiples of a standard unit. Overall, this does not suggest the use of numerical unit of measurement, but probably implies other method of measuring. This possibility is analysed further below.

Thus far, after applying Kendall's formulation, I have found significant quanta in certain areas. Exploratory analysis has shown that quantal properties tend to be present over relatively smaller areas, especially within blocks of enclosures that are spatially contiguous (as at Shaugh Moor, Shovel Down, Windtor Down and Kestor South). Respect for the quantum is inconsistent however, even within these areas. Based on these findings it is clear that some kind of measuring was involved, but it seems unlikely to be a standard numerical unit or 'coaxial yard'. On the same grounds a 'coaxial pace' also seems unlikely. In the next section I suggest what measuring practices are evidenced by these results.

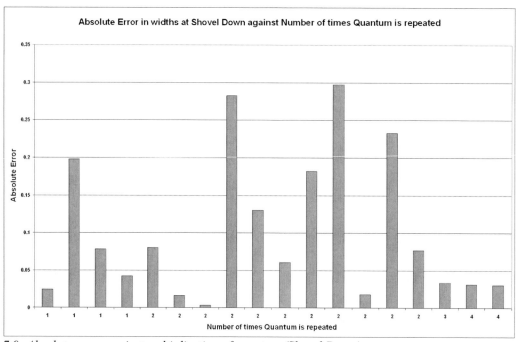

7.9: Absolute error against multiplication of quantum (Shovel Down)
(0 = minimum deviation from quantum, 0.5 = maximum deviation from quantum).

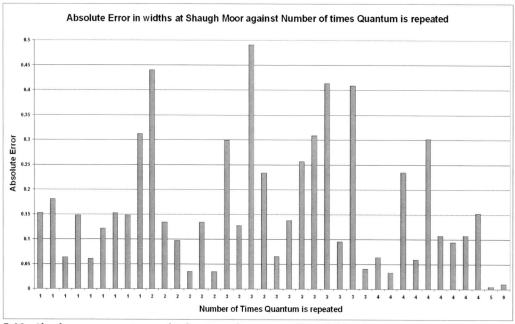

7.10: Absolute error against multiplication of quantum (Shaugh Moor)
(0 = minimum deviation from quantum, 0.5 = maximum deviation from quantum).

7.4 Measuring Practices in Coaxial Landscapes

I begin this section by investigating the results of the metrological analysis in the context of coaxial pattern. The findings imply that the quanta identified in the last section result from fractional and analogical rather than numerical measuring methods. I then suggest what kinds of equipment may have been involved in these practices. Lastly I discuss what these forms of measurement indicate concerning practical mathematics at the time coaxial landscapes were laid out.

Coaxial Pattern and Quantal Landscapes

It has been widely observed that land division on Dartmoor seems to proceed with reference to topographically bounded 'blocks' (Barnatt, 1989; Fleming, 1978b; Fleming, 1983). Within these blocks three basic principles underlie coaxial pattern:

i) repetition of strips or blocks of roughly equal widths;
ii) subdivision of these widths;
iii) strips that do not repeat or sub-divide, but repeat fractions of existing widths.

The most noticeable aspect of coaxial layout is the use of proportion and fractions. 7.11 and 7.12 illustrate these processes of repetition and fractional subdivision at work on Shaugh Moor and Shovel Down (further examples are illustrated in Appendices X and Y, and documented in Appendix K).

Patterns generated through subdivision and repetition can also be observed in parts of other coaxial landscapes (see Appendix K, X and Y). This can be shown using a Chi Square test. Widths in seven coaxial areas were measured once at the terminal reave (see Appendix K) and compared with the widths that would have results from exact subdivision on a map. In all areas the actual widths were found to have a strong relationship with a population of expected widths (see 7.4).

It is possible that coaxial pattern bestowed quantal properties on coaxial landscapes, without there ever having been a numerical unit of measurement. Table 7.14 shows that the significant quanta at Windtor, Shaugh Moor, Shovel Down and Kestor South are very close to the widths of the smallest enclosures in these layouts. These findings viewed in conjunction with evidence for inconsistencies of quanta it seems most likely that the significant quanta do not reflect a numerical unit of measurement but instead emerge from measuring practices that paid great attention to already existing spaces. The 'quanta' identified through application of Kendall's formula represent the lowest level of a hierarchy of self-similar spaces, some of which have been subdivided.

Lay-outs based on subdivision combined with repetition of regular widths suggest fractional and analogical methods of measurement. These forms of measurement would have been based in local characteristics of terrain and this explains why quanta tend to be found in smaller areas with contiguous enclosures. The failure to find plausible quanta at Corndon Down, Holne Moor and Throwleigh Common seems likely to reflect the large area of these layouts.

7.13: Chi Square Test of subdivision in coaxial landscapes

Field System	Degree of freedom	Chi Square Statistic	Probability
Halsanger Common	6	0.79	0.992
Windtor Down	8	0.91	0.999
Shaugh Moor	7	0.99	0.995
Kestor	10	0.99	1.000
Throwleigh Common	22	0.08	1.000
Shovel Down	7	0.93	0.996
Holne Moor	15	0.06	1.000

7.14: Widths of smallest enclosures

Location	Smallest enclosures	Quanta
Shaugh Moor	33.1m, 33.1m, 30.5m 32.9m, 30.4m, 32.2m, 37.7m	27.8m
Shovel Down	25.1m, 29.3m, 26.4m, 25.5m	24.5m
Kestor (South)	27.6m, 27.6m, 31.5m	25.3m
Windtor Down	35.2m, 38.3m, 38.5m, 40.5m	46.5m

7.11: Subdivision on Shaugh Moor (Data from English Heritage, topographic data ©Crown Copyright/database right 2004. An Ordnance Survey/EDINA supplied service)

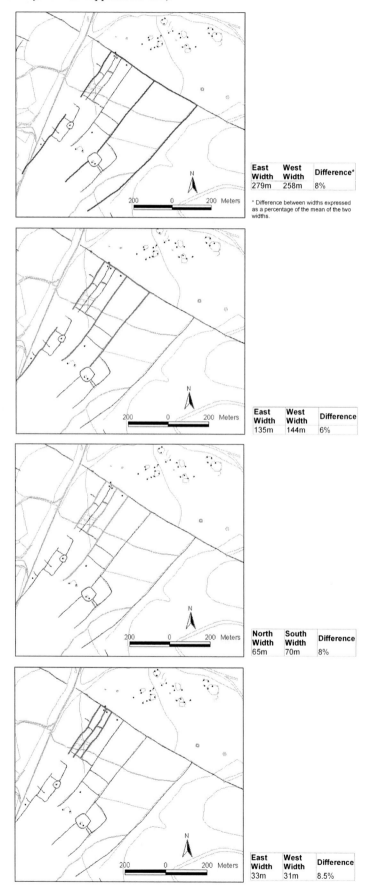

East Width	West Width	Difference*
279m	258m	8%

* Difference between widths expressed as a percentage of the mean of the two widths.

East Width	West Width	Difference
135m	144m	6%

North Width	South Width	Difference
65m	70m	8%

East Width	West Width	Difference
33m	31m	8.5%

7.12: Subdivision on Shovel Down (Data from English Heritage)

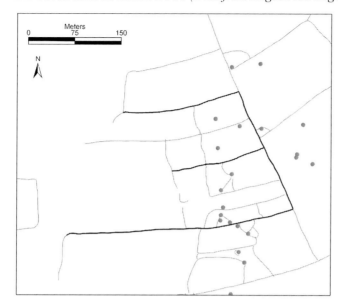

North Width	South Width	Difference
106m	112m	5%

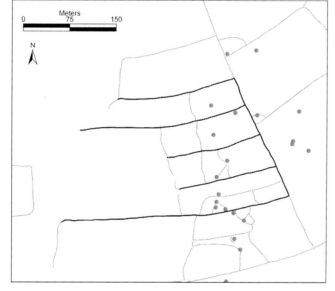

(W)	North Width	South Width	Difference
	46m	60m	27%
(E)	North Width	South Width	Difference
	57m	55m	2%

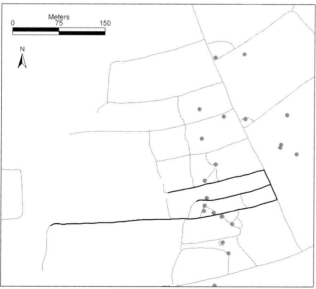

North Width	South Width	Difference
25m	29m	16%

Measuring by Eye and Using Rope

By what practical means might analogical and fractional measuring have proceeded? The analyses of coaxial pattern above demonstrate that measuring was accurate and must have been executed with some care (see 7.11, 7.12, 7.13). How likely is it that lay-outs of this precision were achieved simply by estimating distance by eye? To gauge the degree of accuracy with which it is possible to survey by eye, I laid out several experimental widths on Dartmoor, and compared the accuracy of these with prehistoric enclosures. An unmarked line of 80m was laid

out and subdivided by eye. The test was carried out twenty times in twenty locations for a line of 80m, and then for a length of 100m. The results are shown in 7.15.

Subdividing by eye results in errors of c.0.3% to 17% (on 80m) and c. 1% to 20% (on 100%). Table 7.16 lists actual instances of subdivision producing widths comparable with those subdivided in the experiment. The prehistoric data show less error than the experiment, but the two datasets are roughly comparable. The prehistoric sample could indicate greater practical surveying skill and better observation of terrain.

7.15: Errors on lengths subdivided by eye

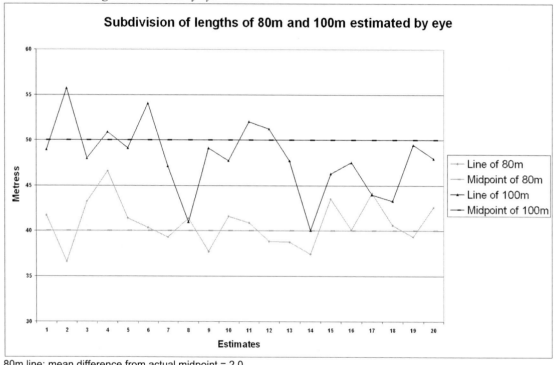

80m line: mean difference from actual midpoint = 2.0
mean difference expressed as a percentage of 40m = 5.01%
100m line: mean difference from actual midpoint = 3.33
mean difference expressed as a percentage of 100m = 6.66%

7.16: Errors in actual examples of subdivision

Location where comparable widths of c40m can be found	Widths in metres	Differences between widths as a percentage of the average of the widths
Windtor, three adjacent strips	40.5m, 38.5m, 38.4m	5.6%
Throwleigh Common, subdivision	38.6m, 37.4m	2.9%
Kestor, subdivision	42.6m, 40.8m	4.4%
Holne Moor, subdivision	59.0m, 56.4m	4.6%
Shovel Down, subdivision	57.1m, 54.9m	4.0%

Subdividing by eye is much easier where both ends of the area to be subdivided are visible simultaneously. Where both ends are not intervisible we might expect far less accuracy in surveying. However, on Dartmoor there are numerous instances where widths are accurately reproduced or subdivided and reference points are out of sight. One of the most striking examples is the remarkable alignment of two reaves on Hamel Down:

Although the reaves are 1.2km apart and are not intervisible for much of their length a consistent width is maintained between them, and they share a common orientation of 075 degrees for over 900m (Butler, 1991a: 142-3). These examples suggest that, in places, measuring practices involved more than gauging distances by eye alone.

Viewshed analysis on the high resolution DEM produced at Kestor/Shovel Down (see section 2.4) reveals several places where the full length of the width to be subdivided would not have been visible from end to end. This would have made measurement difficult to perform by eye. In several places there are only small overlaps in the viewsheds from either end of the subdivided width, and other parts of the layout which could have acted as visual guidelines are also lacking (see 7.17, 7.18). It would not be absolutely impossible to reproduce widths by eye under conditions of restricted visibility like these, but the use of additional devices such as a length of rope would have made the exercise much easier.

Use of rope and pole has been suggested by previous studies (Fleming, 1988; Butler, 1997a:89), and is certainly a feasible solution. Short lengths of rope are known from sites contemporary with reaves elsewhere in England (Brennand & Taylor, 2003: 30-1). Rope and pole seem to have been used to lay out certain 'symmetrical stone circles' from Dartmoor, whose perimeters seem to have circumscribed by rope attached to a central peg (Barnett 1989). Butler points to striking similarities in the diameters of some circles (Butler 1997:

151-3): 'Without invoking megalithic yards', he argues 'some common measurement was used at these sites' possibly 'the same rope and even the same design team' (Butler, 1997a: 152). Intriguingly, Butler's clusters in circle-diameters are comparable with the quanta identified through my analysis (at c.20.5m, c.24.9m and c.32.9m). However, a length of rope was clearly not operating as a 'local unit of measurement' in coaxial lay outs. The range of deviation from the quanta is simply too great (see 7.8 and 7.9). Our prehistoric surveyors would have been poor indeed if such mistakes were to appear when regularly applying a standard rope length (compare 7.8 and 7.9 with 7.15 and Appendix V).

I envisage some kind of 'analogical' method using eye and/or rope, (with rope used as a comparative length not as a standard unit). Nonetheless, if rope were used to aid the surveying of coaxial lay-outs this suggests some simple use of counting. Coaxial landscapes are very extensive, and rope would need to be doubled several times. Use of rope would therefore have required some kind of score or tally – either in number or some other form of recording.

7.17: Viewshed analysis showing non- intervisibility of ends of subdivided enclosures (Kestor) (data from English Heritage and Shovel Down Project)

7.18: Viewshed analysis showing non- inter-visibility of ends of subdivided enclosures (Shovel Down)

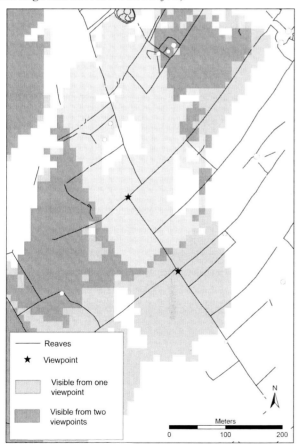

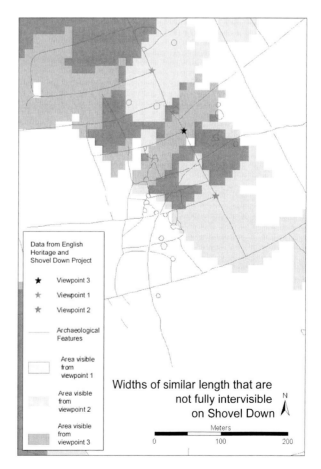

Measuring and Practical Mathematics

In conclusion, application of Kendall's formula and exploratory analysis of the results proves that no standard unit of measurement was used to layout coaxial landscapes, nor, I suggest, were there any local units of measurement. Where significant quanta are found these indicate analogical and fractional measuring methods that subdivide and reproduce widths among spatially related enclosures. These methods involved careful observation of terrain and possibly used a rope.

What do these findings imply in the light of previous interpretations of coaxial layouts? These have tended to follow either a 'mental template' or a 'social context' perspective. Standard units of measurement would have fit well within scenarios envisaged by those who favour a 'mental template' or 'plan' (Fleming 1978, 1988; Earle 2002). However, the results of my analysis show there is no need to postulate surveying specialists (cf Butler 1997: 68). The capacities necessary to layout new boundaries would have been available to most people, and, given the emphasis on subdivision, seem likely to have been employed by different people at different times rather than laid out by a specialist workforce all in one go. Simple measuring techniques nonetheless produced layouts which display some variety. Neither the landscapes nor the methods used to produce them are standardised in ways that suggest they were held entire as a plan in someone's head. Fractional and analogical

measuring would not have been preserved as mental templates but would have inhered in the already existing landscape. New reaves necessarily referenced older reaves so that effectively the layout demanded that the builders 'participate in the unfolding life' of the coaxial landscape (Gell, 1998: 242). Mathematics in this context was not so much a property of individual minds as a capacity distributed about the landscape. The referencing of the system to itself extended this capacity across time and space.

If the 'mental template' perspective finds little support here, investigation of measuring and pattern does not sit easily within the 'social context' perspective either. Measuring was carried out with considerable care and was clearly important in ways not fully captured by existing accounts (cf Bradley 2002; Johnston 2005). The question is, what was the importance of this action? Why was pattern laid out in these specific ways? These are questions to which the social context perspective attends little, because it tends to see pattern as a reflection of (territorializing) social forces.

In the next section I interpret the measuring practices bound up in coaxial landscapes. I return to the discussion of mathematics with which I opened this chapter connecting mathematical practices to valuing processes and personhood. I explore what this kind of practical mathematics might imply about tenure and the development of coaxial landscapes.

7.5 Mathematics, Value and Tenure

I have highlighted how mathematics permeates and configures personhood and economy. Mathematical thinking is not only interiorised in the mind, but is regenerated and redistributed throughout the material world. The way in which people engage with constructed landscapes, I have argued, stimulates certain mathematical capacities. I emphasised the connections between practical mathematical capacities and 'economic' life. Mathematics indexes and orders objects and relations, the practical mathematics of measurement is a process of valuing. I related these operations to what Strathern calls the 'Arithmetic of Ownership'. In this section I bring these observations on mathematics together with theories of value discussed at the end of chapter four (section 4.4) and accounts of Bronze Age personhood and tenure developed in chapter six (section 6.5). I begin with a discussion of the importance of the actions of measuring practices I have identified. This leads onto a discussion of the 'arithmetic of ownership'. Lastly I put forward a new account of the development of coaxial layouts.

Measuring Practices and Valuing Processes

In chapter four I outlined Graeber's theory of value – which sees value as the importance of actions (Graeber,

2001). I introduced an approach that used the idea of value to analyse landscapes (Hirsch, 2004a). Hirsch argues that environments and economies should be seen as mutually interconnected projects of value. Landscapes are 'created artefacts' which act as 'media of value', allowing people to assess their relationships with one another. Constructing landscapes can thus be seen as involving processes of valuing.

The connections between laying out landscapes and valuing processes are perhaps easiest to visualise initially in the more familiar background of modern land surveying. Valuing land as private property involved a new conjunction between practical mathematics and landscapes. Land division within feudal and monastic estates traditionally proceeded according to yields, rather than land area. Enclosures were valued according to the services rendered by the people they supported. However:

> *'Once land was exchanged for cash, its ability to support people became less important than how much rent it could produce. And to compare the value of rent produced by different estates, it was essential to know their exact size'*
> (Linklater, 2002: 12)

As a commodity, private property must be quantified in units that can be evaluated as price (see Abramson, 2000) . The important of the actions of measuring now became their capacity to abstract and quantify accurately.

The measuring practices I have uncovered through my analysis suggest different ways of valuing. Within coaxial landscapes there is little attempt to standardise or quantify the areas of enclosures (see section 3.4), however, widths are carefully measured so that reaves and enclosures retain or reproduce resemblances to earlier layouts. The importance of actions of measurement is in how each reave refers to others spatially related to it. Measuring thus values a certain historicity embodied in particular places. This is not only a matter of referring backwards, but also of anticipating the lay-out of possible future land division. Once one or more axial boundaries are in place, analogical and fractional measuring inevitably reproduces coaxial pattern. Once coaxial pattern is in place additions are necessarily patterned by earlier features, (unless the whole block of enclosures are entirely replaced with a new pattern; see section 5.4). If the use of universal standard units quantifies a priced commodity, fractional and analogical measuring tends to qualify the relations that are embodied in media of value. What is measured here, I suggest, are the relationships involved in constructing and using enclosures.

This interpretation should be seen in the context of arguments developed throughout this monograph: In chapter three I argued that the size and growth of settlement was influenced by developing networks of social ties more than by attempts to maximise ownership of quantities of land. In chapter four I linked coaxial landscapes to increasing flexibility in the use of grazing resources, which necessitated the ability to flexibly negotiate tenure. In chapter five I discussed how building reaves and houses would have mobilised networks of ties and obligations through contributions required in terms of labour and resources. In chapter six I developed an interpretation of tenure linked to gift exchange. These findings suggest forms of interaction in which relations were valued and it seems plausible to infer that the values of relations might be coagulated in the construction of reaves and enclosures. Reaves and enclosures embody claims that might be engaged at a later date, so that people might mobilise their contributions profitably.

Coaxial layouts thus reflect the 'multiple authorship' of reaves. Coaxial land division produced places that were laid out so as to reveal their connections with other places as part of their value. Part of what had the potential to be realised as value was the way that actions integrated multiple contributions in the make-up of places. These multiple contributions were signs of the relationships that composed that place, and of the claims and liabilities over, as well as the capacities of the personages linked to it.

Multiple Authorship and the Arithmetic of Ownership

Multiple composition and authorship can be identified in many different areas of Bronze Age life. It is possible to link such processes back to the practical mathematics I have identified in coaxial layouts. For example, in the Middle Bronze Age, Brück observes that many technological processes involve the deliberate fragmentation of objects and their re-composition into multiply constituted wholes (Brück 2001; Brück, 2006). She points to the fragmentation and grinding up of ceramics which go on to form new vessels; the fragmentation and melting down of bronzes, which go on to form new bronzes; the grinding up of cereals which go on to become food; and the fragmentation of bodies in cremation rites that go on to form deposits at barrows cairns and cemeteries. It is not difficult to see these kinds of material processes as regenerating and redistributing the 'fractal' mathematics described above. If mass production accumulates objects infinitely these technological processes imply a concern with reproduction and multiplication, as one thing contains and reveals another. These are the everyday concerns of livestock management, where the ability to imagine multiplication is necessary to a range of practices including prediction of pasture requirements, control of breeding, and forecasting of herd increase (Gietema, 1998). It is even possible that the kinds of analogical and fractional measuring I have found in coaxial layouts may be an aspect of other pattern making processes, as, for example in the patterns on Collared Urns (Tomalin, 1995; Law, 2005) and in textile technologies and basketry (Owoc et al., 2004; Hurcombe, 2002).

Situations of multiple authorship - where the relationships that go into producing entities are valued – do not fit within conventional notions of property objects or the mathematics which goes with them. Conventional 'western mathematics' indexes and orders a world of property objects and individuals. Strathern conjures this mathematics when she writes of the 'arithmetic of ownership' at the heart of modern concepts of (private) property (Strathern, 2005a). In what Strathern calls 'Euro-American' theories of property, property is always one plus one; one singularised owner relates to one singularised property object. However, where relationships are valued, the arithmetic of ownership is potentially very different. Relationships proliferate and multiply within a network, so that one relationship inevitably leads on to to others. When commodities circulate as media of value the primary relationship is between the commodity and other commodities; the relationships that compose the object tend to be truncated. However, within gift exchange, relationships are part of what is exchanged. The historicity of relationships congealed within the gift is not absolutely truncated. The construction of media of value in the Dartmoor landscape created entities that were valued because they were multiply composed. When value circulated, the multiple contributions that made up entities also circulated.

Identity, too, can be seen as multiply composed; as valuing relationships. In chapters one and six I discussed Bronze Age archaeologies which argued that personhood in this period could be seen as 'fractal' (Brück, 2004; Fowler, 2004; Jones, 2004c). In societies where entities are multiply composed, things and people circulate as fragments of persons; things may be treated like persons and persons treated like things (Mauss, 1970; Strathern, 1984). Transactions involve parts of persons becoming detached from one composite entity or 'dividual' and reattached to another (Chapman, 2000; Fowler, 2004). What I am arguing here is that the measuring practices materialised in coaxial landscapes, because they value relationships, both emerged from and generated 'fractal' notions of personhood.

Interpreting Coaxial Pattern and Tenure

How do processes of measuring layouts that I have identified here fit within previous accounts of the development of land division? As was discussed in chapter five, many previous accounts see coaxial landscapes as emerging through processes of 'fragmentation' and territorialisation as territories become attached to households and lineages. Both the 'mental template' perspective and the 'social context' perspective share this view. Spatial boundaries map onto social boundaries. It is possible to see the patterns I have described in this chapter entirely within these narratives. Processes of subdivision in particular appear to reflect the traditional preoccupation with inheritance found in territorializing accounts. Thus we could see coaxial layouts as reflecting groups settling down and defining themselves within spatial territories and then subdividing land between different segments of the lineage (see Barrett, 1994). However, I consider that this interpretation does not engage sufficiently with the implications of multiple compositions, fractal personhood and the arithmetic of ownership these entail. When spatial boundaries are interpreted as social territories the implied arithmetic of ownership is one plus one: One social group, lineage, 'community' is related to one territory, and this is represented as 'summing up' tenure. But territorialisation is not enough to explain tenure. Tenure involves more than territorialisation. Tenure also involves 'translocation' - allowing media of value to circulate

through loan, transfer and exchange. It makes the 'created artefacts' of environments and economies fungible.

The alternative arithmetic of ownership engaged by relational identities suggests tenure was orientated more towards exchange and the proliferation of relations than towards territorialisation. In chapter four I linked the emergence of coaxial landscapes to the development of greater flexibility in tenure. Before reaves, I suggested, the landscape was characterised by a range of pastures, some of which were occupied seasonally, with tenurial arrangements negotiated between groups. There was already a certain linearity to these pasturing arrangements created by 'axes of movement' between lowlands and uplands (see section 4.3). With the construction of coaxial landscapes, possibilities for greater flexibility in tenure were enhanced. Coaxial landscapes facilitated the loan, exchange and transfer of aspects of tenure between parties more intensely than ever before (see chapter six). The 'arithmetic' of this kind of tenure would have involved relationships multiplying and proliferating. What is valued in tenure, as in other 'gifts', is the value of the relationships that compose it. The ability to access usufruct, for example, would enmesh the holder in a new network of relationships. The arithmetic of ownership here is not one plus one, but instead involves the multiplication of one order of 'fractal' relations with another.

Previous accounts have tended to assume that boundaries signify 'fragmentation'. This assumption, as Barth points out, reflects English speakers particular notions of boundaries as entities that separate (Barth, 1969, 2000). I propose that coaxial boundaries did not separate social groups into lineage segments or spatially distinct 'communities' that can be read off from maps. Instead, as Barth implies, boundaries represent opportunities for proliferating relationships. In this context the way that measuring practices build on relations with pre-existing spaces seems understandable. Relationships are built into reaves, in the forms of the multiple contributions that make them up. They are valued 'economically' and in terms of tenure, because relationships, not resources *per se*, are productive. The relationships that are entered into through tenurial transactions are more important than abstract quantities of land and measuring practices reflect their importance.

Conclusions

In this chapter I approached mathematics as a practical activity, a form of concretised thinking, which depends on engagement with material worlds. I related mathematics to processes that configure personhood and economy. The practical mathematics of measurement, I argued, is a process of valuing. I identified three types of measuring – numerical, analogical and fractional. Metrological analysis of eight coaxial landscapes showed at least four examples had significant quantal properties, but exploratory analyses suggested that these quantal

properties did not result from use of a standard numerical unit, but from a combination of analogical and fractional measuring. Measuring could have been accomplished by careful observations and trail and error, and where visibility was limited a rope may also have been used. I related these measuring processes to the ways that entities were valued within coaxial landscapes. Fractional and analogical measuring, I argued, materialised the relationships involved in building and using these landscapes within their layouts. Relationships were part of the value congealed in landscape artefacts. I linked the multiple composition of objects to an alternative arithmetic of ownership, suggesting that tenure allowed relationships to proliferate as capacities linked to landscapes were loaned and exchanged.

I have approached tenure as part of the constitution of identity. I argued that the fractal mathematics materialised in coaxial landscapes was linked to the wider realities of Bronze Age life; to the ways in which identities were relational. Relationality is poorly understood using conventional theories of property. Classical and Labour theories envisage owners as singular bounded individuals related to singularised bounded property objects. When the property object is land, it tends to be understood as a singularised as a bounded territory related to a bounded social group. The continuing influence of these theories leads tenure to be seen as territorialisation. I have developed an alternative to these approaches based on ideas of personhood that are not singularised or bounded but 'fractal' and proliferating. In the course of my journey through tenure theory I have also developed an interpretation of the archaeology of land division during the second millennium BC. In the next chapter I summarise and evaluate this contribution, placing it in the context of wider debates within archaeology.

Chapter 8

From one 'becoming' to another:
Contribution and Future Projects

At the start of this monograph I set out two aims:

1. To develop existing approaches to tenure
2. To interpret tenure and land division on Dartmoor during the second millennium BC

In this chapter I show how I have met the second of these aims – interpreting prehistoric Dartmoor. I begin with a summary of the findings from analyses carried out in each chapter of the monograph. These findings are used to suggest a new interpretation of tenure and land division. I then reflect on the contribution of my research to existing debates in Bronze Age archaeology. I point to new directions emerging in the study of exchange and economy, subjects with exciting potential for further work. Lastly I recommend more research and outline several future projects.

8.1 Findings of the Study

In this section I review my analysis and the conclusions I have drawn from this work. First, I review the findings of my analyses chapter by chapter. I then draw the conclusions of this work together in a review of my interpretations.

Summary of Results

Dartmoor has a wealth of previous interpretations of tenure and land division. In **chapter two** I argued that Dartmoor was a good place in which to explore the archaeology of tenure. There is a large database of excavations, although most were carried out without modern techniques. Over the last twenty years, several new sources of evidence have been produced, including new palaeoenvironmental studies and survey data. I recalibrated the existing dates for the region showing that reaves began to be built early - around c1850 BC - and continued to be constructed until c1350 BC and probably later. There was a long period of overlap between dates from reaves and cairns.

Chapter three presented analyses that re-evaluated commonsense 'economic' explanations of land division: I assessed the common assumption that fields are built to protect crops from animals - that they are primarily functional to arable farming. Review of palaeoenvironmental data showed that land use within reave landscapes was dominated by pastoral farming with low levels of cereal cultivation. Next, I evaluated the extent to which land scarcity drove the construction of coaxial landscapes. Three related analyses were applied:

i)   I modelled the location of coaxial land division against selected environmental variables. The results suggested that land

division did not take up all suitable, available land.

ii)   I examined the density of land division and settlement. Finding that, rather than spreading out to maximise land holdings, reaves and buildings tended to crowd together, distributed in unevenly dense 'clusters'.

iii)   I compared the results with evidence from palaeoenvironmental studies. This data did not suggest that land was under greatly increased environmental pressures at the time coaxial landscapes were constructed.

The findings of these analyses contradicted commonsense 'economic' explanations in two important ways:

a)   Firstly, the results suggest the construction of coaxial land division was probably not driven by land scarcity to any great extent;

b)   Secondly the builders were not motivated by a desire to maximise individualised land-holdings.

I presented evidence that suggested social ties were much more important in shaping prehistoric settlement patterns than land availability or maximisation of land-holdings. Analysis of the settlement pattern found that the distribution of buildings described a power law. Power law distributions characterise processes of 'scale-free growth'. This result confirmed the idea that landscapes were not ordered around individualised 'family farms. I concluded that obtaining exclusive ownership over singularised plots of land was not an important factor governing the locations of buildings. Settlement was not directed by land availability. The scale-free properties of settlement patterns on Dartmoor suggest that buildings were located according to a network of social ties. Social networks are characteristically scale-free, and often lead to power law distributions. In this scenario the locations of new buildings would follow the ties prospective occupants shared with pre-existing occupants. Settlements with lots of connections would tend to attract even more, so that some locations became densely packed with reaves and buildings while others were much less dense. In conclusion, the results of this analysis did not suggest territorial attitude to tenure which was closed to 'outsiders', but an expansive and flexible situation in which social ties were actively fostered.

The last section of chapter three examined the idea that parcels of land were periodically reallocated as part of a 'redistributive chiefdom' system. Analysis of the sizes of enclosures suggested that land parcelling was very uneven, and that redistribution would therefore be difficult to organise from the 'top-down'.

Chapter four assessed the idea that coaxial division emerged from intensification. Verifying intensification required that increased labour input per unit area be demonstrated. I reviewed evidence for occupation and palaeoenvironmental change in the Neolithic into the Bronze Age, and experimental reconstruction was used to calculate the labour hours involved in building reaves. Ultimately, I found that it was impossible to establish the parameters necessary to prove intensification on the basis of the available data. It was impossible to ascertain the unit area of land involved in agricultural systems before and after reaves, and comparing labour inputs ultimately rested on assumptions concerning the nature of productive 'work'.

Rather than concentrating on intensification I focused on the flexibility of agricultural systems. I compared the elevation ranges incorporated in different kinds of enclosure. The results showed that coaxial enclosures encompassed a much greater range of elevations than either randomly located quadrangles or aggregate enclosures. I suggested that this property of coaxial landscapes was linked to flexible use of grazing resources including pasture rotation. Because coaxial enclosures bundled together different habitat types land division could have gradually increased the productivity of pastures through rotation grazing. This result did not prove intensification. Instead, it suggested coaxial landscapes would have increased flexibility in the management of agricultural systems. I argued that flexibility in agricultural management would have encouraged flexible tenurial arrangements allowing tenure to circulate within and between different persons and groups.

In **chapter five** I investigated the occupancy of prehistoric buildings. I summarised features recovered by excavations of buildings. Analysis showed 'cooking pits' and paving were more prevalent in 'pound' type settlements, whereas 'hearths' and 'pot-boilers' were more common among densely packed high-altitude 'field networks'. Early excavators uncovered ambiguous features that may relate to the burnt mound tradition, possibly linked to the use or reuse of some buildings for communal feasting.

I explored the extent to which evidence supported the notion of 'territorialisation' of the landscape as people gradually became more fixed to occupation of the same spaces. Exploration of this question involved three kinds of analysis:

i) Firstly I analysed evidence for lifecycles of excavated buildings. Previous studies of buildings across southern Britain have revealed a neolocal residence pattern, with houses only occupied for a single generation. Although excavations of timber buildings within coaxial landscapes fit this pattern, other buildings did not. The analysis was limited by the poor quality of most excavations and the difficulties of separating continuous occupations from reoccupation and reuse. The poor quality of the data meant it was impossible to find a conclusive pattern.

ii) Secondly I analysed the relationship between locations of buildings and reaves. I found that the layout of coaxial landscapes was not determined by the locations of buildings to any great extent. Although short lengths of reaves often linked structures to axial reaves, and demarcated 'yard' spaces around the building.

iii) Thirdly, review of excavations of reaves confirmed previous accounts showing a long history of construction, maintenance and use at many sites. Nonetheless there is also evidence for the wholesale demolition of landscapes, and their replacement with new layouts.

I concluded that continuous territorializing processes fixing people to land were only one aspect of the story of Bronze Age landscapes. Occupation could also be discontinuous, involving processes of de/reterritorialisation. Although many previous accounts have seen land tenure as coterminous with territorialisation, tenure also involves the loan and exchange of reproductive capacities linked to land.

Chapter six studied Bronze Age exchange, mortuary rites, and treatment of metalwork. Review of current evidence for exchange underlines the importance of long distance communications in Bronze Age societies. At the time reaves were built artefact distributions suggest a series of interlocking gift exchange networks operating throughout the South-West region. There is good evidence for regular communications with Ireland and Northern France, and even some evidence for direct contact with the Mediterranean.

Previous accounts of barrows and cairns interpreted them as property markers, as the graves of high-status lineage heads reinforcing claims over territory. Recent reappraisals of mortuary rites suggest that these sites were not the 'graves' of individuals but evidenced relational identities in the Bronze Age. I analysed evidence from excavations of cairns on and around Dartmoor. The findings matched recent studies on mortuary practices across the South West, which show that cairns are not primarily 'graves' but communal loci involving a range of depositional activities.

I analysed evidence from metalwork finds. Review showed that after c1600 BC an increasing range of locations were appropriate for deposition of metalwork. Evidence reinforced the importance of dryland locations and of findspots with only one or two artefacts. There was no absolute distinction between human remains and metalwork; instead, I argued metal objects might have circulated as 'persons and parts of persons'. I interpreted evidence for deposition using previous notions of 'gifts to the gods'. The memory of such gifts, I suggested, linked land inalienably to the identity of persons and groups. However, I suggested that this very inalienable identification between people and land allowed the reproductive capacities of land to be loaned or exchanged.

Finally I linked the 'keeping' of land with the 'giving' of tenure within exchange networks. Expanding such networks of exchange, I argued would have been important in Bronze Age societies since local exchange relations were ultimately the grounds for success in long distance voyages and transactions.

In chapter seven I analysed how coaxial land division was laid out. I developed a method of metrological analysis that applied Kendall's cosine-based formula. The results showed that there was no overall unit of numerical measurement in use. Investigation of individual areas showed that several had significant quanta. These areas were comparatively smaller in size, and had many spatially inter-related reaves. Exploratory analysis revealed that significant quanta could be isolated spatially within particular areas of sample landscapes. Further analysis showed that, within landscapes with significant quanta, only some reaves were close multiples, while other reaves were such inaccurate multiples that it seemed unlikely that a unit of measurement had been used. Analysis of subdivision and replication of widths suggested that the significant quanta were the result of processes of analogical and fractional measurement based on existing properties of each landscape. I related these processes of measuring to the way that land was valued

among the people who constructed reaves. I argued that the importance of reave-building was the network of debts and obligations such communal activities set up. Coaxial layouts materialised the value of relationships. I argued that the layout of coaxial landscapes expressed the relational or 'fractal' characteristics of Bronze Age personhood.

Conclusions of the Interpretation

Reaves emerged in the final centuries of the Early Bronze Age and the beginning of the Middle Bronze Age when the size of exchange networks and the velocity of exchange was increasing. Tenure allowed land and its reproductive capabilities to be distributed and circulated as parts of persons in exchange. It was part of the constitution of identity which involved two sets of relations:

i) relations with the gods, ancestors or supernatural forces which preserved the identification of people with land;

ii) relations of people with each other which involved the proliferation of relations through exchanges of the reproductive capacities of land.

Exchange networks provided the means to proliferate social ties, which were the basis of economic life. Loan and exchange of access to pastures allowed land to be used more flexibly, and coaxial landscapes may have increased this flexibility, allowing spare capacity to be shared productively. Landscapes of land division do not signal 'fragmentation' into individual territories but instead, provide evidence for expanding interconnections between groups.

Tenurial exchanges are likely to have been part of the small-scale interlocking exchange networks which characterised exchange within the South-West region. However this does not mean such exchanges were purely 'local'. Tenure sustained networks through which the communal activities necessary for long distance communications were organised. The value of tenurial exchanges could be translocated – much as Munn describes the value of tenurial exchanges being translocated in long distance kula exchange (Munn 1987: 267-71). What contribution does this interpretation make to existing ideas of Bronze Age land division and tenure? How is it different to previous accounts? The next section takes up these questions beginning on Dartmoor and then looking towards wider debates in the archaeology of Bronze Age societies.

8.2 Contribution of the Interpretation and Methodology

In this section I assess how my interpretation contributes to current debates in the Bronze Age of Dartmoor and southern Britain and the advantages and disadvantages of

the methodology I used. I begin by examining how my work contributes to existing literature on Dartmoor landscapes. I then discuss changing ideas of what the so-called 'Middle Bronze Age transition' signifies, and how my work fits within these debates. Lastly I assess the methodology, and application of GIS in the study.

Contribution to Archaeologies of Dartmoor

Any study of Dartmoor will engage with Fleming's important work in the region. This study builds on Fleming's interpretation and its findings support many of his conclusions. Like Fleming, I have rejected the assumption that prehistoric land division represents a generalised social evolutionary progression towards private property. My findings support Fleming's insistence that reaves did not define individualised 'family farms' (see Fleming, 1978b, 1988, and chapter three). Just as Fleming found evidence for pastoral land uses and commons, so have I (see Fleming, 1979; Maguire et al., 1983, and chapter four). Like him, I have stressed the importance of the small scale 'community' and flexible management of agricultural systems from the 'bottom up'(see Fleming, 1982, 1984 and chapter four). I have pointed to the importance of exchange networks in tenurial relations, and Fleming also emphasised exchange, particularly gifts of labour and produce, and pooling of resources including communal shepherds and pastures (see Fleming, 1984, 1985b, and chapter seven).

Nonetheless, the findings of this study advance archaeologies of the region in certain ways, and the interpretation differs from previous literature. To bring out this contribution I return to a series of issues raised in chapter two (section 2.3). Here, I reviewed existing literature on Dartmoor and identified debates concentrated around the following:

- Issues arising from Fleming's social model and critique by others. Critique has focused on the structural image of social organisation in some of Fleming's work, which makes it difficult to incorporate social dynamics (Brück, 1999a; Johnston, 2005).
- Issues arising from Fleming's spatial model and its critique in subsequent work. The debate here has revolved around the extent to which land division was planned, and if not, how the striking pattern of coaxial landscapes can be explained (Bradley, 2002; Johnston, 2005).
- Debate concerning the extent to which Dartmoor evidences 'Bronze Age chiefdoms' – 'top down' control of tenure and the economy (Pearce, 1983; Kristiansen, 1998: 367-8; Earle, 2002: chapter 12-4; cf Fleming, 1982).
- The issue of how land division and tenure are connected to exchange networks (Pearce, 1983, 1999; Kristiansen, 1998)

Discussion centres on how each of these debates has been advanced by this study.
Fleming's social model begins by assuming certain categories, especially that of the 'household' (Fleming,

1985b, 1988). After Sahlins (1972), (and ultimately Chayanov (Shanin, 1986)), the household is seen as *contradicting* the wider community and neighbourhood group. The 'household' tends towards privatisation, whereas the 'community' entails obligations towards the collective. This produces 'tension' between household and community, private and collective (Sahlins, 1972; Fleming, 1984).

My interpretation has made much less of the distinctions between domains like 'households' and 'communities'. I have been more inclined to emphasise the way entities permeate one another. This is an effect of the way I have drawn on recent ideas of personhood and relational identity (e.g. Chapman, 2000; Brück, 2004; Fowler, 2004). According to these ideas 'persons' can be human bodies or families or groups. Each entity is multiply composed and hence each contains something of the others. The distinction between 'individual' and 'community' has therefore been much less definite in this account. When ideas of personhood are applied to concepts of tenure they collapse the conventional opposition between private and common property. Instead tenure becomes more or less inclusive according to the ways in which persons relate to other persons. As a result there has been much less emphasis on social structure in my study and much more on processes like exchange. Exchange is a process that has the potential to generate claims and obligations and hence to make tenure inclusive in different ways (Kalinoe & Leach, 2004; Hirsch & Strathern, 2004). The advantage of this approach is that it does not rely too much on predefined social levels, and is therefore more mutable. The disadvantage is that it offers much less specific characterisation of form.

Although Fleming made it clear that social structure could not be 'read off' from spatial boundaries (1978b, 1988), some of his texts produce diagrammatic accounts of social order that clearly relate to what I have called his 'spatial model'. Fleming's spatial model is inscribed on the landscape through diagrammatic maps of boundaries and territories (Fleming 1978b, 1984, 1988, 1994b). It offers a 'total' image of the landscape, explained as a series of interlocking zones of land use and tracts of territory. Boundaries tend to separate rather then unite in this model and reaves are seen as commonsense 'boundaries' in the manner criticised by Barth (see section 6.1). This model is a territorializing account of land division, in which bounded territories indicate singular 'communities'.

In this monograph I have tried to break away from territorializing accounts of tenure. Accordingly I have tried not to singularise territories or 'owners', but to multiply outwards from boundaries towards networks of relationships. Instead of reading spatial boundaries as 'symbols' or encodings of social units I tried to approach them as indicating processes of building and measuring. Because of this emphasis on processes I have not produced a 'total' model of the landscape. This might be seen as a limitation of my study. However, it should be remembered that Fleming's spatial model is not 'total' either. Fleming's diagrammatic maps have the effect of making the evidence appear much more integrated and less messy than detailed survey data (see section 2.3 and Butler, 1997b). To explain all of the existing detail within a 'total' model we would require much better information on dates and sequences of construction. Without sustained programmes of excavation and analysis conclusions are inevitably partial.

Critique of Fleming's spatial model has focused on the extent to which a 'system' of land division was 'planned' or not. While Fleming supports the idea of a 'template' behind construction (Fleming, 1978b, 1994b) later writers envisage a gradual and contingent process based on the locations of pre-existing features (Bradley, 2002; Johnston, 2001b, 2005). Explaining coaxial pattern has been a problem for these recent studies. My analysis of measurement in coaxial landscapes suggested a middle way between these two camps: Coaxial pattern was not only 'planned', nor was it only a by-product of the gradual imposition of social forces. Instead, division of pastures against the contour led to particular ways of measuring emerging from the ways that boundaries themselves were built and understood. Coaxial pattern emerged through fractional and analogical forms of measurement that were linked to how reaves were built. The building of reaves involved exchanges of labour and resources that generated future claims over people (including tenurial claims). The measuring of coaxial landscapes thus referred to a history of transactions and to the way relations were valued.

This study has found little support for hierarchical elite management of the Dartmoor landscape. There is no evidence for an architecture that would support centralised accumulation and redistribution of agricultural surpluses at the time of reaves (cf Pearce, 1983, 1999; see section 3.5) and no evidence that land was parcelled to allow periodic redistribution of tenure (cf Earle, 2002; see section 3.5). Furthermore, I found excavations of cairns and barrows did not offer a great deal of evidence to support the notion that these were the graves of high status individuals (cf Kristiansen, 1998: 352; see section 6.3). Although Fleming (1984) argued that reaves were 'planned' by some form of central authority, (either a chief or something more akin to a council of commoners) I have rejected this idea of 'top-down' centralised planning (see chapter 7). I suggest networks that were much more fluid and unstable than these structural models of hierarchy imagine. Inequality emerged from differential access to social ties and hence to tenure and exchange networks. Power was not a property that 'individuals' 'possessed', in the way some previous accounts have suggested (cf Kristiansen, 1998) but had to be built through the efforts of wider networks. Only through communal activities could powerful persons travel forth.

My interpretation of land division has emphasised exchange of tenure over the territorialisation of exclusive 'property'. In particular I drew on theories of gift exchange that pointed to the personification of objects and the creation of enduring connections stemming from the inalienability of gifts (Mauss, 1970; Gregory, 1982; Strathern, 1988; Godelier, 1999). I used evidence derived from metalwork to suggest what kinds of exchanges may have been taking place, making no necessary distinction between exchanges over access to land and resources and exchanges of objects or people. This differs from some previous approaches that have suggested that agricultural produce and metal 'wealth' represent two different classes of object. Such accounts imply that intensifying agricultural production led to surpluses that could be translated into metal 'wealth' (e.g. Pearce, 1983, 1999). My emphasis on gifts has led me to an alternative view that focuses on the value of relationships rather then on the value of objects in-themselves. This approach was informed by the theory of value that I discussed in chapter four, which saw value as the importance of action (Graeber, 2001). The actions of building were gift exchanges materialised in the form of reaves. These gifts ensured that tenurial exchanges were ones of 'keeping-for-giving' since, whilst tenure was given away, it remained inalienably linked to a particular group.

The Middle Bronze Age Transition

In chapter two I discussed how, (despite the early dates of most reaves), Dartmoor land division is often discussed as marking a 'transition' taking place c.1500 BC. The Middle Bronze Age transition is understood as a period during which the mobile groups of the Late Neolithic and Early Bronze Age settle down in permanent homesteads, 'fragmenting' into extended family groups. Influential accounts of this transition have understood it as part of a transformation in the nature of 'subjectivity' (Gosden, 1994; Barrett, 1994). My interpretation, with its emphasis on the constitution of identities, clearly owes much to this tradition. However, in chapter two, I discussed new evidence that challenges some previous accounts. For example, Barrett envisages a transition away from subjectivities of 'becoming' towards increasingly territorialized, place-bound senses of 'being' (Barrett, 1994, 1999). But several sources of evidence for this transformation have recently been reassessed:

i) Firstly the life-cycles of many Middle Bronze Age buildings suggest that people were perhaps not as 'settled' as some accounts of the Middle Bronze Age imply (Brück, 1999a) – the landscape was not gradually territorializing, but was still mobile in significant ways.

ii) Secondly environmental evidence for Bronze Age intensification on the chalk of southern Britain has been overturned, and it now seems that these landscapes were largely pastoral (French et al., 2003).

iii)   Lastly, the evidence for 'individuating' burial practices has been re-examined (Woodward, 2002; Brück, 2004; Jones, 2004c; Jones, 2005). These new studies show that many mortuary sites are not the graves of individuals.

This study examined Dartmoor landscapes in the light of these recent debates. In particular, I sought to challenge notions that linked tenure to territorialisation. In chapter five I found that it was difficult to reconstruct the lifecycles of many buildings. No uniform 'lifecycle' could be established, although there was enough evidence to suggest that the landscape was not everywhere dominated by long-term sedentarisation. Intensification was assessed in chapter four. Here, I found that, like Cranborne Chase, Dartmoor was a predominately pastoral landscape. Land division, I concluded was not de facto evidence for intensification, and intensification could not be proved from existing data. Lastly, in chapter six I argued that rites at barrows and cairns were not 'individuating', but could equally be considered communal and/or 'dividuating'. The findings of the this study, therefore suggest that previous ideas of the Middle Bronze Age transition based on the transformation from 'becoming' to 'being' should be revised.

Previous accounts have seen land division as indicating a period in which identity became 'fixed' in space and time (Barrett, 1994, 1999). I argue that, on the contrary, land division evidences new ways of allowing personhood to be more distributed and expanded. When land division is read as territorialisation than it is seen as heralding 'social fragmentation' into small groups 'fixed' to soil. I have tried to engage with the ways that tenure allows de/reterritorialisation as well as territorialisation. Instead of seeing the changes of the Early to Middle Bronze Age as indicating 'fragmentation' I consider this period as one in which more flexible ways of expanding personhood around exchange networks became possible. Land division facilitated tenurial exchanges and exchange of labour. The value of exchanges in tenure, labour and resources could be translocated to allow people to enter into longer distance transactions. I suggest that the Middle Bronze Age is best seen not as a transition from 'becoming' to 'being'; but as change from one sort of 'becoming' to another.

Methodology and Use of GIS

'...applications of GIS must be carefully shaped around specific archaeological questions, themselves embedded in an explicit body of archaeological theory.'

(Wheatley & Gillings, 2002: 237)

In the early days of archaeological GIS, Gillings and Wheatley report, studies were characterised by 'profound lack of imagination' and 'technological-determinism' (ibid, emphasis removed). Research was driven by the kinds of analysis offered by software packages rather than by questions of archaeological interest. However they predict that, in the future, studies will be guided by specific theoretical questions. When research proceeds from theory rather than method GIS-based studies will make 'their own contribution to the development of archaeological theory' (ibid.).

The methodology of this study did not foreground GIS, but integrated spatial analyses within a 'method assemblage' (Law, 2004). Analysis took place as part of the development of larger conceptual themes. Because no single method was pursued, the text did not follow a method-results-conclusion structure, but was organised thematically around different approaches to tenure. This structure had both advantages and disadvantages. The chief advantage was that there was a relatively good match between data and theory – something that is often difficult to achieve in GIS studies. A disadvantage is that there has not been room in the text to dwell at length on the details of each analysis. Had GIS been foregrounded there would undoubtedly have been greater exegesis of each application and the statistical operations involved. However, this would have shifted the balance of the research, which has always been trying to find a way to develop interpretation and theory, rather than to advance a single technology or method.

As was indicated in the Preface, this methodology emerged from my philosophical understanding of the status of knowledge claims. I did not begin with a notion of using method to discover a pre-existing determinate coherent reality of prehistoric tenure. Instead I argued that method involved creating networks that, more or less precariously, constructed or stabilised realities (see Latour, 1987, 1999; Law, 2004). From previous studies I inferred that prehistoric tenure was likely to be a heterogeneous multi-dimensional reality, poorly described by a single clear-cut method. Therefore the methodology was exploratory and interpretative rather than purely hypothesis-testing. The limitation of this approach is that it can never lead to the satisfying conclusion of an absolute claim to truth. Instead, I have offered a series of findings constructed from inevitably partial and provisional datasets and theories. Future work is needed to reinforce or challenge these unstable realities.

8.3 Critique of 'Personhood' Approaches and Further Work

'The mind-set which currently dominates British Archaeology' Shennan argues, 'belongs to a long tradition of constructing 'noble savages' in opposition to ourselves, and more generally of generating rhetorical opposites to 'western society'...' (Shennan, 1999: 352). 'Thus' he continues 'if *We* engage in exchanges to make some sort of profit, *They* do so in order to cement social relationships; *We* trade commodities, *They* give gifts' (ibid. sic). While I do not agree with Shennan's solution, (a return to neoclassical value theory), there no denying the ring of truth in his characterisation of British Archaeology. Some of the personhood literature in archaeology steers rather close to the dichotomies he describes (see Fowler, 2004; Brück, 2006). The danger is that this literature implies that 'they' (primitives) are multiply composed persons, while 'we' (moderns) are sovereign individuals. In chapter one I discussed this danger (section 1.5). I made clear that it was not my intention to perpetuate this kind of 'primitivism'. I illustrated the value of approaches that focused on relational identity and distributed personhood for studying modern property phenomena like biotechnology, Open Source Software and the internet. However, there might be one area in which both this study and recent archaeologies of personhood, have not escaped this danger; that is in the way gifts have been opposed to commodities.

In this section I criticise the archaeologies of personhood that I have used in this study. I argue that these approaches are so preoccupied with a Strathernian version of reciprocal gift exchange that they have failed to engage with other kinds of transaction. In particular they have little to say about the significant evidence for commodity exchanges in the Bronze Age. I discuss this problem, and then I introduce some ideas that might be developed by further work.

Dichotomies of Gifts and Commodities and Archaeologies of Personhood

The personhood literature tends towards rhetorical dualisms between 'dividuals' and 'individuals', gifts and commodities. This is in part because such literature is intended to rehabilitate dimensions of identity that have been suppressed by conventional approaches. The once suppressed element is elevated by opposing it to the 'modern', 'western' and 'capitalist'. The emphasis on reciprocal non-agonistic gifts in recent personhood literature is intended as a 'remedial' critique that rectifies the reductionism of many previous accounts of prehistoric 'economics'. Thus Brück rightly argues that traditional accounts 'impose aspects of Capitalist economics onto the past' (Brück, 2006). However, the solution – the elevation of gift exchange at the expense of commodity transactions – constructs an opposition that is ultimately unhelpful. The current personhood literature unfortunately implies that the commodity is a 'modern' 'western' 'capitalist' phenomenon –that is of no interest to prehistorians (cf Appadurai, 2005). There are two risks here;

i) Firstly that archaeologies of personhood perpetuate an social evolutionary account of

transactions with gift exchange at one end and commodity exchange at the other;

ii) Secondly, that this literature, by ignoring commodity transactions, misses out on an area to which it could make an important contribution.

Just as tenure is traditionally thought to evolve from common to private property, so exchange has long been thought to evolve from gift to commodity transactions (Mauss, 1970). Polanyi's idea of the 'Great Transformation' invoked the differences between modern 'market' societies and previous economies based on reciprocity, redistribution and house-holding (Polanyi, 1944: chapter 4; Sahlins, 1972). Archaeologies of the Bronze Age have sometimes represented this period as one of increasing commodity exchange (Bradley, 1984, 1998a; Shennan, 1993; Earle, 2002: chapter 12). The principal sources of evidence for increasing emphasis on commodity exchange come from studies of metalwork, in particular from:

i) fragmentation of objects into potentially tradable 'scrap' (Bradley, 1998a)

ii) ingots and 'axe-ingots' of standardised shape and/or metal content (Bradley, 1998a; Northover, 2006)

iii) standard weights and the beginnings of a 'weighed metal economy' (Malmer, 1992; Pare, 2000; Ruiz-Galvez, 2000)

iv) suggested 'pre-monetary' forms including torcs, bracelets and 'ring-money' (Eogan, 1997).

These various sources of evidence, different in different parts of Europe, have been integrated within general social evolutionary approaches, as potential 'commodities'. Within such 'world systems' approaches commodity exchange is seen as spreading outwards from the Mediterranean and south-central Europe almost as if it were an evolutionary wave of advance (Kristiansen, 1998). Commodity exchange, this approach implies, was always the same everywhere, and is principally significant as indicating a new economic era which will eventually displace primitive gift societies. The current literature on 'personhood' perpetuates the notion that commodity exchange is a 'modern' phenomenon. It thus continues in this social evolutionary vein. Furthermore, by seeing commodities as the 'flip-side' of gifts, it perpetuates the presumption that commodity transactions are everywhere the same, and are significant principally as tokens of advance towards the modern.

This is unfortunate since it might be very interesting to apply the concept of relational identity developed in archaeologies of personhood to all this evidence for Bronze Age 'commodification'. Recent theories of commodification and economics outside archaeology suggest how this might be accomplished.

New Approaches to Exchange

People of all times and places have the potential to engage in a range of transactions including both gift and commodity exchange. Commodity exchange is a feature of a great many, possibly all, societies (Appadurai, 2005). As Polanyi pointed out long ago, this is a very different thing from saying that all economies are 'controlled and regulated by markets' (Polanyi, 1944: 44) - clearly they are not. If the general potential for both commodity and gift exchange is accepted it no longer seems adequate to simply identify and oppose 'societies of the gift' to 'societies of the commodity' as archaeologies of personhood have been wont to do. Nor can archaeologists presume that just because a number of Bronze Age objects (ingots or 'pre-monetary forms') resemble 'commodities' that they were only transacted in commodity exchanges. Gift and commodity exchange are relations, not innate properties of certain classes of object. Commodification is 'a situation … that can characterise many different kinds of thing at different points in their social lives' (Appadurai, 2005: 36). The task for the analyst is not to find 'gifts' or 'commodities', nor to oppose general models of 'gift societies' and 'commodity societies' but to identify contexts in which certain different kinds of 'exchangeability' become the 'socially relevant' features of things (Appadurai, 2005: 37).

The account of inalienability that I gave in chapter six is an important part of identifying how transactions are framed. In chapter six I stressed that land was not inalienable by virtue of it being a particular category of thing (cf Weiner, 1992). What made land, or other things, inalienable were context of previous exchanges. Following Godelier (1999), I suggested that land tended to be inalienable because it was often understood to have been given by gods or other supernatural agencies. Because land was a gift that could never be repaid it permanently retained something inalienable of the sacred. The imaginary realm of original gifts was important in framing what was exchangeable and how. Several recent studies of contemporary societies have shown how modern markets are framed by creating strong distinctions between things which are inalienable and 'commodities' (see Ertman & Williams, 2005). Accordingly the world of 'commodities' and 'economic' value is represented as the negative inverse of a 'pure' realm of social and moral 'uneconomic' values. However these recent studies point out how the act of purifying non-market 'culture', 'heritage', 'charity' or 'family life' implicitly frames and supports market capitalism (Joseph, 2005; Harding, 2005). What is needed, these critics insist, is an examination of how and when gifts and commodities, inalienable and alienable are able to transform into one another; 'an examination of the social conditions that frame market exchanges' (Williams & Zelizer, 2005: 363, see also Carrier, 1995).

What archaeologists might bring to this project is an enduring interest in the part that material things play in framing transactions. The materiality of modern markets is something that has been studied by Callon (1998). He points to the network of material things environments and people that are necessary to allow modern market exchanges to be performed. Particularly important, he demonstrates are material technologies of measuring – quantifying and qualifying – value (Callon, 1998; Callon et al., 2002). Also important are architectures that promote certain relations between artefacts; relations that allow comparisons and equivalences to be drawn between them. In the context of prehistoric societies it is extremely unlikely that all the evidence for the networks that framed exchanges will be preserved. However, there are some obvious places to begin to look; with artefact assemblages that suggest ways of realising value, for example, with weights and measures. Archaeologies of personhood - with their focus on relations and networks - have much to contribute to studies of how transactions are framed. Future research is needed into Bronze Age exchange that engages with evidence for commodity transactions as well as with gift exchange.

8.4 Future Projects Emerging from the Study

In this section I outline the directions suggested by the findings of this study. Beginning with Dartmoor, I offer some recommendations for future projects in the region. The interpretation of tenure and land division I have produced could be developed through comparative study looking further afield in Britain and Ireland. Lastly I consider new directions in the study of Bronze Age exchange.

Future Research on Dartmoor

The lack of recent excavations on Dartmoor significantly limits the kinds of analysis that can be undertaken in this region. The principal problem is that - for the size of the known resource - there are very few sites with good dating sequences or detailed stratigraphic information available. The Shaugh Moor project still stands out as the major Bronze Age excavation (Balaam et al., 1982). Holne Moor supplies another important site, but it has no full excavation report (Fleming, 1988). Both these excavation projects are over twenty-five years old and took place before modern techniques of radio-carbon dating that can obtain dates on small samples and peat samples. The palaeoenvironmental record has a good coverage of samples, but many cores lack good absolute dates, and relatively few are tied into excavated sites. Previous excavations have not left the region exhaustively researched (cf Griffith, 1990), rather, due to the poor quality of much of this work, they have simply produced more unanswered questions. There are therefore two main priorities for future work:

i)   New excavation projects

ii)   Scientific studies of materials from early excavations – especially new dating programmes.

Excavations currently underway on Dartmoor begin to address the need for new excavations. Work is currently in progress at Teigncombe and on Shovel Down. The Teigncombe project focuses on a single building, with the aim of assessing the damage caused by bracken to archaeological deposits (Gerrard, 1997b). It will provide detailed stratigraphic information on the lifecycle of a Bronze Age building. The aims of the Shovel Down Project are closely allied with the concerns raised by my research. The project has three main aims:

i)   examine the socio-economic basis of land-use practices;

ii)   investigate the interplay between subsistence, social relations and environmental conditions; and

iii)   obtain a detailed understanding of the chronology and historical context of land enclosure (Brück et al., 2005).

Following the successes of the Shaugh Moor and Holne Moor projects, which both examined large areas of land division, this project focuses on an area four square kilometres in extent. The first phase of the fieldwork, completed in 2005, involved evaluative geophysical, earthwork and geochemical survey, palaeoenvironmental investigation, test pitting and exploratory trenching of reaves designed to improve the focus and success of more intensive methodologies. Trenches dug in mires revealed reaves stratigraphically associated with environmental sequences. Dates on peat from these trenches are currently being processed. Subsequent phases of the project will involve open area excavation focusing on two zones of buildings and reaves. This intensive site-focused phase of the project will tie into the results of the earlier 'off-site' phase. The Shovel Down Project is thus designed to allow greater appreciation of the chronological depth of land division, the relations between life-cycles of reaves and buildings and the processes of laying out and constructing reaves. These projects will hopefully encourage a revival in archaeological interest in the region.

Considerable potential exists for re-examining sites investigated before 1950. Plymouth Museum contains an archive of finds and other material left by the Dartmoor Excavation Committee that represents an opportunity to revisit early excavations and obtain supplementary information. Quinnell is currently undertaking a programme of absolute dating from charcoal residues on the ceramics in this collection (Quinnell, 1996; pers. comm.). A programme making use of new techniques that allow dates on cremated bone would also prove helpful, giving some indication of the pattern of mortuary practices in the region (Jones, 2005: 143).

New excavations designed to complement work on the archives of early and unpublished sites could enhance the existing resource. Techniques for studying palaeoenvironments and soil geochemistry were either unknown or infrequently applied before the 1960s and a great deal of work could be done tying these early excavations into the wider sequences currently available. Future work should re-examine the trenches of previous excavators through targeted excavations. Documentary records indicate that deposits survive intact on many sites including:

i)   Deposits beneath the level of the 'calm' (judged by previous excavators to correspond to the floors of the buildings)

ii)   Fills of features incompletely excavated

iii)   Deposits beneath stones that were not removed (including the walls of all buildings and large fallen stones)

iv)   Buildings which were never totally excavated

Appendix Z lists sites where records indicate the survival of prehistoric deposits.

The extent of the distribution of known prehistoric sites is so vast it is unlikely that a truly synoptic understanding of the region's archaeology will be obtained anytime soon. While I was writing this monograph a new stone row was discovered beneath deep peat at Cut Hill raising the possibility that many more sites lie undiscovered in the high moors (Greeves, 2004). Here, again is an important opportunity for future work, work that could revolutionise our current understanding of the spatial distribution of prehistoric sites.

Future Research in Prehistoric Tenure and Land division

This study has focused on one region - albeit a significant one for interpretations of prehistoric tenure. It has not looked in any detail at land division outside the region. There are therefore questions concerning how my interpretations from the current findings would fare in other regions? Landscapes of land division are now known to have existed in many parts of southern Britain from the Thames Valley to the Scilly Isles. Land division dated to the second millennium BC is also present in the southern Netherlands and in Ireland. Previous accounts have tended to extract the landscapes with evidence for 'coaxial' land division, and to deploy them within generalising narratives of centralised 'planning' and elite power. However, the category 'coaxial' may mask as much as it reveals about the various processes involved in constructing landscapes. Nonetheless, given my interpretation of coaxial layouts in chapter seven it is a valid to ask how other coaxial layouts in southern Britain compare to the Dartmoor landscapes?

Initial inspection of survey data from Salisbury Plain and the Thames Valley suggest that at least some layouts show similar patterns to the Dartmoor systems and metrological analysis may reveal similar processes of laying out (Bradley et al., 1994; Crutchley, 2001; Yates, 1999). Yet many Bronze Age landscapes were not laid out in this way. Traces of land division across most of Cornwall for example, are not coaxial (Johnson & Rose, 1994; cf Brisbane & Clews, 1979). An obvious question for future work concerns the significance of different layouts and how they relate to local tenurial systems.

Answering these questions requires a larger research project comparing between areas. Evidence for land division should be considered alongside differences in exchange networks, mortuary and depositional practices, settlement patterns and lifecycles of occupation, agricultural systems and environmental histories. This project would further refine the approach developed in this research, evaluating it against a range of different datasets. The archaeologies of personhood that have influenced the approach taken here tend to produce broad brush characterisations, based on dichotomies (e.g. between dividuals or individuals, gifts and commodities). A comparative approach based on comparing different areas might explore more subtle variations in personhood linked to the different ways tenure was materialised.

New Directions in Bronze Age Exchange

Some of the methods developed in my research might prove applicable to the study of commodity transactions. The method of metrological analysis in chapter seven could be used to investigate evidence for weights, measures and standardisation in Bronze Age metalwork. Previous metrological study has focused on gold objects that do not lose weight from corrosion, although it has also been applied to well-preserved examples of bronze axes and palstaves (Pare, 2000). More work would be needed to define a suitable dataset for such a study.

Studying commodification should not involve simply identifying likely commodities. Instead this project requires the examination and comparison of how exchanges are framed differently in different circumstances. Why for example are weights materialised in different kinds of objects in different places? How do they embody values as well as value (Graeber, 2001)? It is no longer enough to evoke a 'world system' that supposes commodification is the same everywhere. Just because there is a transaction this does not mean that each party to the transaction understands it in the same way. The ethnographic record is full of examples of transactions between and within groups, sometimes continuing over long periods, which are nonetheless understood entirely differently by either party. We need to understand the importance of the act of exchange in each case. What are the projects of value involved? How are media of value finally realised as value? What totalities must be constructed in order for values to be realised? Answering these questions necessitates detailed studies of the conditions that frame transactions in particular times and places. We need to generate interpretations of specific historically constituted 'economics' and value systems. Transactions in the past involved webs of partial overlapping networks which allowed different values to be translocated, and different value systems to interact. This approach has the potential to challenge dominant 'world systems' models and, perhaps, to re-invent existing notions of Bronze Age 'economics'.

Conclusions

This chapter discussed how the study met one of its aims: interpreting tenure and land division on Dartmoor during the second millennium BC. I reviewed the findings of the analyses. These findings demonstrated a landscape in which relationships seemed to be valued more than individualised 'property' holdings. I interpreted land division as an architecture that materialised the value of relationships, facilitating tenurial arrangements that allowed persons to expand relations and exchange networks more flexibly. This interpretation moved away from the emphasis on territorialisation seen in existing interpretations of the reave landscapes. I argued that building boundaries united more than separating groups. This led me to question the ways some previous interpretations had 'read' reaves as diagrams of social structure. My findings correspond to those of a series of recent studies that are challenging established accounts of the Middle Bronze Age transition. Instead of seeing the Bronze Age as a period in which identities were spatially and temporally 'fixed' within boundaries, I have pointed to the ways that tenure translocates and expands personhood. However, I identified some weaknesses in archaeologies of personhood, particularly the failure of this literature to engage with evidence for commodity transactions. I suggest further work is needed in this area. Finally, I outlined a number of future projects, on Dartmoor, and other landscapes of land division, that will develop and refine the interpretation presented here.

Fleming ends *The Dartmoor Reaves* by summoning the wider community of interest in tenure. 'For prehistorians' he observes, 'the world is shrinking':

> *Instead of simply reconstructing local sequences, [we] are concerned to find out how similar archaeological problems have been tackled in other parts of the world, how far the processes which we are thinking about have occurred elsewhere'*
> (Fleming, 1988: 123).

The relevance of the problems we tackle, Fleming argues, should be global. My attempts to develop approaches to tenure in this monograph were influenced by this spirit in Fleming's work. My research has gathered together ideas from different disciplines to help me think anew about tenure. Along the way I have summoned examples from many different times and places to illustrate each theme.

In the next chapter I consider how the approach to tenure I have developed here contributes to current thinking in the rapidly changing field of tenure studies. As Fleming continues (ibid.), 'I had started my study on a misty Dartmoor hillside, but who could say where it might end?'

Chapter 9

Tenure and How Persons Matter:
Contribution to Tenure Studies

In this chapter I return to the first aim of the research – to develop existing theories of tenure. I begin by reviewing the findings of the study, and discussing the implications of my conclusions for existing archaeologies of tenure. I then suggest how archaeologies of tenure might contribute to wider tenure studies. I advocate approaches that explore tenure as relations through which persons matter, and I highlight how these approaches connect with the wider interest in materiality currently apparent across the social sciences. I suggest that this approach

supplies a critical perspective on some other approaches to tenure: Classical theories of property can themselves be understood as part of networks that constitute persons as sovereign rights-bearing individuals. While territorializing approaches participate in networks that make persons matter as 'indigenous'. Lastly, I examine the trajectories along which this rapidly changing field is travelling, suggesting new directions for future research.

9.1 Findings of the Study and their Implications

The methodology of the research applied approaches, informed by series of different 'themes' in tenure theory, to data from prehistoric Dartmoor. This method allowed me to reflect critically on each theme. Four themes were identified from the historical background of tenure studies:

1   Classical theories of property,
2   The labour theory of property
3   Tenure as territorialisation
4   Tenure as part of the constitution of identity

In this section I report on how each of these themes was developed through application to the data, and what critical insights emerged on each set of approaches. I then review the implications of my findings for archaeological approaches to tenure.

Classical Theories of Property

Following Rose (1990) I described 'classical' theories of property. The definition of property, according to classical theories, is that property is an 'exclusive individual right' (MacPherson, 1978). This body of property-thought includes 'neoclassical' economic, as well as what might be described as commonsense 'economic' accounts. 'Classical' theories assume that property arises from self-interested individuals maximising utility in conditions of scarcity. However, they also characterise property as a jural institution of 'rights'. These two assumptions contradict one another because jural institutions could not be set up if individuals were purely selfish (see section 1.2). Partly to get over this contradiction, Rose argues, classical theorists tend to tell 'stories' of the origins of property. Evolutionary narratives tell how institutional change is

driven by increasing scarcity and associated negative externalities. Classical theories thus leave three important legacies that have been inherited in neoclassical and other 'economic' approaches:

i)   resources defined by scarcity
ii)   self-interested maximisation by individuals
iii)   property as a legal structure of 'rights'

In chapter three I explored classical theories of property in relation to the evidence from Dartmoor. The analytical work contradicted the dominant narratives of classical theories: there was little evidence that land division was driven by evolution towards cereal cultivation - the most 'maximal' form of agriculture when it comes to short-term calorific yields. Land division need not seem to be driven by land scarcity to any great extent. Coaxial landscapes were not characterised by individualised family-farms spreading out to maximise their land-holdings. Instead settlement seemed to grow in a scale-free manner, with new buildings probably located on the basis of social ties to other inhabitants. These processes suggest growth was influenced more by abundant resources (relationships) than scarce goods. The findings suggest that classical theories of property - and the commonsense 'economic' explanations they inspire- are poor descriptions of Dartmoor land division. Classical theories define property as an exclusive individual right, but these landscapes suggest a more flexible and inclusive system.

Classical theories of property fail to allow for the full diversity of tenure. Insisting on property as an 'exclusive individual right' they presume that individuals exist everywhere in the same way, driven by 'economic' self-interest to maximise what is theirs. This image of *Homo economicus* has long been challenged by anthropologists and is questioned even by neoclassical economists. Classical theories assume that scarcity leads to property, but some writers suggest that rather than scarcity causing tenure, certain forms of tenure cause scarcity. Scarcity may best be seen as a phenomenon generated by specific networks, rather than an inherent attribute of the world. It should be noted that tenure can exist even where goods are superabundant and unlimited. Analyses of the Dartmoor data cast doubts on the universal claims of classical theories.

In chapter three I identified a tendency to 'lurch' from an 'under-socialised' to an 'over-socialised' viewpoint within classical theories of property: Property is either explained at the level of individual self-interest, or at that of authoritarian social institutions. Classical narratives of property see it as a legal institution, travelling along a trajectory of social evolution. Influenced by these ideas, several commentators have seen reaves as evidence for hierarchical social structures, with social elites administering property institutions. In chapter three I argued that these over-determined images of structure tended to be unwieldy for archaeologists trying to understand transformation and change.

The Labour Theory of Property

The labour theory of property considers that owners obtain rights to land when they invest labour in improving or making it productive. Usually linked to the writings of Locke (Locke, 1690) this theory was developed by Boserup into a theory of intensification (Boserup, 1965). Intensification theory described progressively increasing attachment to land as labour inputs per unit area increased.

In chapter four I examined the premises of Locke's labour theory of property and Boserup's intensification theory. Proving intensification requires the demonstration of increased labour input per unit area of land – a measure that is very difficult to ascertain archaeologically. Furthermore intensification depends on only one kind of dynamic, when most analyses of agricultural systems suggest they comprise multiple dynamics, often involving intensification, extensification and diversification simultaneously. I suggested that archaeologists make more use of the alternative approaches that emphasise innovation and flexibility in agricultural systems.

I found that the labour theory of property drew on a narrow category of what it constituted as 'productive' work. This category excluded the so-called 'non-productive' activities that ethnographers suggest are important aspects of tenure in many societies. In chapter four, I developed the labour theory, suggesting that this narrow category of productive work be radically broadened using recent theories of value. Graeber's (2001) theory of value suggested how practices that fall outside the conventional category of 'work' could still be understood as 'productive'. The importance of such actions was the way in which they shaped personhood, reproducing social networks. Moving from the labour theory towards this 'anthropological' theory of value and identification broadened the focus of inquiry away from its narrow concern with 'subsistence' and 'land use'.

Tenure-as-Territorialisation

Some archaeological accounts of tenure assume that tenure and territorialisation are effectively the same things. Commonly this idea of tenure-as-territorialisation emerges in narratives that describe gradually solidifying attachments between a descent group and its territory. This idea of tenure-as-territorialisation was explored in chapter five, where I examined evidence from excavated buildings, and extended in chapter six, with examination of excavated barrows and cairns. I argued that the tendency to see tenure-as-territorialisation emerged from the influence of modern nationalisms: Archaeologies of traditional tenure naturalise a 'national order of things' (Malkki, 1992). Ironically, this idea of territorialized identities itself depends on the deterritorialized image of territories arranged as segments of space like nations in a school atlas (ibid). I argued that tenure was not always and only territorializing, but equally involved important re/deterritorializing movements, movements that 'translocated' aspects of the person in space and time.

Tenure as part of the Constitution of Identity

This theme was defined in chapter one by integrating a wide range of sources from psychology, sociology, economics, philosophy of law, anthropology and archaeology. From this literature, I identified a concept of possession based on self-extension into objects and places. At the same time, however, I raised the question of what 'self-extension' might mean? The concept of 'individual' selves offers only one among many alternative ways of understanding the person (Strathern, 1988; Busby, 1997). Persons may be approached as sovereign individuals, or equally, they may appear as multiply-composed or multiply-authored 'dividuals'. Several recent archaeologies have suggested that Neolithic and Bronze Age selves may be more appropriately viewed using these alternative notions of personhood than conventional notions of sovereign individuals (Chapman, 2000; Brück, 2004, 2006; Jones, 2004c; Fowler, 2004). Ethnographies suggest that where personhood is understood differently, tenure is also altered. Evidence for these differences was presented from a wide range of sources – from recent studies of tenure in Papua New Guinea (Kalinoe & Leach, 2004; Hirsch & Strathern, 2004) to Biotechnology, Open Source Software and web-based publishing (Strathern, 2001a; Leach, 2002).

This theme was developed in chapter six through investigation of mortuary practices, metalwork, and exchange on and around Dartmoor. I suggested that tenure on Dartmoor involved processes of 'keeping-for-giving' allowing persons to retain identification with objects and places while they were exchanged. I argued that this allowed persons to expand the networks around which aspects of 'selves' circulated. In chapter seven I linked the processes of measuring and building coaxial landscapes to the ways that persons and objects were valued through the relations that went into composing them. The importance of these actions was realised as claims over the holder(s) of tenure and obligations that were owed to the wider network that contributed to their future successes. Personhood was thus distributed around a wider network of relations through tenure.

This theme offered a critical perspective on the other three. I observed that classical and labour theories demanded that the subjects and objects of property relations be singularised as individual owner(s) and bounded territories. Only once subjects and objects are singularised in this way can property appear as an individual right to exclude. However, when the subject and object are understood as an intersection of relations – as multiply composed - they cannot be posited in the way the classical theory requires. Instead of property based on exclusion, relations tend to be inclusive and to proliferate along networks.

Implications for Archaeologies of Tenure

'How should archaeologists approach tenure?' This was I question I posed at the beginning of the preface. Having reviewed the findings of my exploration of tenure I now return to this question. The research has revealed a number of limitations within traditional approaches based on classical, labour theory, and territorializing notions of property. These approaches assume that there is a single 'pan-cultural' definition of property that can be applied everywhere. For example Earle argues that property is:

> *'the right to exclude ... equivalent to*
> *'get your cotton pickin' hands off my*
> *whatever'*
> (Earle, 2000: 40, brackets removed,
> citing Neale, 1998)

These kinds of definition simply restate the universalising premises of the classical and labour theories current in most mainstream legal and economic literature. However, I have pointed out that the 'pan-cultural' assumptions of classical theories are nothing of the sort. In fact the ethnographic literature is full of situations where tenure is not based on the individual's right to exclude, but the way different networks direct inclusion (see Anderson, 1998; Sneath, 2004: 168-9; Verdery, 2003: 177-189).

When property is taken as the same thing everywhere variety appears only in the way property is 'expressed' in each 'social context'. Anthropologists catalogue the different ways in which kinship groups give individuals rights of access or the means by which different rights to relations through an object are determined or managed socially, while the fundamental question of what property *is* in each case is taken as given (Alexander, 2004: 252). The same assumptions are reproduced in the many tautologous social evolutionary accounts of property (see Demetz, 1967, 2002; Gilman, 1998; Earle, 2000). Such approaches all begin with a pre-given category of property which can then be shown to have 'evolved' alongside social institutions and hierarchies.

I prefer to adopt a less prescriptive approach. When tenure is investigated as part of the constitution of relational identity it appears less of a known quantity, and more like a set of relations. This approach does not seek to place societies within generalising social evolutionary narratives; instead, it assumes that tenure exists in all societies, but less as a unitary phenomenon, and more as problem stabilised by the analyst.

This approach has certain implications. It means that tenure studies are necessary in all kinds of contexts, not just where there is evidence for agricultural 'land use' or land division. The continuing prominence of land division in archaeologies of tenure reflects the way boundaries *symbolise* property within contemporary discourses (Barth, 1969, 2000; see chapter one). But, as Barth shows, boundaries are no more or less indicative of tenure than, say, mortuary rites or long distance transactions. The pre-eminence given to boundaries as symbols of ownership reflects the legacies of classical theories of property, social evolutionism and nationalism. 'Boundaries' appear as 'natural' symbols of territorial attitudes to space and identity across the globe because of the way that modern nationalisms have inculcated territorialized notions of identification across the globe. This is not to say that traces of land division are not relevant to archaeologies of tenure *at all* – clearly, they are. However I have tried to show that archaeologies of tenure should not focus only, or primarily, on evidence for land division. There is still a tendency for tenure to suddenly become a pressing issue when archaeological evidence for boundaries is present, but tenure should be a concern when dealing with all kinds of evidence.

The notion that tenure should primarily be sought in the realms of 'land use' and the 'subsistence economy' (cf Sherratt, 1999), reflects the historical legacy of the labour theory of property and the social and moral values historically bestowed on cultivation. I have tried to get away from this land-bound perspective, with its narrow definition of production. The advantage of approaching tenure as part of the constitution of identity is that it opens up the possibilities for the kinds of evidence that might be considered 'productive'. Production becomes a question of what activities shape persons rather than a matter of subsistence land use. This approach implies that tenure has very little to do with 'land' as it has been traditionally understood, and much more to do with networks of relations, exchange and the 'economy' in its widest possible sense.

I have concluded by advocating approaches that see tenure as part of the constitution of identity, however, my study also suggests how this approach, outlined in chapter one, may be developed further to make it of wider relevance to tenure studies. This is the aim of the next section.

9.2 Contribution of Archaeology to Tenure Studies

'Archaeology' Gosden reminds us '…is good with artefacts' (2005: 183). This, he argues, places archaeologists in the vanguard of a new interest in materiality developing across the social sciences (cf Olsen, 2003): 'Suddenly, and for the first time since the 1890s, we find ourselves not lagging behind other disciplines, but out in front' (ibid). It is this facility with, and access to, the material that is the key contribution of archaeology to wider tenure studies.

I begin this section by showing how archaeologies that approach tenure as part of the constitution of identity produce tenure as *how persons matter*. I then discuss how tenure can be approached from a perspective based on observations of networks including relations between people and other living and material things. I discuss how ideas of value and landscape construction contribute to these perspectives. Lastly, I outline to role that theories or discourses play in regulating and performing networks, suggesting that theories of property, actively participate in the networks that they describe.

Archaeologies of Tenure and how Persons Matter

Tenure describes particular relations within networks. The networks at issue here are material as well as social, involving relations between people and things as well as between people and people (cf Bohannan, 1963). Relations can be recognised as tenure because of how they regulate and frame the way persons extend into (are identified with) other entities. Similarities between relations can be found even where the networks concerned are very different. Thus the relations described by 'tenure' are not just the relations of private property, but include relations from other sorts of network. As was discussed in the preface to this study, dictionary definitions show that the word 'tenure' connotes 'holding' of all kinds. It also captures the conditions on relations of holding. 'Tenure' thus describes both relations and relations of relations. The usage and etymology of the word shows how the sets of relations it describes shape and transform personhood.

I suggest that what archaeologies contribute to wider tenure studies is a focus on the materiality of tenure. Archaeologists, especially prehistorians, necessarily explore how material things make a difference. Hence they can lend this perspective to interdisciplinary research on tenure. Although some commentators consider that archaeology has been led away from material culture by textual analogies borrowed from other disciplines (Olsen, 2003; Jones, 2004b) it is difficult to imagine an archaeology entirely disentangled from concern with material things. This makes archaeology well placed to contribute to the recent burgeoning of interest in materiality across a range of disciplines (Pels et al., 2002). Archaeologies that approach tenure as part of constitution of identity are therefore projects that describe the 'mattering' of persons within networks of people and material things.

Approaches which sees tenure as part of the constitution of identity were developed in chapter one of this study from readings of Hegel by thinkers like Radin (1982, 1995) and Miller (1987, 1995a). Both these thinkers however are largely concerned with studies of modern capitalist societies. Miller's work on objectification seeks to show how material culture, particularly commodities, are appropriated and used in processes that constitute identities, including 'selves'. Recently, Miller had made an explicit connection between objectification, self-creation and property under modern capitalisms. He suggests that persons are *made to matter* through private property which gives them greater 'relative materiality' within capitalist networks of relations (also see Rowlands, 2005: 72; Myers, 2005):

> *'Owners of private property … have greater consequences as a result of their extended presence in the material world; those who do not possess property are by comparison rendered insubstantial'*
> (Miller, 2005: 17).

While Miller (and Radin) concentrate on how persons matter in capitalist societies, I have sought to understand non-capitalist contexts as well. In both cases, I suggest, tenure can be approached as part of how persons come to matter, although the processes of 'mattering' and kinds of person that result may be quite different. Archaeologies that approach tenure as part of the constitution of identity thus approach tenure as part of how persons come to matter in different networks.

Network Perspectives on Tenure

The emphasis on materiality in recent studies is often expressed in approaches that describe 'networks' of people and material artefacts. For example, Callon describes how property is constituted within modern market networks (Callon, 1998). Such networks involve humans, nonhumans, artefacts, technologies, social arrangements and, even disciplinary theories which act together as 'collectives'. Entities must be continually constructed and configured to allow them to be recruited by the network. Callon describes how market-networks use socio-technical devices of quantification and qualification (of measuring and valuing) to constitute property objects, and use other devices (e.g. money, trading halls) to bring property into relations that allow it to be bought and sold (Callon et al., 2002). Entities configured within the network are not just property objects, but also property subjects. Thus Callon points to the work of the network in configuring persons as *Homo economicus*: 'Homo economicus', Callon argues 'does exist, but not as an ahistorical reality; he does not describe the hidden nature of the human being' (Callon, 1998: 22). For *Homo economicus* to emerge and act within the network he had to be 'formatted, framed and equipped with prostheses which help him in his calculations' (Callon, 1998; 22-57). *Homo economicus* is the result of networks that make this kind of person matter.

A similar network perspective has been applied by Sneath to understand tenure among nomadic pastoralists in Mongolia (Sneath, 2004). Sneath argues that tenure should be seen within a 'socio-technical network' which includes the relations between herders and animals, technical equipment used to move animals, fodder and people, pastures and their distribution, the seasons, as well as theories of moral authority and governance. Mongolian socio-technical networks make persons matter in terms of their capacity to include or encompass other entities (people, animals and land). Words for tenure also translate as terms for custodianship, governance and authority (Sneath, 2004: 168-9).

Archaeologies of tenure that investigate processes of landscape construction in the widest sense offer their own network perspectives, bringing together aspects of environments, economies, artefacts, technologies and architecture. In this study I have stressed approaches that explore the co-production of environments and economies through processes that materialise value (Graeber, 2001; Hirsch, 2004a). In chapter four I introduced a theory of value (see section 4.4) that I used to interpret processes of landscape construction in chapter seven. While traditional approaches to value tended to reduce, abstract and particularise value, by separating 'economic' value from social and cultural values, I deployed theories which treated 'economic' value as only one form of valuing. Following Graeber, I suggested that projects of value are ways of constructing what life should be, and are therefore moral and economic at the same time. Using this theory it is possible to see how value is part of how things matter, relating to the historicity of actions congealed in objects (Graeber, 2001; Sutton, 2004).

Participation of Property Theory within Networks

Callon makes the important point that theories are not separate from networks of people and material things. In

fact, he argues, disciplinary discourses and knowledge practices are integral components of networks, often playing important roles in configuring entities or making persons matter. For example, Callon points to the important role that Economics plays in configuring and constructing entities so that they fit within market-networks. Economics is not outside the marketplace; it actively participates in shaping the entities that it describes (Callon, 1998). Butler's work offers useful perspectives on how hegemonic discourses like those of law, economics or 'biological' sex, construct entities, making them matter at the same time as they are realised within a world of meaning and value:

> 'To speak ... of bodies that matter is not an idle pun, for to be material means to materialise, where the principle of that materialisation is precisely what "matters" about that body, its very intelligibility ... "to matter" means at once "to materialise" and "to mean"'
> (Butler, 1993b: 32, her emphasis).

Processes of 'mattering', Butler argues, instantiate phenomena at the same as they name them. (For example, consider the statement 'I now pronounce you husband and wife'. This speech act effectively produces husbands and wives at the same time as it names them). To live within networks is to take up a compulsory subject position, to be 'taken into a chain of prior usages' which makes one matter at the same time as it produces disciplinary knowledge (Butler, 1993b: 219).

Butler highlights the ongoing work of discourses as part of the way that networks continuously reproduce themselves. The example she gives is of legal performances (Butler, 1993b: 106-9). She observes how, within legal discourses, the person who invokes the law refers outwards to a chain of prior usages, in a potentially infinite process of citation. It is the very absence of an actual ground for authority within the network that constitutes the authority of law – its 'groundless ground'. The impossibility of final closure produces the effect of the performance's necessity; the hegemonic practices of ruling and judging must be reproduced, reiterating the same subject positions, but always creating more 'overspills' that need more law to correct them. In the same way, Butler argues, the fact that identities can never be finally or absolutely fixed produces the necessity of continuing to name, stabilise and reproduce them through discourses that 'continually reconstitute what they enjoin and protect' (Butler, 1993b: 192).

Theories of property are disciplinary practices rather like those described by Callon (1998, 2002) and Butler (1993b). Theories of property do not just describe tenure – they participate in networks that actively produce certain types of relation. Theories of property play a part in making persons matter in certain ways. This has important implications for the kinds of theories that archaeologists identify and enact, for archaeology too participates in the networks of relations that include those of tenure and property. In the next two sections I offer two case studies which show how tenure can be approached as part of the constitution of identities – as

making persons matter in particular ways. In the section that follows I argue that classical theories of tenure participate in networks that make persons matter as 'individuals'.

9.3 Classical Theories make Individuals matter

This study has compared four different themes in approaches to tenure. It concluded that the fourth theme – approaches which saw tenure as part of the constitution of identity – had the most potential for extending archaeologies of tenure in future studies. In this section I use this fourth theme to critique other theories of tenure. I argue that classical theories of property are themselves part of constituting identity. They thus further illustrate and exemplify the usefulness of approaching tenure from this direction.

I begin with a historical perspective on the kinds of work that classical theories achieve within networks of relations, suggesting how they contribute to networks which make persons matter as individuals bearing property rights. The second part of this section discusses recent studies of 'transition economies' in Post-Soviet societies. These case studies examine how classical theories of property operated within recent privatisation reforms, transforming persons into 'individual' property owners.

Classical Theories of Property and the Emergence of the Individual

The transformations associated with the 'rise of the individual' and the emergence of private property are recorded by MacPherson: Transformation 'came with the spread of the full capitalist market from the seventeenth century on, and the replacement of the old limited rights in land and other valuable things by virtually unlimited rights'. In law, the 'rights' of the individual became 'more absolute' as 'parcels of land became more freely marketable commodities'. Common property formerly recognised within philosophical discourse as property, 'drops virtually out of sight' within theoretical debates (MacPherson, 1978: 7-10).

Changes in theory and law are only part of wider changes in materialities in this period. Transforming material things and technological processes also had a hand in the development of new property relations. Associated with the 'rise of the individual' were wholesale (if discontinuous and contested) transformations in the ways that landscapes were constructed and valued. Enclosure in Britain, plantation architectures, and colonial land division all effected dramatic changes in property networks (Gosden, 2004: 27-30; Linklater, 2002). Processes of mapping, measuring and enclosing were integral to the institution of networks and the operation of new legal, commercial and civic discourses which configured property objects. The changes in property

objects also effected changes in property's subjects: Positing land and other things as unitary enabled 'the appearance of unity for persons to whom the things were linked' (Verdery & Humphrey, 2004a: 7).

These processes have been described by Maurer as work of 'purification'. Classical theories of property work in and through networks of modern capitalisms, sorting out the 'messy morality' of these worlds to produce 'clear and natural relations between subjects about objects' (Maurer, 2004: 315). From a network perspective, entities within any network of relations can never be fully separated (see Latour, 1993). However these overspills make the ongoing work of purification all the more necessary. Hence classical theories and property law continually reproduce effects that require their re-enactment (see Butler, 1993b). Rose observes this process of purification in action when she notes how 'courts and legislation, routinely strip away any odd or unexpected arrangements when property changes hands,' negating purported property interests that do not fit the law's requirement for singularised 'owners' (Rose, 2004: 290). Classical theories of property operate within networks like algebraic equations, continually working out property's subjects and objects in relation to one another, so that they always add up to the same (Maurer, 2004).

The networks of relations within which classical property theories operate make persons matter as 'individuals' bearing singularised property rights. Appearing as an 'individual' is to an extent compulsory because persons cannot 'matter' without being configured in this way. If an entity cannot be separated, configured, formatted, measured, valued or named within a network it becomes difficult to incorporate within that network. The price of not appearing sufficiently 'individual' - not sufficiently self-possessed or self-controlled - is that of not holding recognised property rights and hence of not 'mattering'. Rowlands has recently suggested that this kind of inequality might be understood through the notion of 'relative materialities': 'We can' he argues, 'be more or less material in our being, more or less ephemeral, massive and condensed in material presence' (Rowlands, 2005: 72). Some people and things are 'more material than others' as different networks engender the experience of 'inequalities in a materiality of being' (ibid).

Historically, some persons have found it easier to be 'individuals' than others. Women, blacks and the working classes have all been considered insufficiently rational, self-contained or self-controlled to constitute property subjects in various times and places (Jamoussi,

1999; Penningroth, 2003). For example, in the nineteenth century southern states of the US slaves *were* property. According to classical theories of property, they could not, therefore, own it. To this extent, slaves, their belongings and their everyday tenurial systems, did not matter within dominant property discourses (Penningroth, 2003). Changes in the relations between entities effectively change what those entities *are*. Thus the emergence of new forms of property constitutes new kinds of entity. For example copyright law was part of constructing the 'author'. Copyright law instituted a new form of person; an individual who could displace the claims of all the other people involved in book production and distribution. The labour theory of property allowed the author to configure the printed word as 'the expression of his own – unique – mind' (Woodmansee, 1984: 447). Creativity, 'genius' and 'originality' came to be linked to individuality and private property claims. Contestation of property's subject is ongoing, since property law continues to exclude what cannot be singularised. For example, while intellectual property laws currently protect the copyright of individuals, they fail to protect the 'traditional' or 'folk' music of the 'rural, poor, non-literate, populations' because such subjects are not sufficiently individualised (Seeger, 2004).

Classical Theories of Property in the Transition Economies

Post-socialist societies have presented social scientists with important environments in which to study transformations in property and value. Recent studies have found these societies important for the study of exchange and property markets (Heller, 1998; Seabright, 2000), governance and identity (Anderson, 2000; Alexander, 2004), and theories of property and tenure (Anderson, 1998; Verdery, 2003; Verdery & Humphrey, 2004b). Classical theories of property played a pre-eminent role in recent upheavals in these societies and several recent studies suggest how such theories work to change the way that persons matter; reconfiguring persons as 'individuals' through new property relations.

As Soviet support was increasingly withdrawn after 1989, regimes increasingly embarked on 'reform' and 'privatisation' programmes. The international agencies and consultancies that advised and guided these programmes were committed to a particular idea of what tenure is (see Verdery, 2003: chapter one). They saw property as an exclusive individual right – as private property – according to the premises of classical and labour theories. To the extent that they did not fit these preconceived models of private property, existing forms of tenure were rendered invisible. Because there was no 'property' it was supposed that there was no tenure of any kind; it was imagined that a new frontier of *terra nullius* had opened up in these societies. Ethnographers, however, disagree with this characterisation of post-socialist societies (Verdery, 2003; Verdery & Humphrey,

2004a). Instead of situations of 'no property' they describe various pre-existing forms of tenure that, while they were invisible to those who enacted privatisation reforms, had important consequences for the social impacts of such reforms.

Ethnographers suggest that classical and labour theories of property within privatisation reform composed a new 'ideology' (Verdery, 2003; 14; Verdery & Humphrey, 2004a:3-5). Property as an exclusive individual right – private property – was assumed to be 'natural'. It was assumed that governments had only to remove state interference and private property would emerge 'naturally' from individual self-interest. Ideologically driven enthusiasm for privatisation, belief that private property was 'natural' (and therefore required little planning) and belief that equity was ultimately not all that important (Rose, 2004), led to transformations in tenure systems with unforeseen and undesirable consequences for many ordinary people (Verdery, 2003, 2004; Alexander, 2004; Sneath, 2004).

Modifying networks of relations to contain and enact classical theories, involved the re-materialisation of relations. This necessitated that persons and property objects be posited as 'unitary', and that ways of 'purifying' property objects and subjects were instituted. Across the 'transition economies' re-materialising property objects also re-materialised personhood: Material changes in the fabric of things and places were linked to changing concepts of the person. For example in Kazakhstan, Alexander records how the 'physical disintegration' of workplaces into new property objects was 'part and parcel of the disintegration of the Soviet worker' (Alexander, 2004: 263). Privatisation involved 'tearing off' profitable elements from places, 'abandoning the rest to the wind and the rain' (ibid.). The worker was fragmented into an 'individual' capable of selling their labour. In Romania, Verdery records how new persons emerged through privatisation; 'owners' and 'entrepreneurs' were defined in relation to new property 'rights' (Verdery, 2003). Through the work of classical theories of property persons came to matter as individuals.

Classical theories cannot be enacted anywhere at will, however, because tenure is a relation within a network of relations. For example, despite the efforts of the Asia Development Bank and other international agencies, it has not yet proved possible to fully privatise land in Mongolia. Although farm equipment, herds and infrastructure were privatised in the 1990s, what Sneath calls the 'socio-technical network' of pastoral life here makes it difficult to re-materialise land and personhood in the ways that classical theories of property require (Sneath, 2004). The first efforts to enact privatisation failed, and they were followed by famine. The famines, coupled with deeply held beliefs concerning tenure, have thus far ensured that politicians who intend to privatise pastures have not been re-elected. Networks of relations constrain how theories participate in their transformation.

In this section I argued that classical theories of property can be approached as part of the constitution of identity: Classical theories make persons matter as individuals with exclusive individual rights. However, I have also stressed the way that theories like this depend on wider networks, processes or 'materialities' (Rowlands, 2005; Miller, 2005). From this 'network perspective' one can see that classical theories do not always participate everywhere in the same way. In the next section I examine another facet of western 'folk theories' of tenure, one related to this classical view, but differing from it in important ways. I argue that the assumption of tenure-as-territorialisation, like classical theories, can be seen as part of the constitution of identity, making persons matter.

9.4 Territorializing Tenure makes the 'Indigenous' matter

'Land' is among the most important national *sacra* (Smith, 2000). Land offers imagery that can be used to link people and land in ways that refer back to distant origins. Landed estates, territories and fields offer homologies of the nation; little nations, exclusively owned, passed on from father to son. In this section I suggest that the assumption that tenure is a process of territorialisation can itself be seen as a way of constituting identity. Tenure-as-territorialisation, I argue, participates in making persons matter as 'indigenous' 'natives'. It offers a kind of 'traditional' 'authentic' version of classical theories of property, in which groups, (rather than individuals), are property's subject, and cultural heritage / ancestral homelands, (rather than abstract 'rights'), are property's object. I begin by discussing how tenure-as-territorialisation feeds into mainstream notions of 'traditional' and 'indigenous' tenure. I then illustrate this discussion using recent studies of indigenous land law in Australia, and the repatriation of cultural heritage in North America.

Territorialisation and concepts of the 'Traditional' in Tenure

Increasingly, mainstream property literature recognises 'traditional' or 'indigenous' property alongside private property. Even neoclassical economists, who once saw the inception of private property as the 'origin' of property *per se*, now make some accommodation to alternative 'non-modern', 'non-western' forms (Demetz, 2002; cf Demetz, 1967). These kinds of 'indigenous' 'traditional' forms are often characterised as forms of common property that link groups to home territories (Ostrom, 1990; Rose, 1998; United Nations, 2005). Increasingly, national and global property law seeks to incorporate this kind of tenure into existing frameworks and procedures, defined largely in terms of classical theories.

Povinelli observes that the price of this 'recognition' of indigenous tenure is a kind of 'violence' perpetrated on the post-colonial subject (Povinelli, 2004). Legislation of 'traditional' and 'indigenous' property by the state demands that persons fit the state's externally defined notions of what is 'traditional' and 'indigenous'. The assumption of tenure-as-territorialisation within dominant property discourses, works to stabilise and singularise the 'native' as outside the dominant mainstream 'modern'

world. Increased recognition of 'traditional' and 'indigenous' tenure requires that persons matter as 'traditional' and 'indigenous' in ways defined by the state and by dominant society, not directly by the subjects themselves.

Territorializing narratives of tenure work to stabilise and construct group identities in relation to blocks of land. In chapter five I pointed to the importance of these territorializing narratives to national identities and the way they supported a 'national order of things' (Malkki, 1992). I also suggested that such narratives fit into networks of private property, because they singularise group identities against singularised blocks of land, just as classical theories singularise individuals in relation to singularised rights. Tenure-as-territorialisation, thus feeds into and informs ideas of 'traditional' or 'indigenous' property. This can be seen in the characteristics of such tenure which can be summarised as follows:

i) 'traditional' tenure is linked to membership of a group, defined by residence or descent;
ii) it refers to a bounded area, definite territory, or homeland.
iii) it is seen as 'traditional' to the extent that it is distinct from the modern
iv) it is sometimes understood as 'inalienable' in contradistinction to modern alienable forms.

The important point about these characteristics is that they are defined primarily by the dominant society's view of what is 'traditional' rather then by that of indigenous people themselves. The 'traditional' here does not reflect what any particular indigenous society considers customary. Instead it reflects reactions that the dominant society has to its own history; its own 'inauthentic' 'modern' 'commodified' way of life and its own (nationalist inflected) notion that tenure-as-territorialisation represents a more authentic, ancient, non-commodified source of identification that should be preserved.

Tenure-as-territorialisation in Indigenous Property Law

Characteristics ascribed to 'traditional' tenure become requirements that indigenous people must show they meet in the context of land claims adjudication. We could say, that in this context persons must 'matter' in a particular way. Of course, indigenous people have the 'option' of not taking up land claims at all; however, since this 'option' is at the expense of being able to live fully within an indigenous identity, people are keen to make their performances effective (cf Butler, 1993b). By insisting on such performances, land claims adjudication breaks open the internal logic of indigenous relations. It becomes necessary for indigenous people to make their 'self-contained and implicit' knowledge and relations 'steadily more explicit and external' 'showing and telling' in ways that meet the demands of outside evaluation (Strang, 2000: 280). Recent studies of Australian land claims illustrate how notions of tenure-as-territorialisation, translated into ideas of 'traditional' tenure, constitute identities as 'indigenous' in particular ways. In this sense, we could say this network makes persons matter as 'indigenous' and 'traditional' according to the characteristics of 'traditional' tenure outlined above.

From their earliest inception, Australian land claims instruments have required that traditional tenure revolve around a group defined by local residence and descent. This is so even where land claims are made by individuals (Povinelli, 2004: 190). In the very first land claims report the Commissioner accepted that 'all traditional Indigenous societies reckoned the descent of territorial rights through the father and the father's father (patrilineally) and that an indigenous person could belong in a full sense only to one local descent group and thus only to one territory' (ibid). Although courts now accept a wider range of kinship diagrams, this does not change the fact that it is still *descent* that is the principal criterion rather then any other sort of relation: 'Spiritual and material relationships ... to land, to the dead, and to the unborn', are 'reduced in the last instance' to the genealogical diagram' (Povinelli, 2004: 190). This priority, Povinelli observes, does not reflect the relations of aboriginal societies, but the historical preoccupations of British and Australian anthropologists. Through indigenous land law archaeology and anthropology participate in constituting 'native' identities according to their own 'official' kinship diagrams (see section 5.1).

Successful land claims require land configured as bounded territory, regardless of local concepts of landscape. Land must be singularised into unitary property objects. Although this process 'denies the more fluid reality of Aboriginal relations to land', aboriginal communities realise that land claims will affix bounded territories, and that land presented as a territory on a map, will carry 'perceptual authority'(Strang, 2000: 278). As a result 'hybrid forms of representation' such as OS maps inscribed with aboriginal place names, are commonly used (ibid.). These forms of representation reflect the 'national order of things' producing space as a tessellating mass of blocks of territory (Malkki, 1992). Land is configured as property and homeland for the courts in ways that reflect the spatiality of post-colonial nation states.

Successful land claims depend on the inheritance of unchanging structures from the past: 'Authentic and traditional Aboriginality lies only in the distant pre-colonial past' if anything has been changed since that time, it is no longer 'traditional' (Harrison, 2000: 35). The law, (in keeping with the classical assumption that property is a jural institution), treats aboriginal tenure as itself a form of 'law'. Demonstrating continuity allows customs to become legal property 'deeds' handed down over generations. However unlike the state's law (which is continually modified) indigenous groups must demonstrate that their customary 'law' is unchanged. To be authentic, traditions must be handed down among people related by descent and occupying the same territory, people, land and traditions must remain unchanging, outside modernity (Harrison, 2000).

The idea that the 'traditional' is defined primarily through opposition to modernity is also enacted in cultural heritage law. Like land law in Australia, the legal framework concerned with repatriation of 'cultural patrimony' in the United States requires that the 'traditional' manifest itself as 'non-modern'. Whereas modern societies commodify objects and circulate them in markets, 'traditional' societies are supposed to treat land and heritage as inalienable; outside the realm of exchange. Harding records a 'single dominating narrative' of agencies concerned with implementing this law, one that envisages 'return' as the 'de-commodification' of objects supposed to be originally 'inalienable' (Harding, 2005: 144). The dominant narrative of repatriation law thus 'fixes cultural identity to a point in the distant past' as if Native Americans were outside the flow of modern life and the cut and thrust of exchange relations (Harding, 2005: 151).

The aim of this section and the last has been to show how classical theories and notions of tenure-as-territorialisation can both be seen as part of the constitution of identity, in slightly different, though related, ways. Classical theories, I argued participated in networks that made persons matter as individuals bearing exclusive rights. Territorializing assumptions led persons to matter as 'indigenous', in ways consonant with dominant society's notions of what 'indigenous' should mean. None of this is intended to deny the positive results of indigenous people's campaigns for land law reform. However, it is to acknowledge that, while better than not mattering at all, 'recognition' still exacts a price when the terms of that recognition are not equal.

The case studies explored here and in the last section illustrated the wider applicability of approaches that see tenure as part of the constitution of identity. They also indicate the potential contribution that archaeology, as the study of material worlds, might make when tenure is understood as relations of 'mattering'. In the final section of this monograph I look to the future of tenure studies and suggest how approaches to tenure might be developed next.

9.5 The Future of Tenure Studies

The 'age of property' is over. The new era is the 'age of access' (Rifkin, 2000). The 'new economy' and the 'network society' are transforming contemporary tenure relations (Castells, 2000). Property relations are increasingly information-based, digital, 'off-shored', 'out-sourced' and 'intangible'. Intellectual property and service provision predominate. Instead of alienating their property within markets many firms now keep hold of what they own and lease, rent or charge an admission or membership fee for short term use of it. Hence, in the 'age of access':

> *'The exchange of property by buyers and sellers – the most important feature of the modern market system – gives way to short-term access between servers and clients operating in a network relationship'* (Rifkin, 2000: 4).

What do these transformations in global economies mean for the future of tenure studies? In this section I explore the future of tenure studies (including archaeologies of tenure) in the context of the changes now underway in contemporary tenures. I begin with a discussion of the emphasis on 'immaterial' and 'virtual' objects in the new economy. Do these changes make archaeological approaches less useful for future tenure studies? I argue that, on the contrary, archaeology – with its focus on materiality – is more important than ever. Next, I point to recent studies suggesting how the new economy and network society are changing the ways that identity is constituted. New forms of personhood are coming to matter, partly through new tenurial relations. I suggest that the approach to tenure that I have favoured here offers a useful perspective on these transformations.

Transforming Tenure and the New Economy

> *'Property – like other 'native concepts' essential to the self-understanding of Euro-American societies ('race', 'nation', 'market' and so on) – is a protean idea that changes with the times'* (Verdery & Humphrey, 2004a: 1)

Tenure is a description of relations that are always changing, and consequently, it never stands still. Approaches to tenure and property are necessarily of their time. At the time of writing commentators suggest that tenure networks are undergoing profound transformations around the globe (Verdery & Humphrey, 2004a). More and more new areas are entering into capitalist economic circuits under the rubric of classical theories of property (Rifkin, 2000: chapter 6). New domains opening up to 'commodification' and 'privatisation' reconfigure

property objects including: aspects of culture and identity (Austin, 2005; Chasin, 2005); relationships of intimacy and care (Hernandez, 2005; Stone, 2005); living things, embryos and body parts (Strathern, 2001b; Williams, 2005); intellectual property, brands, information and bio-information (Brown, 2004; Parry, 2004) formerly common goods (e.g. public space, bandwidth, broadcast spectrum) and/or capacity to pollute or damage those goods (e.g. tradable fisheries or emissions allowances) (Coombe & Herman, 2004; Rose, 1998). Each of these new kinds of object create their own 'overspills' and network effects, changing the relations of contemporary tenure.

Commentators often suggest that the new property is 'dematerialising'. Property, is becoming 'weightless'; less physical and more intellectual. Capital is increasingly deterritorialized, aspatial, circulating around networks outside the regulation of the nation state (Maurer, 2004; 2005):

> *'tangible property is becoming increasingly marginal to the exercise of economic power, and intangible property is fast becoming the defining force of an access-based era. Ideas in the form of patents, copyrights, trademarks, trade secrets, and relationships – are being used to forge a new kind of economic power, composed of mega-suppliers in control of expanded networks of users.'* (Rifkin, 2000: 57).

The 'dematerialisation' of property is accompanied by increasing 'virtuality'. This 'virtual' property has been presented as an innovation in recent press reports, illustrated by the emergence of online games like Linden Lab's 'Second Life'. Property bought and sold in Second Life is valued in 'Linden dollars' convertible into 'real life' hard currency. Second Life is not just a simulation, but is also a 'real life' emerging property market valued at around 60 million US dollars (The Economist, 2006). The message is clear – property is 'dematerialising'. What contribution can object-centred disciplines like archaeology make in this context? Should they restrict themselves to the material-bound past?

Several recent commentators have argued that, on the contrary, the new network economy does *not* signal 'dematerialisation'. Instead, it is suggested, important changes are taking place in contemporary materialities. Property is not 'dematerialising' but being 're-materialised' (Parry, 2004 her emphasis; Miller, 2005: 20-9). Tenure networks which involve the new electronic technologies (software, digital information, the internet and World Wide Web) appear to be becoming more 'virtual', which is taken to mean that they are becoming 'less real'.

However, recent studies of actual uses and experience of these technologies suggests that this is not the case. Dealing with the new technologies necessarily depends on physical engagements among electronic devices, screens and communications environments which are transforming material worlds. The virtual, it seems, does not displace the real. Instead the virtual increasingly supplements and supports the real. For example, email does not displace phone and paper but encourages more phone calls, more memos; teleworkers travel more rather than less; online museums stimulate more visits to actual museums (Woolgar, 2002: 267-8). Instead the virtual making the material irrelevant, analysts suggest that the rule of virtuality is 'the more virtual the more real' (Woolgar, 2002: 267). Contrary to contemporary 'cyperbole' virtual property is not new. Paper money, for example, is 'virtual' property, its value operating through the trust people place in the nation state. Nor is virtual property a special characteristic of 'western' capitalisms. Ethnographers are able to catalogue numerous examples of non-western societies and non-capitalist economies where tenure in intangibles is at least as important if not more so, than tangible entities (Strathern, 2005b). Returning to Second Life, the property that Linden Lab sells is actually computing power stored in materials, which it rents out according to the conventional premises of classical theories; here as much as anywhere the more 'virtual' the more real (Diski, 2007).

What is important in these rematerialisations is not the displacement of material property, but the construction of new categories of 'real' and 'virtual', material and the 'immaterial' and the emergence of new ways of managing the intersection of these categories. It is the boundary work between these realms that is increasingly significant in how persons matter. For example, Knorr Cetina and Bruegger show how the rematerialisation of foreign exchange markets on screens configure new forms of relationship between traders and the market, making both traders and market matter in new ways (2002). Property is not dematerialising but is undergoing rematerialisations. These rematerialisations mean that disciplines that can make sense of materiality are more important than ever.

New Tenure, New Personhood

Several analysts point out how the new economy and network society are leading to changes in personhood:

'The people of the twenty-first century are as likely to perceive themselves as nodes embedded in networks of shared interests as they are to perceive themselves as autonomous agents ... For them personal freedom has less to do with the right of possession and the ability to exclude others

and more to do with the right to be included in webs of mutual relationships' (Rifkin, 2000: 12).

Networking within and between companies is the organisational form on which the new economy is based (Castells, 2000). A new 'network sociality' is emerging (Wittel, 2001). Self-interest in the new economy is not amassing property and excluding others, but securing access to a network of mutually beneficial reciprocal relationships – (Rifkin 2000: 19). Increasingly unstable patterns of work mean that employment has become 'flexible' and relations between management and workers have become individualised.

The economic and social conditions of property relations in the new economy are reworking how identities are constituted. The classical private property of industrial capitalisms derived partly from an idea of the person as the owner of rights in themselves. Each man 'has a *property* in his own *person*' as Locke put it, and 'the *labour* of his body and the work of his hands ... are properly his' (Locke, 1690). In the employment contract workers traditionally alienated 'their' labour in exchange for a wage. However in the new economy, Adkins argues, 'property rights regarding labour are more akin to …contemporary forms of authorship' branding or patenting (2005; 118). Increasingly rights of 'ownership' can only be claimed by the audience's (or 'customer's') perception of a 'brand', rather than from property rights that individuals hold in themselves. At the same time previously essentialised notions of sex and species now appear more fluid, contingent and relational (Haraway, 1991, 1992; Braidotti, 2003).

In the context of the new economy and network sociality, approaches to tenure which see it as part of the constitution of identity – as how persons matter – are more appropriate than traditional 'property' approaches. The new economy makes such approaches more relevant than ever both in studies of the contemporary world and the past. For analysts looking to understand how changing tenure and personhood might be related, archaeology and anthropology are useful places to look. The best parallels are not to be found by looking to histories of western property law, which are overwhelmingly inflected by western 'native categories' of property. Instead they may be found in studies of tenure elsewhere, and in the past (Strathern, 1999). Archaeology and anthropology are disciplines that can examine tenure networks in the widest possible field, and they increasingly throw up unexpected comparisons and connections between property relations in the new economy and those found in non-western societies and in the past (Strathern, 2005b).

It may be that it is the circumstances of the new economies that have made it possible for analysts to identify 'relational identities' and 'networks', encouraging the approach I have favoured here. The theories of tenure that I have preferred here, just like classical theories of property, participate in networks of tenure that are emerging right now. Prehistories of tenure are not outside the modern world. The restructured property relations of the new networked world will inevitably change what tenure is in the present and thus the ways we construct tenure in the past.

Conclusion

At the beginning of this monograph I asked how archaeologists might approach tenure. Throughout the study I have explored this question, applying a range of different approaches, reflecting on different theories of tenure. In this chapter I reviewed the results. I suggested an approach that saw tenure as part of the constitution of identity was the most useful. I turned to previous readings of Hegel to understand how relations between people and material things that are part of tenure might be figured as processes that constituted persons. I argued that this emphasis on mutual constitution – on the 'mattering' of persons and things – allowed archaeologies to contribute to a revival of interest in relations with material things currently taking place across disciplines (Pels et al., 2002; Olsen, 2003; Gosden, 2005). The middle part of this chapter reinforced my conclusion, showing how alternative theories of tenure could themselves be approached as examples of how tenure participates in networks which make persons matter differently. Classical theories of property, I argued, were part of processes that made individuals matter. The assumption that tenure only represents territorialisation is part of networks that make persons matter as indigenous, through the state's regulation of what is properly 'traditional' and 'native. Finally, I argued that this approach could also be used to study the way that tenure is changing in the present, as the 'new network economy' introduces dramatic changes in property relations across the globe.

Tenure describes certain kinds of relations, relations that involve the 'holding' of entities – land, objects, productive capacities, people, ideas. I have chosen an approach that focuses on how these relations constitute identities and 'persons'. Of course this is not the whole story. Personhood is only a sort of gathering point from which to understand relations and processes. Inevitably this gathering point pulls certain phenomena ('persons' and 'things') into prominence, and, to this extent it may be insufficiently 'relational' for some; retaining vestiges of dualisms that recent thinkers are attempting to overcome (Woolgar, 2002; Ingold, 2006). However, because my approach has emphasised the distribution of persons and the relational processes of their constitution it has departed from previous approaches based on taken-for-granted notions of land, property and individuals. In this way I have tried to free tenure from traditional narratives of territorialisation, intensification and scarcity. Instead of routinely identifying tenure only in land use and property, approaches are needed that allow us to see tenure more widely. Only when discussions of tenure are as common in studies of art, kinship, exchange, as they are in studies of land division and farming will tenure be 'translocated'.

Appendix A: Excavations of Dartmoor Settlements

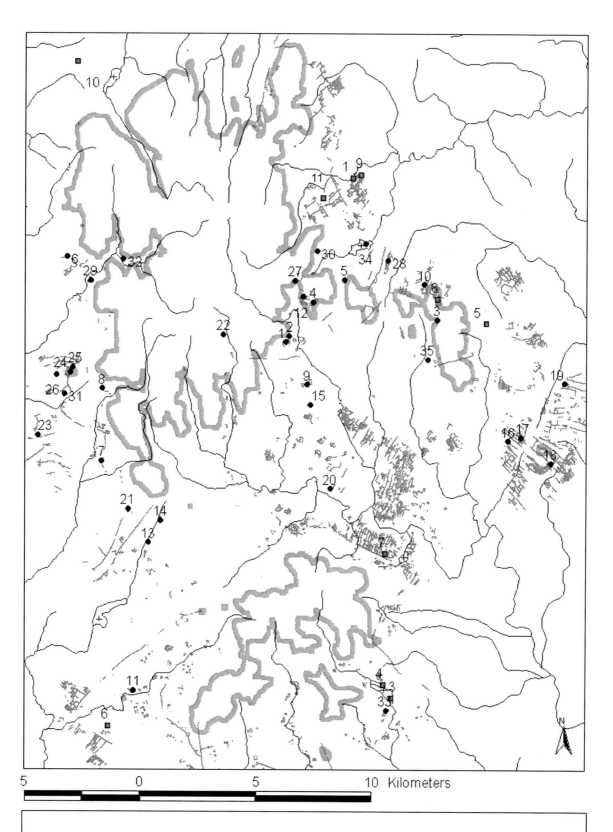

Excavations since 1950
Excavations before 1950
Reaves recorded by Butler
450m OD

Sites Excavated Before 1950

Number	Name of Settlement
1	Broadun Ring
2	Broadun
3	Grimspound
4	White Ridge
5	Assycombe
6	Ger Tor
7	Merrivale
8	Langstone Moor
9	Krapps Ring
10	Cullacombe
11	Legis Tor
12	White Ridge
13	Hart Tor
14	Raddick Hill
15	Lakehead Hill
16	Tunhill Rocks
17	Foales Arrishes
18	Halsanger Common
19	Smallacombe Rocks
20	Huccaby
21	Yes Tor Bottom
22	Rough Tor
23	Cox Tor
24	White Tor Fort
25	White Tor North
26	White Tor West
27	Lade Brookhead
28	Chagford Common
29	Stannon Down
30	Hemstone Rocks
31	Wedlake
32	Watern Oke
33	Riders Rings
34	Metheral
35	Challacombe

Sites Excavated After 1950

Number	Name of Settlement
1	Kes Tor
2	Owley Gate
3	Grippers Pound
4	Dean Moor
5	Heatree
6	Shaugh Moor
7	Holne Moor
8	Gold Park
9	Teigncombe
10	Sourton Down
11	Shovel Down

Appendix B: Relocating Early Excavations of Prehistoric Buildings

It is now difficult to locate many excavated buildings with certainty. Where there is no survey published the reports generally include a grid reference to the Ordnance survey maps, however, these grid references are sometimes only of two figures and the round houses are not always located on the maps. A typical reference is that for the seven roundhouses "lying above Lade Hill Bottom and below the Vitifer Mine Leat, near 1543 on Ordnance (hut circles not marked thereon)" (Baring Gould et al 1899: 153) five of these roundhouses were excavated but exactly which of the seven these were is not recorded. Nonetheless as Butler notes excavated

buildings are "… easy to recognise from their uneven floors and lowered interiors…" (Butler 1997b: 63); Quinnell (1991) reports that Mrs Minter's trenches at Heatree from 1968 are still clearly visible despite having been backfilled. Butler has relocated many of the excavated roundhouses using the descriptions from the reports combined with the Ordnance Survey first edition maps. Site reports which allow the exact relocation of buildings and those which do not are listed in the table below. Where there is no plan locating the trenches further survey and geophysical work could be undertaken to relocate the trenches.

Reports with plans enabling excavated roundhouses to be relocated	Reports with no overall plan of excavated roundhouses
Grimspound (Baring Gould et al 1894)	Broadun Ring and Broadun (Burnard 1894)
Merrivale (locations of excavated buildings not identified) (Baring Gould et al 1895)	Tavy Cleave (Baring Gould 1894)
Cullacombe Head (Shapely Common) (elevation drawing of common and plans of some roundhouses) (Baring Gould et al 1895)	Langstone Moor (Baring Gould et al 1895)
Whittor "Fort" (White Tor) (Baring Gould et al 1899)	Krapp's Ring (Baring Gould et al 1895)
Standon Down or Stannon Down (Anderson et al 1902)	Whiten Ridge (Baring Gould et al 1895 and 1896)
Wedlake (Anderson et al 1905)	Lake Head Hill (Baring Gould et al 1896)
Watern Oke (Anderson et al 1906)	Legis Tor (Baring Gould et al 1896)
Riders Rings (Harris et al 1935)	"Hut circles in and about the Rifle Range, between the main road at Devils Gully near Princetown and Har Tor" (Hart Tor) (Baring Gould et al 1896: 189)
Metherel (Harris et al 1935)	Tunhill Rocks (Baring Gould et al 1897)
Challacombe (photographs in excavation report in Shorter 1948 show which half of building was excavated, building located in survey in Shorter 1938)	Foales Arrishes (Baring Gould et al 1897)
Heatree, Manaton (excavated in 1968, published by Quinnell 1991)	Halsanger Common (Baring Gould et al 1897)
	Smallacombe Rocks (Baring Gould et al 1897)
	Berry Field, Huccaby (Baring Gould et al 1898)
	Yes Tor Bottom (Baring Gould et al 1898)
	West Dart Head (Baring Gould et al 1898)

	Cox Tor (Baring Gould et al 1898)
	Broadmoor Pound (Baring Gould et al 1899)
	"… above Lade Hill Bottom and below the Vitifer Mine Leat…" (Baring Gould et al 1899: 153)
	"… hut circles at Hemstone Rocks…" (Anderson et al 1901: 135)
	"… hut circles between Devils Gully and the Princetown Railway" (Anderson et al 1901: 135)
	Chagford Common "… a hut circle…" (Anderson et al 1901: 137)
	"… a small group of four on the newtake south east of Fernworthy" (Anderson et al 1902)
	"The Croft", Pater Tavy (Anderson et al 1906)

Appendix C: Methodology and Quality of Archaeological Excavations before 1950

Excavations at Metheral in 1936, under the reformed DEC, supervised by R. N. Worth (Reproduced with permission of Devon Library and Information Services)

Excavation reports and photographs of excavations recently digitised from the Burnard archive suggest that excavations of cairns, circles and buildings may have proceeded in a similar way; generally driving a single linear trench into the centre of the site, and then clearing areas to the left or right of this. Illustrations indicate this technique used in the excavation of barrows in 1871 on Hameldown (Spence Bate, 1872) and in 1898 at Halwill (Baring-Gould et al., 1898). It appears to have been standard practice to sieve all the soil suggesting that finds are unlikely to have been missed. Burnard states that at Broadun and Broadun Ring: 'All the meat earth was carefully examined as it was thrown out and when nearly on the 'calm' the excavated soil and subsoil was passed through a sieve with a mesh of a quarter of an inch' (Burnard 1984: 187). That this became standard practice is suggested by the references to 'sifting' soil in later reports, as, for example, at Langstone Moor, where the conditions of the excavation were far from ideal and it was therefore decided to '...uncover the floors of the huts and leave the sifting of the floors of the huts till Mr. George French could be secured in the spring' (Baring-Gould et al., 1895: 84). Sieves are also present in photographs of early excavations (see photographs of Metheral excavations in Worth, 1994).

The DEC maintained standards of excavation quality; this is demonstrated by their recognition of times when the work underway was failing to meet them; for example at Langstone Moor: 'The exploration was not carried out as happily as at Grimspound, as the workmen employed were changing every day, so that the same men could not be secured sufficiently long to be trained to dig intelligently' (Baring-Gould et al., 1895: 84). As ever, the foreman ran the show; Mr George French developed some important archaeological skills, recognised by the authors of the Grimspound report:

'... he had acquired a knowledge of the sort of work that had to be done, and he added thereto an enthusiasm not surpassed by that of any of the members of the committee ; added to which, his long experience in wall-building, and his general practical knowledge, rendered his judgment in disputed matters of the highest consequence' (Baring-Gould et al., 1894: 102).

The indispensability of George French is shown by the fact that the excavation at Langstone Moor was abandoned until his assistance could be secured (Baring-Gould et al., 1895: 84). The continuity of personnel undertaking excavations on Dartmoor before 1950 encourages the belief that methods of excavation were fairly consistent. George French advanced interpretations that the clergymen and gentlemen scholars reporting on the excavations might not have arrived at themselves - for example, at Hart Tor, where he suggested that large pits full of charcoal in buildings No 12 and 14 were "baking places for pottery" (Baring-Gould et al., 1896: 191).

Overall, the quality of the excavation fieldwork seems to have been very good by the standards of its time. However the tiny amount of time expended on the excavation of each building betrays an absence of detailed on site recording. The standard allowance was one day or less per structure. Spending longer than a day on a building is sufficiently remarkable to excite comment, as at Hut circle No 2, Yes Tor Bottom: "... a most interesting hut, and justified the two days which were spent over its thorough exploration" (Baring-Gould et al., 1898: 103). The absence of detailed on site recording led to some peremptory reports, suffering most from a dearth of drawings. Despite some interesting post excavation analysis (R H Worth's chemical and microscopic examination of pottery fabrics (Baring-Gould et al., 1897) is possibly the first ever petrological analysis in archaeology) the reports are difficult to use. Lack of standard terminology means there is sometimes uncertainty over what is being described.

Appendix D: Key for Map of Pollen Sampling Sites in and around Dartmoor

1	Sandyford and Okement	Caseldine 1983
2	Broad Amicombe Hole	Maguire Unpub.
3	Black Ridge Brook	Staines 1979, Caseldine and Maguire 1986, Hatton Unpub.
4	Pinswell	Caseldine and Hatton 1993
5	Black Lane Brook	Simmons 1964a, Simmons, Rand and Crabtree 1983
6	Blackabrook	Smith et al 1981
7	Okehampton Park	Austin, Daggett and Walker 1980
8	Wotter Common	Smith et al 1981, Balaam et al 1982
9	Saddlesborough Reave	Smith et al 1981, Balaam et al 1982
1	Trowlesworthy	Smith et al 1981
1	Houndtor	Austin and Walker 1985
1	Taw Marsh	Simmons 1964a, Thorndycraft et al 2003
1	Taw Head	Simmons 1964a,
1	Postbridge	Simmons 1964a,
1	Holne Moor	Maguire, Ralph and Fleming 1983
1	Okement Hill	Godwin [pre 1939] in Simmons 1964a
1	Kestor	Blackburn in Fox 1954
1	Tor Royal	Coombe 1958, West et al 1996
1	Stallmoor Down Stone Row	Simmons 1961
2	Rattlebrook	Simmons 1962
2	Throwleigh	Simmons 1962
2	Raybarrow Pool	Simmons 1964a
2	Cholwichtown Stone Row	Simmons 1964b
2	Clay works	Staines 1979
2	Nuns Cross	Staines 1979
2	Shapley	Staines 1979
2	Princes Hall	Staines 1979
2	Piles Hill	Staines 1979
2	Whittenknowle	Staines 1979
3	Cuckoo Ball	Staines 1979
3	Moorgate	Staines 1979
3	Chagford Common	Staines 1972
3	Walkhampton	Staines 1972
3	Wistman's Wood	Staines 1972
3	Fox Tor	Staines 1972
3	Lee Moor	Smith et al 1981
3	Bellever	Caseldine and Hatton 1996
3	Black Tor Copse	Pinnington Unpub.
3	Sourton Down	Straker in Weddell and Reed 1997
4	Aveton Gifford	Thorndycraft et al 2004

4	Ermington	Thorndycraft et al 2004
4	Rundlestone Pipeline	Straker in Reed 1994
4	Rundlestone Pipeline	Straker in Reed 1994
4	Batworthy Pipeline	Gibson 1990
4	Shovel Down	Fyfe and Amesbury 2004, Brück et al 2005
4	Shovel Down	Fyfe and Amesbury 2004, Brück et al 2005

Appendix E: Dealing with the lie of the land

At an early stage in the project Frances Griffiths suggested a problem with my GIS based approach. The data I was using had either been projected to lie in two dimensions, or (in the case of the English Heritage GPS data) had its 3D attributes removed. Obviously Bronze Age people themselves measured their land on the ground, wouldn't this make a map based approach incorrect?

I needed to understand the extent of the impact of this problem on my data, so I first calculated where this error was and the degree to which it was likely to impact on my measurements. Using a slope map and applying basic trigonometry I was able to calculate what the percentage error on my data caused by slope would be. I then classified my map into a range of error classes. The

resulting map showed where the terrain was likely to introduce problems.

Based on this model I was able to find out the proportion of the total lengths of reaves which fell within each error class. As you can see from the pie chart the longest amount of reaves fell into error classes of under 2%. This means that on a length of 100m the error caused by slope could cause the actual three dimensional measurement to differ from the two dimensional length by up to 2m. Of course on a length of 50m the error would be up to 1m and so on. However around 14% of the data has errors that might affect the types of analysis it is possible to carry out on this data.

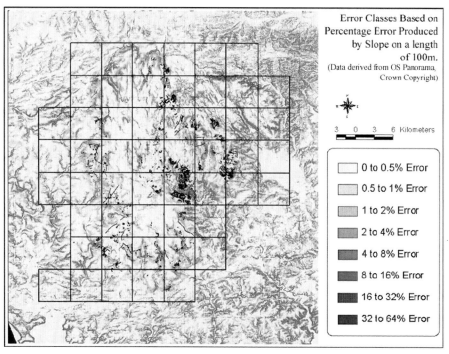

Error Classes Based on Percentage Error Produced by Slope on a length of 100m.
(Data derived from OS Panorama, Crown Copyright)

3 0 3 6 Kilometers

☐ 0 to 0.5% Error
☐ 0.5 to 1% Error
▨ 1 to 2% Error
▨ 2 to 4% Error
▨ 4 to 8% Error
▨ 8 to 16% Error
▨ 16 to 32% Error
▮ 32 to 64% Error

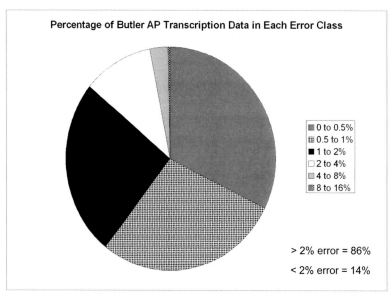

Percentage of Butler AP Transcription Data in Each Error Class

▨ 0 to 0.5%
▦ 0.5 to 1%
▮ 1 to 2%
☐ 2 to 4%
▨ 4 to 8%
▨ 8 to 16%

> 2% error = 86%

< 2% error = 14%

I then started to think more about how I might be able to get around the problem of slope. GPS instruments were not available for my work, and Total Station hire was costly. The other options were either to measure boundaries directly using tapes or to drape the data over the DEM before measuring. However I was uncertain which of these options was the best way of dealing with the problem. A pilot study was therefore carried out in order to evaluate different approaches. The three options I evaluated were

i) Using uncorrected map data

ii) Measuring boundaries directly through tape measure survey

iii) Using data corrected to a three dimensional DTM recorded at 1:50,000.

Field work was carried out with a team of twenty volunteers at Kestor, North East Dartmoor. This area was selected because it offered many boundaries and showed a wide range of the error classes I had generated. Using the data from the tape measure survey I was able to compare two solutions to the problem of slope. The results were surprising. The three dimensional representation of the AP transcription data did exactly what I expected in that all the boundaries were slightly longer. However, if you look at the mean percentage differences for the tape measure survey you can see that it is generally closer to the two dimensional data (at 9.39%) than it is to the corrected data (where it stands at 10.18%).

As you can see from this graph, generally the results from the tape measure survey bore some relationship to the two dimensional data, but there were some significant disparities. This suggests that the tape measure survey must have been picking up some form of random disturbance not attributable to slope. The comments on the recording forms of Katy and Amy sum up factors that might be introducing this error: '*Strong wind; gorse 4ft high - Oh my God we can't walk through it, help!*'

I conclude from this study that tape measure survey is not a very efficient solution to the problems of slope. This is one instance where dwelling in the landscape is not necessarily going to get me any closer to land measurement in the Bronze Age; in fact, it is likely to introduce a lot of poorly constrained error. Although the DEM I am using is not of particularly high resolution, it still offers a better way of dealing with the lie of the land.

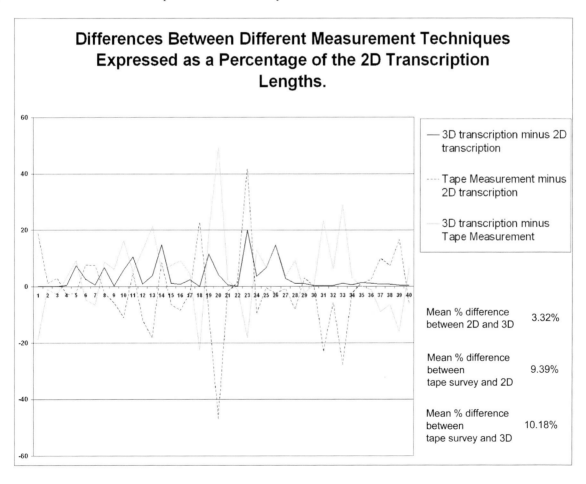

Appendix F: Recalibration of Dates for Enclosures and Buildings

1. Shaugh Moor, Enclosures 15 and 25

Recalibration of Dates from Enclosures 15 and 25, Shaugh Moor

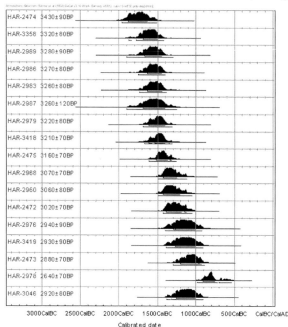

Enclosure 15, Shaugh Moor				
Context	Name	Sigma 1	Sigma 2	Mid point of date at Sigma 2
Charcoal from post hole, House 15 - phase 1	HAR-2474	1880BC (68.2%) 1630BC	1960BC (95.4%) 1510BC	1735
Charcoal from House 67 - phase 2	HAR-3358	1690BC (68.2%) 1500BC	1780BC (94.0%) 1420B	1630
Charcoal from fill of pit 633	HAR-2989	1670BC (68.2%) 1450BC	1900BC (95.4%) 1300BC	1600
Charcoal from beneath enclosure wall	HAR-2986	1630BC (68.2%) 1450BC	1750BC (95.4%) 1400BC	1575
Charcoal from gully flanking E wall of House 66	HAR-2983	1630BC (68.2%) 1440BC	1740BC (95.4%) 1390BC	1565
Charcoal (bulked sample) from drain fill in House 18	HAR-2987	1690BC (68.2%) 1410BC	1900BC (95.4%) 1250BC	1575
Charcoal from drain fill, House 67 - phase 1	HAR-2979	1610BC (68.2%) 1410BC	1690BC (95.4%) 1310BC	1500
Charcoal from old land surface beneath enclosure wall	HAR-3418	1610BC (8.1%) 1570BC 1540BC (60.1%) 1410B	1670BC (92.8%) 1360BC	1515
Charcoal assoc with enclosure wall	HAR-2475	1520BC (63.8%) 1370BC	1610BC (95.4%) 1260BC	1435
Charcoal from drain fill, House 15 - phase 1	HAR-2968	1430BC (68.2%)	1500BC (95.4%)	1310

		1250BC	1120BC	
Charcoal, id as Alder, from hollow beneath wall of House 66	HAR-2960	1430BC (68.2%) 1210BC	1500BC (95.4%) 1050BC	1275
Charcoal between phase 2 flagstones of House 18	HAR-2472	1390BC (66.0%) 1190BC	1430BC (95.4%) 1050BC	1240
Charcoal from post hole of structure 804	HAR-2976	1270BC (66.8%) 1010BC	1400BC (95.4%) 920BC	1160
Charcoal from surface of trampled soil in drain area, House 15 (phase 2)	HAR-3419	1270BC (68.2%) 1000BC	1390BC (95.4%) 910BC	1150
Charcoal assoc with floor of House 19	HAR-2473	1200BC (63.2%) 970BC	1300BC (95.4%) 890BC	1095
Charcoal from phase 1 drain fill, House 19	HAR-2978	910BC (68.2%) 760BC	980BC (80.0%) 720BC	850
Context	**Name**	**Sigma 1**	**Sigma 2**	**Mid point of date at Sigma 2**
Charcoal (from earlier excavations by Plymouth Museum) from house in Enclosure 25, N slope of Saddlesborough, Shaugh Moor Site 209, Devon, England.	HAR-3046	1220BC (61.3%) 1000BC	1320BC (92.1%) 910BC	1115

2. Holne Moor Houses 1 and 2

Recalibration of Dates from Houses 1 and 2, Holne Moor

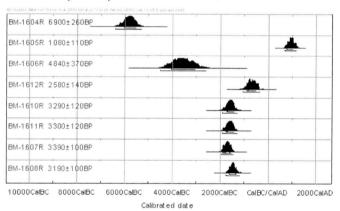

House 1				
Context	**Name**	**Sigma 1**	**Sigma 2**	**Mid point of date at Sigma 2**
Charcoal from below wall, House 1	BM-1604R	6030BC (68.2%) 5550BC	6400BC (95.4%) 5300BC	5850 BC
Charcoal from outside entrance to House 1	BM-1605R	770AD (68.2%) 1040AD	680AD (95.4%) 1170AD	945 AD
Charcoal from upper fill of house 1 ditch	BM-1606R	4050BC (68.2%) 3050BC	4500BC (95.4%) 2600BC	3550 BC
Charcoal from inner edge of House 1 wall, sealed by House 2	BM-1612R	900BC (2.8%) 870BC 850BC (65.4%) 510BC	1050BC (95.4%) 350BC	700 BC
House 2				
Context	**Name**	**Sigma 1**	**Sigma 2**	**Mid point of date at Sigma**

				2
Charcoal sealed by N wall of House 2	BM-1610R	1730BC (2.1%) 1710BC 1700BC (66.1%) 1430BC	1900BC (95.4%) 1300BC	1600 BC
Charcoal sealed by wall of House 2	BM-1611R	1740BC (4.7%) 1710BC 1700BC (63.5%) 1440BC	1900BC (95.4%) 1300BC	1600 BC
Charcoal from floor of House 2	BM-1607R	1870BC (5.3%) 1840BC 1820BC (1.5%) 1800BC 1780BC (49.4%) 1600BC 1590BC (12.0%) 1530BC	1940BC (95.4%) 1450BC	1695 BC
Charcoal from doorway, House 2, sealed by debris	BM-1608R	1610BC (65.9%) 1380BC 1340BC (2.3%) 1320BC	1750BC (95.4%) 1200BC	1475 BC

3. Gold Park, Timber and Stone Platform Buildings

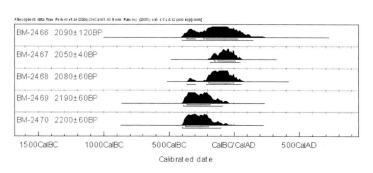

Stone house			
Information	**name**	**Sigma 1**	**Sigma 2**
Charcoal, sample 9, id by G Morgan as gorse, hazel and oak, from patch of charcoal on floor of stone hut Comment (lab, JA): large margin of error is due to low carbon content of sample.	BM-2466	210BC (57.2%) 30AD	400BC (95.4%) 150AD
Charcoal, sample 6, id by G Morgan as gorse, hazel and oak, from patch of charcoal on floor of timber hut, sealed below wall of stone hut.	BM-2467	120BC (65.8%) 10AD	180BC (95.4%) 50AD
Charcoal, sample 17, id by G Morgan as oak, hazel, gorse, poplar, from patch of charcoal in stone hut.	BM-2468	190BC (66.3%) 20BC	210BC (89.5%) 60AD
timber house			
Charcoal, sample 28, id by G Morgan as gorse and hazel, from central hearth F11 assoc with timber hut	BM-2469	360BC (68.2%) 180BC	390BC (95.4%) 90BC
Charcoal, sample 29, id by G Morgan as gorse, hazel, oak and poplar, from section 22 of bedding trench of timber hut.	BM-2470	370BC (68.2%) 190BC	400BC (95.4%) 100BC

Appendix G: Recalibration of Dates from Reaves on Dartmoor

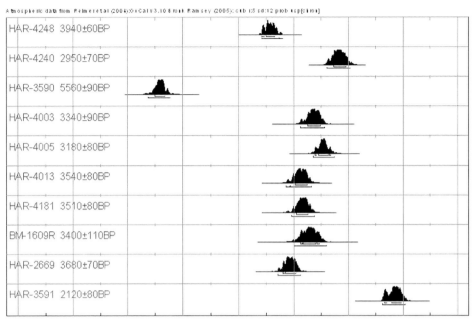

Atmospheric data from Reimer et al (2004);OxCal v3.10 Bronk Ramsey (2005); cub r:5 sd:12 prob usp[chron]

HAR-4248 3940±60BP

HAR-4240 2950±70BP

HAR-3590 5560±90BP

HAR-4003 3340±90BP

HAR-4005 3180±80BP

HAR-4013 3540±80BP

HAR-4181 3510±80BP

BM-1609R 3400±110BP

HAR-2669 3680±70BP

HAR-3591 2120±80BP

7000CalBC 6000CalBC 5000CalBC 4000CalBC 3000CalBC 2000CalBC 1000CalBC CalBC/CalAD 1000CalAD

Calibrated date

Saddleborough Main Reave				
Context	Lab Code	Sigma 1	Sigma 2	Mid point of date at Sigma 2
Peat from peaty surface horizon of buried soil beneath Saddlesborough Main Reave	HAR-4248	2570BC (9.7%) 2530BC 2500BC (58.5%) 2340BC	2580BC (92.4%) 2270BC 2260BC (3.0%) 2200BC	2425 BC
Peat from peaty surface horizon from soil immediately below Saddlesborough Main Reave.	HAR-4240	1270BC (68.2%) 1040BC	1390BC (95.4%) 970BC	1180 BC
Charcoal from lens, context 385, within peat under reave at Saddlesborough Main Reave	HAR-3590	4500BC (68.2%) 4330BC	4620BC (95.4%) 4230BC	4425 BC
Wood from stake on ditch bottom, Phase II of reave (Trench AE)	HAR-4003	1740BC (68.2%) 1510BC	1880BC (95.4%) 1430BC	1655 BC
Peat from OGS beneath primary bank (Phase I) of reave (Trench AJ) at Saddlesborough Main Reave, Shaugh Moor, Devon, England.	HAR-4005	1610BC (2.4%) 1590BC 1540BC (62.7%) 1370BC 1340BC (3.1%) 1320BC	1640BC (95.4%) 1260BC	1450 BC
Peat from animal footprint layer in ditch bottom, reave Phase I (Trench AK)	HAR-4013	1980BC (68.2%) 1750BC	2140BC (3.6%) 2080BC 2060BC (91.8%) 1680BC	1870 BC
Peat from OGS below bank of parallel reave (Phase I, Trench AF at junction with Saddlesborough reave) at Saddlesborough Main Reave, Shaugh Moor, Devon, England.	HAR-4181	1950BC (68.2%) 1740BC	2040BC (95.4%) 1620BC	1830 BC

Holne Moor Parallel Reave near House F				
Context	**Lab Code**	**Sigma 1**	**Sigma 2**	**Mid point of date at Sigma 2**
Charcoal from top 10cm of pre-reave bank at Holne Moor, Devon, England. Coll A Fleming. Comment (lab): Is revision of earlier determination BM-1609.	BM-1609R	1880BC (7.8%) 1840BC 1830BC (52.5%) 1600BC 1580BC (7.9%) 1530BC	2000BC (95.4%) 1400BC	1700 BC
Parallel Reave on Wotter Common				
Context	**Lab Code**	**Sigma 1**	**Sigma 2**	**Mid point of date at Sigma 2**
Charcoal from puddle-like depression below boundary wall S of Enclosure 13 at Shaugh Moor - Wotter Playground (Site 201)	HAR-2669	2200BC (3.3%) 2170BC 2150BC (64.9%) 1960BC	2290BC (95.4%) 1880BC	2085 BC
Clearance for cultivation terrace				
Context	**Lab Code**	**Sigma 1**	**Sigma 2**	**Mid point of date at Sigma 2**
Charcoal, id as oak, from clearance for cultivation terrace in later Iron Age at Shaugh Moor - Wotter Playground (Site 201).	HAR-3591	350BC (13.0%) 300BC 210BC (55.2%) 40BC	380BC (95.4%) 30AD	205 BC

Appendix H: Recalibration of Dates from Cairns and Barrows at Shaugh Moor, Upton Pyne and Dainton

Recalibration of Dates from Cairns at Shaugh Moor, (Atmospheric data from Reimer et al (2004);OxCal v3.10 Bronk Ramsey (2005)

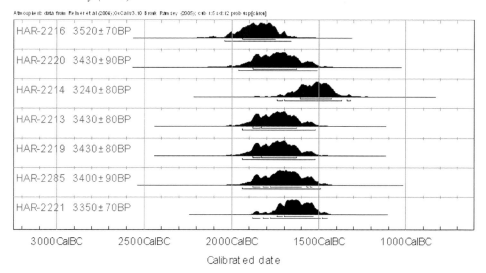

Recalibration of Date from Upton Pyne, (Atmospheric data from Reimer et al (2004);OxCal v3.10 Bronk Ramsey (2005)

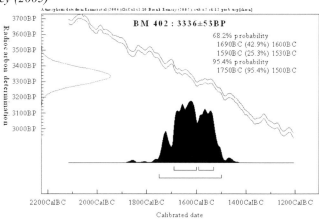

Recalibration of Dates from Cairn at Dainton, (Atmospheric data from Reimer et al (2004);OxCal v3.10 Bronk Ramsey (2005)

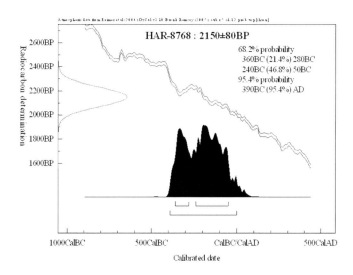

Context	Name	Sigma 1	Sigma 2	Midpoint of Date at Sigma 2
Charcoal from central pit, Ring cairn (No. 1)	HAR-2216	1940BC (68.2%) 1750BC	2040BC (95.4%) 1660BC	1850 BC
Charcoal from central pit with faience beads, Ring cairn (No. 2).	HAR-2220	1880BC (68.2%) 1630BC	1960BC (95.4%) 1510BC	1735 BC
Charcoal from pit below stone ring, Ring cairn (No. 2).	HAR-2214	1610BC (68.2%) 1430BC	1740BC (1.3%) 1710BC; 1700BC (93.0%) 1370BC; 1340BC (1.0%) 1320BC	1535 BC
Charcoal from central pit with pottery, Kerbed cairn (No. 71) at Shaugh Moor, Dartmoor, Devon, England.	HAR-2213	1880BC (11.2%) 1840BC; 1830BC (57.0%) 1630BC;	1940BC (95.4%) 1520BC	1730 BC
Charcoal from central pit, Kerbed cairn (No. 70).	HAR-2219	1880BC (11.2%) 1840BC; 1830BC (57.0%) 1630BC;	1940BC (95.4%) 1520BC	1730 BC
Charcoal from central pit (lower fill) Kerbed cairn (No. 126).	HAR-2285	1880BC (7.3%) 1840BC; 1820BC (3.9%) 1790BC; 1780BC (53.8%) 1600BC; 1570BC (2.0%)1560BC; 1550BC (1.2%) 1540BC	1940BC (95.4%) 1490BC	1715 BC
Charcoal from central pit (upper fill) Kerbed cairn (No. 126).	HAR-2221	1740BC (7.3%) 1710BC; 1700BC (60.9%) 1530B	1880BC (2.7%) 1840BC; 1820BC (1.2%) 1790BC; 1780BC (90.2%) 1490BC; 1480BC (1.3%) 1450BC	1635 BC
Oak charcoal from Urn 4, inverted at Upton Pyne	BM 402	1690BC (42.9%) 1600BC; 1590 (25.3%) 1530BC	1750BC (95.4%) 1500BC	1625 BC
Charcoal, id as Prunus avium (Wild Cherry) and Pomoideae (Apple, Pear, Hawthorn) twigs, c 5 yr old, from the fill of a posthole sealed by stone rubble of cairn (English Heritage 1987).	HAR-8768	360 (21.4%) 280 BC; 240 BC (48.8%) 50 BC;	390 BC (95.4%) 0 AD	195 BC

Appendix I: Condensed Version of Needham's Chronological Framework

Needham's Periodisation of the British Bronze Age (from Needham, 1996)

Period	Material Culture Traits	Archaeological Sites
Period 1 (2500-2300 cal BC)	Metal Using Neolithic 1; Grooved Ware, Beakers	Continued construction and elaboration of timber circles and linear ceremonial sites.
Period 2 (2300-2050 cal BC)	Metal Using Neolithic 2; End of Grooved Ware (c2100 BC), Beakers, Migdale metalwork starts (c2300 BC)	Crouched inhumation burial often with grave goods. Only beakers regularly placed in graves.
Period 3 (2050-1700 cal BC)	Food vessels appear (c2000 BC), Collared Urns appear (c2000 BC), Migdale metalwork ends (c1900 BC)	Urned cremation and "marked diversification" in funerary pottery. "Late currency" of Beakers – now sites include Food vessels and Collared Urns, also new 'rich' grave goods including "special cups, varied ornaments and developed weapons".
Period 4 (1700-1500 cal BC)	Beakers end, Food Vessels end (c1700 BC), Camerton-Snowhill metalwork (c1600-1400 BC), Deverel Rimbury and Trevisker starts (c1700 BC), Arreton metalwork and Acton Park starts	Increased focus on cremation. Beakers and Food Vessels disappear from graves. Urned cremation in Collared Urns continues. "Profusion of metalwork types" with overlap between EBA and MBA types.
Period 5 (1500-1150 cal BC)	Deverel Rimbury and Trevisker continue, Collared Urns disappear, Acton Park, Taunton and Penard metalwork	Settlement sites "come to the forefront". First rampart at Rams Hill built.
Period 6 (1150-950 cal BC)	Post Deverel Rimbury starts, Wilburton metalwork begins (c1200 BC)	Earliest ringforts
Period 7 (950-750 cal BC)	Ewart Park Metalwork, Post Deverel Rimbury continues, decorated PDR (c800-600 BC)	Some hilltops given ramparts, iron working may begin, many more hoards appear in record
Early Iron Age (750-450 cal BC)	Llyn Fawr metalwork,	Hillforts proliferate

Appendix J: Frequencies of Enclosure areas within size classes

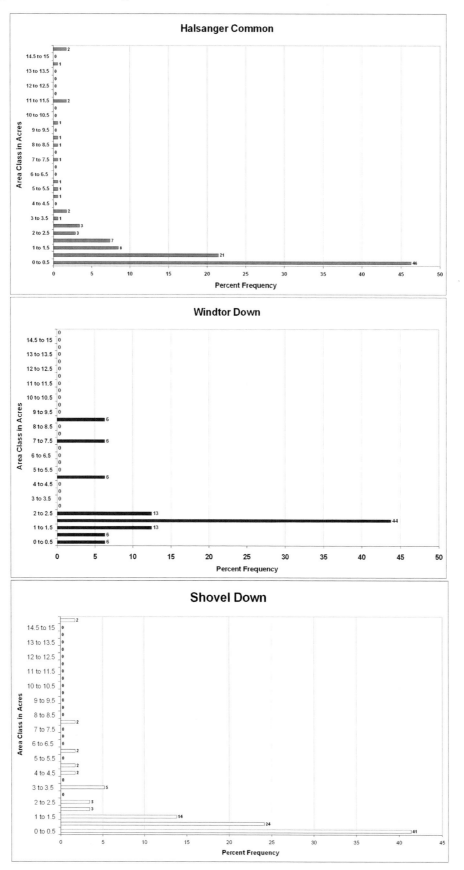

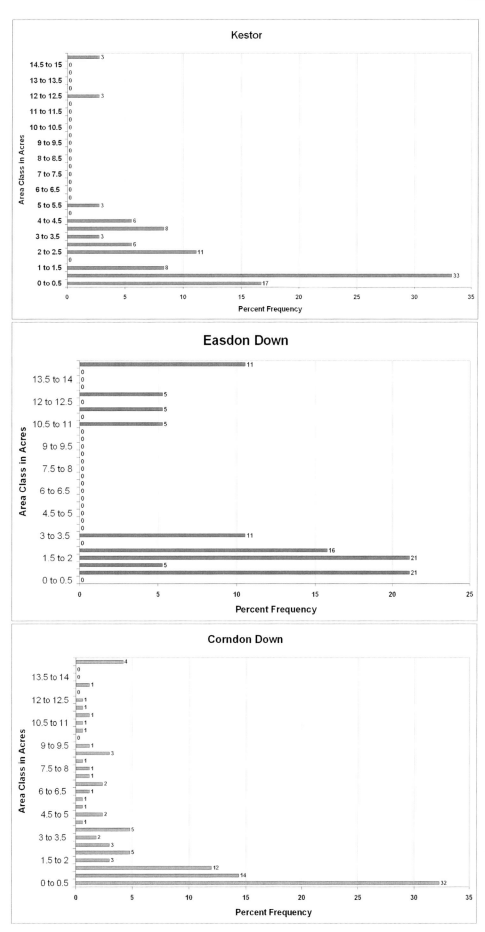

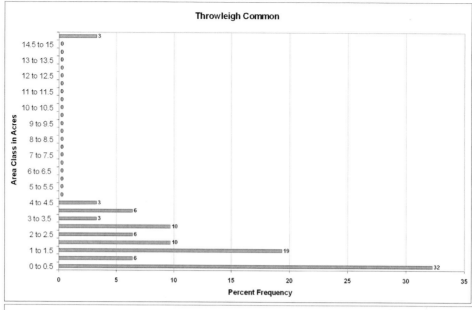

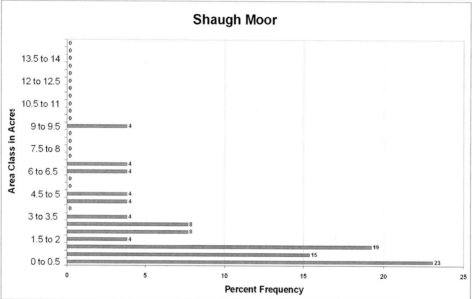

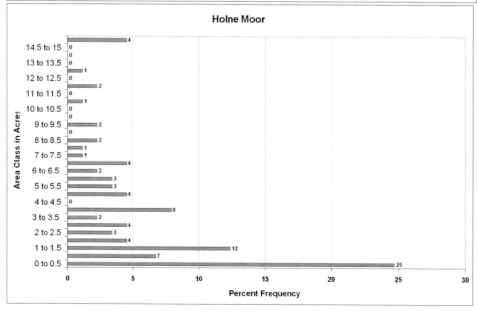

Appendix K: Measurements of Strip Widths

Case Study 1: Windtor Down

Strip width measured from West to East.

	Strip 1	Strip 2	Strip 3	Strip 4	Strip 5	Strip 6	Strip 7	standard deviation
Terminal width	38.442	41.114	34.377	null	null	null	35.195	2.684419
field width 1	52.509	null	39.74	51.787	50.722	37.456	45.859	5.911076
field width 2	51.899	null	null	54.957	40.366	53.925	44.828	5.655212
field width 3	56.41	null	null	null	null	66.874	58.028	4.599093

Case Study 2: Shaugh Moor

Three main areas of subdivision are preserved at Shaugh Moor. The westernmost block is composed of four strips, only the middle two of which now meet the terminal reave. The strips are roughly equal but vary in width and are less even then those of the second block below. The middle block of fields is made up of two large blocks of roughly equal width. This area has an interesting pattern of subdivision. Of the two large blocks (level 1), one is subdivided into two strips (level 2) one of which is then subdivided into two further strips (level 3) the most westerly of which is then divided down again (level 4).

The standard deviation of the widths is slightly smaller at the terminal reave at levels 2, and 3 but not at 4. There are not enough transverse boundaries to judge the significance of this finding. The westernmost area of land division at Shaugh Moor is made up of a group of sub-rectangular enclosures which are arranged alongside each other in a way that suggests some traces of a strip like structure. There are also some curvilinear enclosures in this group. The area is not sufficiently 'coaxial' to be used in the analysis.

Shaugh Moor: Westernmost Area (strips form West to East)

	strip 1	strip 2	strip 3	strip 4	standard deviation
terminal width	null	92.55	118.345	null	12.8975
field width 1	116.57	89.644	116.754	108.092	11.03186
field width 2	106.385	null	null	113.861	3.738

Shaugh Moor: Middle Area - Level 1 (Strips from West to East)

	strip 1	strip 2	Standard Deviation
terminal widths	278.98	257.864	10.558
field width 1	253.333	null	0
field width 2	null	null	null

Shaugh Moor: Middle Area – Level 2

level 2	strip 1	strip 2	Standard deviation
terminal widths	135.34	143.64	4.15
field width 1	135.046	118.287	8.3795
field width 2	null	117.561	null

Shaugh Moor: Middle Area – Level 3

	strip 1	strip 2	Standard Deviation
terminal widths	64.932	70.408	2.738
field width 1	63.124	71.922	4.399

Shaugh Moor: Middle Area – Level 4

	strip 1	strip 2	Standard Deviation
terminal widths	33.837	31.095	1.371
field width 1	33.255	32.934	0.1605
field width 2	32.601	30.523	1.039

Case Study 3: Throwleigh Common

The preservation of a large area of boundaries on Throwleigh Common means that something can be adduced of the 'landscape structure' of land division in this region. The terrain is divided into three blocks which delimit an area of ridge, valley and then ridge again. A similar structure can be observed at Shovel Down. These blocks are not fully enclosed, and only one is traversed by a 'terminal reave'. Interestingly they have the appearance of very large parallel strips in themselves. The block containing the coaxial field system is not delimited by a boundary on the southern side, which means that its width cannot be measured. However the other two blocks are each around 580m wide.

The northernmost block is divided into three strips. The furthest north does not have any transverse divisions, so cannot be measured. Measurement of the transverse divisions in the other two strips suggests that they are not very evenly matched. The southernmost block is divided into two by a boundary that follows the line of the ridge. This boundary is also a droveway for the upper part of its length. At this level the two parts of the field system are not very similar in width, and this may be because the width of the second strip has not been correctly measured

– it is interrupted by an enclosure at its southern end that does not have an outer limit. Enclosure in the northern half of this block runs right up to the terminal reave, but there is a large 'reserved area' behind the terminal in the southern half. This area is delimited by another long boundary that makes its own 'mini-terminal'. The latter is considered separately below. The northern half of the block is again divided into two strips. One of these strips is then divided in half forming another two strips Finally the southern strip is subdivided into two again. This strip gradually widens as it travels downhill causing strip 1 above to narrow. The effect of this is that the subdivision at level 3 above - from being a bipartite division - becomes closer to a division into thirds. The southerly half of the coaxial field system begins behind a large square enclosure next to the terminal. A few rectangular and sub rectangular fields are built within this enclosure. Four roughly even strips meet at the edge of this enclosure. Strip three of the above has a subdivision within it which runs across roughly a third of its width. Dividing the remainder of the field into two gives a result of 24.681, indicating that the subdivision is only an approximate rather than a precise third.

Throwleigh Common: Northernmost Block

	Strip 1	strip 2	strip 3	Standard Deviation
terminal width	Null	null	null	null
field width 1	null	186.903	224.814	18.9555

Throwleigh Common: Southernmost Block - Level 1

	strip 1	strip 2	Standard Deviation
terminal width	236.531	215.408	10.5615

Throwleigh Common: Southernmost Block - Level 2

	strip 1	strip 2	Standard Deviation
terminal width	111.633	124.898	6.6325
field width 1	163.921	120.843	21.539
field width 2	139.758	137.035	1.3615
field width 3	145.995	148.821	1.413
field width 4	null	160.278	null

Throwleigh Common: Southernmost Block - Level 3

	strip 1	strip 2	Standard Deviation
terminal width	null	null	null
field width 1	66.877	97.044	15.0835
field width 2	54.643	85.115	15.236
field width 3	46.27	99.725	26.7275
field width 4	54.067	null	null

Throwleigh Common: Southernmost Block - Level 4

	strip 1	strip 2	Standard Deviation
terminal width	null	null	null
field width 1	46.217	50.827	2.305
field width 2	43.237	41.878	0.6795
field width 3	52.088	47.637	2.2255
field width 4	36.888	null	null
field width 5	39.31	null	null
field width 6	42.715	null	null

Strips beginning behind enclosure

Level 1	strip 1	strip 2	strip 3	strip 4	Standard Deviation
terminal width	73.411	83.879	76.874	93.425	7.649605
field width 1	96.783	90.778	68.476	null	12.17796

Subdivision in Strip Three of above

level 2 (subdivision of strip3)	strip 1	strip 2
terminal width	27.512	49.362
field width 1	null	45.487
field width 2	28.496	39.98

Case Study 4: Kestor

The overall structure of the Kestor system has some aspects of the 'block' type layout seen at Throwleigh Common, but the blocks are not evenly matched. Some 'blocks' are parallel strips which run alongside those of the field system but lack a terminal reave or internal enclosures / subdivisions. The distinction between a area of unbounded land above the level of the terminal reaves and an area of boundaries and fields below is much less here, the enclosures at Kestor continue up onto the moor into the blocks of the Shovel Down system. The northernmost area is divided into two strips. The terminal from the above area is staggered slightly with that of the

next block. This block begins with three strips that are quite even. The width of the strips then changes to around 67m, the middle strip represents two of these widths. The second strip in this system is neatly divided into two. Although the Kestor site is not badly preserved, level 2 of the southernmost block provides the only opportunity to compare widths at the terminal with those further down the system. The standard deviation indicates that the strip has been much more precisely divided at this point. The width of transverse boundaries at the terminal reave is more evenly matched than widths further down the in the bounded landscape.

Northernmost area

	strip 1`	strip2	Standard Deviation
terminal width	177.882	191.333	6.7255

Next block southwards

level 1	strip 1`	strip2	strip 3	Standard Deviation
terminal width	82.316	83.474	87.742	2.333292
field width 1	74.576	null	null	null
field width 2	null	102.045	null	null
field width 3	71.279	null	null	null
field width 4	61.784	null	null	null

Southernmost Block

strip 4	strip 5	strip 6
61.247	138.084	67.555
51	null	null
null	null	null
null	null	null
null	null	null

Standard deviation of strips 4 and 6 = 3.154

Southernmost block, level 2

level 2	strip 2a	strip 2b	Standard Deviation
terminal width	42.645	40.829	0.908
field width 1	null	67.028	null
field width 2	61.023	41.022	10.0005
field width 3	50.628	43.739	3.4445
field width 4	51.904	null	null

Case Study 5: Holne Moor

Unlike Throwleigh Common and Kestor the landscape at Holne Moor is not arranged as series of 'blocks'. Instead the dominate feature of the system is the terminal reave, to which the enclosures are attached on the northern side. At the largest scale the boundaries show a series of large and relatively poorly matched strips. Some of these strips have been 'reconstructed' by combining strips. This may indicate that the important measurement may have been either this width or half this width. The next level consists of a series of 'runs' of strips of similar widths. The standard deviations here do not show any greater attention to precise equality at the terminal reaves. This characteristic is even more marked in the last 'run' of strips at Holne Moor. These strips form a distinct group

isolated by the destruction wrought by the Venford Reservoir. These strips meet the terminal reave at a pronounced angle. The builders at this location seem to have made an effort to ensure that these strips were parallel to those in the rest of the system, but the terminal reave curves to the south. If the terminal reave had continued on its previous orientation the width of strips at the terminal reave would have been more even. This feature is intriguing, because it appears that the terminal reave is here laid out according to a principle that is different to that of the rest of the system. One of the strips is very precisely subdivided into two, but becomes more, rather than less, even away from the terminal reave.

Holne Moor, level 1

	strip 1	strp2	strip 3 (strips 1a and 2a)	strip 4	strip 5 (1b and 2b)	strip 6 (1c and 2c)	Standard Deviation
terminal	265.841	222.8	171.779	181.967	246.12	226.854	33.18297
field 1	null	null	169.102	176.31	236.156	216.637	27.83497
field 2	null	219.444	null	172.485	242.359	null	29.08344
field 3	294.492	227.235	162.825	189.26	null	null	49.51202
field 4	295.505	227.403	null	185.543	null	215.191	40.28047

Holne Moor, level 2

level 2					level 2 next block		
	strip 1	strip 2	strip 3	Standard Deviation	strip 1a	strip 2a	Standard Deviation
terminal widths	104.467	121.546	162.099	24.16997	92.927	78.852	7.0375
field width 1	91.5	null	null	null	89.655	79.447	5.104
field width 2	88.511	null	null	null	94.087	null	null
field width 3	84.178	116.494	null	16.158	92.217	70.608	10.8045

level 2 next block		level 2		
strip 1b	strip 2b	strip 1c	strip2c	Standard Deviation
130.754	115.366	120.72	106.134	8.910186
119.64	116.516	117.051	99.586	7.947337
127.144	115.215	null	null	5.9645
null	null	114.732	100.459	7.1365

	strip 1d	strip 2d	strip 3d	strip 4d	Standard Deviation
terminal width	142.016	147.961	116.742	184.026	24.03306
field width 1	137.103	147.773	112.905	138.977	12.93203
field width 2	149.341	148.289	122.231	null	12.53917
field width 3	153.445	null	null	null	null

level 3 (subdivision of strip 2b)			
	1	2	Standard Deviation
terminal width	59.006	56.36	1.323
field width 1	56.525	59.991	1.733
field width 2	57.946	57.269	0.3385

Appendix L: Lithic Scatters from Dartmoor

Review revealed some problems in the record. Recent work on a lithic scatter at Batworthy Corner close to Shovel Down (Brück et al., 2005) has shown that the location Miles and Devon SMR record for the Batworthy scatter is incorrect and probably results from a confusion in the literature over place names. A collection of over 8,000 lithics was picked up at Batworthy Corner by a Mr Budd in the 1880s (Budd, 1889, Burnard, 1986) the Shovel Down Project has recently carried out a programme of test pitting at this location and found several hundred pieces of flint in the fields described by Mr Budd confirming that this is indeed the site of the scatter. It appears that later work has confused Batworthy Corner with the larger Batworthy village. Batworthy Corner has therefore been added to the Data tables collected from Devon SMR, and the incorrect Batworthy location has been excluded from further analyses. Important early work detailing lithic scatters on Dartmoor was done by Burnard of the DEC (Burnard, 1986), but unfortunately much of the material mentioned by Burnard cannot now be located (Miles, 1976). Recent work on

collections in Plymouth and Torquay museums confirms that quantities of flint from some of the largest collections have been discarded with only some of the more attractive pieces retained (Brück et al., 2005).

It should be noted that the data presented here mainly focuses on places where lithics have been found without excavation. Many excavated sites also contain chipped stone artefacts and including these sites might significantly change the distribution. In addition there is currently a large body of lithic material held in museums in Devon which has never been looked at (John Allen pers. com.) and there are many private collections that have not been examined or recorded. There is clearly an opening for future work on this material.There is a distinct cluster of presumed Neolithic activity in the North East especially around the valley of the North Teign. Two chamber tombs have been identified here; Gidleigh North and South, along with three possible chamber tombs and some large lithic scatters.

Number	Place Name	MESO	NEO	EBA	Circumstances of Recovery	Quantity
1	Gidleigh Moor	y	y	y	not given	1700
2	Batworthy	y	y	y	ploughing	8000
3	Carapitt Farm	no	y	y	not given	1
4	Higher Snowdens Well	unknown	unknown	unknown	not given	null
5	Reservoir	no	y	no	water erosion	large numbers
6	Runnage Farm	y	y	y	not given	>10
7	Sampford Courtenay	no	y	y	ploughing	1
8	Grove Park Housing Estate	no	y	y	excavation	11
9	Widecombe in the Moor	y	y	y	ploughing and fieldwalking	12
10	Widecombe in the Moor	no	no	y	ploughing and fieldwalking	6
11	Widecombe in the Moor	y	y	y	ploughing and fieldwalking	49
12	Widecombe in the Moor	y	y	y	ploughing and fieldwalking	7
13	Widecombe in the Moor	y	y	y	ploughing and fieldwalking	13
14	Field called Daggers, Ashburton	y	y	y	ploughing and excavation	null
15	Buckfast Abbey Vegetable Field	no	y	y	ploughing and fieldwalking	30
16	Southbrook Farm	no	y	y	not given	>5
17	Hedgemoor Farm	y	y	y	ploughing	large numbers
18	Hedgemoor Farm	no	y	y	not given	132
19	Dean Moor	no	y	y	excavation	32
20	Tavistock	no	y	no	not given	null
21	Yalland Farm	y	y	y	not given	large numbers
22	Round Warrens, Shipley Tor	no	y	y	not given	>11

23	Hedgemoor Farm	no	y	y	not given	80
24	Postbridge	y	y	y	peat erosion	large numbers
25	Brownberry	y	y	y	not given	75
26	Fernworthy Reservoir	y	y	y	water erosion	>800
27	East Week	y	y	y	ploughing and fieldwalking	4870
28	Welstor Estate, Ashburton	y	y	y	not given	>70
29	Little Hays Farm	no	y	y	ploughing	>100
30	Carrapit Farm	no	y	no	not given	2000
31	Hedgemoor Farm	no	y	no	digging of pond	2
32	Furzeland	no	y	y	not given	null
33	White Tor Fort	unknown	unknown	unknown	excavation	0
34	Batworthy Corner	y	y	y	ploughing and excavation	>8000
35	South Tawton	no	y	no	ploughing	1
36	South Tawton	no	y	no	ploughing	1
37	Widecombe in the Moor	unknown	unknown	unknown	ploughing	1
38	Lydford	no	y	no	not given	1
39	Challacombe	no	y	y	ploughing	3
40	Devonport Leat	no	no	y	not given	1

Appendix M: Areas of Blocks of Pastureland

The size ranges of these blocks vary, but they generally fall within the expected ranges for communal cattle herds and sheep flocks. Stocking rates for upland pasture are currently set at around 5-7 ewes per hectare (National Sheep Association, 2005) but it should be noted that prehistoric sheep were less than half the size of their modern counterparts and would have been much more numerous (Pryor, 1998: 106). For prehistoric cattle it is suggested that stocking rates would have been of the order of one livestock unit per hectare (i.e. one cow and calf, one yearling and a two year old, or a single three year old cow), and that a 'family farm' of c25 hectare would have been viable for a beef crop on upland pasture (Caulfield, 1983). A dairy herd would require less. The size range of the 'blocks' below might have accommodated around 150 to 200 sheep/goats or c50 cattle permanently but more for shorter lengths of time. Used permanently areas of this size could support one or more large extended family groups (Caulfield, 1983, Abu-Rabia, 1994).

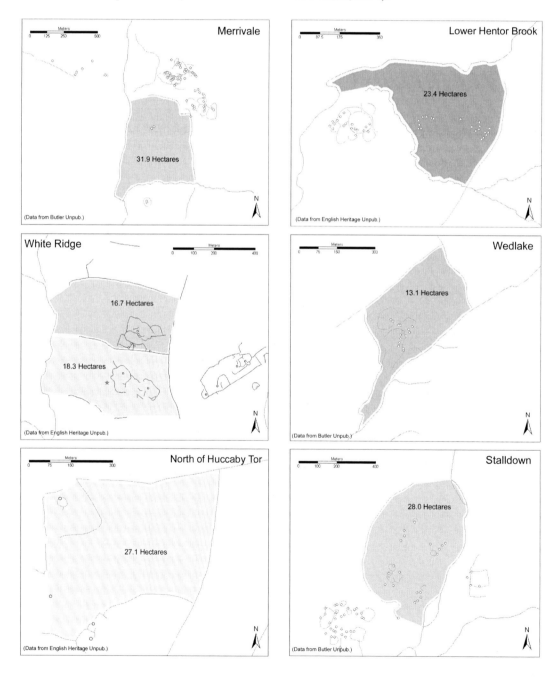

Appendix N: Possible Common Pastures in Different Types of Land Division

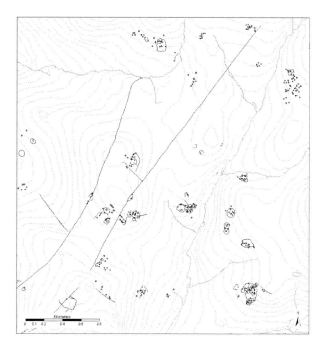

Appendix O: Characteristics of Hearth Architecture from Excavations after 1930

Name of Settlement	Building No.	length at long axis in metres	Description
Riders Rings	2	0.9144	"… a granite slab, erect on edge … leaning slightly inward … carefully trigged on the side toward the centre of the Hut with small flat stones. Against the slab … there had evidently been one of the fireplaces, represented by a shallow pit filled with charcoal and ash." (Harris et al., 1935: 119).
Challacombe	1		"… a quantity of ashy and very black soil lying near two stones…" (Shorter, 1938: 105).
Dean Moor	1	0.762	"concentration of charcoal" (Fox, 1957)
Dean Moor	2	1.2192	"… two fine-grained granite slabs with a kerb of small stones bedded into the subsoil" (ibid: 41)
Dean Moor	3	1.0668	"… laid on four granite paving slabs, crazed by heat …" (ibid: 43).
Dean Moor	4	0.6096	No description
Dean Moor	5a	0.4572	"A boulder had been left in position as a fire-back…" (ibid: 46).
Dean Moor	5b	0.6096	"… backed by a natural boulder and paved in front…" (ibid: 47).
Dean Moor	6	0.9144	"… had a paved surround" (ibid: 48).
Dean Moor	7	0.762	"… made on a bedded slab and edged by small upright stones as a fender…" (ibid: 50).
Dean Moor	8	0.762	"… with a paved surround" (ibid: 53).
Kes Tor	1	0.9144	"… the fire had been made on three bedded slabs. There was a scatter of small pieces of charcoal around them, and of a fine grey soil which was probably peat ash" (Fox, 1954b: 30)
Kes Tor	Round Pound	0.762	"… a small hearth on the clean raised floor at the back of the hut for a smoulder fire…" (ibid: 39).
Heatree	2	0.5	"… a burnt area surrounded by a rough oval of small stones" (Quinnell, 1991: 9).
Heatree	3	0.6	"(18) was a grounder; both its surface and that of the subsoil around it were burnt and it may have been a hearth" (ibid: 14).

Appendix P: Early Excavations of Charcoal-filled 'Troughs' or 'Cooking Chambers'

Site and Reference	Structure No.	Description
Hart Tor (Baring-Gould et al., 1896)	No. 12	Large 'stone-lined' feature 'measuring, when the lining was taken out, 3ft. 6in. in diameter and 1ft 2 in. deep. It extended down to a bed of china clay that showed indications of fire. A wheelbarrow and a half of charcoal were taken out' (ibid: 190)
	No 14	Another 'stone-lined' feature 'like that in No.12. This was 3ft in diameter, and 1ft 3in. in depth. The china clay in which it had been sunk was reddened with fire. Two wheelbarrow-loads of charcoal and burnt stones were removed from this hole' (ibid: 191).
Yes Tor Bottom (Baring-Gould et al., 1898)	No 5	The 'feature of this dwelling' was a large trough '4 feet long, 2 feet wide, and 15 inches deep. It contained much charcoal' (ibid: 103).
Watern Oke (Amery et al., 1906	Between nos 14 and 15	'circular pit of stones, about 6ft in diameter, which was evidently used as a fireplace' situated between two roundhouses
	Excavation 36	A 'large cooking chamber', which was '...very rough, more like a quarry than anything else...' containing 'many cooking stones' (ibid: 108).
	No 40	A large 'cooking pit' 12ft long by 7ft wide roughly constructed of large rocks (ibid: 108)
	No 46a	A 'cooking place, constructed amongst the rocks, impossible to measure or delineate, for it had no shape' and containing 'much burnt granite' (ibid: 109).
	No. 52	A 'rough', 'oblong' structure 12ft by 7ft made of large stones and 'burnt on all sides', containing charcoal and cooking stones (ibid: 110).
	No 54	A 'cooking pit' with a floor of 4ft by 5ft and 3ft deep, having no entrance and with 'fire all over floor' (ibid: 110).
	No 61	A 'circular pit' 4ft deep, 8ft in diameter at the top and 6ft at the base, with 'traces of fire all over the bottom'. It was 'formed of large stones' and contained 'several dozen' cooking stones, as well as flint (ibid: 111).

Appendix Q: Numbers and Percentages of Excavated Buildings Associated with Hearths, Cooking Pits, Pot-Boilers and Paving Compared Between Settlement Types

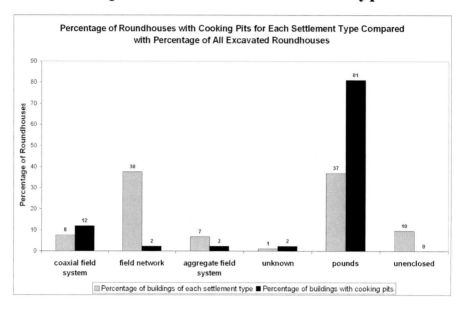

	No. of Excavated Buildings	No. of Buildings with Cooking Pits
Coaxial Land Division	25	5
Field Networks	122	1
Aggregate Land Division	22	1
Pounds	120	34
Unenclosed	31	0
Unknown	4	1

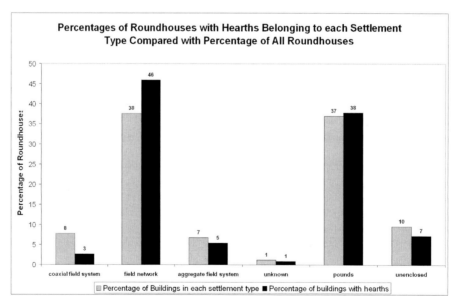

	No. of Excavated Buildings	No. of Buildings with Hearths
Coaxial Land Division	25	3
Field Networks	122	51
Aggregate Land Division	22	6
Pounds	120	42
Unenclosed	31	8
Unknown	4	1

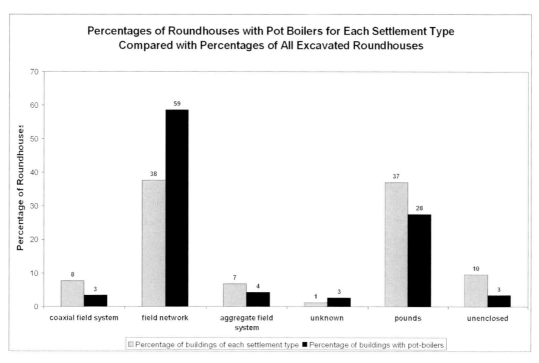

	No. of Excavated Buildings	No. of Buildings with Pot-Boilers
Coaxial Land Division	25	4
Field Networks	122	68
Aggregate Land Division	22	5
Pounds	120	32
Unenclosed	31	4
Unknown	4	3

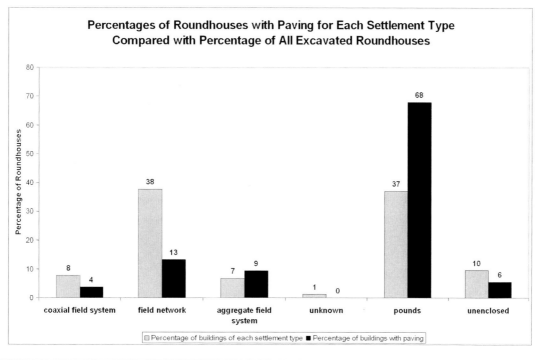

	No. of Excavated Buildings	No. of buildings with paving
Coaxial Land Division	25	2
Field Networks	122	7
Aggregate Land Division	22	5
Pounds	120	36
Unenclosed	31	3
Unknown	4	0

Appendix R: Frequencies of Excavated Buildings with Different Features at various Elevations

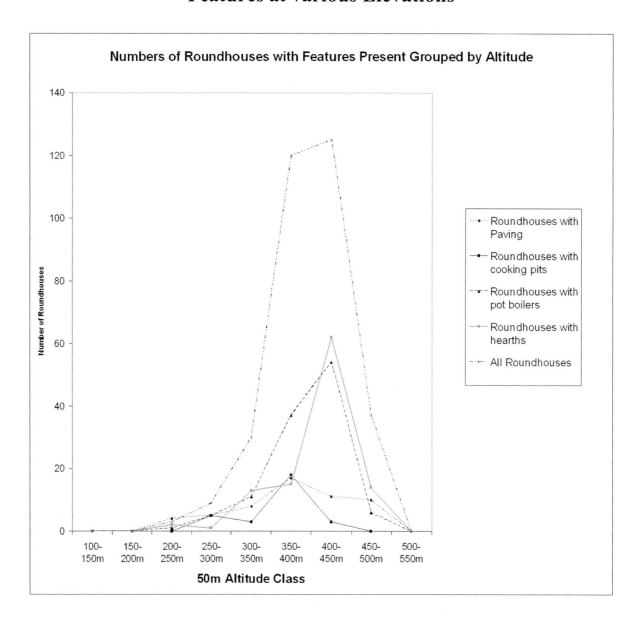

Appendix S: Cumulative Frequency Graphs Comparing the Numbers of Buildings at a range of Distances from Boundaries with Nine Random Simulations.

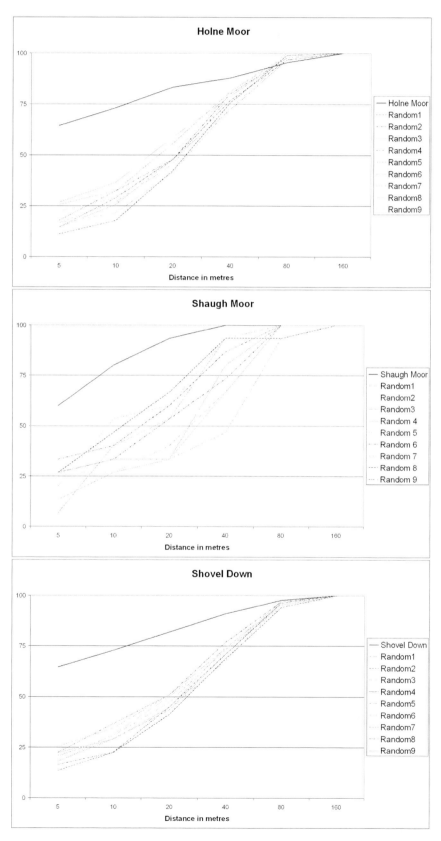

Appendix T: Database of Metalwork for Dartmoor and its Surrounding Area

Early Bronze Age

LOCATION	CONTEXT	TYPOLOGICAL INFORMATION	NUMBER	OBJECT
Near Corringdon Ball	old lane	Low Flanged Axe	single	Axe
Fernworthy	cairn	Harlyn Knife Dagger	single	Dagger
Hameldown	cairn	Camerton Dagger	with EBA pommel	Dagger
Heatree	settlement	Dagger	single	Dagger
Lustleigh	cist	Dagger	with blue beads	Dagger
Moor Barton	cist	Dagger	with blue beads	Dagger
Drewsteignton	unknown	Migdale Flat axe (unfinished)	single	Axe
Fingle Bridge	cist	Daggers	multiple	Dagger
Lannacombe	Estuary	Low Flanged Axe	single	Axe
Ipplepen	unknown	Thin-butted Flat Axe	single	Axe
Hameldown	cairn	Amber Pommel	with later Dagger	Amber Pommel
Red Barrows	cairn	Bronze fragments	single	Bronze fragments

Middle Bronze Age

LOCATION	CONTEXT	TYPOLOGICAL INFORMATION	NUMBER	OBJECT
Plymstock	under rock	Arreton Flanged Axe	multiple 1	Axe
Yealm Bridge	unknown	Early Shield Pattern Palstave	single	Palstave
Fices Well	unknown	Triple Arris Rapier	single	Rapier
Broadall Head	peat cutting	Flat Rib Rapier	single	Rapier
Dean Moor	settlement	Tin Ore	single	Tin Ore
Yarde Farm	unknown	Low Flanged Palstave	single	Palstave
Oxenham	unknown	Palstave	single	Palstave
Ashburton	unknown	High Flanged Palstave	single	Palstave
Horridge Common	field	Imported Palstave	single	Palstave
Near Ashburton	unknown	SW looped palstave	single	Palstave
New Quarry	Quarry	Early Plain Palstave	double 1	Palstave
Quintertown Quarry	Quarry	Crediton Palstave	double 1	Palstave
Chagford	unknown	Double looped palstave	single	Palstave
Chagford	unknown	Crediton Palstave	single	Palstave
Week, N. Bovey	old hedge bank	Crediton Palstave	double 1	Palstave
Moretonhampstead	unknown	High Flanged Palstave	single	Palstave
Moretonhampstead	unknown	Low Flanged Unlooped Palstave	single	Palstave
Lustleigh	unknown	Palstave	single	Palstave
Drewsteignton	unknown	Early Plain Palstave	single	Palstave
Honeyford	unknown	Rapier	single	Rapier
Plumley	under rock	Hi flanged looped palstave	multiple 1	Palstave
Heathfield	unknown	Taunton-Penard Socketed Tool	single	Tool
Bovey Tracey	unknown	Low Flanged Palstave	single	Palstave

Heathfield	unknown	Palstave	single	Palstave
Chudleigh Knighton	field	Rapier Moulds	multiple	Rapier Moulds
Bridford	unknown	Hi flanged looped palstave	single	Palstave
Scatter Rock Quarry	quarry	High Flanged Palstave	double 1	Palstave
Torr Lane, Plymouth	old hedge bank	Palstave	multiple 1	Palstave
Brixham	unknown	Early shield pattern palstave	single	Palstave
Teignmouth	unknown	Flanged Axe	single	Axe
Dawlish	unknown	Early shield pattern palstave	single	Palstave
Dawlish	unknown	Crediton Palstave	single	Palstave
New Quarry	unknown	Crediton Palstave	double 2	Palstave
Plymstock	under rock	Arreton Flanged Axe	multiple 2	Axe
Plymstock	under rock	Arreton Flanged Axe	multiple 3	Axe
Plymstock	under rock	Arreton Flanged Axe	multiple 4	Axe
Plymstock	under rock	Arreton Flanged Axe	multiple 5	Axe
Plymstock	under rock	Arreton Flanged Axe	multiple 6	Axe
Plymstock	under rock	Arreton Flanged Axe	multiple 7	Axe
Plymstock	under rock	Arreton Flanged Axe	multiple 8	Axe
Plymstock	under rock	Arreton Flanged Axe	multiple 9	Axe
Plymstock	under rock	Arreton Flanged Axe	multiple 10	Axe
Plymstock	under rock	Arreton Flanged Axe	multiple 11	Axe
Plymstock	under rock	Arreton Flanged Axe	multiple 12	Axe
Plymstock	under rock	Arreton Flanged Axe	multiple 13	Axe
Plymstock	under rock	Arreton Flanged Axe	multiple 14	Axe
Plymstock	under rock	Arreton Flanged Axe	multiple 15	Axe
Plymstock	under rock	Arreton Flanged Axe	multiple 16	Axe
Quintertown Quarry	Quarry	Low Flanged Palstave	double 2	Palstave
Plumley	under rock	Hi flanged looped palstave	multiple 2	Palstave
Week, N. Bovey	old hedge bank	Hi flanged looped palstave	double 2	Palstave
Scatter Rock Quarry	quarry	SW looped palstave	double 2	Palstave
Plumley	under rock	Low flanged looped palstave	multiple 3	Palstave
Torr Lane, Plymouth	old hedge bank	Palstave	multiple 2	Palstave
Plymstock	under rock	Tanged Spearhead	multiple 17	Spearhead
Torr Lane, Plymouth	old hedge bank	Rapier	multiple 3	Rapier
Torr Lane, Plymouth	old hedge bank	Rapier	multiple 4	Rapier
Torr Lane, Plymouth	old hedge bank	Rapier	multiple 5	Rapier
Plymstock	under rock	Plymstock Tanged Chisel	multiple 17	Chisel
Torr Lane, Plymouth	old hedge bank	Taunton-Penard Socketed Tool	multiple 6	Tool
Salcombe Moorsands	wreck	Sword	multiple 1	Sword
Pinhoe	unknown	Palstave	multiple 1	Palstave
Salcombe Moorsands	wreck	Palstave	multiple 3	Palstave
Salcombe Moorsands	wreck	gold bracelet	multiple 4	Gold Bracelet
Salcombe Moorsands	wreck	chisel	multiple 5	Chisel
Salcombe Moorsands	wreck	Sword hilt	multiple 2	Sword
Pinhoe	unknown	Palstave	multiple 2	Palstave

Pinhoe	unknown	Palstave	multiple 3	Palstave
Pinhoe	unknown	Bronze Armlet	multiple 4	Bronze Armlet
Pinhoe	unknown	Bronze Armlet	multiple 5	Bronze Armlet
Pinhoe	unknown	Bronze Armlet	multiple 6	Bronze Armlet
Pinhoe	unknown	Bronze Armlet	multiple 7	Bronze Armlet
Pinhoe	unknown	Bronze Armlet	multiple 8	Bronze Armlet
Pinhoe	unknown	Bronze Armlet	multiple 9	Bronze Armlet
Pinhoe	unknown	Bronze Armlet	multiple 10	Bronze Armlet
Pinhoe	unknown	Bronze Armlet	multiple 11	Bronze Armlet

Late Bronze Age

LOCATION	CONTEXT	TYPOLOGICAL INFORMATION	NUMBER	OBJECT
Near Tavistock	unknown	Stogursey Socketed Axe	single	Axe
Gawler Bottom	peat cutting	Spear Ferrule	single	Spear Ferrule
Hazard Hill	Neolithic hilltop settlement	Late Pegged Spearhead	single	Spearhead
Bloody Pool	pool	Late Pegged Spearhead	multiple 1	Spearhead
Haytor	unknown	Amorican Socketed Axe	single	Axe
Haytor	unknown	British Type Socketed knife	single	Knife
Near Chagford	unknown	Late Pegged Spearhead	multiple 1	Spearhead
Bovey Tracey	garden	Faceted Socketed Axe	with stone axe	Axe
Bovey Tracey	unknown	Stogursey Socketed Axe	single	Axe
bank of River Teign	River bank	Lozenge sectioned spearhead	with wooden idol	Spearhead
Place, Chudleigh	unknown	Socketed Axe	double 1	Axe
Trendlebere Camp	Hillfort	Faceted Socketed Axe	multiple 1	Axe
Near Plymouth	unknown	SE Socketed Axe	unknown	Axe
Off Plymouth	unknown	Socketed Axe	unknown	Axe
Mountbatten	settlement	Linear Faceted Socketed Axe	multiple 1	Axe
Churston Court Farm	excavation	Ingot fragment	multiple 1	Ingot fragment
Churston Ferrers	excavation	Ingot fragment	multiple 2	Ingot fragment
Kents Cavern	cave	Socketed Axe	multiple 1	Axe
Totnes Area	unknown	SE Socketed Axe	single	Axe
East Hillerton Farm	unknown	Stogursey Socketed Axe	single	Axe
Stoneycombe Quarry	settlement	Mould Fragments	multiple	Mould Fragments
Stoneycombe Quarry	settlement	Faceted Socketed Axe	single	Axe
Kingsland, Torquay	unknown	Basel looped spearhead	single	Spearhead
Mountbatten	settlement	Amorican Socketed Axe	multiple 2	Axe
Mountbatten	settlement	Amorican Socketed Axe	multiple 3	Axe
Mountbatten	settlement	Socketed Axe Fragment	multiple 4	Axe
Kents Cavern	cave	Socketed Axe	multiple 2	Axe

Alphington	unknown	Late Pegged Spearhead	single	Spearhead
Near Chagford	unknown	Late Pegged Spearhead	multiple 2	Spearhead
Bloody Pool	pool	Barbed Spearhead	multiple 2	Spearhead
Bloody Pool	pool	Barbed Spearhead	multiple 3	Spearhead
Bloody Pool	pool	Barbed Spearhead	multiple 4	Spearhead
Bloody Pool	pool	Spear Ferrule	multiple 5	Spear Ferrule
Bloody Pool	pool	Spear Ferrule	multiple 6	Spear Ferrule
Bloody Pool	pool	Spear Ferrule	multiple 7	Spear Ferrule
Mountbatten	settlement	Elaborated Chisel	multiple 5	Chisel
Mountbatten	settlement	Taunton-Penard Socketed Tool	multiple 6	Tool
Mountbatten	settlement	Socketed Gouge	multiple 7	Gouge
Mountbatten	settlement	Socketed Gouge	multiple 8	Gouge
Kents Cavern	cave	Socketed Gouge	multiple 3	Gouge
Mountbatten	settlement	Tanged Knife	multiple 9	Knife
Mountbatten	settlement	British Type Socketed knife	multiple 10	Knife
Mountbatten	settlement	British Type Socketed knife	multiple 11	Knife
Mountbatten	settlement	British Type Socketed knife	multiple 12	Knife
Kents Cavern	cave	British Type Socketed knife	multiple 4	Knife
Mountbatten	settlement	Tanged Sickle	multiple 13	Sickle
Kents Cavern	cave	Swans Necked Pin	multiple 5	Pin
Kents Cavern	cave	Coiled Finger Ring	multiple 6	Ring
Kents Cavern	cave	Finger Ring	multiple 7	Ring
Kents Cavern	cave	Finger Ring	multiple 8	Ring
Kents Cavern	cave	Finger Ring	multiple 9	Ring
Mountbatten	settlement	Penannular D section Torc	multiple 14	Torc
Mountbatten	settlement	Vessel Fragment	multiple 15	Vessel
Mountbatten	settlement	Vessel Fragment	multiple 16	Vessel
Mountbatten	settlement	Vessel Fragment	multiple 17	Vessel
Mountbatten	settlement	Cast Vessel	multiple 18	Vessel
Mountbatten	settlement	Vessel Fitting	multiple 19	Vessel
Kents Cavern	cave	Ingot Fragments	multiple 10	Ingot Fragments
Mountbatten	settlement	Bronze Cake Fragments	multiple 20	Bronze Cake Fragment
Place, Chudleigh	unknown	Socketed Axe	double 2	Axe
Colaton Raleigh	pit	Gold clipping	multiple 1	Gold clipping
Colaton Raleigh	pit	Gold bracelet	multiple 1	bracelet
Colaton Raleigh	pit	Gold bracelet	multiple 1	bracelet
Colaton Raleigh	pit	Gold bracelet	multiple 1	bracelet

Appendix U: Metalwork Findspots in North East Dartmoor

An important cluster of findspots is found in North East Dartmoor (see below). This area comprises the largest cluster of Middle Bronze Age metalwork in the south-west. An interesting tendency seen this region is the pairing of 'sets' of palstaves at deposition. Chapman has discussed 'sets' as groupings which can easily be fragmented (Chapman, 2000). Evidence for this is recorded in the Plumley Hoard where palstaves were paired in two sets of four (Pearce, 1983: 433). The double finds of paired palstaves, and mostly consist of a distinctive local type - the Crediton Palstave - paired with a palstave of another type. For example, at Quintertown Quarry one Crediton Palstave is accompanied by one

Low Flanged Looped Palstave, at Week one Crediton Palstave is accompanied by one High Flanged Looped Palstave, at New Quarry one Crediton Palstave is accompanied by one Early Plain Palstave (Pearce, 1983: 433-452); and at Scatter Rock Quarry, two palstaves of two different types were found - a South Western Looped Palstave and a High Flanged Palstave. This interesting pattern suggests that construction of sets in this area, but the records of recovery of for these finds are poor (several are from nineteenth century quarrying) and this means the exact circumstances of recovery are difficult to reconstruct.

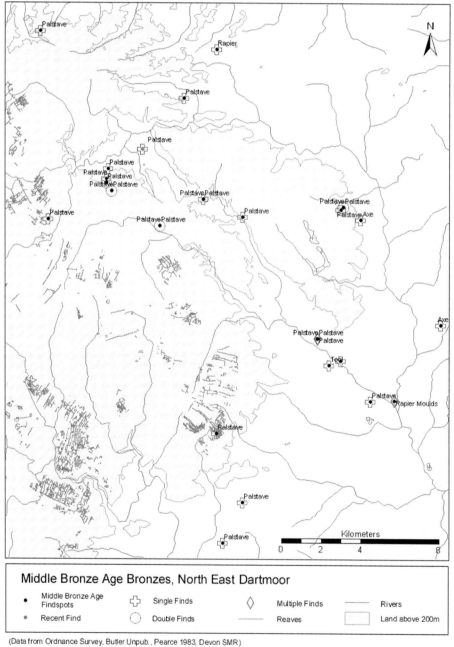

Middle Bronze Age Bronzes, North East Dartmoor

- Middle Bronze Age Findspots
- Recent Find

✛ Single Finds
◯ Double Finds

◇ Multiple Finds
—— Reaves

—— Rivers
▢ Land above 200m

(Data from Ordnance Survey, Butler Unpub., Pearce 1983, Devon SMR)

Note: The recent finds of an additional palstave and a 'formless blob' of bronze have been reported to me by a local metal detectorist (Mr John Smith pers. com) the location has been added to the map

Appendix V: Pacing Experiments

Today British prehistorians point out that the size of the megalithic yard (2.72 ft or 0.83m) is around that of the average pace, and suggest that Thom's megalithic yard is 'actually a megalithic pace' Bradley, 1984: 77, Pitts, 2001: 228). Implicitly pacing is seen as more 'natural', less 'scientific' alternative to Thom's whalebone rod; hence one that is less 'calculating' and tolerant of a greater degree of error. Thus Pitts suggests that an 'unconscious pace' may have been used in the laying out of stone circles (Pitts, 2001: 230). In an attempt to determine the degree the amounts of error that are found in paced measurements a number of experiments were carried out. The first experiment involved 100 students and staff of UCL. Participants were asked to pace two distances of the same length, each of 30 paces. The actual lengths of the journeys were then measured and recorded using a tape measure. The results showed that many staff and students of UCL were frankly useless at this task (see below). The differences between the lengths, expressed as a percentage of the lengths had a mean error of 12%.

Comparing the differences between journeys with the differences between widths laid out in the field systems of similar lengths shows that the laying-out of axial reaves was often a good deal better then the accuracy of the UCL pacers. As a result of this experiment it became obvious that people who had experience of pacing in

basic surveying were better at reproducing similar lengths. I therefore decided to take two friends who had some experience of pacing in their work, and the three of us paced 60 journeys of 80 paces each. We found that were each as capable at this task to the degree with which we had been required to use it in our working lives; my friends were able to reproduce similar lengths with a mean error of only 6.0% and 7.4% - my error was a not very impressive 11.6%. The errors introduced by good pacing are around the same as are found where similar lengths are adjacent to one another in the field systems.

Neither of these experiments is really representative of the precision obtained by experienced pacers. Good pacing is far too accurate to be distinguished statistically from a unit of measurement at most prehistoric sites (Kendall, 1974: 258). If pacing of this sort was a habitual aspect of prehistoric surveying it should have shown up as a consistent quantum around 0.8m in the metrological analyses presented in chapter 5. Whether pacing was used on a more ad hoc basis for reproducing widths where reaves are not intervisible depends on what 'pacing' is taken to be. It seems difficult to exclude the possibility that an 'unconscious pace' might have entered into the laying out of reaves - although it is difficult to envisage exactly what such a phenomenon would be.

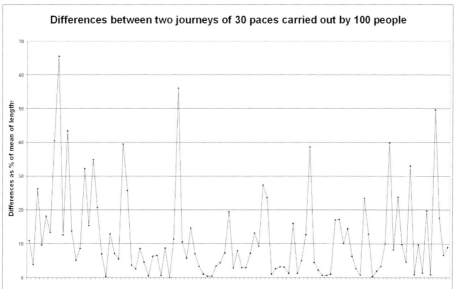

Location	Widths in metres	Differences between widths as a percentage of the average of the widths
Windtor, three adjacent strips	40.5m, 38.5m, 38.4m	5.6%
Throwleigh Common, subdivision	38.6m, 37.4m	2.9%
Kestor, subdivision	42.6m, 40.8m	4.4%
Shaugh Moor subdivision	33.8m, 31.1m	8.4%
Shaugh Moor, subdivision into two strips	64.9m, 70.4m	8.0%
Horridge Common, three adjacent strips	77.9m, 79.9m, 82.2m	4.3%
Kestor, three adjacent strips	82.3m, 83.5m, 87.7m	5.4%

Appendix W: Metrological Analysis Using Kendall's Formulation. Cosine Quantograms for Eight Sample Coaxial Landscapes

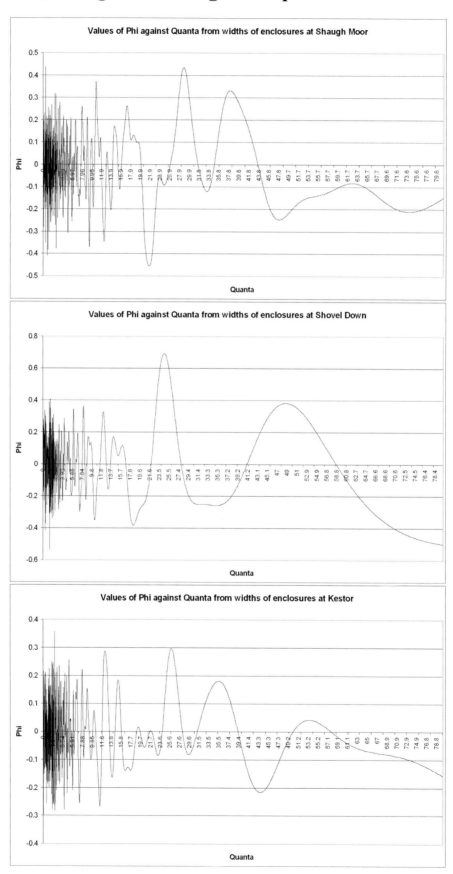

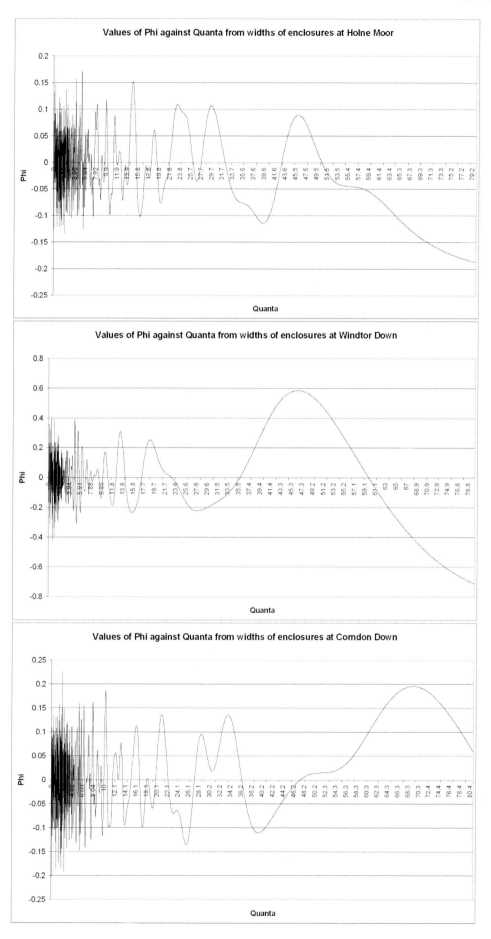

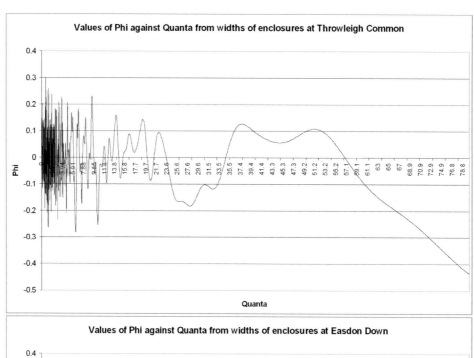

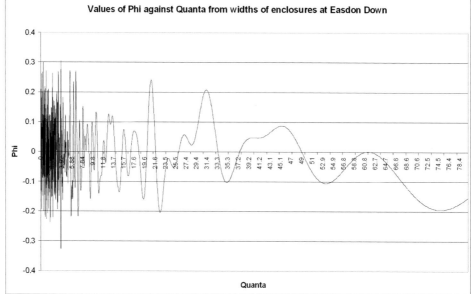

Appendix X: Coaxial Pattern at Kestor South

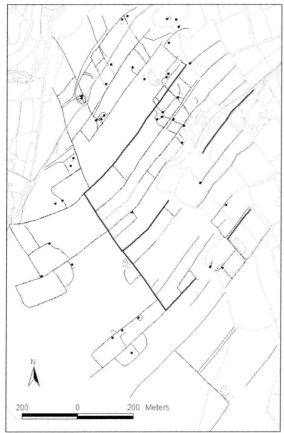

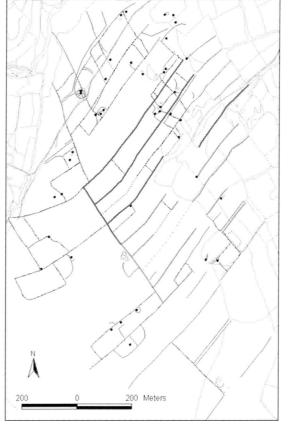

Northernmost half at terminal reave = 253.5m
Southernmost half at terminal reave = 266.9m

Red strips: standard deviation at terminal reave = 2.333
Green strips: standard deviation at terminal reave = 3.154

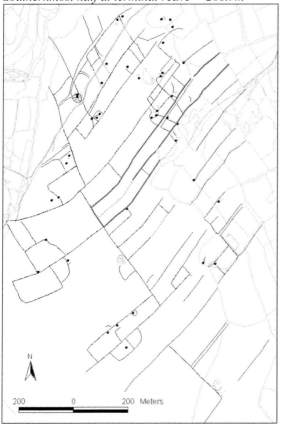

Exact Widths Unknown (poor preservation)

Appendix Y: Coaxial Pattern at Halsanger and Horridge Commons

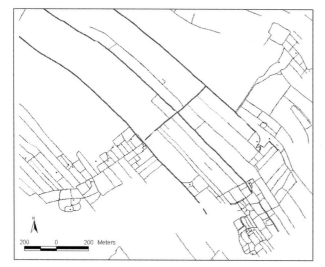

Subdivision of Block on Halsanger and Horridge Commons (prehistoric and fossilised reaves)

Half 1 = 282.6m
Half 2 = 242.5m

Subdivision and repetition of widths - exact widths unknown due to poor preservation of reaves.

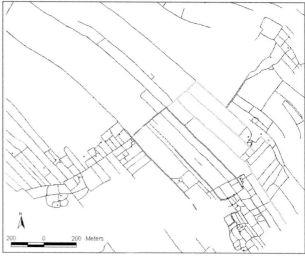

Appendix Z: Potential for Further Work on Partially Excavated Buildings

Deposits beneath the level of the 'calm'

The prehistoric floors of the buildings appear to have been the chief object of the search, and it is thus unlikely that excavation continued much below this level. For example at Grimspound hut iii was reconstructed and left "with the floor exposed" and with an iron rail around it "for its protection against cattle" (Baring Gould et al 1984: 119). This suggests that the floors of some buildings were not comprehensively destroyed and there is potential that some archaeological material still exists at these sites that may have been missed by the original excavators.

Fills of features that have been incompletely excavated

There is also potential that some features may have been incompletely excavated. At Grimspound, for example, a visit by the Devon Association caused the excavators to return to the site and re-excavate the cooking hole in hut 19. This feature was "cleared out more thoroughly than it had been before, and adhering to the side was found a piece of pottery..." (Baring Gould et al 1896: 192). It may be that there are other examples of features that still contain remnants of prehistoric material, including

charcoal to which a range of modern techniques, including AMS dating might be applied.

Deposits beneath stones that were not removed and beneath walls

Following these imperatives, early excavators on Dartmoor did not remove in situ wall material. Only at Metherel, where the buildings were to be submerged beneath a reservoir did Worth section a wall (Worth 1935: 122). It is therefore reasonably certain that archaeological deposits beneath walls, and perhaps beneath internal stone built features are largely intact and may have potential for future study. Very large stones were left in situ at some sites (eg Halsanger Common (Baring Gould et al 1897: 156 see table below) and prehistoric buried soils may be preserved beneath these stones.

Buildings which were never totally excavated

Several trenches were abandoned unfinished because the excavators felt they were unproductive. It is possible that these buildings still contain untouched deposits. A list of buildings that may still contain material is given in the table below.

Site and References	Records
Tavy Cleave (Baring Gould 1894)	"Of the huts themselves I was able to examine but four, and of these only one exhaustively." (ibid: 198)
"Hut circles in and about the rifle range, between the main road at Devil's Gully, near Princetown and Har Tor" (Baring Gould et al 1896)	No. 2 "... only partially explored, for no trace of charcoal was found, and it did not seem to have been a human habitation" (ibid: 189) No. 11 "This hut was not thoroughly explored" (ibid: 190). No. 13 "No traces of charcoal having been found, it was abandoned" (ibid: 190).
Foales Arrishes (also known as Torr Town or Tor Hill) (Baring Gould et al 1897)	No 1 "... about one third was laid bare, together with patches on the eastern and south-eastern sides" (ibid: 152)
Halsanger Common (Baring Gould et al 1897)	In the first circle to be examined a very large stone was found that had fallen inwards and was "too heavy to move without levers, which were not at the time available" (ibid: 156). Deposits should still be sealed beneath this stone.
Smallacombe Rocks (Baring Gould et al 1897)	Hut circle No 4: "As the summer work of the Committee was now terminating, the further exploration of this hut was suspended" (ibid: 159). There is no mention of a return to Smallacombe Rocks in any subsequent reports; the roundhouse may have been left incompletely excavated.
Hemstone rocks (Anderson et al 1901)	"One at Hemstone Rocks was explored, and trial pits were dug in others, with the result that some charcoal only was discovered. A thunderstorm on July 16th, 1900, drove the explorers off the ground" (ibid: 135).

"between Devil's Gully and the Princetown railway" (Hart Tor) (Anderson et al 1901)	"It was found that these huts had been much pulled about by stone-cutters, and their further examination was abandoned" (ibid: 135).
Watern Oke (Anderson et al 1906)	94 buildings were excavated here, but some were left unexcavated: Hut circle 3a: "Unexplored … did not look worth trying. It was left till the last, and then overlooked" (ibid: 103). Hut circle 27c: "… being somewhat covered with heather, it was overlooked and not excavated." (ibid: 107). "A hut circle is marked on the Ordnance Map NE by N of the top of Fur Tor at a distance on plan of about 800 yards. We located this and marked it for excavation, but were unable to carry out our intention, though we attempted to do so" (ibid: 113).
Riders Rings Harris et al., 1935	Building/enclosure Y: "A trench cut across the court marked "Y" on Fig 2 revealed nothing but undisturbed natural ground". Hut No 3: "A small area … was excavated, sufficient only to uncover a patch of the floor. It was hoped that the fireplace might be found, but, failing this, the excavation was abandoned since piecemeal excavations are not to be encouraged" (ibid: 119).
Challacombe (Shorter 1938)	"… inclement weather curtailed the programme … and it proved possible to work on only thirteen days. The project for 1939 had to be abandoned because of the imminence of war … In all, one half of the hut was cleared…" (ibid: 104-5).
Heatree (excavated 1968) (Quinnell, 1991)	"In Hut 4 (a dubious site) a single trench was cut downhill. All rubble was removed from the interiors of two further hut circles in the enclosure… E1 and E2, exposing possible floor levels, which were not investigated further; the only drawn records are simple cross sections" (ibid: 2).

Bibliography

Abramson, A. (2000). Mythical land, legal boundaries: Wondering about landscape and other tracts. In *Land, Law and Environment: Mythical land, legal boundaries*, eds. Abramson, A. & Theodossopoulos, D., pp. 1-30. London, Sterling, Virginia: Pluto Press.

Abu-Rabia, A. (1994). *The Negev Bedouin and Livestock rearing: Social, economic and political aspects.* Oxford: Berg

Adams, W.M. & Mortimore, M.J. (1997). Agricultural intensification and flexibility in the Nigerian Sahel. *The Geographical Journal 163*, 150-160.

Adkins, L. (2005). The New Economy, Property and Personhood. *Theory, Culture and Society 22*, 111-130.

Adler, M.A. (1996). Land tenure, Archaeology, and the Ancestral Pueblo Social Landscape. *Journal of Anthropological Archaeology 15*, 337-371.

Agarwal, B. (1994). *A field of one's own: Gender and land rights in South Asia.* Cambridge: CUP.

Alcorn, S. & Solarz, B. (2006). The Autistic Economist. *Yale Economic Review*

Alexander, C. (2001). Legal and Binding; Time, change and long-term transactions. *Journal of the Royal Anthropological Institute (New Series) 7*, 467-485.

Alexander, C. (2004). Value, Relations, and Changing Bodies: Privatisation and property rights in Kazakhstan. In *Property in Question: Value Transformation in the Global Economy*, eds. Verdery, K. & Humphrey, C., pp. 251-274. Oxford: Berg.

Allen, C. (1982). *A Mountain in Tibet.* Futura / Andre Deutsh.

Allen, M.J. (1997). Environment and Land-use: The economic development of the communities who built Stonehenge (an economy to support the stones). In *Science and Stonehenge: Proceedings of the British Academy 92*, eds. Cunliffe, B. & Renfrew, C., Oxford: Oxford University Press.

Amery, J.S., Anderson, I.K., Burnard, R., Baring-Gould, S., Pode, J.D., Brooking-Rowe, J., Thomson, B. & Hansford Worth, R. (1906). Eleventh report of the Dartmoor Exploration Committee. Hut circle settlement at Watern Oke, explored July, 1905. Buried hut circle or barrow at 'The Croft', Peter Tavy. *Report and Transactions of the Devonshire Association for the Advancement of Science 38*, 101-113.

Amesbury, M., Charman, D.J., Fyfe, R. & Langdon, P. (2005). *Upland settlement in southwest England: Testing the climate change hypothesis.* Unpub. Manuscript

Anderson, B. (1983). *Imagined Communities: Reflections on the origins and spread of Nationalism.* London: Verso.

Anderson, D.G. (1998). Property as a way of knowing on Evenki lands in Arctic Siberia. In *Property Relations: Renewing the anthropological tradition*, ed. Hann, C.M., pp. 64-84. Cambridge: CUP.

Anderson, D.G. (2000). *Identity and Ecology in Artic Siberia: The Number One Reindeer Brigade.* Oxford: Oxford University Press.

Anderson, R.I.K., Burnard, R., Baring-Gould, S., Pode, J.D., Brooking-Rowe, J. & Worth, R.H. (1902). Eighth Report of the Dartmoor Exploration Committee. *Report and Transactions of the Devonshire Association for the Advancement of Science XXXIV*, 160-165.

Anderson, R.I.K., Burnard, R., Baring-Gould, S., Pode, J.D., Brooking-Rowe, J. & Worth, R.H. (1903). Ninth Report of the Dartmoor Exploration Committee. *Report and Transactions of the Devonshire Association for the Advancement of Science XXXV*, 143-145.

Appadurai, A. (1988). Putting Hierarchy in its Place. *Current Anthropology 3*, 36-49.

Appadurai, A. (2005). Commodities and the Politics of Value. In *Rethinking Commodification: Cases and readings in Law and Culture*, eds. Ertman, M.M. & Williams, J.C., pp. 34-45. New York: New York University Press.

Arnsperger, C. & Varoufakis, Y. (2006). What is Neoclassical Economics? *Post-Autistic Economics Review 38*, 1-10.

Austin, R. (2005). Kwanzaa and the Commodification of Black Culture. In *Rethinking Commodification: Cases and Readings in Law and Culture*, eds. Ertman, M.M. & Williams, J.C., pp. 178-190. New York and London: New York University Press.

Axelrod, R. (1980a). Effective Choice in the Prisoner's Dilemma. *Journal of Conflict Resolution 24*, 3-25.

Axelrod, R. (1980b). More Effective Choice in the Prisoner's Dilemma. *The Journal of Conflict Resolution 24*, 379-403.

Bailey, D.W., Gross, J.E., Laca, E.A., Rittenhouse, L.R., Coughenour, M.B., Swift, D.M. & Sims, P.L. (1996). Mechanisms that result in large herbivore grazing distribution patterns. *Journal of Range Management 49*, 386-400.

Balaam, N.D. (1982). Soil Pollen Analyses. *Proceedings of the Prehistoric Society 48*, 203-278.

Balaam, N.D., Smith, K. & Wainwright, G.J. (1982). The Shaugh Moor Project: Fourth Report - Environment, context and conclusion. *Proceedings of the Prehistoric Society 48*, 203-278.

Barber, J. (1997). *The Archaeological Investigation of a Prehistoric Landscape: Excavations on Arran, 1978 - 1981*. Edinburgh: The Scottish Trust for Archaeological Research.

Barber, M. (2003). *Bronze and the Bronze Age; metalwork and society in Britain c2500 - 800 BC*. Stroud: Tempus.

Barger, E. (1938). The present position of studies in English field-systems. *The English Historical Review 53*, 385-411.

Baring-Gould, S., Burnard, R., Brooking-Rowe, J., Pode, J.D. & Worth, R.H. (1896). Third Report of the Dartmoor Exploration Committee. *Report and Transactions of the Devonshire Association for the Advancement of Science 28*, 174-199.

Baring-Gould, S., Burnard, R., Brooking-Rowe, J., Pode, J.D. & Worth, R.H. (1897). Fourth Report of the Dartmoor Exploration Committee. *Report and Transactions of the Devonshire Association for the Advancement of Science 29*, 145-165.

Baring-Gould, S., Burnard, R., Brooking-Rowe, J., Pode, J.D. & Worth, R.H. (1898). Fifth Report of the Dartmoor Exploration Committee. *Report and Transactions of the Devonshire Association for the Advancement of Science XXX*, 97-115.

Baring-Gould, S., Burnard, R., Brooking-Rowe, J., Pode, J.D. & Worth, R.H. (1899). Sixth Report of the Dartmoor Exploration Committee. *Report and Transactions of the Devonshire Association for the Advancement of Science XXXI*, 146-155.

Baring-Gould, S., Burnard, R., Worth, R.N., Brooking-Rowe, J., Pode, J.D. & Berry, G.B. (1895). Second Report of the Dartmoor Exploration Committee. *Report and Transactions of the Devonshire Association for the Advancement of Science XXVII*, 81-92.

Baring-Gould, S., Burnard, R., Worth, R.N., Gordon Gray, W.A. & Worth, R.H. (1894). The Exploration of Grimspound: First report of the Dartmoor Exploration Committee. *Report and Transactions of the Devonshire Association for the Advancement of Science XXVI*, 101-121.

Barnatt, J. (1989). *Stone circles of Britain: Taxonomic and distributional analyses and a catalogue of sites in England, Scotland and Wales. B.A.R. British Series 215*. Oxford: Archaeopress.

Barnatt, J. (1998). Monuments in the landscape: Thoughts from the Peak. In *Essays in Honour of Aubrey Burl: Prehistoric ritual and religion*, eds. Gibson, A. & Simpson, D., pp. 92-107. Stroud: Sutton.

Barnatt, J. (1999). Taming the Land: Peak District farming and ritual in the Bronze Age. *Derbyshire Archaeological Journal 119*,

Barnatt, J. (2000). To each their own: Later prehistoric farming communities and their monuments on the Peak. *Derbyshire Archaeological Journal 120*,

Barrett, J.C. (1990). The monumentality of death: The character of Early Bronze Age mortuary mounds in southern Britain. *World Archaeology 22*, 179-189.

Barrett, J.C. (1994). *Fragments from Antiquity: An archaeology of social life in Britain, 2900-1200 BC*. Oxford: Blackwell.

Barrett, J.C. (1999). Rethinking the Bronze Age Environment. *Quarternary Proceedings 7*, 493-500.

Barrett, J.C., Bradley, R. & Green, M. (1991). *Landscape, Monuments and Society. The prehistory of Cranbourne Chase*. Cambridge: Cambridge University Press.

Barth, F. (1969). Introduction. In *Ethnic Groups and Boundaries; The social organisation of cultural difference*, ed. Barth, F., pp. 9-38. London: Allen and Unwin.

Barth, F. (2000). Boundaries and Connections. In *Signifying Identities: Anthropological perspectives on boundaries and contested values*, ed. Cohen, A., pp. 17-36. London and New York: Routledge.

Baxandall, M. (1972). *Painting and Experience in Fifteenth Century Italy: A primer in the social history of pictorial style*. Oxford: Oxford University Press.

Baxter, M. (2003). *Statistics in Archaeology*. London: Hodder Arnold.

Bayliss-Smith, T. (1999). Comments. *Current Anthropology 40*, 323-324.

Beeson, M. & Greeves, T. (1993). The image of Dartmoor. *Transactions of the Devonshire Association for the Advancement of Science 125*, 127-154.

Belk, R.W. (1988). Possessions and the Extended Self. *The Journal of Consumer Research 15*, 139-168.

Bell, D. (1998). The social relations of property and efficiency. In *Property in Economic Context. Monographs in Economic Anthropology, No. 14.*, eds. Hunt, R.C. & Gilman, A., pp. 29-46. Lanham, New York, Oxford: University Press of America.

Bender, B. (1986). *The Archaeology of Britany, Normandy and the Channel Islands: An Introduction and Guide*. London and Boston: Faber and Faber.

Bender, B. (1993). Landscape - Meaning and Action. In *Landscape: Politics and perspectives*, ed. Bender, B., pp. 1-17. Oxford: Berg.

Benkler, Y. (2004). Sharing Nicely: On Sharable Goods and the emergence of sharing as a modality of economic production. *Yale Law Journal 114*, 273-358.

Bentley, R.A., Lake, M.W. & Shennan, S. (2005). Specialisation and wealth inequality in a model of a clustered economic network. *Journal of Archaeological Science 32*, 1346-1356.

Bentley, R.A. & Maschner, H.D.G. (2003). *Complex Systems and Archaeology: Empirical and Theoretical Applications*. Salt Lake City: University of Utah Press.

Berkes, F., Feeny, D., McCay, B.J. & Acheson, J.M. (1989). The benefits of the commons. *Nature 340*, 91-93.

Bishop, A.J. (1995). Western Mathematics: The secret weapon of cultural imperialism. In *The Post-Colonial Studies Reader*, eds. Ashcroft, B., Griffiths, G. & Tiffin, H., pp. 71-75. London and New York: Routledge.

Bohannan, P. (1963). 'Land', 'tenure' and land-tenure. In *African Agarian Systems: Studies presented and discussed at the Second International African Seminar, Lovanium University, Leopoldville, January 1960*, ed. Biebuyck, D., pp. 101-111. Oxford: OUP.

Boserup, E. (1965). *The Conditions of Agricultural Growth: The economics of agrarian change under population pressure*. London: Earthscan.

Bouquet, M. (1996). Family Trees and their affinities: The visual imperative of the genealogical diagram. *Journal of the Royal Anthropological Institute (New Series) 2*, 43-66.

Bourdieu, P. (1977). *Outline of a Theory of Practice*. Cambridge: Cambridge University Press.

Bowen, H.C. (1961). *Ancient Fields: A tentative analysis of vanishing earthworks and landscape*. London: The British Association for the Advancement of Science.

Bowen, H.C. (1975). Pattern and interpretation: a view of the Wessex landscape from Neolithic to Roman times. In *Recent Work in Rural Archaeology.*, ed. Fowler, P.J., pp. 44-56. Bradford-on-Avon: Monnraker Press.

Bradley, R. (1977). Prehistoric field systems in Britain and north-west Europe - a review of some recent work. *World Archaeology 9*, 265-280.

Bradley, R. (1984). *The Social Foundations of Prehistoric Britain*. London: Longman.

Bradley, R. (1998a). *The Passage of Arms: An archaeological analysis of prehistoric hoard and votive deposits, Second Edition*. Oxford and Oakville: Oxbow Books.

Bradley, R. (1998b). *The significance of monuments: On the shaping of human experience in Neolithic and Bronze Age Europe*. London: Routledge.

Bradley, R. (2000). *An Archaeology of Natural Places*. London and New York: Routledge.

Bradley, R. (2002). *The Past in Prehistoric Societies*. London: Routledge.

Bradley, R. (2005). *Ritual and Domestic life in Prehistoric Europe*. London and New York: Routledge.

Bradley, R., Entwistle, R. & Raymond, F. (1994). *Prehistoric Land Divisions on Salisbury Plain: The work of the Wessex Linear Ditches Project*. London: English Heritage.

Bradley, R. & Sheridan, A. (2004). Croft Moraig and the chronology of stone circles. *Paper given at Bronze Age Forum*

Bradshaw, M. & Williams, S. (1999). Scales, Lines and Minor Geographies: Whither King Island? *Australian Geographical Studies 37*, 248-267.

Bradstock, A. (2000). *Winstanley and the Diggers, 1649-1999*. Frank Cass: London and Portland, Oregon.

Braidotti, R. (2003). Becoming Woman: or Sexual Difference Revisited. *Theory, Culture and Society 20*, 43-64.

Brailsford, J.W. (1938). Bronze Age stone monuments of Dartmoor. *Antiquity 12*, 444-463.

Brennand, M. & Taylor, M. (2003). The survey and excavation of a Bronze Age timber circle at Holme-next-the-Sea, Norfolk, 1998-9. *Proceedings of the Prehistoric Society 69*, 1-84.

Brisbane, M. & Clews, S. (1979). The East Moor systems, Altarnun and North Hill, Bodmin Moor. *Cornish Archaeology 18*, 33-56.

Brongers, J.A. (1976). *Air photography and celtic field research in the Netherlands.* Amersfoort: Uitgave Rijksdienst voor het Oudheidkundig Bodemnderzoek.

Brookfield, H.C. (1972). Intensification and Disintensification in Pacific Agriculture: A theoretical approach. *Pacific Viewpoint 13*, 30-48.

Brookfield, H.C. (1984). Intensification Revisited. *Pacific Viewpoint 25*, 15-44.

Brookfield, H. (2001). Intensification and alternative approaches to agricultural change. *Asia Pacific Viewpoint 42*, 181-192.

Brown, G.O. (2004). Commentary. *Anthropological Quarterly 77*, 575-580.

Brown, P. (1998). Simbu Property. In *Property in Economic Context. Monographs in Economic Anthropology, No. 14*, eds. Gilman, A. & Hunt, R.C., pp. 269-287. Lanham, New York, Oxford: University Press of America.

Brück, J. (1995). A Place for the Dead: The role of human remains in Late Bronze Age Britain. *Proceedings of the Prehistoric Society 61*, 278

Brück, J. (1999a). Houses, lifecycles and deposition on Middle Bronze Age settlements in Southern England. *Proceedings of the Prehistoric Society 65*, 145-166.

Brück, J. (1999b). Ritual and Rationality: Some problems of interpretation in European Archaeology. *European Journal of Archaeology 2*, 313-344.

Brück, J. (1999c). What's in a settlement? Domestic practice and residential mobility in Early Bronze Age southern England. In *Making Places in the Prehistoric World: Themes in settlement archaeology*, eds. Brück, J. & Goodman, M., pp. 52-75. London: UCL Press.

Brück, J. (2000). Settlement, landscpe and social identity: The Early-Middle Bronze Age transition in Wessex, Sussex and the Thames Valley. *Oxford Journal of Archaeology 19*, 273-300.

Brück, J. (2001a). Body metaphors and technologies of transformation in the English Middle and Late Bronze Age. In *Bronze Age Landscapes: Tradition and transformation*, ed. Brück, J., pp. 149-160. Oxford: Oxbow.

Brück, J. (2001b). Monuments, Power and Personhood in the British Neolithic. *Journal of the Royal Anthropological Institute (New Series) 7*, 667

Brück, J. (2004). Material Metaphors: The relational construction of identity in Early Bronze Age burials in Ireland and Britain. *Journal of Material Culture 4*, 307-333.

Brück, J. (2005). Homing instincts: Grounded identities and dividual selves in the British Bronze Age. In *The Archaeology of Plural and Changing Identities: Beyond identification*, eds. Casella, E. & Fowler, C., New York: Kluwer.

Brück, J. (2006). *Death, exchange and reproduction in the British Bronze Age - Forthcoming paper.*

Brück, J., Fyfe, R., Johnston, R., Lewis, H. & Wickstead, H. (2005). *A Divided Land: Field systems, land use and society on Bronze Age Dartmoor.* Privately published Summary Report.

Brück, J., Johnston, R. & Wickstead, H. (2003). Excavations of Bronze Age field systems on Shovel Down, Dartmoor, 2003. *PAST: Newletter of the Prehistoric Society 45*,

Buckley, V. (1990). *Burnt Offerings: International contributions to Burnt Mound Archaeology.* Dublin: Wordwell.

Budd, F.N. (1889). Notes of a find of flint implements at Batworthy. *Report of the Proceedings of the Teign Naturalists' Field Club 8-9.*

Budd, P., Haggerty, R., Ixer, R.A., Scaife, B. & Thomas, R.G. (2000). *Copper deposits in south-west England identified as a source of Copper Age metalwork.* http://www.rosiehardman.com/provenance.html.

Burleigh, R., Matthews, K., Ambers, J. & Kinnes, I. (1981). British Museum natural radiocarbon measurements XII. *Radiocarbon 23*, 14-23.

Burnard, R. (1894). Exploration of the hut circles in Broadun Ring and Broadun. *Report and Transactions of the Devonshire Association for the Advancement of Science XXVI*, 185-196.

Burnard, R. (1896). Fifteenth Report of the Barrow Committee. *Report and Transactions of the Devonshire Association for the Advancement of Science XXVIII*, 84-89.

Burnard, R. (1986). *Dartmoor Pictorial Records, Limited Edition Facsimile.* Newton Abbott: Devon Books.

Busby, C. (1997). Permeable and Partible Persons: A comparative analysis of gender and body in South India and Melanesia. *Journal of the Royal Anthropological Institute (New Series) 3*, 261-278.

Butler, J. (1991a). *Dartmoor Atlas of Antiquities. Volume 1 - The East.* Exeter: Devon Books.

Butler, J. (1991b). *Dartmoor Atlas of Antiquities. Volume 2 - The North*. Exeter: Devon Books.

Butler, J. (1993a). *Dartmoor Atlas of Antiquities. Volume 4 - The South-East*. Exeter: Devon Books.

Butler, J. (1994). *Dartmoor Atlas of Antiquities. Volume 3 - The South-West*. Tiverton: Devon Books.

Butler, J. (1997a). *Dartmoor Atlas of Antiquities. Volume 5 - The Second Millennium BC*. Exeter: Devon Books.

Butler, J. *The Prehistoric Settlement of Dartmoor*. Unpublished PhD Thesis. 1997b. University College London.

Butler, J. (1993b). *Bodies That Matter: On the discursive limits of 'sex'*. London: Routledge.

Callon, M. (1998). *The Laws of the Market*. Oxford: Blackwell.

Callon, M., Meadel, C. & Rabeharisoa, V. (2002). The economy of qualities. *Economy and Society 31*, 194-217.

Carrier, J.G. (1995). *Gifts and Commodities: Exchange and western capitalism since 1700*. London: Routledge.

Carrier, J.G. (1998). Property and social relations in Melanesian anthropology. In *Property Relations: Renewing the anthropological tradition*, ed. Hann, C.M., pp. 85-103. Cambridge: CUP.

Carrington, N.T. (1826). *Dartmoor: A descriptive poem*. London: Murray.

Carsten, J. (2004a). *After Kinship*. Cambridge: Cambridge University Press.

Carsten, J. (2004b). The substance of kinship and the heat of the hearth: Feeding, personhood and relatedness among Malays in Pulau Langkawi [first published 1995]. In *Kinship and Family: An Anthropological Reader*, eds. Parkin, R. & Stone, L., pp. 309-328. Oxford: Blackwell.

Carsten, J. & Hugh-Jones, S. (1995). Introduction. In *About the House: Levi-Strauss and Beyond*, eds. Carsten, J. & Hugh-Jones, S., pp. 1-46. Cambridge: Cambridge University Press.

Caseldine, C.J. (1999). Archaeological and environmental change on prehistoric Dartmoor - current understandings and future directions. *Journal of Quarternary Science 14*, 575-583.

Caseldine, C.J., Coles, B., Griffith, F.M. & Hatton, J.M. (2000). Conservation or Change? Human influence on the mid-Devon landscape. In *People as an agent of environmental change: Symposia of the Association for Environmental Archaeology*, eds. Nicholson, R. & O'Connor, T., pp. 60-70. Oxford: Oxbow.

Caseldine, C.J. & Hatton, J.M. (1994). Into the mists? Thoughts on the prehistoric and historic environmental history of Dartmoor. *Devon Archaeological Society Proceedings 52*, 35-47.

Caseldine, C.J. & Hatton, J.M. (1996). Vegetation History of Dartmoor - Holocene development and the impact of human activity. In *Devon and East Cornwall Field Guide*, eds. Charman, D.J., Newnham, R.M. & Croot, D.G., pp. 48-61. London: Quarternary Research Association.

Caseldine, C.J. & Macguire, D.J. (1981). A review of the prehistoric and historic environment on Dartmoor. *Devon Archaeological Society Proceedings 39*, 1-16.

Caseldine, C.J. & Maguire, D. (1981). A review of the prehistoric and historic environment on Dartmoor. *Proceedings of the Devon Archaeological Society 39*, 1-16.

Casimir, M.J. (1992). The dimensions of territoriality: An introduction. In *Mobility and Territoriality: Social and spatial boundaries among foragers, fishers and peripatetics*, eds. Casimir, M.J. & Aparna, R., pp. 3-22. New York and Oxford: Berg.

Castells, M. (2000). *The Institutions of the New Economy. Address to Delivering the Virtual Promise? Conference. Edited by Peter Watts*. London: http://virtualsociety.sbs.ox.ac.uk/events/castells.htm.

Caulfield, S. Neolithic Fields: The evidence. In *Early Land Allotment, British Series 48*. eds. Bowen, H.C. and Fowler, P.J. 137-144. 1978. Oxford: British Archaeological Reports.

Caulfield, S. (1983). The Neolithic settlement of north Connaught. In *Landscape archaeology in Ireland. British Archaeological Reports, British Series 116*, eds. Reeves-Smyth, T. & Hamond, F., pp. 195-215. Oxford: British Archaeological Reports.

Caulfield, S., O'Donnell, R.G. & Mitchell, P.I. (1998). C14 dating of a Neolithic field system at Ceide Fields, County Mayo, Ireland. *Radiocarbon 40*, 629-640.

Cederholm, M. (2005). *Random Points in Polygon, Arcview GIS 3.x Extension*. *http://www.pierssen.com/arcview/arcview.htm*.

Chamberlain, A.T. & Williams, J.P. (2001). A Gazetteer of English Caves, Fissures and Rock Shelters Containing Human Remains. *Cave Archaeology and Palaeontology Research Archive 1*,

Bibliography

Chapman, J. (2000). *Fragmentation and Archaeology: People, places and broken objects in the prehistory of south-eastern Europe.* London: Routledge.

Chapman, J. & Shiel, R.S. (1993). Social change and land use in prehistoric Dalmatia. *Proceedings of the Prehistoric Society 59,* 61-104.

Chasin, A. (2005). Selling Out: The Gay and Lesbian movement goes to market. In *Rethinking Commodification: Cases and Readings in Law and Culture,* eds. Ertman, M.M. & Williams, J.C., pp. 213-221. London and New York: New York University Press.

Childe, V.G. (1942). *What Happened in History.* London: Penguin.

Childe, V.G. (1981). *Man Makes Himself.* Bradford-on-Avon: Moonraker Press.

Christie, A. (1931). *The Sittaford Mystery.* London: Collins Crime Club.

Clark, P. (2004). The Dover boat ten years after its discovery. In *The Dover Bronze Age Boat in Context: Society and water transport in prehistoric Europe,* ed. Clark, P., pp. 1-12. Oxford: Oxbow.

Clayden, B. & Manley, D.J.R. (1964). The soils of the Dartmoor Granite. In *Dartmoor Essays,* ed. Simmons, I.G., pp. 117-140. Plymouth: Devonshire Association for the Advancement of Science.

Coleman, G. (2004). The political agnosticism of free and open source software and the inadvertent politics of contrast. *Anthropological Quarterly 77,* 507-519.

Collier, W.F. (1894). Dartmoor for Devonshire. *Report and Transactions of the Devonshire Association for the Advancement of Science 26,* 199-208.

Collis, J. (1978). Fields and settlements on Shaugh Moor, Dartmoor. In *Early Land Allotment in the British Isles: A survey of recent work,* eds. Bowen, H.C. & Fowler, P.J., pp. 23-27. Oxford: British Archaeological Reports.

Conan Doyle, A. (1996). *The Hound of the Baskervilles.* Harmondsworth: Penguin.

Coombe, R.J. & Herman, A. (2004). Rhetorical Virtues: Property, speech, and the commons on the world-wide web. *Anthropological Quarterly 77,* 559-574.

Coucelis, H. (1999). Space, Time, Geography. In *Geographical Information Systems and Science,* eds. Longley, P.A., Goodchild, M.F., Maguire, D. & Rhind, D.W., pp. 29-38. Chicester: John Wiley and Sons.

Crampton, J.W. (2004). Critical GIS: Rethinking GIS and (Homeland) Security. *Geoworld Magazine*

Crawford, O.G.S. (1953). *Archaeology in the Field.* London: Phoenix House Ltd.

Crutchley, S. (2001). The landscape of Salisbury Plain, as revealed by aerial photography. *Landscapes 2,* 46-64.

Cummings, S., van Dam, H., Khadar, A. & Valk, M. (2001). *Gender Perspectives on Property and Inheritance: A global sourcebook.* Oxford: Oxfam GB.

Curry, M.R. (1998). *Digital Places: Living with Geographical Information Technologies.* London: Routledge.

Curwen, E.C. (1946). *Plough and Pasture.* London: Cobbett Press.

Curwen, E.C. (1927). Prehistoric agriculture in Britain. *Antiquity 1,* 261-289.

Curwen, E.C. (1929). *Air-Photography and Economic History: The evolution of the corn-field.* London: Economic History Society.

Curwen, E.C. (1932). Ancient Cultivations. *Antiquity 5,* 389-406.

Curwen, E.C. (1938). The early development of agriculture in Britain. *Proceedings of the Prehistoric Society 4,* 27-51.

Curwen, E. & Curwen, E.C. (1923). Sussex lynchets and their associated field-ways. *Sussex Archaeological Society Collections 64,* 1-65.

Cutter, S.L., Richardson, D.B. & Wilbanks, T.J. (2003). *The Geographical Dimensions of Terrorism.* New York and London: Routledge.

Dartmoor National Park Authority (2004). *A Guide to the Archaeology of Dartmoor.* Tiverton: Halsgrove.

Dawson, A. & Johnson, M. (2001). Migration, Exile and Landscapes of the Imagination. In *Contested Landscapes: Movement, Exile and Place,* eds. Bender, B. & Winer, M., pp. 319-332. Oxford: Blackwell.

De Hingh, A. (1998). The archaeology of the agricultural landscape: Land-use and access to land in later prehistoric society in North-West Europe. In *Landless and Hungry? Access to land in early and traditional societies,* eds. Haring, B. & de Maaijer, R., pp. 1-18. Leiden: CNWS Publications.

Deininger, K. (2003). *Land Policies for Growth and Poverty Reduction.* Oxford and New York: World Bank and Oxford University Press.

Deleuze, G. & Guattari, F. (1987). *A Thousand Plateaus: Capitalism and Schizophrenia*. London and New York: Continuum.

Demetz, H. (1967). Toward a Therory of Property Rights. *The American Economic Review 57*, 347-359.

Demetz, H. (2002). Toward a Theory of Property Rights II: The competition between private and collective ownership. *Journal of Legal Studies XXXI*, 653-672.

Demian, M. (2004). Disputing damage versus disputing ownership in Suau. In *Rationales of Ownership: Transactions and claims to ownership in contemporary Papua New Guinea*, eds. Kalinoe, L. & Leach, J., pp. 27-41. Wantage: Sean Kingston Publishing.

Diski, J. (2007). Jowls are available (review of Second Life). *London Review of Books 8th February*,

Drewett, P. (1982). Later Bronze Age downland economy and excavations at Black Patch, East Sussex. *Proceedings of the Prehistoric Society 48*, 321-400.

Earle, T. (2000). Archaeology, property and prehistory. *Annual Review of Anthropology 29*, 39-60.

Earle, T. (2002). *Bronze Age Economics: The first political economies*. Boulder, CO: Westview Press.

Earle, T. (2004). Culture Matter: Why Symbolic Objects Change. In *Rethinking Materiality: The engagement of mind with the material world*, eds. DeMarrias, E., Gosden, C. & Renfrew, C., pp. 153-167. Cambrige: MacDonald Institute.

Economist (2006). Living a Second Life. *The Economist Sept. 28th 2006*,

Ellis, L. (1985). On the rudiments of possessions and property. *Social Science Information 24* , 113-143.

Ellison, A. (1981). Towards a socioeconomic model for the Middle Bronze Age in southern England. In *Pattern of the Past: Studies in honour of David Clarke*, eds. Hodder, I., Issac, G. & Hammond, N., pp. 413-439. Cambridge: Cambridge University Press.

Engels, F. (2005). *The Origin of the Family, Private Property and the State [published 1884]*. http://www.marxists.org/archive/marx/works/1884/origin-family/ch01.htm (accessed 7th February 2005).

English Heritage (1987). *The Work of the Central Excavation Unit 1986-7*. London: HBMCE.

Eogan, G. (1964). The excavation of a stone alignment and circle at Cholwichtown, Lee Moor, Devonshire, England. *Proceedings of the Prehistoric Society 30*, 25-38.

Eogan, G. (1997). 'Hair-rings' and European Late Bronze Age society. *Antiquity 71*, 308-320.

Ertman, M.M. & Williams, J.C. (2005). *Rethinking Commodification: Cases and readings in Law and Culture*. New York: New York University Press.

Evans-Pritchard, E.E. (2004). The Nuer of Southern Sudan. In *Kinship and Family: An Anthropological Reader*, eds. Parkin, R. & Stone, L., pp. 64-78. Oxford: Blackwell.

Evans, C. (1997). Sentimental Prehistories: The construction of the Fenland past. *Journal of European Archaeology 5*, 105-136.

Evans, C. & Knight, M. (2001). The 'community of builders': The Barleycroft post alignments. In *Bronze Age Landscapes: Tradition and transformation*, ed. Brück, J., pp. 83-98. Oxford: Oxbow Books.

Evans, J.G. (1999). *Land and Archaeology: Histories of human environment in the British Isles*. Stroud: Tempus.

Farquharson, J.E. (1976). *The Plough and the Swastika: The NSDAP and agriculture in Germany 1928-45*. London: Sage.

Fitzpatrick, A.P. (2002). The Amesbury Archer: "King of Stonehenge". *PAST: Newletter of the Prehistoric Society 41*,

Fitzpatrick, A.P., Butterworth, C. & Grove, J. (1999). *Prehistoric and Roman sites in East Devon: The A30 Honiton to Exeter improvement DBFO, 1996-9*. Salisbury: Wessex Archaeology.

Fleming, A. (1971). Territorial Patterns in Bronze Age Wessex. *Proceedings of the Prehistoric Society 37*, 138-166.

Fleming, A. (1975). Prehistoric land boundaries in upland Britain: an appeal. *Antiquity 49*, 215-216.

Fleming, A. (1978a). Dartmoor reaves: a nineteenth century fiasco. *Antiquity LII*, 16-20.

Fleming, A. (1978b). The prehistoric landscape of Dartmoor. Part 1: South Dartmoor. *Proceedings of the Prehistoric Society 44*, 97-123.

Fleming, A. (1979). The Dartmoor reaves: Boundary patterns and behaviour patterns in the second millennium BC. *Devon Archaeological Society Proceedings 37*, 115-131.

Fleming, A. (1982). Social boundaries and land boundaries. In *Ranking, resource and exchange: Aspects of the archaeology of early European society*, eds.

Renfrew, C. & Shennan, S., pp. 52-55. Cambridge: Cambridge University Press.

Fleming, A. (1983). The prehistoric landscape of Dartmoor. Part 2: North and East Dartmoor. *Proceedings of the Prehistoric Society 49*, 195-241.

Fleming, A. (1984). The prehistoric landscape of Dartmoor: wider implications. *Landscape History 6*, 5-19.

Fleming, A. (1985a). Dartmoor Reaves. *Devon Archaeology 3*, 1-6.

Fleming, A. (1985b). Land tenure, productivity and field systems. In *Beyond domestication in prehistoric Europe: investigations in subsistence archaeology and social complexity*, eds. Barker, G. & Gamble, C., pp. 129-146.

Fleming, A. (1987a). Coaxial field systems: some questions of time and space. *Antiquity 61*, 188-202.

Fleming, A. (1987b). Prehistoric tin extraction on Dartmoor: A cautionary note. *Transactions of the Devonshire Association for the Advancement of Science 119*, 117-122.

Fleming, A. (1988). *The Dartmoor Reaves: Investigating prehistoric land divisions*. London: Batsford.

Fleming, A. (1994a). Medieval and post-medieval cultivation on Dartmoor: A landscape archaeologist's view. *Devon Archaeological Society Proceedings 52*, 101-117.

Fleming, A. (1994b). The reaves reviewed. *Devon Archaeological Society Proceedings 52*, 63-73.

Fleming, A. (1998a). *Swaledale: Valley of the Wild River*. Edinburgh: Edinburgh University Press.

Fleming, A. (1998b). The Changing Commons: The case of Swaledale (England). In *Property in Economic Context. Monographs in Economic Anthropology, No. 14*, eds. Hunt, R.C. & Gilman, A., pp. 186-214. Lanham, New York, Oxford: University Press of America Inc.

Fleming, A., Collis, J. & Jones, R.L. (1973). A late prehistoric reave system near Cholwich Town, Dartmoor. *Devon Archaeological Society Proceedings 31*, 1-21.

Ford, S., Bowden, M., Gaffney, V. & Mees, G.C. (1994). The 'Celtic' field systems on the Berkshire Downs, England. In *The Archaeology of Garden and Field*, eds. Miller, N.F. & Gleason, K.L., pp. 153-167. Philadelphia: University of Pennsylvania Press.

Foucault, M. (1980). Questions on Geography. In *Power/Knowledge: Selected interviews and other writings 1972-1977*, ed. Gordon, C., Brighton: The Harvester Press.

Fowler, C. (2001). Personhood and social relations in the British Neolithic, with a study from the Isle of Man. *Journal of Material Culture 6*, 137-163.

Fowler, C. (2004). *The Archaeology of Personhood: An anthropological approach*. London: Routledge.

Fowler, P.J. (1971). Early prehistoric agriculture in Western Europe: some archaeological evidence. In *Economy and Settlement in Neolithic and Early Bronze Age Britain and Europe. Papers delivered at a conference held in the University of Leicester, December 1969.*, ed. Simpson, D.D.A., pp. 153-182. Leicester: Leicester University Press.

Fowler, P.J. & Blackwell, I. (1998). *The Land of Lettice Sweetapple: An English countryside explored*. Stroud: Tempus.

Fowler, P.J. (1983). *The Farming of Prehistoric Britain*. Cambridge: Cambridge University Press.

Fowler, P.J. (1984). Wildscape to Landscape: 'Enclosure' in Prehistoric Britain. In *Farming Practice in British Prehistory*, ed. Mercer, R., Edinburgh: Edinburgh University Press.

Fox, A. (1948). The Broad Down (Farway) Necropolis and the Wessex Culture in Devon. *Devon Archaeological Society Proceedings 4*, 1-16.

Fox, A. (1954a). Celtic fields and farms on Dartmoor, in the light of recent excavations at Kestor. *Antiquity 20*, 87-102.

Fox, A. (1954b). Excavations at Kestor, an early Iron Age settlement near Chagford, Devon. *Transactions of the Devonshire Association for the Advancement of Science 86*, 21-49.

Fox, A. (1955). Huts and Enclosures on Gripper's Hill, in the Avon Valley, Dartmoor. *Report and Transactions of the Devonshire Association for the Advancement of Science LXXXVII*, 55-62.

Fox, A. (1957). Excavations on Dean Moor, in the Avon Valley, 1954-1956, The Late Bronze Age settlement. *Transactions of the Devonshire Association for the Advancement of Science 89*, 18-77.

Fox, A. (1961). Twenty-fifth report on the Archaeology and Early History of Devon. *Report and Transactions of the Devonshire Association for the Advancement of Science 93*, 61-80.

Fox, A. (1973). *South west England 3500BC to AD600.* Newton Abbot: David and Charles.

Fox, A. (1996). *Prehistoric Hillforts in Devon.* Tiverton: Devon Books.

Fox, A. & Britton, D. (1969). A continental palstave from the ancient field system on Horridge Common, Dartmoor, England. *Proceedings of the Prehistoric Society XXXV*, 220-228.

Framework Archaeology (2002). *Press Release .* Thursday July 17th.

French, C., Lewis, H., Allen, M.J., Scaife, R.G. & Green, M. (2003). Archaeological and Palaeo-environmental investigations of the Upper Allen Valley, Cranbourne Chase, Dorset (1999-2000): A new model of Earlier Holocene landscape development. *Proceedings of the Prehistoric Society 69*, 201-234.

Fulbrook, E. (2000). *Translation of the original student's petition circulated in France.* www.paecon.net: Post Autistic Economics Movement.

Fyfe, R., Brown, A.G. & Coles, B. (2003). Mesolithic to Bronze Age vegetation change and human activity in the Exe Valley, Devon, UK. *Proceedings of the Prehistoric Society 69*, 161-181.

Gaffney, V. & Van Leusen, M. (1995). Postscript - GIS, environmental determinism and archaeology: A parallel text. In *Archaeology and Geographical Information Systems: A European perspective*, eds. Lock, G. & Stancic, Z., pp. 367-381. London: Taylor and Francis.

Gallant, L., Luxton, N. & Collman, M. (1985). Ancient fields on the South Devon limestone plateau. *Proceedings of the Devon Archaeological Society 43*, 23-38.

Gardner, D. (2001). Intensification, social production and the inscrutable ways of culture. *Asia Pacific Viewpoint 42*, 193-207.

Gawne, E. & Somers Cocks, J.V. (1968). Parallel reaves on Dartmoor. *Transactions of the Devonshire Association for the Advancement of Science 100*, 277-291.

Geertz, C. (1963). *Agricultural Involution: The processes of ecological change in indonesia.* Berkley, Los Angeles: University of California Press.

Gell, A. (1985). How to Read a Map; Remarks on the practical logic of navigation. *Man 20*, 271-286.

Gell, A. (1998). *Art and Agency: An anthropological theory.* Oxford: Clarendon Press.

Gerrard, S. (1997a). *Dartmoor: Book of Dartmoor landscapes through time.* London: Batsford / English Heritage.

Gerrard, S. (1997b). *Meavy Valley Archaeology. Interim Report for 1996.* Privately published by Dr. Sandy Gerrard.

Gerrard, S. (2000). *The Early British Tin Industry.* Stroud: Tempus.

Gerritsen, F. (1999). To build and to abandon: The cultural biography of late prehistoric houses and farmsteads in the southern Netherlands. *Archaeological Dialogues 6*, 78-114.

Gibbs, P. (2006). *Missionaries and Culture.* http://www.sedos.org.

Gibson, A. (1990). *Excavations at the Kestor Field System, Dartmoor, July 1989, Unpublished Report.*

Gibson, A. (1992). The excavation of an iron age settlement at Gold Park, Dartmoor. *Proceedings of the Devon Archaeological Society 50*, 19-46.

Giddens, A. (1986). *The Constitution of Society: Outline of the Theory of Structuration.* Cambridge: Polity.

Gietema, B. (1998). *Basic Calculations in Agriculture and Animal Production.* Wageningen: STOAS.

Gillings, M. & Goodrick, G. (1996). Senuous and Reflexive GIS: Exploring visualisation and VRML. *Internet Archaeology 1*,

Gilman, A. (1998). Reconstructing property systems from archaeological evidence. In *Property in Economic Context. Monographs in Economic Anthropology, No. 14*, eds. Hunt, R.C. & Gilman, A., pp. 215-236. Lanham, New York, Oxford: University Press of America Inc.

Gingell, C. (1992). *The Marlborough Downs: A Later Bronze Age landscape and its origins.* Devizes: Wiltshire Archaeological and Natural History Society in co-operation with the Trust for Wessex Archaeology.

Godelier, M. (1986). Territory and property in some pre-capitalist societies. In *The Mental and the Material: Thought, economy and society*, Anonymouspp. 71-121. London: Verso.

Godelier, M. (1999). *The Enigma of the Gift.* Oxford: Polity Press.

Goldstein, L. (1981). One-dimensional archaeology and multi-dimensional people; Spatial organisation and mortuary analysis. In *The Archaeology of Death*, eds.

Chapman, R., Randsborg, K. & Kinnes, I., pp. 53-70. Cambridge: Cambridge University Press.

Goody, J. (1976). *Production and Reproduction: A comparative study of the domestic domain.* Cambridge: Cambridge University Press.

Goody, J. (1998). Dowry and the rights of women to property. In *Property Relations: Renewing the anthropological tradition*, ed. Hann, C.M., pp. 201-213. Cambridge: CUP.

Gosden, C. (1985). Gifts and Kin in Early Iron Age Europe. *Man 20*, 475-493.

Gosden, C. (1994). *Social Being and Time.* Oxford: Blackwell.

Gosden, C. (2004). *Archaeology and Colonialism: Cultural Contact from 5000 BC to the present.* Cambridge: Cambridge University Press.

Gosden, C. (2005). Comments III: Is science a foreign country? *Archaeometry 47*, 182-185.

Graeber, D. (2001). *Toward an Anthropological Theory of Value; The False Coin of our own Dreams.* New York: Palgrave.

Graeber, D. (2005a). Fetishism as social creativity, or, Fetishes are gods in the process of construction. *Anthropological Theory 5*, 407-438.

Graeber, D. (2005b). Value as the Importance of Action. *The Commoner 10*, 5-65.

Graeber, D. (2006). Turning Modes of Production Inside Out, Or, Why Capitalism is a Transformation of Slavery. *Critique of Anthropology 26*, 61-85.

Granovetter, M. (1985). The Impact of Social Structure on Economic Outcomes. *Journal of Economic Perspectives 19*, 33-50.

Gray, J. (1999). Open spaces and dwelling places: Being at home on hill farms in the Scottish borders. *American Ethnologist 26*, 440-460.

Greeves, T. (2004). Megalithic Stone Row discovered on Dartmoor's remotest hill. *PAST: Newletter of the Prehistoric Society 47*,

Gregory, C. (1982). *Gifts and Commodities.* London: Academic Press.

Griffith, F.M. (1990). Aerial reconnaisance in mainland Britain in the summer of 1989. *Antiquity 64*, 14-33.

Griffiths, D. (1994). 'A field to the spoiler': A review of archaeological conservation on Dartmoor. *Devon Archaeological Society Proceedings 52*, 271-285.

Grinsell, L.V. (1978). Dartmoor Barrows. *Devon Archaeological Society Proceedings 36*, 85-119.

Hambleton, E. (1999). *Animal Husbandry Regimes in Iron Age Britain: A comparative study of faunal assemblages from British Iron Age sites. BAR British Series 282.* Oxford: Archaeopress.

Hammond, J.L. & Hammond, B. (1911). *The Village Labourer - Volume 1.* London: Guild Books.

Hammond, M. (1987). *The Iliad by Homer, translated and with an introduction by Michael Hammond.* London: Penguin.

Hamond, F. (1979). Settlement, economy and environment on prehistoric Dartmoor. *Proceedings of the Devon Archaeological Society* 146-175.

Hann, C.M. (1998). Introduction: the embeddedness of property. In *Property Relations: Renewing the anthropological tradition.*, ed. Hann, C.M., pp. 1-47. Cambridge: Cambridge University Press.

Haraway, D. (1991). A Cyborg Manifesto: Science, Technology and Socialist-Feminism in the Late Twentieth Century. In *Simians, Cyborgs and Women: The Reinvention of Nature*, ed. Haraway, D., pp. 149-181. New York and London: Routledge.

Haraway, D. (1992). The Promises of Monsters: A regenerative politics for Inappropriate/d Others. In *Cultural Studies*, eds. Grossberg, L., Nelson, C. & Triechler, P.A., pp. 295-337. New York and London: Routledge.

Hardin, G. (1968). The Tragedy of the Commons. *Science 162*, 1243-1248.

Harding, A.F. (1989). Interpreting the evidence for agricultural change in the Late Bronze Age in northern Europe. In *Bronze Age Studies*, eds. Nordstrom, H.-A. & Knape, A., pp. 173-181. Stockholm: Statens Historiska Museum.

Harding, A.F. (1999). North-South Exchanges of Raw Materials. In *Gods and Heroes of the European Bronze Age*, eds. Demakopoulou, K., Eluere, C., Jensen, J., Jockenhovel, A. & Mohen, J.-P., pp. 38-43. London: Thames and Hudson.

Harding, S. (2005). Culture, Commodification, and Native American Cultural Patrimony. In *Rethinking Commodification: Cases and readings in Law and Culture*, eds. Ertman, M.M. & Williams, J.C., pp. 137-155. New York and London: New York University Press.

Harmer, R. & Gill, R. (2000). Natural Regeneration in Broadleaved Woodlands: Deer Browsing and the establishment of advance regeneration. *Forestry Commission Research Information Notes* 1-6.

Harmer, R. & Kerr, G. (1995). Natural Regeneration of Broadleaved Trees. *Forestry Commission Research Information Notes 275*, 1-6.

Harris, G.T., Radford, C.A.R. & Worth, R.H. (1935). Dartmoor Exploration Committee, Twelfth Report. *LXVII* 115-130.

Harrison, P.A., Berry, P.M. & Dawson, T.P. (2001). *Climate Change and Nature Conservation in Britain and Ireland: Modelling natural resource responses to climate change (The MONARCH Project)*. Oxford: UK Climate Impacts Programme Technical Reports.

Harrison, R. (2000). Challenging the authenicity of antiquity: Contact archaeology and native title in Australia. In *Native Title and the Transformation of Archaeology in the Postcolonial World*, ed. Lilley, I., pp. 35-53. Sydney: University of Sydney.

Hatt, G. (1931). Prehistoric fields in Jylland. *Acta Archaeologica 2*, 117-158.

Hatt, G. (1939). The Ownership of Cultivated Land. *Det Kogl.Danske Videnokabernes Selskab Historisk-filogiske Meddelelser XXVI*, 1-22.

Hatt, G. (1949). *Oldtidsagre*. Kobenhaven: I Kommission Hos Ejnar Munksgaard.

Hawkes, J. (1951). *A Land*. Harmondsworth: Penguin.

Hedeager, L. (1992). *Iron Age Societies: From tribe to state in Northern Europe, 500 BC to AD 700*. Oxford: Blackwell.

Hegmon, M. (1989). Risk reduction and Variation in Agricultural Economies: A computer simulation of Hopi agriculture. In *Research in Economic Anthropology: A Research Annual*, ed. Issac, B.L., pp. 89-122. Greenwich, London: JAI Press.

Heller, M.A. (1998). The Tragedy of the Anticommons: Property in the transition from Marx to Markets. *Havard Law Review 111*, 621-688.

Henrich, J., Boyd, R., Bowles, S., Camerer, C., Fehr, E., Gintis, H. & McElreath, R. (2001). In Search of Homo Economicus: Behavioural expreiments in 15 small-scale societies. *The American Economic Review 91*, 73-78.

Hernandez, T.K. (2005). 'Sex in the [Foreign] City?' Commodification and the Female Sex tourist. In *Rethinking Commodification: Cases and Readings in Law and Culture*, eds. Ertman, M.M. & Williams, J.C., pp. 222-242. London and New York: New York University Press.

Hirsch, E. (2004a). Environment and Economy: Mutual connections and diverse perspectives. *Anthropological Theory 4*, 435-453.

Hirsch, E. (2004b). Mining boundaries and local land narratives (tibide) in the Udabe Valley, Central Province. In *Rationales of Ownership: Transactions and claims to ownership in contemporary Papua New Guinea*, eds. Kalinoe, L. & Leach, J., pp. 13-26. Wantage: Sean Kingston Publishing.

Hirsch, E. & Strathern, M. (2004). *Transactions and Creations: Property debates and the stimulus of Melanesia*. Oxford and New York: Berghahn books.

Hobbes, T. (1660). *Leviathan*. http://oregonstate.edu/instruct/phl302/texts/hobbes/leviathan-contents.html (accessed 7th February 2005).

Hume, D. (1896). *A Treatise of Human Nature*. Oxford: Clarendon Press.

Hunt, R.C. (1998). Properties of property: Conceptual issues. In *Property in Economic Context. Monographs in Economic Anthropology, No. 14*, eds. Hunt, R.C. & Gilman, A., pp. 3-6. Lanham, New York, Oxford: University Press of America.

Hurcombe, L. (2002). *Making an Impression: Basketry and cordage from pots*. Paper given at the Bronze Age Forum, Newcastle 2002.

Hutchinson, S.E. (1996). *Nuer Dilemmas: Coping with Money, War and the State*. Berkley, Los Angeles, London: University of California Press.

Hutchinson, T.P. (1993). *Version 2 (History and Archaeology) of Essentials of Statistical Methods*. Adelaide: Rumsby Scientific Publishing.

Ingold, T. (1986). *The Appropriation of Nature: Essays on human ecology and social relations*. Manchester: Manchester University Press.

Ingold, T. (2000). *The perception of the environment: Essays in livelihood, dwelling and skill*. London: Routledge.

Ingold, T. (2004). Culture on the Ground: The world perceived through the feet. *Journal of Material Culture 9*, 315-340.

Ingold, T. (2006). *Overcoming the Modern Invention of Material Culture: Summary Discussion*. Exeter: Paper Given at T.A.G. Conference 17th December.

Jamoussi, Z. (1999). *Primogeniture and Entail in England: A survey of their history and representation in literature*. Paris: Centre de Publication Universitaire.

Jarvis, K. (1976). The M5 Motorway and the Peamore-Pocombe Link. *Proceedings of the Devon Archaeological Society 34*, 209-266.

Jewell, P.A. & Grubb, P. (1974). Movement, daily activity and home range of Soay sheep. In *Island Survivors: The ecology of the Soay Sheep of St Kilda*, eds. Jewell, P.A., Milner, C. & Morton Boyd, J., pp. 160-194. London: Athlone Press.

Johnson, M.H. (1996). *An Archaeology of Capitalism*. Oxford: Blackwell.

Johnson, N. & Rose, P. (1994). *Bodmin Moor: An archaeological survey. Volume 1: The human landscape to c1800*. London: English Heritage.

Johnston, R. (2000). Field systems and the Atlantic Bronze Age: Thoughts on a regional perspective. In *The Prehistory and Early History of Atlantic Europe. British Archaeological Reports International Series 861*, ed. Henderson, J.C., pp. 47-55. Oxford: Archaeopress.

Johnston, R. (2001a). 'Breaking new ground': Land tenure and fieldstone clearance during the Bronze Age. In *Bronze Age Landscapes: Tradition and transformation*, ed. Brück, J., pp. 99-109. Oxford: Oxbow.

Johnston, R. Land and Society: The Bronze Age cairnfields and field systems of Britain. 2001b. University of Newcastle Upon Tyne.

Johnston, R. (2005). Pattern without a plan: Rethinking the Bronze Age Coaxial Field Sytems on Dartmoor, South-West England. *Oxford Journal of Archaeology 24*, 1-21.

Johnston, R. & Wickstead, H. (2005). *Geophysical surveys on Shovel Down and Kestor, Dartmoor, Devon, 2003 and 2004*. Unpublished Report.

Jones, A.M. (2004a). *Cornish Bronze Age Ceremonial Landscapes*. Exeter: Unpublished PhD Thesis.

Jones, A.M. (2005). *Cornish Bronze Age Ceremonial Landscapes c.2500-1500 BC. British Archaeological Reports, British Series 394*. Oxford: Archaeopress.

Jones, A. (2004b). Archaeometry and Materiality: Materials-based analysis in theory and practice. *Archaeometry 46*, 327-338.

Jones, A. (2004c). Matter and Memory: Colour, rememberance and the Neolithic / Bronze Age transition. In *Rethinking materiality: The engagement of mind with the material world*, eds. DeMarrias, E., Gosden, C. &

Renfrew, C., pp. 167-178. Cambridge: MacDonald Institute.

Jordan, D., Haddon-Reece, D. & Bayliss, A. (1994). *Radiocarbon dates from samples funded by English Heritage and dated before 1981*. Northampton: English Heritage.

Joseph, M. (2005). The Multivalent Commodity: On the supplementarity of value and values. In *Rethinking Commodification: Cases and readings in Law and Culture*, eds. Ertman, M.M. & Williams, J.C., pp. 383-401. New York: New York University Press.

Kalinoe, L. (2004). The bases of ownership claims over natural resources by indigenous peoples in Papua New Guinea. In *Rationales of Ownership: Transactions and claims to ownership in Papua New Guinea*, eds. Kalinoe, L. & Leach, J., pp. 57-78. Wantage: Sean Kingston Publishing.

Kalinoe, L. & Leach, J. (2004). *Rationales of Ownership: Transactions and claims to ownership in contemporary Papua New Guinea*. Wantage: Sean Kingston Publishing.

Kendall, D.G. (1974). Hunting quanta. In *The Place of Astronomy in the Ancient World. A joint symposium of The Royal Society and The British Academy*, ed. Hodson, F.R., pp. 231-266. London: Oxford University Press.

Kirsch, S. (2004). Keeping the Network in View: Compensation claims, property and social relations in Melanesia. In *Rationales of Ownership: Transactions and claims to ownership in contemporary Papua New Guinea*, eds. Kalinoe, L. & Leach, J., pp. 79-89. Wantage: Sean Kingston Publishing.

Kitchen, W. (2001). Tenure and territoriality in the British Bronze Age: A question of varying social and geographic scales? In *Bronze Age Landscapes: Tradition and Transformation*, ed. Brück, J., pp. 110-120. Oxford: Oxbow.

Kleine, S.S. & Baker, S.M. (2004). An Integrative Review of Material Possession Attachment. *Academy of Marketing Science Review 1*, 1-35.

Kleine, S.S., Kleine, R.E. & Allen, C.T. (1995). How is a possession 'me' or 'not me'? Characterising types and an antecedent of material possession attachment. *Journal of Consumer Research 22*, 327-343.

Knorr Cetina, K. & Bruegger, U. (2002). Trader' Engagement with Markets: A Postsocial Relationship. *Theory, Culture and Society 19*, 161-185.

Kristiansen, K. (1998). *Europe Before History*. Cambridge: Cambridge University Press.

Kristiansen, K. & Larsson, T.B. (2005). *The Rise of Bronze Age Society; Travels, transmissions and transformations.* Cambridge: Cambridge University Press.

Kuchler, S. (2002). *Malanggan: Art, memory and sacrifice.* London and New York: Berg.

Kuchler, S. (2004). Art and Mathematics. *Archaeological Review from Cambridge 19,* 28-46.

Kuper, A. (2004). Lineage Theory: A Critical Retrospect [first published 1982]. In *Kinship and Family: An Anthropological Reader,* eds. Parkin, R. & Stone, L., pp. 79-96. Oxford: Blackwell.

Kvamme, K.L. (1997). Ranter's Corner: Bringing the camps together: GIS and ED. *Archaeological Computing Newsletter 47,* 1-5.

Kvamme, K.L. (1999). Recent directions and developments in Geographical Information Systems. *Journal of Archaeological Research 7,* 153-201.

Laidlaw, J. (2000). A Free Gift makes no Friends. *Journal of the Royal Anthropological Institute (New Series) 6,* 617-634.

Latour, B. (1987). *Science in Action: How to follow scientists and engineers through society.* Milton Keynes: Open University Press.

Latour, B. (1993). *We Have Never Been Modern .* New York: Harvester Wheatsheaf.

Latour, B. (1999). *Pandora's Hope: Essays on the Reality of Science Studies.* Cambridge MA and London, England: Havard University Press.

Law, J. (2004). *After Method: Mess in Social Science Research.* London and New York: Routledge.

Law, R. (2005). *Making a Mark in the Early Bronze Age: Some thoughts on the social implications of decorating prehsitoric pottery.* Paper given at the Theoretical Archaeology Group Conference 2005.

Leach, E. (1962). On certain unconsidered aspects of double descent systems. *Man 62,* 130-134.

Leach, H.M. (1999). Intensification in the Pacific: A critique of the archaeological criteria and their application. *Current Anthropology 40,* 311-339.

Leach, J. (2002). The generation of the Free / Open Source Community and the conditions for creativity: Social and cultural research agenda. In *Advancing the Research Agenda on Free / Open Source Software ,* Brussels: European Commission.

Leach, J. (2003a). *Creative Land: Place and Procreation on the Rai Coast of Papua New Guinea.* New York and Oxford: Berghahn Books.

Leach, J. (2003b). Owning Creativity: Cultural property and the efficacy of custom on the Rai Coast of Papua New Guinea. *Journal of Material Culture 8,* 123-143.

Leach, J. (2004). Land, trees and history: Disputes involving boundaries and identities in the context of development. In *Rationales of Ownership: Transactions and claims to ownership in contemporary Papua New Guinea,* eds. Kalinoe, L. & Leach, J., pp. 42-56. Wantage: Sean Kingston Publishing.

Lindquist, S.-O. (1974). The development of the agrarian landscape on Gotland during the Early Iron Age. *Norwegian Archaeological Review 7,* 6-32.

Linklater, A. (2002). *Measuring America: How an Untamed Wilderness Shaped the United States and Fulfilled the Promise of Democracy.* London: Rogers, Coleridge and White Ltd.

Lipuma, E. (2000). *Encompassing Others: The magic of modernity in Melanesia.* Ann Arbor: University of Michigan Press.

Locke, J. (1690). *Second Treatise on Government.* http://www.swan.ac.uk/poli/texts/locke/locke04.html (last accessed 7th Febuary 2005).

Lopez Y Royo, A. (2005). Embodying a Site: Choreographing Prambanan. *Journal of Material Culture 10,* 31-48.

Lorimer, H. (2004). *Herding memories of humans and animals.*
http://web.geog.gla.ac.uk/olpapers/hlorimer001.pdf.

Lowenthal, D. (1994). European and English Landscape as National Symbols. In *Geography and National Identity,* ed. Hooson, D., pp. 15-38. Oxford and Cambridge: Blackwell.

Lucas, G. (2001). *Critical Approaches to Fieldwork: Contemporary and historical archaeological practice.* London: Routledge.

Lucas, G. (2005). *The Archaeology of Time.* London and New York: Routledge.

Macfarlane, A. (1991). Some contributions of Maine to History and Anthropology. In *The Victorian Achievement of Sir Henry Maine: A centennial reappraisal,* ed. Diamond, A., Cambridge: Cambridge University Press.

MacPherson, C.B. (1978). *Property: Mainstream and Critical Positions.* Toronto: University of Toronto Press.

Maguire, D., Ralph, N. & Fleming, A. (1983). Early land use on Dartmoor - Palaeobotanical and pedological investigations on Holne Moor. In *Integrating the Subsistence Economy. Symposia of the Association for Environmental Archaeology No. 14. BAR Int. Series 181*, ed. Jones, M., pp. 57-105. Oxford: Archaeopress.

Maine, H.S. (1891). *Ancient Law: Its connection with the early history of society and its relation to modern ideas, 14th edition*. London: John Murray.

Malinowski, B. (1920). Kula ; the Circulating Exchange of Valuables in the Archipelagoes of Eastern New Guinea. *Man 20*, 97-105.

Malinowski, B. (1921). The Primitive Economics of the Trobriand Islanders. *The Economic Journal 31*, 1-16.

Malkki, L. (1992). National Geographic: The rooting of peoples and the territorialisation of National Identity among scholars and refugees. *Cultural Anthropology 7*, 24-44.

Malmer, M. (1992). Weight systems in the Scandanavian Bronze Age. *Antiquity 66*, 377-388.

Malthus, T. (2005). *An Essay on the Principle of Population, as it affects the future improvement on society, with remarks on the speculations of Mr Godwin, M. Condorcet, and other writers [first published 1798]*. http://socserv2.socsci.mcmaster.ca/~econ/ugcm/3ll3/malthus/popu.txt (accessed 9th February 2005).

Maritime and Coastguard Agency (2005). Devon Divers find 3, 000 year old Bronze Age artefacts on shipwreck site. *Devon Archaeological Society Newsletter 91*, 7

Marsh, J. (1982). *Back to the Land: The Pastoral impulse in Victorian England from 1880 to 1914*. London: Quartet Books.

Marx, K. (1976). *Capital: A critique of political economy - Volume 1*. London: Penguin (in association with New Left Review).

Matless, D. (1998). *Landscape and Englishness*. London: Reaktion.

Maurer, B. (2004). Cyberspatial Properties: Taxing questions about Property Regimes. In *Property in Question: Value Transformation in the Global Economy*, eds. Verdery, K. & Humphrey, C., pp. 297-318. Oxford: Berg.

Mauss, M. (1970). *The Gift: Forms and functions of exchange in archaic societies*. London: Cohen and West.

McCay, B.J. & Acheson, J.M. (1987). *The Question of the Commons: The Culture and ecology of communal resources*. Tuscon: University of Arizona Press.

McKean, M.A. (2000). Common Property: What is it, What is it good for, and What makes it work? In *People and Forests: Communities, institutions and governance*, eds. Gibson, C.C., McKean, M.A. & Ostrom, E., pp. 29-55. Cambridge Mass., London, MIT Press.

McKinley, J. (2001). Appendix 2: The Cremated Bone. In A Bronze Age Cemetery at Elburton, Plymouth By Watts, M.A. & Quinnell, H. *Proceedings of the Devon Archaeological Society 59*, 35-38.

Meillassoux, C. (1972). From reproduction to production: A Marxist appraoch to economic anthropology. *Economic and Society 1*, 93-105.

Merrill, T.W. (2002). Introduction: The Demetz thesis and the evolution of property rights. *Journal of Legal Studies XXXI*, 331-338.

Miles, H. (1976). Flint scatters and prehistoric settlement in Devon. *Proceedings of the Devon Archaeological Society 34*, 3-16.

Miller, D. (1995a). Consumption as the Vanguard of History: A polemic by way of an introduction. In *Acknowledging Consumtion: A review of New Studies*, ed. Miller, D., pp. 1-57. London: Routledge.

Miller, D. (1995b). Consumption Studies as the Transformation of Anthropology. In *Acknowledging Consumption; A review of New Studies*, ed. Miller, D., pp. 264-295. London: Routledge.

Miller, D. (2005). Materiality: An Introduction. In *Materiality*, ed. Miller, D., pp. 1-50. Durham and London: Duke University Press.

Miller, D. (1987). *Material Culture and Mass Consumption*. Oxford: Blackwell.

Mimica, J. (1988). *Intimations of Infinity: The mythopoeia of the Iqwaye counting system and number*. Oxford: Berg.

Mizoguchi, K. (1993). Time in the reproduction of mortuary practices. *World Archaeology 25*, 223-245.

Morgan, L.H. (2005). *Ancient Society, or, Researches in the Lines of Human Progress from Savagery through Barbarism to Civilization*. http://www.marxists.org/reference/archive/morgan-lewis/ancient-society/ (accessed 7th February 2005).

Morrison, K.D. (1996). Typological Schemes and Agricultural Change: Beyond Boserup in precolonial South India. *Current Anthropology 37*, 583-608.

Mosko, M. (2000). Inalienable Ethnography: Keeping-while-giving and the Trobriand case. *Journal of the Royal Anthropological Institute (New Series) 6*, 377-396.

Muckelroy, K. (1980). Two Bronze Age cargoes in British waters. *Antiquity 54*, 100-112.

Müller-Wille, M. (1965). *Eisenzeitliche Fluren in den festlandischen Nordseegebieten*. Munster: Im Selbstverlag der Geographischen Kommission.

Munn, N.D. (1986). *The Fame of Gawa: A symbolic study of value transformation in a Massim (Papua New Guinea) society*. Cambridge: Cambridge University Press.

Munn, N.D. (1987). *The Fame of Gawa: A symbolic study of value transformation in a Massim (Papua New Guinea) society*. Cambridge: Cambridge University Press.

Munn, N.D. (1990). Constructing Regional Worlds in Experience: Kula exchange, witchcraft and Gawan local events. *Man (New Series) 25*, 1-17.

Myers, F. (2005). Some Properties of Art and Culture: Ontologies of the image and economies of exchange. In *Materiality*, ed. Miller, D., pp. 88-117. London and Durham: Duke University Press.

National Sheep Association (2005). *Upland Sheep Farming*. http://www.nationalsheep.org.uk/.

Neale, W.C. (1998). Property: Law, Cotton-pickin' hands, and implicit cultural imperialism. In *Property in Economic Context. Monographs in Economic Anthropology, No. 14*, eds. Hunt, R.C. & Gilman, A., pp. 47-66. Lanham, New York, Oxford: University Press of America.

Needham, S. (1980). An assemblage of Late Bronze Age metalworking debris from Dainton, Devon. *Proceedings of the Prehistoric Society 46*, 177-216.

Needham, S. (1996). Chronology and Periodisation in the British Bronze Age. *Acta Archaeologica 67*, 121-140.

Needham, S. (2001). When expediency broaches ritual intention; The flow of metal between systemic and buried domains. *Journal of the Royal Anthropological Institute (New Series) 7*, 275-298.

Needham, S. (2006). *Ringlemere, Precious Cups and the Beginning of the Channel Bronze Age - Paper given at 'Bronze Age Connections: Cultural Contact in prehistoric Europe' - Second Dover Boat Conference*.

Needham, S. & Ambers, J. (1994). Redating Rams Hill and reconsidering Bronze Age enclosure. *Proceedings of the Prehistoric Society 60*, 225-243.

Needham, S., Bronk Ramsey, C., Coombs, D., Cartwright, C. & Pettitt, P. (1997). An independant chronology for British Bronze Age metalwork: The results of the Oxford radiocarbon accelerator programme. *Archaeological Journal 154*, 55-107.

Netting, R.M. (1993). *Smallholders, Householders: Farm families and the ecology of intensive, sustainable agriculture*. Stanford: Stanford University Press.

Niederle, U.-M. (2004). *From Possession to Property: Preferences and the role of culture*. Jena: Max-Planck Institute for Research into Economic Systems, Evolutionary Economics Unit.

Northover, J.P. (1982). The Exploration of long-distance movement of bronze in Bronze and Early Iron Age Europe. *Bulletin of the Institute of Archaeology 45-72*.

Northover, P. (2006). *Ingots and the Bronze Age trade in metals. Paper given at the Dover Boat Conference 2006*. Dover:

Novemsky, N. & Kahneman, D. (2005). The Boundaries of Loss Aversion. *Journal of Marketing Research XLII*, 119-128.

Nowakowski, J.A. (2001). Leaving home in the Cornish Bronze Age: Insights into planned abandonment processes. In *Bronze Age Landscapes: Tradition and transformation*, ed. Brück, J., pp. 139-148. Oxford: Oxbow.

O'Neill, S.H. (1982). *Bronze Age settlement of the Plym Valley*. University of Sheffield: Unpub. MPhil Thesis.

Olsen, B. (2003). Material Culture after Text: Re-Membering Things. *Norwegian Archaeological Review 36*, 87-104.

Openshaw, S. (1991). A view on the GIS crisis in geography, or, using GIS to put humpty-dumpty together again. *Environment and planning A 23*, 621-628.

Openshaw, S. (1998). Towards a more computationally minded scientific human geography. *Environment and planning A 30*, 332

Ormerod, G.W. (1864). On the Hut-Circles of the Eastern side of Dartmoor. *Journal of the Archaeological Association 20*, 299-308.

Ormerod, G.W. (1876). *Rude Stone Remains situate on the easterly side of Dartmoor*. Exeter: Privately published.

Ostereng, G. (2004). *Habitat selection and wolverine depredation-risk in free-ranging sheep at an alpine pasture. Master of Science Thesis*. As: The Agricultural University of Norway.

Ostrom, E. (1990). *Governing the Commons: The evolution of institutions for collective action.* Cambridge: CUP.

Owoc, M.A. (1999). *Munselling the mound: The use of soil colour as metaphor in British Bronze Age funerary ritual. Paper given at the 5th Annual Meeting of the European Association of Archaeologists, 1999 .*

Owoc, M.A. (2001). The times, they are a changin': Experiencing continuity and development in the Early Bronze Age funerary rituals of south-western Britain. In *Bronze Age Landsapes: Tradition and transformation,* ed. Brück, J., Oxford: Oxbow.

Owoc, M.A., Manske, K., Greek, M., Illingworth, J. & Adowasio, J. (2004). *Island Threads: Bronze Age textile production and identity on the Isle of Scilly, UK.* Paper presented at SAA conference 2004.

Paine, T. (2004). Agrarian Justice [first published 1795]. In *Common Sense,* pp. 79-104. London: Penguin.

Pare, C. (2000). Bronze and the Bronze Age. In *Metals Make the World Go Round: The Supply and Circulation of Metals in Bronze Age Europe. Proceedings of a conference held at the University of Birmingham in June 1997.,* ed. Pare, C., pp. 1-38. Oxford: Oxbow Books.

Parham, D., Needham, S. & Palmer, M. (2006). Final Proof of Ancient UK Contact with Sicily? Salcombe and Dover - Bronze Age wrecked cargoes in Devon and Kent. *British Archaeology 91,*

Parker Pearson, M. (1990). The production and distribution of Bronze Age pottery in south-western Britain. *Cornish Archaeology 29,* 5-27.

Parker Pearson, M. (1993). *English Heritage book of Bronze Age Britain.* London: Batsford.

Parker Pearson, M. (1995). South-western Bronze Age pottery. In *Unbaked urns of rudely shape,* eds. Kinnes, I. & Varndell, G., pp. 89-100. Oxford: Oxbow.

Parker Pearson, M. (1996). Food, fertility and front doors in the first millennium BC. In *The Iron Age in Britain and Ireland: Recent trends,* eds. Champion, T.C. & Collis, J., pp. 117-132. Sheffield: Sheffield Academic Press.

Parker Pearson, M. (1999). *The Archaeology of Death and Burial.* Sutton Publishing: Stroud.

Parkin, R. (2004). Descent and Marriage: Introduction. In *Kinship and Family: An Anthropological Reader,* eds. Parkin, R. & Stone, L., pp. 29-42. Oxford: Blackwell.

Parry, B. (2004). Bodily Transactions: Regulating a new space of flows in 'Bio-information'. In *Property in*

Question: Value transformation in the Global Economy, eds. Verdery, K. & Humphrey, C., pp. 29-48. Oxford: Berg.

Pattison, P. & Fletcher, M. (1994). Grimspound, one hundred years on. *Devon Archaeological Society Proceedings 52,* 21-34.

Pearce, S. (1979). The distribution and production of Bronze Age metalwork. *Devon Archaeological Society Proceedings 37,* 136-145.

Pearce, S. (1981). *The Archaeology of South West Britain.* London: Collins.

Pearce, S. (1983). *The Bronze Age Metalwork of South Western Britain. British Archaeological Reports (British Series) 120.* Oxford: BAR.

Pearce, S. (1984). *Bronze Age metalwork of Southern Britain.* Aylesbury: Shire Archaeology.

Pearce, S. (1999). Bronze Age Metalwork. In *Historical Atlas of South-West England,* eds. Ravenhill, W. & Kain, R., pp. 69-73. Exeter: University of Exeter Press.

Pels, D., Hetherington, K. & Vandenberghe, F. (2002). The Status of the Object: Performances, mediations, and techniques. *Theory, Culture and Society 19,* 1-21.

Penningroth, D. (2003). *The Claims of Kinfolk: Afircan American Property and Community in the Nineteenth-Century South.* Chapel Hill and London: University of North Carolina Press.

Petruso, K. (2003). Quantum analysis of some Mycenaean Balance Weights. In *METRON: Measuring the Aegean Bronze Age. Proceedings of the IXth International Aegean Conference, Yale University, 18-21 April 2002. Aegaeum, vol. 24 ,* Liege: Liege University.

Pettit, P. (1974). *Prehistoric Dartmoor.* Torquay: Forest Publishing.

Phillips, S.K. (1984). Encoded in stone: Neighbouring relationships and the organisation of stone walls among Yorkshire Dales farmers. *JASO: Journal of the Anthropological Society of Oxford XV,* 235-242.

Pickles, J. (1995). Conclusion: Toward an economy of electronic representation and the virtual sign. In *Ground Truth: The social implications of Geographical Information Systems,* ed. Pickles, J., pp. 223-240. New York and London: The Guildford Press.

Pierce, J.L. & Rodgers, L. (2004). The Psychology of Ownership and Worker-Owner Productivity. *Group and Organisation Management 29,* 588-612.

Pitts, M. (2001). *Hengeworld: Life in Britain 2000 BC as revealed by the latest discoveries at Stonehenge, Avebury and Stanton Drew*. London: Arrow.

Pluciennik, M. (2001). Archaeology, Anthropology and Subsistence. *Journal of the Royal Anthropological Institute (New Series) 7*, 741-758.

Polanyi, K. (1944). *The Great Transformation: The Political and Economic Origins of our time*. New York: Rinehart and Company Inc.

Pollard, S. & Russell, P.M.G. (1969). Excavation of Round Barrow 248b, Upton Pyne, Exeter. *Proceedings of the Devon Archaeological Society 27*, 49-78.

Povinelli, E. (2004). At Home in the Violence of Recognition. In *Property in Question: Value Transformation in the Global Economy*, eds. Humphrey, C. & Verdery, K., pp. 185-206. Oxford: Berg.

Price, D.G. (1973). Ancient fields on Shaugh Moor. *Report and Transactions of the Devonshire Association for the Advancement of Science 105*, 87-93.

Price, D.G. & Tinsley, H.M. (1976). On the significance of soilprofiles at Trowlesworthy Warren and Wigford Down. *Report and Transactions of the Devonshire Association for the Advancement of Science 108*, 147-157.

Probert, S. & Newman, P. (1998). *Shaugh Moor, Devon: An archaeological survey by the Royal Commission on the Historical Monuments of England*. Exeter: Unpublished Report.

Pryor, F. (1996). Sheep, stockyards and field systems: Bronze Age livestock populations in the Fenlands of eastern England. *Antiquity 70*, 313-324.

Pryor, F. (1998). *Farmers in Prehistoric Britain*. Stroud: Tempus.

Pryor, F. (2001). *Seahenge: New discoveries in Prehistoric Britain*. London: Harper Collins.

Pye, A.R., Noble, S. & Turton, S.D. (1993). *Archaeological survey of part of Crownhill Down, Shaugh Prior. Exeter Musuems Archaeological Field Unit Report Number 93.17*. Exeter Museum.

Quinnell, H. (1991). The late Mrs Minter's excavation of hut circles at Heatree, Manaton in 1968. *Proceedings of the Devon Archaeological Society 49*, 1-24.

Quinnell, H. (1994a). Becoming marginal? Dartmoor in later prehistory. *Proceedings of the Devon Archaeological Society 52*, 75-84.

Quinnell, H. (1994b). New perspectives on upland monuments - Dartmoor in earlier prehistory. *Proceedings of the Devon Archaeological Society 52*, 49-62.

Quinnell, H. Later Prehistoric Pottery Survey (Devon). Unpublished Catalogue. 1996.

Radin, M.J. (1982). Property and Personhood. *Stanford Law Review 34*, 957-1015.

Radin, M.J. (1995). The Colin Ruagh Thomas O'Fallon Memorial Lecture on Reconsidering Personhood. *Oregon Law Review 74*, 423-448.

Ralegh Radford, C.A. (1952). Prehistoric Settlements on Dartmoor and the Cornish Moors. *Proceedings of the Prehistoric Society 18*, 55-84.

Ralph, N. (1982). *Assessment of ancient land use in abandoned settlements and fields - A study of prehistoric and medieval land use and its influence upon soil properties on Holne Moor, Dartmoor, England*. University of Sheffield: Unpublished PhD. Thesis.

Reed, S.J. (1994). *Archaeological recording on the SWW Dousland to Rundlestone water main. Exeter Museums Archaeological Field Unit Report Number 94.40*. Exeter Museum.

Renfrew, C. (1976). Megaliths, Territories and Populations. In *Acculturation and Continuity in Atlantic Europe, Mainly During the Neolithic Period and the Bronze Age*, ed. De Laet, S.J., pp. 198-220. Bruges: De Tempel.

Reynolds, P. (1979). *Iron-Age Farm: The Butser experiment*. London: British Musuem Publications Ltd.

Ricardo, D. (1821). *On the Principles of Political Economy and Taxation*. http://www.econlibrary.org/library/Ricardo [accessed 2005].

Rifkin, J. (2000). *The Age of Access: How the shift from Ownership to Access is transforming modern life*. London: Penguin.

Roberts, B. & Ottaway, B. (2003). The use and significance of socketed axes during the Late Bronze Age. *European Journal of Archaeology 6*, 119-140.

Robertson, J. The Archaeology of the Upper Plym Valley. Unpublished PhD Thesis. 1991. University of Edinburgh.

Rose, C.M. (1990). Property as Storytelling: Perspectives from Game Theory, Narrative Theory, Feminist Theory. *Yale Journal of Law and the Humanities 2*, 37-57.

Rose, C.M. (1998). The Several Futures of Property: Of Cyberspace and Folk Tales, Emission Trades and Ecosystems. *Minnesota Law Review 83*, 129-182.

Rose, C.M. (2004). Economic Claims and the Challenges of New Property. In *Property in Questions: Value Transformation in the Global Economy*, eds. Verdery, K. & Humphrey, C., pp. 275-296. Oxford: Berg.

Rossi, M.A. (2004). Decoding the 'Free / Open Source (F/OSS) Software Puzzle' a survey of theoretical and empirical contributions. *Quaderni, Universita degli Studi Siena 424*,

Rousseau, J.J. (2005). *A discourse on a subject proposed by the Academy of Dijon: What is the origin of inequality among men, and is it authorised by natural law? [first published 1754]*. http://www.constitution.org/jjr/ineq.htm.

Rowe, S. (1985). *A Perambulation of the Antient and Royal Forest of Dartmoor and the Venville precincts or a Topographical Study of their Antiquities and Scenery. Facsimile of 1896 Edition.* Newton Abbott: Devon Books.

Rowlands, M.J. (1980). Kinship, alliance and exchange in the European Bronze Age. In *The British Later Bronze Age. British Archaeological Reports 83*, eds. Barrett, J.C. & Bradley, R., pp. 15-56. Oxford: Archaeopress.

Rowlands, M.J. (1986). Modernist Fantasies in Prehistory? *Man 21*, 745-748.

Rowlands, M.J. (2005). A Materialist Apporach to Materiality. In *Materiality*, ed. Miller, D., pp. 72-87. Durham and London: Duke University Press.

Roymans, N. & Theuws, F. (1999). Long-term perspectives on man and landscape in the Meuse-Demer-Scheldt region: An Introduction. In *Land and Ancestors: Cultural dynamics in the Urnfield period and the Middle Ages in the Southern Netherlands*, eds. Theuws, F. & Roymans, N., pp. 1-32. Amsterdam: Amsterdam University Press.

Ruiz-Galvez, M. (2000). Weight systems and exchange networks in Bronze Age Europe. In *Metals Make the World Go Round: The supply and circulation of metals in Bronze Age Europe. Proceedings of a conference held at the University of Birmingham in June 1997*, ed. Pare, C., pp. 267-279. Oxford: Oxbow.

Ruskin, J. (2004). The Nature of Gothic [first published 1853]. In *On Art and Life*, ed. Ruskin, J., pp. 1-56. London: Penguin.

Sahlins, M. (1972). *Stone Age Economics*. New York: Aldine de Gruyter.

Sayers, D.L. (1930). *Strong Poison*. London: New English Library.

Schneider, D.M. (2004). What is Kinship all about? [first published 1972]. In *Kinship and Family: An anthropological reader*, eds. Parkin, R. & Stone, L., pp. 257-274. Oxford: Blackwell.

Seabright, P. (2000). *The Vanishing Rouble: Barter networks and non-monetary transactions in Post-Soviet societies*. Cambridge: Cambridge University Press.

Seebohm, F. (1914). *Customary Acres and their historical importance. Being a series of unfinished essays by the late Frederic Seebohm*. London, New York, Bombay and Calcutta: Longmans, Green and Co.

Seebohm, F. (1926). *The English Village Community examined in its relations to the manorial and tribal systems and to the common or open field system of husbandry: An essay in Economic History*. Cambridge: Cambridge University Press.

Seeger, A. (2004). The Selective Protection of Musical Ideas: The 'creators' and the dispossessed. In *Property in Question: Value Transformation in the Global Economy*, eds. Verdery, K. & Humphrey, C., pp. 69-84. Oxford: Berg.

Sen, A. (1983). Development: Which way now? *The Economic Journal 93*, 745-762.

Shanin, T. (1986). Chayanov Message: Illuminations, miscomprehensions, and the contemporary 'development theory': Introduction. In *The Theory of Peasant Economy*, ed. Chayanov, A.V., Wisconsin: University of Wisconsin Press.

Shennan, S. (1993). Commodities, Transactions, and Growth in the Central-European Early Bronze Age. *Journal of European Archaeology 1*, 59-72.

Shennan, S. (1999). Cost, Benefit and Value in the Organisation of Early European Copper Production. *Antiquity 73*, 352-363.

Sherratt, A. (1993). What would a Bronze Age World System look like? Relations between Temperate Europe and the Mediterranean in Later Prehistory. *Journal of European Archaeology 1*, 1-57.

Sherratt, A. (1999). Cash-crops before cash: Organic consumables and trade. In *The Prehistory of Food: Appetites for change*, eds. Gosden, C. & Hather, J., pp. 11-34. London: Routledge.

Shils, E. (1991). Henry Sumner Maine in the tradition of the analysis of society. In *The Victorian Achievement of Sir Henry Maine: A centennial reappraisal*, ed.

Diamond, A., pp. 143-178. Cambridge: Cambridge University Press.

Shorter, A.H. (1938). Hut circles and ancient fields near Challacombe, Dartmoor. *Devon Archaeological Exploration Society 4*, 102-105.

Silvester, R.J. (1979). The relationship of first millennium settlement to the upland areas of the southwest. *Proceedings of the Devon Archaeological Society 37*, 176-190.

Silvester, R.J. (1980). The prehistoric open settlement at Dainton, South Devon. *Proceedings of the Devon Archaeological Society 38*, 17-38.

Silvester, R.J. (1986). The later prehistoic and roman material from Kent's Cavern, Torquay. *Proceedings of the Devon Archaeological Society 44*, 9-38.

Simmons, I.G. (1963). The blanket bog of Dartmoor. *Report and Transactions of the Devonshire Association for the Advancement of Science 95*, 180-196.

Simmons, I.G. (1964). Pollen diagrams from Dartmoor. *New Phytologist 63*, 165-180.

Simmons, I.G. (1969). Environment and early man on Dartmoor, Devon, England. *Proceedings of the Prehistoric Society 35*, 203-219.

Simmons, I.G. (2003). *The Moorlands of England and Wales: An Environmental History 8000 BC - AD 2000.* Edinburgh: Edinburgh University Press.

Sklenar, K. (1983). *Archaeology in Central Europe: The first 500 years*. Leicester: Leicester University Press.

Smith, A. (1776). *An Inquiry into the Nature and Causes of the Wealth of Nations.* http://www.econlib.org/library/Smith/smWN1.html (accessed 7 February 2005).

Smith, A.D. (2000). The 'Sacred' Dimension of Nationalism. *Millennium: Journal of International Studies 29*, 791-814.

Smith, A.D. (2001). Authenticity, antiquity and archaeology. *Nations and Nationalism 7*, 441-449.

Smith, E.A. (1988). Risk and uncertainty in the 'original affluent society': Evolutionary ecology of resource-sharing and land tenure. In *Hunter-Gatherers, Volume 1: History, evolution and social change*, eds. Ingold, T., Riches, D. & Woodburn, J., pp. 222-251. New York: Berg.

Smith, K., Coppen, J., Wainwright, G.J. & Beckett, S. (1981). The Shaugh Moor Project: Third Report - Settlement and environmental investigations. *Proceedings of the Prehistoric Society 47*, 205-273.

Smith, K., Wainwright, G.J. & Fleming, A. (1979). The Shaugh Moor Project: First Report. *Proceedings of the Prehistoric Society 45*, 1-34.

Sneath, D. (2004). Property Regimes and Sociotechnical Systems: Rights over land in Mongolia's 'age of the market'. In *Property in Question: Value Transformation in the Global Economy*, eds. Verdery, K. & Humphrey, C., pp. 161-184. Oxford: Berg.

Spence Bate, C. (1872). Researches into some ancient tumuli on Dartmoor. *Report and Transactions of the Devonshire Association for the Advancement of Science 5*, 549-558.

Staines, S. (1979). Environmental change on Dartmoor. *Devon Archaeological Society Proceedings 37*, 21-47.

Stone, D. (2005). For Love nor Money: The Commodification of Care. In *Rethinking Commodification: Cases and Readings in Law and Culture*, eds. Ertman, M.M. & Williams, J.C., pp. 271-290. London and New York: New York University Press.

Stone, G.D. (1993). Agrarian settlement and the spatial disposition of labor. In *Spatial Boundaries and Social Dynamics: Case studies from food producing societies. Ethnoarchaeological Series 2*, eds. Holl, A. & Levy, T.E., pp. 25-38. Ann Arbor: International Monographs in Prehistory.

Stone, G.D. (1994). Agricultural Intensification and Perimetrics: Ethnoarchaeological evidence from Nigeria. *Current Anthropology 35*, 317-324.

Stone, G.D. (1997). "Predatory Sedentism": Intimidation and intensification in the Nigerian Savanna. *Human Ecology 25*, 223-242.

Stone, G.D. & Downum, C.E. (1999). Non-Boserupian Ecology and Agricultural Risk: Ethnic politics and land control in the arid southwest. *American Anthropologist 101*, 113-128.

Stone, L. (2004). The Demise and Revival of Kinship: Introduction. In *Kinship and Family: An Anthropological Reader*, eds. Parkin, R. & Stone, L., pp. 237-256. Oxford: Blackwell.

Strang, V. (2000). Showing and telling: Australian land rights and material moralities. *Journal of Material Culture 5*, 275-299.

Strathern, M. (1984). Subject or Object? Women and the circulation of valuables in Highlands New Guinea. In *Women and Property: Women as Property*, ed. Hirschon, R., pp. 158-175. London and Canberra: Croon Helm.

Strathern, M. (1988). *The Gender of the Gift: Problems with women and problems with society in Melanesia*. Berkley, Los Angeles, London: University of California Press.

Strathern, M. (1991). Partners and Consumers: Making Relations Visible. *New Literary History 22*, 581-601.

Strathern, M. (1999). *Property, Substance and Effect: Anthropological essays on persons and things*. London and New Brunswick NJ: The Athlone Press.

Strathern, M. (2001a). *Imagined Collectivities and Multiple Authorship*. The Arts Council: http://www.artscouncil.org.uk/documents/projects/831.pdf.

Strathern, M. (2001b). The Patent and the Malanggan. *Theory, Culture and Society 18*, 1-26.

Strathern, M. (2004). Introduction: Rationales of Ownership. In *Rationales of Ownership: Transactions and claims to ownership in contemporary Papua New Guinea*, eds. Kalinoe, L. & Leach, J., pp. 1-12. Wantage: Sean Kingston Publishing.

Strathern, M. (2005a). *Kinship, Law and the Unexpected. Relatives are Always a Surprise*. Cambridge: Cambridge University Press.

Strathern, M. Land: Tangible and Intangible Property. Oxford Amnesty Lecture. 2005b.

Strathern, M. and Hirsch, E. Property, Transactions and Creations: New economic relations in the Pacific. Unpublished end of award report for the Economic and Social Reasearch Council. 2002.

Sutton, D. (2004). Anthropology's value(s). *Anthropological Theory 4*, 373-379.

Swedberg, R. (1997). New Economic Sociology: What has been accomplished, what is ahead? *Acta Sociologia 40*, 161-182.

Sweet, R. (2004). *Antiquaries: The Discovery of the Past in Eighteenth-Century Britain*. London: Hambledon and London.

Taylor, C. (2000). *Fields in the English Landscape. Revised Edition*. Stroud: Sutton.

Taylor, J. (1999). The Colaton Raleigh Gold Bracelet Hoard and its significance to the interpretation of the Later Bronze Age. *Proceedings of the Devon Archaeological Society 57*, 205-218.

Theuws, F. & Roymans, N. (1999). *Land and Ancestors: Cultural dynamics in the Urnfield Period and the Middle Ages in the Southern Netherlands*. Amsterdam: Amsterdam University Press.

Thom, A. & Thom, A.S. (1978). *Megalithic Remains in Britain and Brittany*. Oxford: Clarendon.

Thomas, J. (1993). The politics of vision and the archaeologies of landscape. In *Landscape, Politics and Perspectives*, ed. Bender, B., pp. 19-48. Oxford: Berg.

Thomas, J. (1996). *Time, Culture and Identity: An interpretative archaeology*. London: Routledge.

Thomas, J. (2001). Comment: Monuments, Power and Personhood in the British Neolithic. *Journal of the Royal Anthropological Institute (New Series) 7*, 763-766.

Thomas, J. (2004). *Archaeology and Modernity*. London and New York: Routledge.

Thorndycraft, V.R., Pirrie, D. & Brown, A.G. (2004). Alluvial records of Medieval and prehistoric Tin Mining on Dartmoor, Southwest England. *Geoarcheaology: An International Journal 19*, 219-236.

Tilley, C. (1994). *A Phenomenology of Landscape: Places, paths and monuments*. Oxford: Berg.

Timberlake, S. (2001). Mining and prospection for metals in Early Bronze Age Britain - making claims within the archaeological landscape. In *Bronze Age Landscapes, Tradition and Transformations*, ed. Brück, J., pp. 179-192. Oxbow: Oxford.

Tivy, J. (1990). *Agricultural Ecology*. London: Longman Scientific and Technical.

Todd, M. (1989). *The south west to AD1000*. London: Longman.

Tomalin, D. (1995). Cognition, ethnicity and some implications for linguistics in the perception and perpetation of 'Collared Urn art'. In *'Unbaked Urns of Rudely Shape': Essays on British and Irish Pottery for Ian Longworth*, eds. Kinnes, I. & Varndell, G., pp. 101-112. Oxford: Oxbow.

Trigger, B.G. (1989). *A History of Archaeological Thought*. Cambridge: Cambridge University Press.

Turner, J.R. (1990). Ring cairns, stone circles and related monuments on Dartmoor. *Proceedings of the Devon Archaeological Society 48*, 27-86.

United Nations (2005). *World Resources 2005 - The Wealth of the Poor: Managing ecosystems to fight poverty*. The World Bank: United Nations Development Programme, United Nations Environment Programme, World Resources Institute.

Van der Noort, R. (2004). The Humber, its sewn plank boats, their context and the significance of it all. In *The Dover Bronze Age Boat: Society and water transport in prehistoric Europe*, ed. Clark, P., pp. 90-98. Oxford: Oxbow.

Veblen, T. (1898). The Beginnings of Ownership. *American Jounral of Sociology 4*, 352-365.

Velthuis, O. (1999). The Changing Relationship between Economic Sociology and Institutional Economics: From Talcott Parsons to Mark Granovetter. *American Journal of Economics and Sociology 58*, 629-649.

Verdery, K. (1998). Property and power in Transylvania's decollectivization. In *Property Relations: Renewing the anthropological tradition*, ed. Hann, C.M., Cambridge: CUP.

Verdery, K. (2003). *The Vanishing Hectare: Property and Value in Postsocialist Transylvania*. Ithaca and London: Cornell University Press.

Verdery, K. (2004). The Obligations of Ownership: Restoring Rights in land in Post-socialist Transylvania. In *Property in Question: Value Transformation in the Global Economy*, eds. Verdery, K. & Humphrey, C., pp. 139-160. Oxford: Berg.

Verdery, K. & Humphrey, C. (2004a). Introduction: Raising Questions about Property. In *Property in Question: Value Transformation in the Global Economy*, eds. Verdery, K. & Humphrey, C., pp. 1-25. Oxford: Berg.

Verdery, K. & Humphrey, C. (2004b). *Property in Question: Value Transformation in the Global Economy*. Oxford: Berg.

Verran, H. (1999). Staying true to the laughter in Nigerian classrooms. In *Actor Network Theory and After*, eds. Law, J. & Hassard, J., pp. 136-155. Oxford: Blackwell.

Vitruvius Pollio, M. (2005). *The Ten Books on Architecture: de Architectura, Book III (c.90-20 BC)*. http://www.perseus.tufts.edu/cgi-bin/ptext?doc=Perseus:text:1999.02.0073.

Wainwright, G.J. & Smith, K. (1980). The Shaugh Moor Project: Second Report - The Enclosure. *Proceedings of the Prehistoric Society 46*, 65-122.

Walker, A., Young, A., Keyzor, A. & Otlet, R. (1991). Harwell Radiocarbon Measurements IX. *Radiocarbon 33*, 79-86.

Waterbolk, H.T. (1995). Patterns of the peasant landscape. *Proceedings of the Prehistoric Society 61*, 1-36.

Watts, M.A. & Quinnell, H. (2001). A Bronze Age Cemetery at Elburton, Plymouth. *Proceedings of the Devon Archaeological Society 59*, 11-44.

Webster, C. (2003). *South West Archaeological Research Framework: Recent work on the Bronze Age*. English Heritage: www.somerset.gov.uk/media/DC8A7/bronzeage.pdf .

Weddell, P.J. & Reed, S.J. (1997). Excavations at Sourton Down, Okehampton 1986-1991: Roman road, deserted medieval hamlet and othe landscape features. *Proceedings of the Devon Archaeological Society 55*, 39-147.

Weiner, A. (1992). *Inalienable Possessions: The paradox of keeping while giving*. Berkley, Los Angeles, Oxford: University of California Press.

Welinder, S. (1975). *Prehistoric Agriculture in Eastern Middle Sweden: A model for food production, population growth, agricultural innovations, and ecological limitations in prehistoric Eastern Middle Sweden 4000 BC - AD 1000*. Lund: CWK Gleerup.

Were, G. (2003). Objects of Learning: An anthropological approach to Mathematics Education. *Journal of Material Culture 8*, 24-44.

West, S. (1997). Heavy Metals in Holocence peats from South-West England: Detecting mining impacts and atmospheric pollution. *Water, Air and Soil Pollution 100*, 343-353.

Wheatley, D. & Gillings, M. (2000). Vision, perception and GIS: Developing enriched approaches to the study of archaeological visibility. In *Beyond the map: Archaeology and spatial technologies*, ed. Lock, G., pp. 1-27.

Wheatley, D. & Gillings, M. (2002). *Spatial Technology and Archaeology: The Archaeological Applications of GIS*. London and New York: Taylor and Francis.

Whitehead, A. & Tsikata, D. (2003). Policy Discourse on Women's Land Rights in Sub-Saharan Africa: The implications of the return to the Customary. *Journal of Agrarian Change 3*, 67-112.

Widgren, M. (1989). Geographical approaches to field systems in Swedish Prehistory and Early History. In *Approaches to Swedish Prehistory: A spectrum of problems and perspectives in contemporary research. Britsh archaeological Reports International Series 500.*, eds. Larsson, T.B. & Lundmark, H., pp. 353-366. Oxford: British Archaeological Reports.

Widgren, M. (1990). Strip fields in an Iron Age context: a case study form Vastergotland, Sweden. *Landscape*

History: Journal of the Society for Landscape Studies. 12, 5-24.

Wilk, R.R. (1996). *Economics and Cultures: Foundations of Economic Anthropology.* Oxford: Westview Press.

Williams, J.C. & Zelizer, V.A. (2005). To Commodify or Not to Commodify: That is *Not* the Question. In *Rethinking Commodification: Cases and readings in Law and Culture,* eds. Ertman, M.M. & Williams, J.C., pp. 362-382. New York: New York University Press.

Williams, M. (2003). Growing Metaphors: The agricultural cycle as metaphor in the later prehistoric period of Britain and North-Western Europe. *Journal of Social Archaeology 3,* 223-255.

Williams, P.J. (2005). In Search of Pharoah's Daughter. In *Rethinking Commodification: Cases and Readings in Law and Culture,* eds. Ertman, M.M. & Williams, J.C., pp. 68-70. London and New York: New York University Press.

Williamson, O.E. (2000). The New Institutional Economics: Taking stock, looking ahead. *Journal of Economic Literature 38,* 595-613.

Winterhalder, B. (1990). Open field, Common pot: Harvest variability and risk avoidance in agricultural and foraging societies. In *Risk and Uncertainty in Tribal and Peasant Economies,* ed. Casdan, E., pp. 67-234. Boulder, San Franciso, London: Westview Press.

Witcher, R. (1999). GIS and landscapes of perception. In *Geographical Information Systems and Landscape Archaeology,* eds. Gillings, M., Mattingly, D. & Van Dalen, J., pp. 13-22. Oxford: Oxbow Books.

Wittel, A. (2001). Towards a Network Sociality. *Theory, Culture and Society 18,* 51-76.

Woodmansee, M. (1984). The Genius and the Copyright: Economic and legal conditions of the emergence of the 'Author'. *Eighteenth Century Studies 17,* 425-448.

Woodward, A. (2002). *British Barrows; A matter of life and death.* Stroud: Tempus.

Woolgar, S. (2002). After Word? - On some dynamics of duality interrogation. Or: why bonfires are not enough. *Theory, Culture and Society 19,* 261-270.

Worth, R.H. (1994). *Worth's Dartmoor.* Newton Abbott: Penninsula Press.

Yarrow, T. (2003). Artefactual Persons: The relational capacities of persons and things in the practice of excavation. *Norwegian Archaeological Review 36,* 65-73.

Yates, D. (1999). Bronze Age field systems in the Thames Valley. *Oxford Journal of Archaeology 18,* 157-170.

Yates, D. (2001). Bronze Age agricultural intensification in the Thames Valley and Estuary. In *Bronze Age Landscapes: Tradition and transformation,* ed. Brück, J., pp. 65-82. Oxford: Oxbow Books.

Zeitlyn, D. (2003). *Gift economies in the development of open source software: anthropological reflections. http://opensource.mit.edu/papers/rp-zeitlyn.pdf.*